Barbara Dinner

MEHTARS AND MARIGOLDS

A STORY OF FOUR GENERATIONS IN BRITISH INDIA
(1874 TO 1948)

PERKERREN
PUBLISHING

First Edition.

This e-book edition published in 2009
Published by Perkerren Publishing 2009
© Barbara Dinner 2009

Cover illustration by Brent Clark
Typeset and design by Dan Fentiman
www.surface-studio.co.uk

ISBN: 978-0-9561543-1-6

*For all those loved members of my family
who have, in their various ways, inspired me.*

Contents

		Page
One:	The Call of the East	1
Two:	A Fashionable Place to be	12
Three:	A Maid of Kent	22
Four:	Children of the New Century	37
Five:	The First World War	54
Six:	Annual Escapes	63
Seven:	Losing Loved Ones	71
Eight:	A Desire for England	81
Nine:	The Handsome Dragoon	90
Ten:	A New Generation	110
Eleven:	Family Ties	127
Twelve:	Testing Times	142
Thirteen:	New Orders	151
Fourteen:	Rumblings of War	162
Fifteen:	A Dear Brother in Peril	169
Sixteen:	Home and Away on the North-East Frontier	187
Seventeen:	Once Upon a Time	195
Eighteen:	Fortunes of War	206
Nineteen:	A Fortress City	222
Twenty:	Peace and War	235
Twenty-one:	A Time to Grow	245
Twenty-two:	Meanwhile in England	260
Twenty-three:	Prayers are Answered	266
Twenty-four:	The Wake of War	276
Twenty-five:	Trouble Brewing	286
Twenty-six:	Breaking New Ground	300
Twenty-seven:	What Price Independence?	313
Twenty-eight:	Packing for England	323
Twenty-nine:	Farewell Great Jewel	335
Thirty:	Adjustment	341

Postscript

Acknowledgements:	354
Bibliography:	356
Articles and Journals:	358
Notes:	359

List of Illustrations

Page

Front cover   Susannah Bensley (formerly Perren) sipping tea, with friends and a goose! c1900.

19   William's invitation to the Coronation Durbar of King Edward V11 as Emperor of India.

38   Susannah (centre) with granddaughter Hester, Calcutta, 1905 or early 1906, pictured together with Mary, her son William (back row 2nd from the left) and her son-in-law Billy Hayes standing behind her.

45   The Ridge, one of the only two flat pieces of ground in Simla, with Christ Church in the distance backed by Mount Jacko, and the grand post office to the near left of the picture.

113   Clare (about two months pregnant) and Hector. Taken 11 November 1928, just three months after their marriage.

228   100 Grand Parade Road, home to the Perks family between 1943 and 1947. (Note the presence of Barbara, Hector's bicycle and the salamander hot water heater).

87-88   William John Perren, aged eight months, with an Indian gentleman. Simla, 22 June 1875.

    William John Perren and Mary Yates, Calcutta, 19 March 1904.

    Three of the Perren Children: Jackie, Hester and Clare at Kingsway Camp, Delhi, c1915.

    The Mall, Simla.

    A family outing: the Perrens and the Treglowns. Annandale, Simla, c1917.

    A rare picture of Mary and her four children after church. Simla, c1917.

    Clare with Allan, one of her charges. Simla, c1927.

    William John Perren, Simla.

    Clare Perren aged 19 years old. Simla, c1928.

199-200   Hector, a cavalryman of the 4th/ 7th Dragoon Guards in India. Taken while on secondment at Army Headquarters in Simla, c1926.

    Hector (back left) with his family in England prior to his service. 1916 or 1917.

Hector & Clare in their first home together in Ferozepore. 27 December 1928.

Uncle Walter and Aunt Lizzie. Calcutta, Christmas 1938.

Billy with his nephew Peter in the Fellingham's car. Kirkee, c1936.

Mary Perren with son Billy before his posting to the Far East.

George William Perks, a very sick infant. Quetta, 1937.

Hector, the amateur radio enthusiast. Shillong, 1938-39.

Hector on the Assam metre-gauge railway. 1939-4

Barbara with her ayah. Shillong, c1941

Clare buying fruit at the Bara Bazar in Shillong. 1942

The Fort in Agra where the Perks family lived from September 1942 until February 1943.

The Perks family at Hester and Frank's house while in transit from Agra to Shillong in 1943.

351-352   Bill, 5 months after his release from captivity during WW2. Calcutta, January 1946.

Bill's reunion with his sister Clare and her family in Agra in May 1946.

Some of the many dead of the Calcutta massacres. August 1946.

   Nuntollah Burning Ghat

   Unidentified location in Calcutta

Peter and Bruce Blair at the Taj lit by moonlight.

The Perks family at the officers' mess in Agra on Christmas Day 1946.

An occasion for Hector to be garlanded with marigolds at the farewell of Colonel Stevenson. Avadi, 1947.

Bill with his two youngest nieces Barbara and Mary at their new house in Plymouth. The girls are pictured with the Christmas presents they received on the SS Ormonde while in transit.

Hester and Frank at home in Calcutta. November 1950.

Mary Perren on her 81st birthday, a few months after her return to England after 51 years in India. Pictured with her granddaughter Pat at the family home in Plymouth in 1956.

Maps & Plans

Page

India	XI
Malaya and Singapore	174
North-East Frontier, India and North-West Frontier, Burma	183
The Death Railway, Thailand	208
The Bungalow at 100 Grand Parade Road, Agra	223

INTRODUCTION

Three generations of my family were born and lived in India during some of the most sumptuous years of the British Raj. Ever since I was little, I have found fascinating the events of their multifarious lives. For many British people living in India, the years I describe in this book (1874-1948) were a rich and leisurely era in which life was lived, particularly by the well-to-do, with a sense of spaciousness and a carefree spirit. It was a time never to be repeated.

I enjoyed a special privilege to live in India as a child, and remember my life there as golden and exotic. Memories of family members and their doings were kept alive by my mother, father and the eldest of my sisters, who each – despite leaving in 1947, along with me and the rest of my family, following the events of Independence – retained a deep and enduring affection for that country.

In writing the book, it has been my wish to record these events rather than to allow them to fade forever, and one of my main goals has been to provide a means for my own family to learn about and understand the value of our heritage, shown in the pioneering spirit and courage of our family forebears.

Here I have recorded my recollections of what seemed to us to be a rich, colourful and unique life, in the hope that it may afford readers a glimpse into what it meant to be, during that era of history, children of the Empire.

Barbara Dinner
May 2009

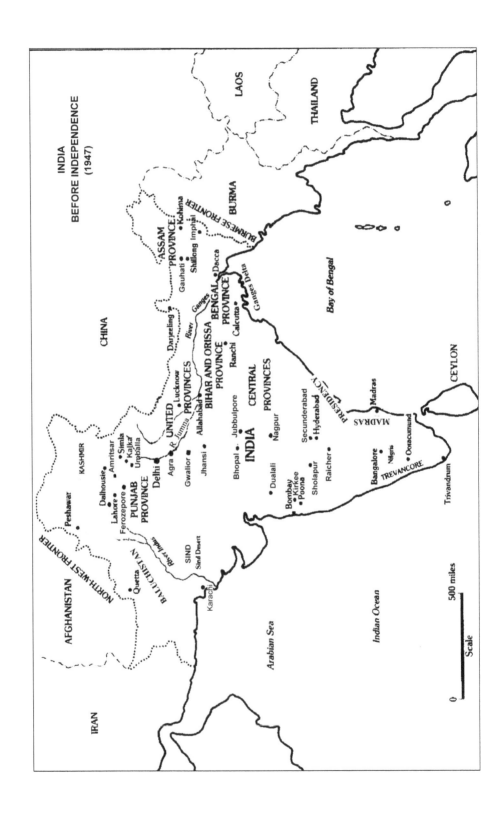

INDIA
BEFORE INDEPENDENCE
(1947)

LAOS

THAILAND

BURMA

CHINA

ASSAM
PROVINCE
• Kohima
Imphal
BURMESE FRONTIER
Shillong
Gauhati •

Darjeeling •
River Ganges
BENGAL
PROVINCE
Dacca
Calcutta •
Ganges Delta

KASHMIR

Dalhousie •
Peshawar •
Amritsar
Lahore • Simla
Ferozepore • Kalka
Umballa
PUNJAB
PROVINCE
Delhi
Agra •
R. Jumna UNITED
PROVINCES
• Lucknow
Gwalior •
Allahabad
Jhansi •
BIHAR AND ORISSA
PROVINCE
Ranchi •

NORTH-WEST FRONTIER

AFGHANISTAN

IRAN

Quetta •
BALUCHISTAN

River Indus
SIND
Sind Desert

Karachi

Bhopal •
Jubbulpore •
INDIA
CENTRAL
PROVINCES
Nagpur •

Secunderabad
• Hyderabad
Raicher •
MADRAS PRESIDENCY
Madras •

Arabian Sea

Dualali •
Bombay •
Kirkee
Poona
Sholapur •
Bangalore •
Nilgris
Ootacamund •
TREVANCORE
Trivandrum •

Bay of Bengal

CEYLON

Indian Ocean

0   500 miles
Scale

ONE

THE CALL OF THE EAST

It was early in the year of 1874 when John and Susannah Perren, newly-weds, left the green and pleasant land of their birth and ancestry to embark upon a new life many thousands of miles away in India. In those days, surely only those with great courage and a sense of adventure and determination could have undertaken such an exploit.

John was the youngest of eight children of William and Ann Perren, and was born on 23rd June 1845 at Widdenham Mill near Colerne, in the county of Wiltshire. The girl who would become his wife was born seven months later – Susannah, the daughter of Charles and Elizabeth Barton, who lived on the high street of nearby Corsham, a small, neat town. At the age of twenty-seven, Susannah married John in the village of Charlcombe, set in glorious countryside surrounding the elegant Georgian city of Bath, Somerset. The date was 8th January 1874 and the ceremony took place in St Mary's Church, a stone building of great antiquity, with a floor worn down by a multitude of pilgrims on their way to Glastonbury to the tomb of Joseph of Arimathea.

John had been an apprentice to the draper and grocer Henry Spackman, part of a talented family famous in Corsham for their musical, educational and sporting prowess. Later, John was reported to have gone into commerce, becoming a merchant. However, even at this time of industrial expansion, opportunities to make one's fortune may not have been abundant in rural Wiltshire. Being the youngest in his family, John may have had little hope of any sort of inheritance. Perhaps for these or similar reasons he began to envisage himself becoming a prosperous merchant and achieving greater success in glamorous India, a land which at that time was attracting many Europeans. He would be a man of enterprise, a fashionable pioneer. He and his new wife Susannah resolved to embark for India – a land that promised substantial rewards to anyone who was prepared to seize the opportunity.

There were two routes to India. One was the long and 'unpredictable voyage of up to six months'[1] around the Cape of Good Hope, a route whose discovery in 1489 was attributed to the explorer Vasco da Gama. This passage, pioneered by early merchant venturers, was becoming hard to maintain against competition from the second, more direct route that had opened up through the Mediterranean and initially involved a land crossing of the Suez Isthmus before re-embarkation for the Arabian sea-crossing. This was shorter by 4,000 miles and took less time.

British trade, and Britain's increasing political and economic control of India, had been developing throughout the 18th century. Prominent in this development had been the work of Robert Clive and the East India Company. 'Company' ships had acquired certain monopolies and privileges and serviced their interests on the subcontinent with a fleet of large, fully rigged sailing ships known as Indiamen. They plied the Cape route around South Africa and, for merchant vessels, were well armed and maintained to counter the depredations of both French and Barbary raiders as well as the fierce storms of the Cape passage. Indeed Good Hope was, for centuries, known as the Cape of Storms.

Voyages were timed so that, once around the Cape, the Indiamen exploited the monsoon winds of the Indian Ocean – a steady southwester for an outward passage between May and September, and an equally reliable northeaster from October to April. However these conditions, while assisting the undertaking of such passages, meant that round trips could extend to one year's duration. Nevertheless, by the standards of the day, these stately Indiamen provided a high level of service and were used extensively by company and government officials, senior members of the military and people from the wealthy classes.

After the defeat of the French fleet at Trafalgar in 1805 and the final defeat of the French in 1815, British command of the seas allowed the development of other sea passages to her dominions, including the Mediterranean. The evolution of the steam engine for marine propulsion was a further important factor in the expansion of trade and the emergence of new shipping companies. The early steamers operated with low-pressure engines that were inefficient by later standards, while ocean-going vessels were fully rigged with masts and sails to conserve coal and exploit favourable winds. Technical progress and trade expansion continued and in 1837, the year of Queen Victoria's accession, the Peninsular Steam Navigation Company was the first shipping line to be awarded a contract to deliver mails – initially as far as Gibraltar. In 1840 the contract was renewed and extended to Alexandria and 'Oriental' was added to the company's name (subsequently known as 'P&O'). By 1845, this now famous company had expanded its service all the way to Calcutta using a land bridge from Alexandria to the Red Sea port of Suez. After the East India Company's loss of the Bombay route monopoly in 1854, P&O operated there, too.

Mail, passengers and cargo had to be landed at Alexandria and taken, by various inconvenient and uncomfortable means, across 150 miles of desert via Cairo to Suez. Additionally, and especially early on, the journey was slow and, at times, dangerous due to its hazardous nature and 'the anti-European stance of the Pasha, Mehemet Ali'.[2] Eventually Thomas Waghorn, the pioneer of this overland transit, won the Pasha's trust and established a regular service between Alexandria and Suez, which P&O subsequently developed. By 1863, a railway across the Isthmus was completed – making it quicker and easier to travel, though 'still far from pleasant',[3] and still involving the awkward and inconvenient need to unload and re-embark both passengers and cargo.

The railway was routed via Cairo and some passengers, with time on their hands, stopped there. Others even proceeded by way of the Nile to see the ruins of Luxor before going on to re-embark at the small Red Sea port of Cossier, rather than Suez, for their onward voyage across the Arabian Sea. Despite these hardships, the Suez route gained in popularity over that around the Cape and most of the passengers who took it, in both directions, were British. The speed and comparative comfort of travel transformed the journey of the men who were serving in India and that of their wives and families. It became the route they chose.

With further technical innovations came the introduction, during the 1860s, of the more efficient compound steam engine operating at higher pressures.

Although vessels became faster, more reliable and less wind dependent, there remained the problems of refueling on route (bunkering) and, in the case of the oriental trade, the land barrier at the eastern end of the Mediterranean. Ships could proceed wherever there was sufficient water depth and within the range of bunkering facilities. These problems were soon to be addressed by two major developments. The first was the establishment of coal stations east of Suez (to which stocks had to be shipped, rather laboriously) and the second was to represent one of the most significant projects of the century.

In 1869, just five years before John and Susannah Perren embarked upon their passage to India, this route underwent a dramatic improvement after the opening of the Suez Canal, which eliminated the vagaries of the overland interlude. Initially a French enterprise, the canal was little more than a ditch about 100 miles long, dug in the sand across the isthmus between Port Said and Suez, but it brought significant benefit to the traveller by ensuring a reliable, continuous passage. A good number of ship owners with ready-built cheaper freighters, who were able to undercut the established rates, began to make regular use of it.

Even the lofty P&O, one of the oldest and smartest lines and one Rudyard Kipling was later to dub 'the exile's line', was ill-prepared and found it difficult to compete with new rivals. Fast mail ships were expensive to build and depended upon regular mail contracts, passengers, and small but valuable cargoes for income to support extensive services and infrastructure. Following the opening of the canal, the company began to flounder – despite all the years of pioneering – because of the overheads arising from these extensive but now redundant investments in Egypt and beyond. There were also losses from the replacement of older vessels by newer ships needed for the canal passage.

P&O regrouped over a relatively short period and by 1873 passengers were no longer landed for the company's overland trek: by now the Cape route had mostly been abandoned by the colonial and army officers, planters, and newly emerging European commercial men. After the opening of the Suez Canal, the company was never again to enjoy its early premiership in India and the East. It had lost its virtual monopoly of passengers and high-value cargoes that, along with its mail contract, had always provided its income. Despite this, it expanded in new directions and by 1884 its fleet had grown so rapidly that it owned 50 ships (most of them twice the average size) and was shipping an increasing volume of freight. The canal, which in 1875 was used mostly by British ships, had even been dredged and widened to take them.

Smart though the company's steamships were, and the providers of a luxurious service, they were not just the preserve of the rich. Many thousands of ordinary British-born soldiers and administrators serving in India in the 1870s travelled on P&O ships between Europe and India. The frequency of the service on these routes indicates the steady demand for berths throughout the year: the luxury end of the market was a small niche and no more. Over the years, whether on their way out to India or going home on leave, the British were said to love P&O and what it stood for. Having already become something of a British institution, it was also considered an important part of the Raj.

Some British customers travelled across France by train to join their ship at Marseilles. It was an option that remained popular after 1869 with those who wished to avoid the possibility of a very uncomfortable crossing through the Bay of Biscay, with its reputation for storms and rough seas (in the days before ships had stabilisers). This option could also shorten the journey from Britain by five to six days, with a proportionate saving in cost for those who did not mind starting their journey to India with several different shipments of their luggage. John and Susannah Perren may well have taken this overland route as far as Marseilles, rather than making the sea journey directly from Southampton, the home port of their most likely carrier, P&O.

Their four-week passage would have ended at Bombay, known as 'the gateway', but even once they were in India, the Perrens' journey was far from over. They now faced the challenge of a journey of several days to the north of India along the railways and roads. There was no direct railway route between Bombay and Simla in 1874: instead, travellers took a long and circuitous route on the Great Indian Peninsular Railway, through Khundwa, Jubbulpoor and Allahabad.

There, they connected with the East Indian Railway bound for Ghaziabad, near Delhi, at the junction at which the Sind, Punjab and Delhi Railway Company operated the Amritsar-to-Delhi line. (It is possible they visited Agra and Delhi, two major cultural centres not far from the main route.) At Umballa, an important junction, they would have disembarked to take the road: there was a cantonment (permanent military station) at Umballa and it was the administrative centre of the district in the eastern Punjab. Umballa was also the station from which all journeys started to that place in the hills for which the Perrens were bound – Simla, the seat of summer government in India.

On leaving the railway, John and Susannah would have travelled the penultimate stage of their long journey either by a large, covered horse-drawn government van or in a privately-operated post cart or carriage (dawk gari). The van or cart would have covered, at just nine or ten miles in a day, the 38 miles through the plains to Kalka. Once there, all that remained between the Perrens and their destination were the 58 miles of steep gradient up the Great Hindustan and Tibet Road.

This road, commonly known as the Cart Road, was completed in 1856 (constructed mainly by 'free labour' – villagers conscripted from neighbouring hill-states) and was a great improvement on its predecessor. Formerly, the mode of transportation to the hills had been by jampan (a sedan chair, designed for ladies and fitted with curtains, which was slung on poles borne by bearers) or by doolie (a litter for children or invalids, consisting of a wooden frame with a couch and curtains, carried on men's shoulders) or – for the men – by pony.

Before the Cart Road was built for wheeled carriages, all luggage and heavy loads were hauled and humped up into the hills by mules, coolies (native porters) or local people. At times, when there was a shortage of manpower, other inhabitants of distant villages were coerced to serve as porters and all of them, of course, were very poorly paid. However, when the new road was operational, enforced labour became a thing of the past and instead of human porters, a bullock cart service for goods was established along with a tonga service for mails and passengers.

At last, after a journey of perhaps six or seven weeks, John and Susannah reached their final destination – Simla – remote and perched high at the roof of the world. There it was, straddling the narrow saddle of one of the mountain ridges deep in the foothills of the Himalayas. In those days of the British Raj, Simla was the summer capital of the government of India. Besides this distinction, it was to bear witness to the births of three generations of this family and the nurturing of two of them into adulthood.

Simla was already a familiar name to many British people who lived in the 19th century. The British Empire in India had its roots in a collection of trading stations that dealt in spices, a trade long dominated by the Portuguese. The famous East India Company was formed in 1599 and granted a charter, a year later, by Queen Elizabeth I. Over the years, it built up a monopoly of British trade and acquired the power, both economic and legal, to defend its interests against competitors and local rulers.

The influential and territorial expansion of the company from its three main trading centres at Calcutta, Madras and Bombay, led to the division of its administrative structure into the three presidencies of Bengal (in which Calcutta was situated), Madras and Bombay, each with its governor and council. Because Bengal expanded faster and had more economic potential, the governor of Bengal, Warren Hastings, was made governor general of Bengal in 1774. The governors of the other two presidencies were subordinate to him in matters of foreign policy.

Trade rivalry was soon to prove to the company how crucial it was to organise Indian soldiers (sepoys) into regular units under European officers. (Until the 1740s, the British had armed Indians solely to guard warehouses.) Shortly after the Battle of Plassey in 1757, when the rich province of Bengal came more securely into British hands, the first Indian regiment was raised in the British service – an historic event. The 1st Bengal Native Infantry was raised from within the Bengal presidency region, although its rank-and-file were men from northern India. This was the origin of the formidable Bengal (Indian) Army, which would leave its mark on India over the next 100 years.

By the middle of the 18th century, the East India Company had become more than just a commercial concern. To secure its trading position – its great cargoes of saltpetre, silk and spices and, later, tea and coffee – against French East India companies who vied for domination of India, it established alliances with native rulers by waging wars on a considerable scale and by acquiring extensive territories. This development, which awarded the company power over millions of Indians, gave rise to a move on the part of the British government to exercise more control over Indian affairs. However, the company remained the agent through which British control of India was exercised and retained the right to appoint governing officials.

By 1819, the conquest of India was almost complete. Among the last territories of India to come under British rule – by 1856 – were the Punjab (a province bounded by the Jumna river to the east, by Kashmir on the north, by the mountains west of the Indus to the west, and by the desert of Rajputana to the south), the North-West Frontier and Oudh, an agricultural province between the Ganges and Nepal. Simla was in the Punjab (meaning 'five rivers' – the Indus and four of its tributaries) and first came to the attention of the British authorities during boundary disputes with Nepal between 1814 and 1816, which saw the British gain the upper hand. At the close of this war, after most of the surrounding district had been given or restored to various states, the British government decided to retain Simla (a small town sited on a 7,000 ft high spur of the lower Himalayas) as a sanatorium.

First came some officers on surveying expeditions. A Lieutenant Ross erected a residence in 1819: a simple, thatched wooden cottage. His successor, Lieutenant Kennedy, built a permanent house in 1822 and was appointed superintendent of the hill states, with instructions to receive tribute from the native hill chiefs and establish rudimentary British-style law and order among them. It appears that the native hill folk (whose traditional occupations were potato growing and fuel-collecting) were submissive and put up little or no resistance.

Others followed Ross and Kennedy, and in 1826 Simla became an official settlement. A year later, Lord Amherst put Simla on the social map by becoming the first governor general to spend the summer there, and from that date the reputation of the sanatorium grew rapidly among Europeans. Lord Combermere was the first commander-in-chief of the Indian Army to travel to Simla in 1828, and so it became a hill-station proper. It could boast a mall (the principal road of any hill-station), though at first this was little more than a winding track, and soon it had more than 100 residences, most of which were perched rather precariously on the slopes of the lofty Mount Jakko, Simla's highest peak.

At its summit was a small shrine dedicated to Hanuman, the monkey-god, for this was the home of troops of native brown monkeys.

Of Simla it was written:

> In the early days when the storms came, paths, roofs and hillside gardens were often washed quite away, and people sometimes tumbled over unparapeted precipices. It was difficult to reach and challenging to build upon; climbing there took your breath away, as did the occasional stupendous sunset over the distant snowy ranges of the Himalayas. The tonic of its clean, high, sharp air was irresistible.[4]

Looking northward, the terrain was rather bleak and ungracious, but in other directions the scenery was majestic:

> Downwards and to your right hand, you looked over the vale formed by faces of the opposite mountains, the whole of which were clothed with wood of the most gorgeous description. The stately deodara, a large oak, and other majestic trees thickly interspersed with rhododendron trees as large as apple trees, in fruit and brilliant scarlet blossoms, giving an idea of looking over a gaudy carpet of scarlet and green.[5]

As time went by, Simla would garner a range of nicknames: from 'Mount Olympus' to 'the viceroy's shooting box', 'the Indian Capua' to 'the abode of the little tin gods'. It would also become 'a dream of coolness in a very hot land; a hope of healthy rest from the burdens of imperial office; a haven of familiarity pinnacled above the alien dust of the plains; a solace for the wounded and the desolate, the ill and the bored; a promise of fun and flirtation; above all, a bitter-sweet memory of home – cuckoos and thrushes, pines in the mist, honeysuckle and roses in the rain'.[6]

Then came the Indian Mutiny in 1857-58: in fact, largely a mutiny of the Bengal Army. It was a revolt by native troops much irritated as a result of the annexation in 1856 of Oudh (a state in which many of them were raised). This irritation was coupled with a widespread report among the natives that the British intended to compel them to become Christians. The situation was inflamed when the troops refused to follow the practice of biting, before loading, the cartridges of their new Enfield rifles, because they believed them to have been greased with beef fat or hog's lard. (To Hindus, the cow was a sacred animal; to Muslims, the pig was unclean; and there was probably some truth in this rumour.)

The initial outbreak of discontent came at Meerut, a large military station about 30 miles from Delhi where the first killings of British civilians took place. Then Delhi itself was captured. There was a massacre at Cawnpore, of a garrison consisting of some 500 soldiers together with their wives and children. At Lucknow, the capital of Oudh, the garrison was besieged for many months. In Simla, however, all remained tranquil and the loyalty of the Indian servants and guards was praised. Many survivors of the conflict, some of them wounded, arrived in Simla bringing 'first-hand accounts of the violence they had witnessed and the perils they had undergone'.[7]

The war ended with the recapture of Delhi and the relief of Lucknow. With that, the British government decided to put an end to the authority of the East India Company by transferring its servants, powers and territories into the name of the British Crown, namely Her Majesty's Government, which would hereafter govern India directly.

As the governor general at the time of the Mutiny, Lord Canning became the first viceroy of India, the representative of Queen Victoria and her successors. This was how he was widely known henceforth, but strictly speaking it was a title of ceremony used specifically when he acted as representative of the Crown. It became particularly appropriate at the Great Imperial Assemblage at Delhi in 1877, an event which included all the various chiefs and princes of India, as well as the maharajahs and rajahs who had been for centuries local rulers of India, building empires throughout vast areas of the country.

Under the British Crown they continued to enjoy various degrees of independence and personal rule, with their rights protected by treaties of alliance. The event, nevertheless, saw Queen Victoria declared Empress of India. (The British had prepared the way by deposing the titular King of Delhi – also known as the Emperor Bahadur Shar – who was the last surviving ruler of the Mughal dynasty. This elderly monarch, who was the last rival to the British Crown in India, was exiled to Burma. His complicity in the Mutiny had sealed his fate.)

The government of India was established under the leadership of the governor general (the viceroy) and his council of members. This council, accountable only to the cabinet of the British government, held supreme authority in India. In 1861, the Indian Council Act gave each member responsibility for a department: these included home, law, finance and the military. (Previously, all council members had deliberated matters of policy jointly). The military member, in charge of the army department, was the commander-in-chief, a position held at the time by Sir Colin Campbell (Lord Clyde). Each department had its own permanent secretariat. The foreign department became the special responsibility of the governor general who, like his council members, was appointed by the crown for a period of five years. The governments of the two minor presidencies, Madras and Bombay, were organised in a similar way to that of the government of India, but on a smaller scale.

Notwithstanding the formal and constitutional arrangements described above, practical considerations demanded some practical administrative developments. Life and human activities in India were ruled by the great dominating seasonal rhythm of the two monsoons, the periodical winds which blew successively and alternately in opposite directions. First, the northeast monsoon, giving the cool, dry season in January and February and the hot, dry season from March to mid-June, and second, the wet southwest monsoon giving the rainy season from mid-June to mid-September as well as the retreating monsoon from mid-September to December which also bears rain. The word 'monsoon', meaning season when used by Europeans, applied now to the rains from June to September. This monsoon set the country awash with frequent, often intense downpours, flooding cities and rendering roads unusable.

In spite of the difficulties of communication and transportation, Simla became the official summer headquarters. Sir John Lawrence, a man with considerable experience of the country who held the position of viceroy for six years from 1863, had decided that Calcutta – because of its great heat – was unsuitable as a year-round location for government, and preferred to move his council and department staff to the hills every summer. 'Of all the hill-stations,' he wrote to the secretary of state in Britain, 'Simla seems to me the best for the Supreme Government'.[8]

Soon after it was established as the summer headquarters of the Indian government, Simla also became home to the army and to the Punjab government, though this in fact continued to function mainly from Lahore. The majority of the town's European population worked in a variety of roles within the government or in the military hierarchies of British India. The numbers that came to Simla every summer continued to grow, and the growth in the expatriate population attracted many others:

> Horse-dealers, grain merchants, sellers of fowls, livestock and spices, came from afar to those bazars and lodged in their ramshackle serai. Several firms from Calcutta ... opened branches there, as had 'wealthy Mussalmen' from Delhi and Lahore so that, in addition to the usual run of shops selling provisions, locally-made furniture and cloth, there were hosiers and milliners, civil and military tailors, gunsmiths, haberdashers, saddlers, confectioners, watchmakers...[9]

Simla was home to a wide range of enterprising retailers, from perfumers and photographers to wine merchants and importers of oilmen's equipment. From 1874 onwards, it was also home to John and Susannah Perren. After their long and tiring journey over ocean and land, it must have been a great relief for them to arrive in Simla at last and to see that it was a place so bustling and full of life, somewhere they could settle and raise a family and perhaps, over time, become prosperous.

TWO

A FASHIONABLE PLACE TO BE

Like many others before them, John and Susannah Perren had come bumping along the Grand Hindustan and Tibet Road, dragging and jolting up the hills in a tonga, a two-wheeled cart drawn by a couple of ponies. The animals were changed every ten miles or so, and this service was provided by the Kalka-Simla Tonga Service, a private enterprise until it was brought wholly under government control in 1881. Throughout, the enterprise carried passengers, goods and parcels between Umballa, Kalka and Simla, the final destination, through the agency of the Post Office. Simla, expanding over a group of hills connected by ridges, could be seen from afar along the route. For the Perrens, it must have been a memorable journey. In the novel *Kim*, Rudyard Kipling (who in his book *Plain Tales from the Hills* demonstrated his familiarity with Simla) describes how his hero would 'remember till he dies that long, lazy journey from Umballa, through Kalka and the Pinjore Gardens near by, up to Simla'.[10]

In fact, John had been to Simla several years before. The 1871 and 1872 entries in the comprehensive Thacker's Directory (then only covering Bengal, the North West Provinces, Oude, the Punjab and British Burma), shows, under Simla, that he was employed as the assistant manager of a wine and spirit merchants' business operating under the name H T Ball & Co, which also imported 'oilman's stores'.

The 1871 listing appears to be the first which mentions John and the firm, which – given that the directory only appeared once a year – seems to suggest that he was with them from the beginning, or nearly so. The firm is listed in exactly the same way in Umballa, indicating two branches, and it seems likely a manager would have been based in one place, and an assistant manager at the other. The assistant manager would have enjoyed some level of responsibility, such as preparing invoices, ordering, stock control, monitoring publicity, and taking oversight of staff, including those in the warehouse.

Perhaps the position that John Perren took in Simla in 1871 had been kept open for him through some family connection, since it seemed that most of those who came to this country did so on temporary assignments – if not as civil servants or military officials, then as merchants. Maybe he was connected with the trade in England and was sent out by his previous employer, or had been offered the job and thought it sounded exciting to travel, or perhaps he had applied to some firm in the trade that had advertised for an enterprising young man to go out to India on its behalf.

One way or another, the chances are that his passage was paid for by somebody else and that he didn't just go out there at his own expense, or simply on spec. A lot would have depended on his prospects in England, or whether he was a man of the temperament to do something just because it sounded interesting. As for the firm of H T Ball & Co itself, it had only recently set up in Simla and Umballa, but had it been established for some time elsewhere in India? John may have worked for them in another capacity, or another location.

What is clear, among all these unknowns, is that John was in India at first as a single man, and that he came home to England, for some reason, and got married. He may even have come home to marry the girl to whom he was already engaged: maybe he had known Susannah before he went out there. It seems likely that there was a plan in place beforehand, since it would have been relatively expensive to travel back to England just to get married on a whim, doubly so if the ceremony was to take place during a possible six-months unpaid leave, whether the wedding was planned or not. It also seems unlikely that such a small firm would hold open a job for John, particularly if neither side felt confident of his eventual return to Simla.

According to the entry in Thackers' directory of 1873, under Simla, John had by now secured the position as manager of H T Ball & Co. If Susannah had already been his fiancée, it might have been expected that she would travel out to him. Perhaps the likeliest explanation for his return to England is that John was offered paid leave of absence for some pressing reason (though it is doubtful that marriage would have qualified as such), or that he came back for another reason: to deal with affairs on behalf of the firm. However, the truth of the matter will never be known.

The couple's first son, William John, was conceived either immediately before or during the journey for India, as he was born later that year of 1874, on 22nd October. The small family lived near the centre of Simla, close to the Anglican Christ Church with its Victorian-Gothic spire, where William was baptised in mid-November.

John was evidently a success in business, as the entries in Thacker's Directory from 1873 onwards continued to describe him as the proprietor of the firm he had joined. Furthermore, the directory in 1876 indicates that he expanded the venture, adding the proprietorship of his own firm – J Perren & Co – although it seems he also introduced a new partner, one J Hudson. Perhaps he brought Hudson in because the businesses did not provide sufficient income, and John Perren wanted to increase turnover by injecting new capital.

This was the year in which Susannah gave birth to her second child – a first daughter – but the Bengal Ecclesiastical Returns (the register of baptisms, marriages and burials) reveal that the infant lived only 18 days and died in early April, of convulsions. The following year, Susannah bore a healthy child – her second daughter, Susie Fanny – who arrived at the end of March and was baptised at Simla on 3rd May.

By 1878, J Perren and Co was conducting its business at Combermere House. This house, beneath Mount Jakko, was situated next to a deep ravine that was crossed by Combermere Bridge, a pine construction named after the commander-in-chief who built it. The aim of the bridge was to connect the main part of Simla to the little neighbourhood out on the long spur that became known as Chota Simla. The town was set at such an angle that the house was just one of those that backed out over the sheer hillside. The windows of these higher buildings looked down over the south side of the ridge and some peered into chimney pots of buildings lower down, as was commonly the case in Simla.

Just a few doors along the road, before the turning up towards Christ Church, could be found one of the most fascinating of Simla's shops. Everyone came here in search of curios and Kipling immortalised the place in his novel *Kim*. Its proprietor was a man of 'uncertain origins'[11] and local fame, who had opened it in 1871. He was an art dealer, jeweller and collector of eastern antiquities, and in the novel he becomes the ambiguous, mesmeric Lurgan Sahib, mentor to the young Kim.

In 1882, an additional list of residences at Simla shows John's occupancy of a property known as Firgrove, a building to which Mahatma Gandhi would be linked when he came to Simla with other important political figures for talks with the viceroy in 1931. This bungalow was above Combermere, up the slope of Jakko, but on the opposite side of the aforementioned ravine. The entry in Thacker's Directory for the following year, and for 1884, now read: 'General: Perren J & Co importers, Combermere House ... Simla: J Perren and Co. wine and spirit merchants and importers of oilman's stores. Props: J Perren and W Hudson. Firgrove.'

Susannah bore another child early in 1880: James Henry who was baptised on 23rd January, oddly not at Simla but at Anarkullee, Lahore. (At the time, John's occupation was listed in the record as 'shopkeeper'.) The Bengal burials for the following year reveal that the same James Henry, aged one year and 15 days, died of pneumonia in January and was buried the next day at the Church of England Cemetery in Lahore.

Two years later, in August 1883, Susannah gave birth to her fifth child at Simla, a fact recorded in the Bengal baptismal register. The child was named Charlotte Heath, but like her brother she lived only a short time and died on 21st May 1885 of water-on-the-brain. Though infant mortality was common, it is clear that Susannah had her fair share of tribulation, losing three of her five young children in a country so far from her original home and family.

By 1885, there are no entries in the specific 'Simla' list in Thacker's Directory under Perren or Hudson but the 'General' list gives the reduced 'J Perren, Simla'. And then, in November of that year, John himself died quite suddenly of an epileptic fit while travelling the 20 miles by road to the railway station at Kathgodam. This was close to the hill-station of Naini Tal in the North West Provinces, and it was also where he was buried.

John Perren was forty-seven years old, and had been in India just 11 years. Tragically, he died three months before the award of an inheritance of £100 or more from his father's will, which made no allowances for any kin of deceased beneficiaries, so that his wife, Susannah, received nothing. It seems clear that the family's troubles had affected his work, for at the time of his death, records list him as 'assistant to Messrs Murray, Naini Tal', a wine and spirit merchant. In 1886, there is no entry at all in Thacker's for 'J Perren'.

On the surface, the facts seem inconsistent. Why does the evidence suggest that the Perren family was living in Lahore, nearly 300 miles away, during a period when the trade directory indicates John to have been in business at Simla? What had happened to this young couple between their arrival in India and John's death? Though there is no extant record of their lives on a daily basis, it is possible to sketch in some details.

Despite the fact that this was an age when all Simla depended on oil lighting or candles, and their associated paraphernalia such as kerosene oil, lamps and lanterns, wicks and tapers, it seems probable that John had fallen on hard times. On his arrival in India, John had been given the manager's post in a retailing and importing business, one that was perhaps already declining. By the following year, he had bought the other proprietors out, becoming the new owner. He tried to make a go of it. He even expanded, with the acquisition of a second firm, taking on a partner (Hudson). For nine years, he struggled on as the businesses waned and then failed. At last, it seems, he was compelled to seek other employment for himself, and went to work for Murray and Co at Naini Tal, a journey of more than 400 miles.

If what is deduced is true, at least in part, it is a moving illustration of the often overwhelming and sometimes insurmountable difficulties which many Europeans faced as they sought to build new lives in India. Health problems, infant death, the climate and the vagaries of business – all of these took their toll on those who had arrived hoping for better things. Much of history, of course, records only the endeavours of those who won through to success.

Susannah Perren was now a widow with two children. It seems likely her financial situation was such that she was forced to find work. Indeed, a Thacker's entry for 1886 lists a 'Mrs Perren' and an 'R A Pymm' as assistants at Williams and Co in Simla, a store which was a 'hairdresser, perfumers, printers, auction and commission agents' all in one, and whose proprietor was listed as J Burton.

She soon moved on. Using skills she had surely acquired as a baker's daughter, Susannah began making and serving cakes and pastries on the terrace at Peliti's Grand Hotel, an establishment known for its first-class fare. Recently opened by the Italian confectioner Peliti, the hotel was described in an item by Cyril Dunn in an Australian magazine as having an 'elegant palm court where even a viceroy might drop in for an [Italian-style] ice'.[12] It quickly became the place for Simla society to take tea and to 'flirt and gossip', with throngs of fashionably-dressed ladies and gentlemen – all 'eating the air', as the Indians put it – who would take their customary stroll along the mall at about five o'clock each afternoon.[13]

William, the elder of Susannah's children, was eleven years old at the time of his father's death. He had probably been at Christ Church School before starting as a boarder at Bishop Cotton School, named after the Bishop of Calcutta who, it was said, had studied under the headmaster Dr Thomas Arnold at Rugby. Boys of 'more elevated circumstances'[14] were sent there, and to reach it from Simla's town centre was to take one of the prettiest walks along Lord Combermere's fine, broad, level road. This road ran for about three miles round Mount Jakko, and began under Simla's town hall (it was in fact an extension of the mall). Travellers would pass Combermere House on the right before crossing the bridge over the Combermere ravine, running down the west face of Jakko, to the south side of the ridge; then the road wound down the lower slopes of the Chota Simla spur to the school's barracks-like buildings, set in acres of playing fields.

When William was fourteen, his mother was married a second time, to the widower Henry Walter Bensley. From her portrait and other photographs, she appears to have been quite a self-assured woman, perhaps as a result of what life's hardships had taught her and through mixing with various echelons of society in her work. Photographs show Susannah socialising and taking tea and cake, so maybe she had met Henry at Peliti's during his annual summer stay in Simla. It was, after all, 'one of the favourite hotels frequented by Europeans, particularly married women and young men'.[15]

Susannah was some six years older than her new husband, who was the son of an apothecary based at a medical depot at Cawnpore. Henry's first wife, three years younger than him, had been Eva Ida Vernieux, and they had married at a Wesleyan chapel in Calcutta. The eight-year union ended in 1884, when Eva died of a ruptured womb while she was giving birth. She was only twenty-nine, and like Susannah she had borne five children, including in 1881 a son called Walter.

Henry Bensley was a clerk in the Indian civil service. This service provided the administrators of British rule at the headquarters of the government of India. The Marquis of Lansdowne was the reigning viceroy (1889-1894), and was to be succeeded by his son Lord Elgin. Henry worked in the commander-in-chief's office in the department of the Indian Army, an office integral to the structure of the Indian civil service. The service itself was said to attract young men of good family and, more importantly, good education. On the other hand, Eurasian clerks and writers – those of mixed blood – occupied a far more 'insecure and lowly'[16] status on the Simla scene.

Henry married Susannah at the Anglican Cathedral in Lahore on 5th January 1889, much to the displeasure of her eldest son William. However, William was making his own way in the world. Just two years later, he became one of the 'competition wallahs' at school, enrolling for an examination known for its difficulty. Succeeding, he followed in the footsteps of his stepfather by embarking upon a career as a clerk in the commander- in-chief's office. It is not clear whether he ever warmed to Henry, despite their professional association.

At that time, the commander-in-chief was Field Marshal Lord Roberts of Kandahar, who had won the Victoria Cross in the 1857-58 Mutiny and was immensely popular with both the British and Indian armies. William Perren's service book shows that for three months in 1892, he acted up for 'Mr H W Bensley', who was on furlough. This arrangement, however, was not to continue. Early in 1895 at Calcutta, the winter base of the government's headquarters, Henry contracted smallpox and died on 4th March, aged only forty-three. The following day, his body was taken from the Lall Bazar Chapel and buried at the Dissenter's Cemetery on the Lower Circular Road, Calcutta.

Susannah, widowed for the second time in ten years, decided to make Calcutta – some 1,170 miles from Simla – her permanent home. She took a house in Royd Street and worked at a tailor's in Old Court Street (W H Phelps & Co) where she sold frocks, suits, coats and hats, and was known affectionately as 'the duchess'. As she was reputedly a no- nonsense kind of person, amply proportioned, stern and with a regal demeanour likely to command respect, this nickname seems apt. Nevertheless she was evidently popular and enjoyed life.

Meanwhile, her only daughter Susie Fanny (known as Fanny), now aged nineteen, had fallen for a young tailor called Sydney Treglown and on 20th April 1896 they were married at the Anglican church of St Thomas (known as the Free School Church) in Calcutta. Their son Sydney John (Jack) was born precisely eight months later that year and baptised at the Old Mission Church in Calcutta. A daughter, Lily Elizabeth, followed in September 1898 and was baptised at the cathedral in Rangoon, Burma.

While Fanny and others like her at the time had all their children baptised, this did not necessarily signify regular churchgoing. Some people felt baptism was sufficient to be on the safe side and that they had done their duty by their children; for others, it was no more than a necessary social convention. There were some, however, who did see baptism as a high priority and who, as part of their religion, had it done without delay, because of the high mortality rate among infants.

The family was in Burma because Sydney had become the manager of a civil, military and naval tailor's, Messrs Harman & Co, but by 1903 they were back in Calcutta, where Sydney occupied a similar role. Calcutta remained the capital of India, being the seat of the government's winter headquarters, and this made it relatively easy for William to stay in touch with his mother and sister for at least part of the year. The great, palace-like government house (completed in 1802) was the official residence of the viceroy, and was situated in six acres of the grassy maidan (parkland) at the centre of Calcutta. More government buildings lay to the west of Government House.

One mile south was the formidable Fort William, the residence of the commander-in- chief. Robert Clive ('Clive of India'), the statesman and soldier who helped Britain to gain such a strong stake in India, had started building it, but it was not completed until 1773, and cost a total of £2m, which was a staggering amount of money for the time. It was octagonal but irregularly so, and while three sides looked onto the Hooghly river, it enclosed an area of two square miles.

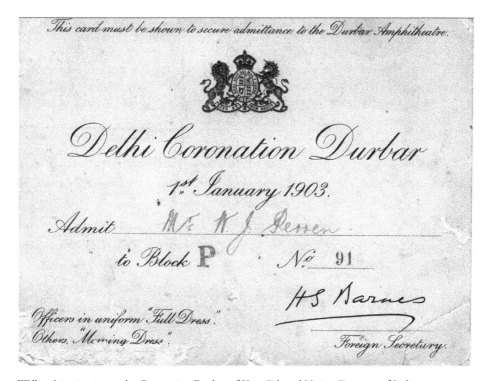

William's invitation to the Coronation Durbar of King Edward V11 as Emperor of India.

When William Perren started working in the office of the commander-in-chief, there were three distinct armies in India, each with a proportion of British army personnel. (Generally, the term 'British Army' referred to the United Kingdom's own land forces, among whom there was always a number serving a tour of duty in India.) These armies were localised under the control of each of the presidencies into which British India was divided, and known respectively as the Bengal, Madras and Bombay armies. After 1895, one army of India replaced these armies and the separate commanders-in-chief and the military departments of Madras and Bombay were disbanded. Their functions were divided between the commander-in-chief, the military department of the government of India and four new divisional commands.

The commander-in-chief (or to give him his full title, the Commander-in-Chief, India) was the chief executive officer of the army. He was an officer of the British army, usually a general or lieutenant general, was appointed for a period of five years and was afforded the title 'Excellency'. Just as the viceroy was the crown's civil and political representative, he was its military representative. T A Heathcote notes in his work *The Indian Army* that:

> Although supreme authority over all the troops in India was vested in the Governor General in Council [the Viceroy], the Commander-in-Chief had a separate responsibility for the manner in which military operations were conducted, and for the efficiency and discipline of the troops which took part in them. The decision to undertake a particular campaign was one taken, on political grounds, by the Governor General, but the Commander-in-Chief alone had the duty to decide what form the campaign should take, what forces were needed, what plans should be made, and what orders issued.[17]

The commander-in-chief and the viceroy each had a military secretary, of the rank of lieutenant colonel or colonel, at the head of their personal staff. The commander-in-chief's military secretary had special responsibility for dealing with appointments, promotions, exchanges and retirements in the regular forces (that is, the British army), while the viceroy's military secretary dealt with these same matters in Indian Army units serving locally.

William Perren served as a member of the personal staff of the commander-in-chief under the military secretary. His career in this office, which was long although interrupted, had begun in 1891 alongside his stepfather, when he became established as a fourth assistant clerk at a monthly starting salary of 75 rupees. After a year, and in subsequent years, he was at various times called upon to 'act up' to superior grades. During these periods he was paid increments and allowances consistent with the additional responsibilities he assumed but his service book shows that he took infrequent and irregular leave, in contrast to modern service conditions. Indeed, his record indicates that his first leave was for three months from March to June in 1897, and it appears to have been unpaid, or what was known as 'privilege absence'. Again in 1900 it seems he had about two months' privilege leave, and a similar amount in 1902. But he must have been working consistently hard because until 1907, this was all the leave he took.

There was certainly much happening. In 1902, Horatio Herbert Kitchener of Khartoum arrived to take up his post as the new commander-in-chief. The next year saw celebrations in Delhi that lasted a fortnight, including a great march-past of British and Indian troops led by veterans of the Mutiny. These culminated with a great assembly on New Year's Day on the Plain of Barwari – a coronation durbar (court) held to declare Queen Victoria's heir, the ageing King Edward VII, Emperor of India. The King himself was absent. Lord George Nathaniel Curzon, as viceroy, declared his sovereign was unable to attend when, in fact, he was cautiously staying away for fear of offending other dominions. Nevertheless, in common with the great Delhi Assemblage of 1877, the event was attended by British rulers and by maharajahs. These latter were resplendent in their traditional finery, in scenes that were said to surpass even the glories of the greatest Mughal emperors.

William Perren received a formal invitation to the durbar, showing the seating arrangement – 'Block P No 91' – in the grand purpose-built amphitheatre. In April 1903, he also achieved his first substantive promotion under a new superior officer, the military secretary Lieutenant Colonel William Riddell Birdwood. William Perren's new grade title is not apparent from the record but by this time, his pay had gone up to about 160 rupees per month. As well as being an eminent soldier (he had served on Kitchener's staff in South Africa), Birdwood was a man with a heart, and he would go on to figure prominently in the career and personal life of William Perren.

THREE

A MAID OF KENT

The new century brought William Perren promotion in his work – and it also brought him love and marriage. In Calcutta, he met and began to court Mary Yates, who was the lady's maid to Barbara Woodroffe, the daughter of the advocate general of Bengal.

Mary, born in Ashford in Kent in 1875, was the youngest of the seven children of Henry and Lucy Yates. As a young woman Mary travelled widely but in her childhood she had spent much of her time at Calehill in Kent, a country estate that for some 500 years (1410-1913) was the family seat of the Darells of Yorkshire. Members of her mother Lucy's family, the Freeds, were gamekeepers associated with this branch of the Darell family over succeeding generations, and for at least a part of her early years, Mary herself grew up under the care of her grandfather Thomas at Calehill in Little Chart, four miles northwest of Ashford.

The Darells were a noble and established Roman Catholic family. Several of its members were knighted and held positions of responsibility until the years of political upheaval in the mid 17th century, when the Civil War, the Restoration and the Jacobite Rebellion culminated in the Glorious Revolution of 1689. The Darells adopted the Protestant faith during the Reformation but embraced the royalist cause during the Civil War and, after the restoration of the monarchy, resumed their ancestral faith. Calehill became one of the outposts of Catholicism in Kent.

As a dissenter, the new Sir John Darell saw it as important to document the births and marriages not only of successive Catholic Darells but also, it seems, of other recusants. Members of the Freed family were mentioned in these early records by Sir John Darell, first in 1711 and then again in 1728, and while there is nothing to show that these individuals were particularly significant, it is clear that even at this time, Mary's family was already deeply intertwined with the lives and land of the Darells, their masters.

The country mansion known as Calehill House was the third to have stood on the site or nearby. Building work had started on it in 1753, though the chapel flanking the house on the right and matching the laundry on the left – both square wings in a style that complemented the main building – were added later. (The ruins of the old Calehill House, lower down at the corner of what was later the garden, also provide evidence of a private chapel.) The first priest to serve in this chapel, between 1769 and 1775, was the Reverend James Darell, a Jesuit and one of the sons of Sir John. Before his ministry at Calehill, there are no records of the names of priests who may have conducted earlier baptisms.

Bishop Douglas's report of 1790 notes that the Darell chapel was one of only five in all Kent, where it was estimated there lived about 600 Catholics. The existence of the chapel is confirmed in the certificate issued to Henry Darell from the General Quarter Sessions of the Peace in 1792 as 'a place of congregation or assembly intended to be set apart for the practice and observance of the Catholick Religion'.[18] By 1814, however, the tide had turned as the number of Kentish Catholics grew to 3,317.[19] In the earliest baptismal register of Calehill dating from 1792, Freed children listed included Thomas (in 1806), the father of Lucy and Mary's grandfather. Calehill was at the time in the Catholic diocese of Southwark (London) and there were confirmations by visiting Vicars Apostolic (delegates with episcopal consecration appointed by the Holy See to govern the church in regions where the ordinary hierarchy is not yet established), the first recorded in 1812.

The Darell family held the Freeds, including Lucy's father Thomas, in high regard. Evidence of this affection remains in a wooded patch of land near to kennels where the working dogs were kept, which became known as Freeds Alders. The Darells may have used this land to breed game for the park shoots. (In medieval times, a 'park' was a large enclosed area where the landowner could hunt game.) It was situated next to the gamekeeper's cottage in which the Freeds lived, one of two (the head gardener occupying the other) under a single roof, and built at around the same time as the third great Calehill House. Although the former cottages still stand as one unit, the big house, with the exception of the square block that was once the chapel, was pulled down in 1951. Completely stripped inside, and with its gothic windows partially occluded, for some years it was a pitiful sight.

The Freeds were deeply involved in the life of Calehill, and were entrusted with many occupations in the daily round. More evidence of the regard in which the Darells held the Freeds is shown by the fact that members of this great family condescended to be godparents to Freed children, apparent from the first entries in the Calehill register (1792) of baptisms for siblings of Lucy's father and, a generation later, Lucy herself; and then, later still, for two of her own children (Mary's siblings). Clearly the shared experience of these devout Catholic families – through the difficulties of recusancy, to emancipation and relative freedom in which they enjoyed the fruits of a thriving community – forged deep mutual bonds of respect, trust and solidarity.

However, Mary herself was baptised not at Calehill Chapel but at the daughter church of St Teresa of Avila in Barrow Hill, Ashford. This church had opened in August 1865, with a service at which Cardinal Manning preached. As a convert from the established (Anglican) church, he was a man of great theological zeal noted for his gift of oratory.

Lady Elizabeth Tufton, also from a great Kent family, contributed £300 towards the expense of building this daughter church. A friend of the Darells, she was also the employer of Mary's father. Henry Yates had formerly worked as a railway porter and clerk in London, but now he became butler to Sir Richard Tufton, 1st Baronet Hothfield, at Hothfield Place. This was another grand country mansion set in its own park, where Queen Elizabeth I once stayed. Henry served Sir Richard until the latter's death in 1871, when his engagement was continued by Sir Henry James, the eldest son and successor in the baronetcy, who was later created 1st Baron Hothfield in 1881.

Henry and Lucy Yates lived in the village but later moved to 7 Barrow Hill

Place, which was close to the church of St Teresa of Avila. It was here that Mary Yates, later to marry William Perren, was born on 20th April 1875. She hardly had any time to get to know her father, for seven months later, after the family had moved out to Westwell, Henry Yates was dead at the age of fifty-three, from leukaemia. As a non-Catholic, he was buried at Hothfield church, which was Anglican.

Lucy Yates, a widow with dependent children, now showed herself to be outstandingly resilient and resourceful. Somehow she managed to find the funds to put herself through midwifery training at Queen Charlotte's Lying-in Hospital, in the 'grand old parish' of Marylebone in London. In doing so, she became a pioneer, qualifying as one of the first hospital midwives.

Whereas in the provinces it was customary for births to be attended by female midwives without any formal training (many of these were incompetent, even a source of danger), London hospitals had begun to accept educated women for instruction in midwifery under the supervision of doctors. The 18th century had seen a surge in organised private philanthropy by active, affluent humanitarians, which created increasing charitable provision for various needy causes. Added to the efforts by medical men to establish centres of study for themselves and their pupils, this led to the opening of the first obstetrical institutions. Most significant among these was the General Lying-in Hospital, later renamed Queen Charlotte's Lying-in Hospital. These infirmaries began as small concerns, which depended upon public donations, and were run by boards of governors elected from among subscribers.

The General Lying-in Hospital was founded in 1739 in Jermyn Street. It was the first maternity hospital in Britain and places were available free of charge 'for the Relief of [25] Poor Women Labouring of Child and During the Lying-in'[20] with the intention that ultimately it would deal with 300 women per year. To qualify, each woman referred had to obtain from a hospital subscriber 'one of the limited number of letters of recommendation allotted according to the yearly sum subscribed'[21] and the sum of two pounds and two shillings to pay for the delivery as well as the customary month of lying-in which followed. Non-subscribers were also permitted to refer patients they considered worthy of admission, and these women had to bring their own fee when they arrived.

By 1809, the date from which records of Queen Charlotte's exist, it is clear the hospital extended aid to out-patients, namely those women who preferred to remain with their families or found it difficult to be removed from home. (It was the first hospital to offer both practices.) In addition, the hospital offered places to 'indigent females during the awful period of Child-birth', women who were the wives of 'industrious Labourers, Mechanics and distressed Housekeepers [householders]'[22]; and it was also associated in particular, throughout its history, with care of the wives of servicemen.

Since 1752, the hospital had admitted unmarried mothers 'in the true spirit of Christian Charity' and 'to facilitate the repentance of a suffering and contrite Sinner, and to preclude every motive of Suicide, the murder of a new born Infant'.[23] However, such women were admitted only on the condition that they were 'penitent'. Even then, it only admitted first-time offenders and these women were strictly segregated in a separate ward so as to prevent 'the possible contagion of evil example'.[24]

Although none of the doctors received a salary or other form of compensation (instead giving their services for free so that they could reap the rewards of public recognition in their private practice), the hospital did manage to maintain a high quality of staff. There was an apothecary who dispensed medicines, and a meticulous categorisation of the various duties of the matron, secretary, and collector of annual subscriptions. Duties of nurses and of patients were also laid down in great detail, but as the doctors tightened their grip on the management of childbirth, resistance to the idea of the female midwife increased.

By the time Lucy Yates went to train as a midwife in the late 1870s, not long after the birth of her own daughter Mary, only about 100 midwife-pupils were being trained annually, throughout the whole of the United Kingdom, in lying-in hospitals. The number of women out-patients in labour who hospital staff attended in their homes had increased over the past decades while the population of the country rose dramatically. For Victorian women spent much of their time producing children. It was also an age when maternal mortality was appallingly high and infanticide common. Newly born illegitimate and unwanted babies were thrown into the Thames as a matter of course or otherwise dispatched.

Queen Charlotte's had been rebuilt in 1857 on the Marylebone Road, and was designed to accommodate about 500 in-patients a year, and eight years later an additional third storey was added, allowing nurses and servants to move out of their unsatisfactory basement accommodation, into rooms on the top floor. Until the 1850s there had been no formal training in midwifery for the medical and nursing staff that passed through Queen Charlotte's. (Records since 1809 indicate there had been few in number of both during the intervening decades.) Things had changed, though, and now an increasingly important part of the hospital's mission was the training it offered in midwifery, mostly to women who were either married or widowed, and sporadically to male doctors who had a special interest in the subject. All were obliged to pay for their instruction.

By 1874, the hospital's Midwifery Training School was established and it soon saw a widespread growth in reputation. Applications for tuition began to increase and in 1875 the hospital trained five pupil-midwives and fifty-two 'monthly nurses', whose job it was to keep watch on a woman throughout her labour and then to care for the mother and baby during the lying-in month. During this training, which lasted for about three months (a definite period introduced in 1851) the pupil-midwives received theoretical instruction from the physicians and the resident medical officer, and practical experience under the eye of the matron and in-patient midwives. Trainee midwives who achieved success in an examination at the end of the course received the hospital's diploma that qualified them to act as midwives during normal deliveries; in the event of complications, the resident medical officer would be called in.

In the late 1870s, there was great concern at Queen Charlotte's over what was known as childbed fever, a virulent puerperal fever for which there was at the time no effective treatment, and which often proved fatal. It was commonly held that a lack of ventilation on wards, and failure to adequately isolate infected women, were at least partly to blame. On the tenth day after giving birth, a woman would be put into a crowded convalescent ward if she felt well enough, and was allowed to wander about the corridors and perhaps to undertake domestic duties.

However, wards were generally unclean and bacteria flourished. Florence Nightingale, in her *Introductory Notes on Lying-in Hospitals* (1871), was critical of the design of several establishments, including Queen Charlotte's. Unsurprisingly, there was no reduction in mortality despite the attempts to improve ventilation. The flow of air from one ward to another was facilitated through a large open space over each door, and noxious odours and air could easily circulate between lavatories in communicating corridors and in the stairwells linking different floors.

Indeed, in 1876 (the year after Henry Yates's death, when it is likely that Lucy was training to be a midwife), an epidemic occurred in the hospital 'of so severe and fatal a nature', according to the Committee of Management's Annual Report, that 'it became necessary to close the wards for many weeks in order that they may be disinfected'.[25] Intensive efforts were made to combat the scourge of infection. These included a new ventilation system: windows were to be opened at stated times, day and night, when previously they had been kept firmly closed for fear the patients might catch cold. There was to be immediate disinfection of dirty linen prior to its being sent to the laundry and a new system of non-resident midwives was introduced to prevent contamination from mixing with other nurses.

Under the new arrangements, Mrs Newns, formerly known as the matron, became lady superintendent and was relieved of most of her midwifery duties. Deliveries apart, she supervised all other nursing in the hospital and on each floor, she was aided by a skilled assistant to superintend and instruct the pupil midwives who had immediate charge of two patients each. Each of these nurses was forbidden to pass from ward to ward. When a pupil's patients were well (the report disclosed), she could go off duty for 'an interval of a day or two' though it was stipulated that during this time she should keep 'out in the open air as much as possible',[26] presumably as a way of staying healthy!

In 1877, with only six deaths among the 466 women delivered and nine in the 592 in the following year, there was hope that the changes were helping to stamp out infection. But by 1879, puerperal fever had once again become an extremely serious matter. (This reversal was at least partly because alterations in the previous year had increased the hospital capacity to the 'extreme limit' of 600 patients in order to try to cater for a huge rise in the number of women wishing to give birth at the hospital, as well as for the increase in applications from women wanting to train as midwives or monthly nurses.) Investigations found fault with Mrs Newns, who had been in office for nearly 20 years, and hitherto had been considered an excellent matron: it was said that she had allowed the stock of linen to fall below requirements and had failed to observe proper rules regarding the use of linen. In what must have been seen as something of a scandal, she was relieved of all her duties.

Between the opening of the new hospital in 1857 and the severe epidemic of 1879, some 9,000 women were delivered of their babies at Queen Charlotte's. Interestingly, more than half of this total were single mothers, many of them (it was reported) 'poor deserted homeless girls'[27] manifesting acute physical and mental distress. A remaining 3,632 patients were married, and a small number were widowed.

A further statistic of these years is also noteworthy: one in 20 widows died in childbirth, according to the records, compared with one in every 27 single women and only one in 48 married women. Even so, such figures illustrate the nature of life in a lying-in hospital at that time: antenatal care was virtually non-existent, and all women were at risk of picking up serious infectious disease, as well as suffering – or their babies suffering – complications such as the deformities of rickets. Dental caries, widespread in those days, was only one result of the conditions of chronic ill health among pregnant women.

However, the 1870s were also a time of discovery. Pasteur and Kock, following Lister's precepts of antisepsis in 1867, were working to combat infection, and while nitrous oxide and ether had both been used as anaesthetic agents, chloroform was already in use at Queen Charlotte's for manipulative procedures and operations. In fact, by 1880 the high mortality rates of the previous decade had dropped at Queen Charlotte's and were to level out in the next few years.

As a well-trained midwife, Lucy, like most others in her position, could have stayed in London or another large town in a salaried or fee-paying post. As well as in the hospitals, there may have been employment opportunities at workhouse infirmaries or on the staff of one of the unions or another charity. She might well have chosen to stay within the sphere of influence provided by London or a provincial obstetric centre, while engaging in her own private practice. Instead she returned to a remote rural district of Kent, to the village of Westwell near West Ashford, Kent, as revealed by the national census of 3rd April 1881. This describes her as follows: 'Lucy Yates. Head. Widow. 48. Professional Nurse.' It shows there were just three of her children with her that night: Annie (19), William (15) and Mary (five).

Two of Lucy's grandchildren (Clare and Hester) recall that she attended well-to-do patients in their own homes, and, providing there were enough patients to generate an income, it is certainly possible that she built up a private practice from home in the district in which she lived. She would probably have directed her services mainly at wealthier families who could afford the fees of a professional midwife.

However, the majority of women in rural areas were poor, often living in squalid conditions and in desperate states of health, and Lucy may also have ministered to them, managing home deliveries alone in most cases. In this, she was not unlike the traditional, untrained midwife; typically a local, older, working-class woman. (Such a woman might also tend to the sick and the dying and lay out the dead. Sometimes she might also offer domestic services to eke out a living.) Only in dire circumstances, if a woman were dying in childbirth, would a doctor be called. Even then, some doctors were unauthorised and unqualified, and fees were likely to be high unless the doctor was feeling charitable enough to overlook payment.

Necessity must have forced Lucy to place some of her children in an orphanage while she was training in London. One can only imagine how she must have felt about this. Mary, the youngest, just a baby or a small child when her mother went to train as a midwife, was to some extent brought up at Calehill by her maternal grandfather Thomas, for whom she developed a great love. A male cousin, thought to also have been called Thomas and to have succeeded his father as gamekeeper, shared the task of childcare. Sometimes Mary would help with picking in a hop field that was among the oldest in the country, adjacent to the Park's oast houses; hops that were used in the brew-house within the great house itself.

In December 1884, Mary received her first holy communion at Calehill Chapel, after being confirmed at St Augustine's Church in Ramsgate the month before. She may already have started her convent school education by this time: in any case, the 1891 census listing St Edmund's Convent and House of Mercy in Blandford Square, London, shows the names of nuns followed by girls whose occupation was 'being trained for service'. Among these was an entry stating, rather cryptically, 'Mary Yates unm (unmarried) 15 will be servant...'

A year later, on 24th March 1892, at The Convent of Mary at Blandford Square, she received recognition in a book she won called *The School of Jesus Crucified*. This was 'A reward for great improvement in needlework' and was a book she was to cherish for her whole life, along with other religious books given to her at about the same time by her 'loving mother', Lucy.

On finishing at the convent, Mary became first of all a parlour maid, and then a nanny. At one large residence in London where she and her sister Emily were employed, there were several nurse maids – known as 'over-maids' and 'under-maids' – who looked after the children. It was after this job that her travels began, for on another appointment she accompanied a family to America, going with them by paddle-steamer on the Mississippi and visiting New Orleans, as well as Guatemala and Belize (a colony of British Honduras) in Central America. These new and great adventures, however, were marred by her contempt for the 'old man', her ever-present employer and master, for his over-familiarity and improper behaviour towards her.

Her next engagement was far happier, and was to last for a decade. She became lady's maid to Barbara, a daughter of James Tisdall Woodroffe, who had been barrister-at-law and advocate of the Supreme Court of Calcutta in 1860 and was now, in 1892, the officiating advocate general of Bengal. Like the Darells, the Woodroffes were an armorial family and it seems certain that Mary Yates's commitment to them began on their return to England. This occurred not long before the death in 1894 of James's wife Florence, who was the mother of Barbara.

At first, Mary accompanied Barbara, who was a year or two younger than her, on her travels around Europe. The record of one such journey is a brown rosary kept in an envelope upon which she wrote: 'My Brown Rosary has been in my possession since the year 1893 and was given to me by a French Priest when I was leaving St Jean de Luz. I took it with me to Rome in the winter of 1895-96. It was blessed by Pope Leo XIII and also touched the tombs of the Apostles and other holy places. The Crucifix attached to the Rosary was in my Brother William's pocket when he was killed on the railway'. (Mary's brother William Yates, a railway porter with the London, Chatham and Dover Railway Company, died in 1887 in hospital at the age of twenty-one. He sustained multiple injuries at Wandsworth Road Station, having been knocked down while crossing the line at the rear of a metropolitan train into the path of a train in motion coming up on the main line.)

Another account in Mary's vivid handwriting describes how she accompanied 'Miss Barbara and Miss Agnes' through France, Switzerland and Italy to Rome, where they stayed during the winter of 1896-97. (Mary describes it as her 'first season' there.) This, together with a certificate indicating that she saw Pope Leo XIII inside the Vatican on 23rd December 1896, indicates that she made a mistake when she later labelled the first envelope. (Miss Agnes, Barbara Woodroffe's sister, later married Francis Mathew, a nephew of Lord Justice Mathew, and became the mother of David Mathew, who was to be an archbishop in Africa and later the first vicar of the armed forces.)

It is clear from the way Mary wrote that, even though she was travelling abroad and expanding her horizons, she maintained close connections with Ashford. At the end of the same exercise book in which she recorded the account of her journey on the continent, she wrote a most poignant poem, entitled 'The dear Homeland', which read:

The land was sweet with sunshine after April rain
There were blossoms in the woodside, sang the birds again
But my heart cried out in longing, all was sad to me
And I wondered, if 'twas springtime far across the sea
In the dear homeland far across the sea
I wondered was it springtime, where I loved to be
Did the sunlight shine on the old sweet strand
Were the birds of April singing in the dear homeland.

I could not find the blossoms that at home all grew
And I missed the happy dear ones that of old I knew
There were kindly faces round me, but they knew not me
And I wondered if they missed me far across the sea.
In the dear homeland far across the sea.
Did they wonder was I happy, did they dream of me
Did they sometimes long just to clasp my hand
Or perchance was I forgotten in the dear homeland.
I dreampt I crossed the waters, for my heart cried go
It was springtime & the dear ones they had missed me so
They came with smiles to greet me, & to me it seemed
My heart with joy was breaking in the dream I dreamed
I awoke once more, on my way I went
And my soul in overflowing with a deep content
In the dear homeland, far across the sea
They remember me, they miss me
And they pray for me.

In 1899, Mary was with the Woodroffes in India where, in December, Barbara's father James took office as His Majesty's Advocate General of Bengal. Additionally, in 1900 and again in 1902, he took service as a member of the legislative council of Bengal. Calcutta, together with the rest of Bengal, had been under the jurisdiction of the lieutenant governor since 1854. When, because of the climate, the viceroy and his officials abandoned Calcutta for Simla during certain months of the year, the governor of Bengal and his secretariat also left Calcutta (during May, June, September and October) and went to Darjeeling, the most important sanatorium town in Bengal and from which breathtaking views of the Himalayan giants, including Mount Everest and the Kinchinjanga peaks, could be seen.

The Woodroffes frequently made this 17-hour excursion. In her role as lady's maid, Mary went with them, and lived life on the fringe of high society in Calcutta and the hill station, for this was a time of 'immense leisure and spaciousness in India'.[28] James Woodroffe continued to serve in India until 1904 when he retired. He and his wife had converted to Catholicism around 1880 and he clearly supported and fostered Catholic worship wherever he was engaged. A decorative scroll was presented to him in the April of his retirement year, which pronounced him 'a devout Christian, a true and loyal son of the Church' while at the same time commanding 'a high social and official position'. His devotion to the Church was recognised as far back as 1890 when Pope Leo XIII made him a Knight Commander of St Gregory. The family retired to Uplyme, Dorset where

James continued in public service serving on the bench and in other fields. He died in London in 1908.

It was during her service in Calcutta that Mary Yates met William Perren, the first- born son of the pioneering Wiltshire Perrens and now an official in the Indian Army department. He was handsome, standing 5ft 5in tall and of stocky build, but how their paths crossed is not known; neither is any detail of their courtship, although it was clearly interrupted from time to time when Mary was obliged to accompany her mistress during the Woodroffe family's periodic leave in England and, presumably, during the hot season's sojourn at the hill station.

Mary's last journey to England in those early days was undertaken for a melancholy reason; one that would no doubt have caused William Perren some anxiety, since the couple was by then engaged to be married. Mary had contracted tuberculosis and was returning to England to be cured and to convalesce in Lyme Regis, which had become a seaside resort in the 18th century. James Woodroffe also went home on leave in April 1903, for medical reasons, and conceivably he would have escorted his daughter's maid. (His residence was only two miles away at Uplyme just outside Lyme Regis, so Mary's convalescence may even have been in his home.) Mary recovered and returned to Calcutta and to William, shortly before finally parting from the Woodroffe family early in 1904.

In these early years, Mary's unfolding new life must have seemed as exciting to her as the unfolding of a new century. On 19th March 1904, as a devout Catholic, she married William at St Thomas's Roman Catholic Church; a handsome 60-year-old building in Middleton Row in Calcutta. In order to obtain a dispensation to marry a non-Catholic, Mary had to undertake to continue in the faith and have any of her children brought up in it; similarly, William would have been required to undertake to facilitate this spiritual way of life. Sydney Treglown (his brother-in-law) and William Hayes were witnesses at the wedding of 'Will and Mollie', as they were known. Both William and Mary knew Calcutta well, but no sooner were they married, with the cool season over and little if any time for a honeymoon, than the two of them had to get ready to be on the move.

A week later, the viceroy and officers of the government, including the commander- in-chief (as well as all their staff), left Calcutta. Special trains were reserved for this retinue and their families and, because of the logistics involved, the transfer of people and luggage was made over a number of days. This time Mary, like William, was to make the journey northwest from this eastern corner of India firstly by means of the East Indian Railway system to Benares, that pilgrim city for millions of Hindus. Across the Ganges and almost opposite was Mughal Serai on the Oudh and Rohilkund Railway. This route via Lucknow and, more importantly, via Umballa was the most direct from Calcutta to the cities of the Punjab and to the North-West Frontier.

By now, communications between Simla and the outside world were much easier. In 1891, a rail line from Umballa up to Kalka at 2,154ft had been completed. Then in November 1903 came the introduction of by far 'the most up-to-date and long-wished for' amenity whose fame was to become legendary: a railway line laid all the way from Kalka up to Simla, which climbed 'where only tongas and bullock carts had gone before'.[29] This railway trailed up precipitous heights and for most of the way followed and criss-crossed the Cart Road, that well trodden but slow-winding trail.

With all its exciting changes, this was the spring in which William Perren brought his new wife Mary to Simla. They travelled as part of the government entourage in transit from Calcutta, up the new mountain railway not yet six months old. To William, it was simply a matter of returning home. Furthemore, he was an insider, for this was the place – as a correspondent of *The Times* in London noted as early as 1858 – where 'each man depends on his position in the public service, which is the aristocracy; and those who do not belong to it are out of the pail (sic), no matter how wealthy they may be, or what claims they may advance to the consideration of the world around them'.[30] Simla would now be Mary's home too, for the best part of each year.

The new railway was not the only talking point in Simla. At the time, a bitter controversy was in progress between Lord George Nathaniel Curzon, who ruled as viceroy until 1905, and Lord Horatio Herbert Kitchener of Khartoum, who was commander-in-chief. This feud concerned the division of responsibility in military matters between the commander-in-chief's department and the government of India. Not surprisingly, the supporters of each of these men were drawn into the dispute.

Specifically, the feud concerned a number of planned alterations to be made by the military member (the equivalent of a war minister) of Curzon's council in the disposition of the North-West Frontier. This challenged Kitchener's authority; and Kitchener was a general with a great deal of public support, a celebrity in an age before celebrity, whose recent triumphs in the Sudan and South Africa had made him one of the most famous soldiers of the British army.

William Perren, as the subordinate of Kitchener and Birdwood (Kitchener's military secretary), would have enjoyed at least some degree of contact and familiarity with these men. Kitchener was at the centre of the quarrel, reacting against Curzon's suggestions and becoming determined to depose the military member, and even his entire department. He proposed that the government of India should instead have just one advisor on all military matters, and that this advisor should be him, for he was the most senior soldier in the government. He should be in charge not only of operations, training and discipline, he suggested, but also of overseeing administrative needs and all supplies. Heathcote, in his book *The Indian Army*, gives details of what happened next:

> Eventually a compromise seemed to have been reached. An Army Department was set up, headed by the Commander-in-Chief as a full member of Council, to deal with all military business of the Government of India except stores and supplies. The Military Department was renamed the Military Supply Department, and its powers were curtailed. However, the Military Supply Member was still to be a serving general, and Kitchener insisted on the right to nominate him. This negated the principal for which Curzon had been fighting, the right to have independent advice. He threatened to resign, and to his chagrin his resignation was accepted.[31]

However, Kitchener was also to be disappointed. The British government refused to confirm his appointment to Curzon's post as viceroy, a rebuff that was a lasting source of bitterness to Kitchener. However, he did not give up. By 1909, in the year he was created field marshal under the new viceroy Lord Minto (Curzon's successor), he managed to secure the abolition of the military supply department and to sit as the only soldier in the government of India, as commander-in-chief and member for the army department.

> After the abolition of the separate Military Member, much of the correspondence between the Governor General and the Commander–in–Chief... was carried on through their respective military secretaries.[32]

Meanwhile, Simla itself was thriving. There had been an increase in the town's population so that, by the summer, there were about 7,000 Europeans and Eurasians among some 38,000 people who were counted as resident. Several new districts had been developed, along with a better road network between the different parts of this steep, scattered hillside resort; each of its various suburbs now had its own distinctive name. Consequently, the irregular–shaped ridge road (known as the mall) was extended to six miles in length and new European-style dwellings were built, in addition to large hotels and more and better civil amenities to cater for the upsurge in numbers.

A token given to William by Birdwood at that time, suggesting the high regard in which he was held, was a solid silver cigarette case inscribed 'FROM COL W R BIRDWOOD TO W PERREN 1909'. For both William and Mary, this gift would have provided a source of great delight and a reason to celebrate. They were young and in love and they had everything to live for, and they must have felt that here in Simla, they too could thrive.

FOUR

CHILDREN OF THE NEW CENTURY

W illiam and Mary Perren's first home together was in the lovely area of Simla known as Annandale. From the north side of the main road (the mall) there were paths leading down to it and a neighboughing glen, 'where a stream tumbled over great rocks shaded by magnificient deodars'.[33] They lived at Stanley Cottage, and it was here that they conceived their first child Emily Hester, who was born at the Ripon Hospital in July of 1905.

The hospital had been named after the Marquis of Ripon, who succeeded Lord Lytton as viceroy of India; he had laid the foundation stone in 1882, two years after he came to power. But things for Mary were not straightforward. The birth of Emily (or Hester as she later came to be known) was a breech delivery, a position with potential complications that must in those years have had life-threatening implications, particularly for the baby.

In fact, Mary believed that the breech position was caused by the

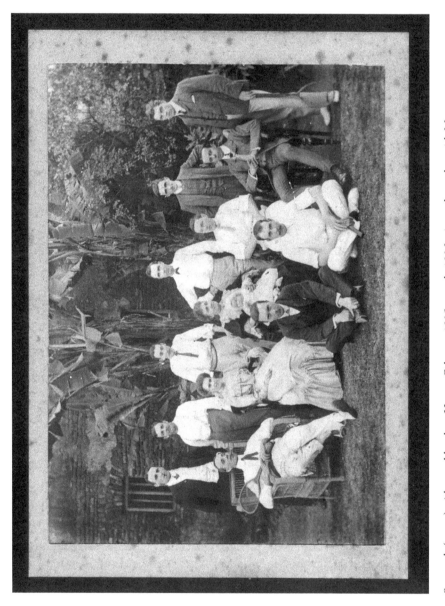

Susannah (centre) with granddaughter Hester, Calcutta, 1905 or early 1906, pictured together with Mary, her son William (back row 2nd from the left) and her son-in-law Billy Hayes standing behind her.

trauma of 'an awful earthquake' that took place earlier that year, on 3rd April. It happened at six in the morning, and was followed by tremors that continued for an hour. Throughout the next day and night, 15 smaller shocks were recorded, until at last the movement seemed to subside.

The earthquake had disastrous effects. Some 1,500 people died in Simla and its neighbouring province, and many buildings were damaged. High up on Observatory Hill, at the extreme eastern end of the mall, Viceregal Lodge, the three-storey summer residence and headquarters of the viceroy, suffered heavy falls of masonry. This stately lodge represented the highest seat of imperial power – Simla's very own Mount Olympus – in British India, and as a symbol of British rule, the union jack flew overhead. Beneath, the plains lay smothered in heat but up here the 'white gods' took it upon themselves to make decisions about the welfare of around a fifth of the human race. Symbolically enough, streams trickled downwards from the lodge into the Sutlej, the great River Indus and the Arabian Sea; and in the other direction, into the Ganges and the Bay of Bengal.

One can imagine how frightening the day of the earthquake must have been for the viceroy's wife Mary Curzon, who was in the lodge alone with her children while Lord Curzon, in Agra, supervised the restoration of the Taj Mahal. She is on record as having remarked about the lodge that 'a Minneapolis millionaire would revel in it',[34] but after the quake it took some 300 workmen a period of three months to restore this building.

Along with the new railway, the town was also being wired to enable private houses to enjoy electric lighting. Electricity as a source of light had come to Simla in 1888 – to Viceregal Lodge in its first year of occupation – although initially it was used only in the public buildings, and later to power a system of street lighting. Now homes themselves could be lit with a switch, and over time the use of oil lamps would cease.

Meanwhile, William and Mary's own family was growing. Their first son John Henry (known as Jackie) was born in October 1906 when Hester was 15 months old, after they had moved to Melville Cottage. This was a dwelling just above Firgrove (where William's parents had once lived) on the slopes of that 'deodar-crowned Jakko, shouldering the stars'[35] which Kipling had brought to life in *Kim* a few years before. At night there were 'house-lights, scattered on every level'.[36] By day, residents of Jakko, with its widened circular road and tiers of small villas looking as if they might at any minute tumble off the slopes, enjoyed some of the finest views in this panoramic wonderland of the foothills.

Just weeks later, before the onset of winter, Mary made the journey with her two small children down to Calcutta to join William, who had already gone in about mid-November with his government colleagues. A postcard to Mary, sent on 28th December 1906 from Stockwell in south London and picturing her brother Thomas's wife Sally, two of the couple's daughters and a niece, was addressed: 'Mrs Perren, 28 Marquis St, Calcutta'. (She had also received a similar picture postcard from Thomas and Sally the year before, this one addressed to her care of the 'Commander-in-Chief's Office, Fort William, Calcutta'.)

There are other cards addressed to Mary at Marquis Street from this period. One, which was posted in Simla, illustrated the fort in Agra and was sent by a friend in February 1907. This came with a somewhat cryptic handwritten message: 'What luck in the lucky bag – hope you have won the elephant or something'. (A 'lucky bag' was a popular attraction at bazars and fetes; customers paid a small sum to dip their hands in and retrieve a prize, which could be of low or high value.) William's sister Fanny Treglown wrote later that same month, on a card that featured 'The Mall & Post Office in Winter'. She wrote: 'Simla's welcome to the old lady – everything with snow – a beautiful sight'.

Fanny was not the Perrens' only correspondent. William's spinster Aunt Charlotte, the oldest sister of his father John, seems to have been close to the family and wrote to each of them from Hope Cottage, Hastings Road, in distant Corsham, Wiltshire, first enclosing a gift and then expressing sadness at not being able to see her great-nephew and great-niece.

The note to Mary ran:

My Dear Niece, I have enclosed the spoons for William. I have sent them to get you to get the lady to take them and if any expence (sic) I will pay you. The initials are T. G. P. Please do let us know if you receive them safely as soon as possible as I am anxious for William Perren to have them. With my love to you. I am keeping fairly well. Your affectionate Aunt Charlotte Perren.

Her letter to William read:

My Dear Nephew, I was very pleased to receive your nice letter and congratulate you on the arrival of Johney and oh how I should like to see Johney, and also Hester. Glad you got each nice children. I am glad you have a Hester as it is a favourite name of mine as it is so old. But oh I should so like to see the second Johney. Of course I cannot see but I could feel if I could only get out where you are. I like to hear about your wife. I like her name

Molly. The spoons with initials T. G. P. is Thomas & Grace Perren, they were your Great Grandfather and Grandmother. The spoons with initials W. A. P. were William & Ann Perren, your Grandfather & Grandmother. Dear Nephew & Niece, I am very ill. Just now I am under Dr Crisp perhaps the medicine will do me good. But of course I don't expect to be much longer here as my health is very bad. How very much I should like to see you all but that will never be now. With my very fond love and kisses for the dear children. I remain your affectionate but unfortunately blind Aunt Charlotte Perren. I am writing to your Mother. It is bitterly cold but I am in bed. Been in bed 12 weeks.

Not long after this letter was written, in March 1907, Charlotte died. It is fascinating to think that these same spoons, family heirlooms of the Wiltshire Perrens, found their way back to England, many decades later, in the possession of Mary, who by then was in her dotage.

This was the year in which William was again called upon to serve various periods in a temporarily promoted position. It seems he was a trustworthy employee who could be counted on to do others' work if necessary. By now, his salary had risen to 225 rupees per month, with a further 25 rupee allowance for each month he was 'acting up'. In September, he was granted a month's privilege leave.

The following year, Mary was pregnant again and at the end of August there was a new addition to the family: Clare Mary Perren, a little sister for Hester (three) and Jackie (two), born at the Ripon Hospital. By this stage, Mary had an ayah to help look after the children, as was the custom in India. Madhu, typically, was kind, gentle and responsible. (Only the ayah was called by her first name: other servants were referred to by their occupation.) She was to become so attached to the Perrens that for years, even after the children were all but grown up, she would return to visit them from her village and bring gifts such as nuts. The family continued for the next few years to live on Jakko, the hill above the town, and with their dog Nancy they enjoyed many happy times together.

Fanny Treglown, Mary's sister-in-law and correspondent, wrote to her even while both were living in Simla. (Fanny, now married, had returned to Simla from Calcutta with her family.) A card dated 12th August 1910, and addressed to Melville Cottage, depicts the interior of Simla's Catholic Co-Cathedral of St Michael and St Joseph where Mary attended mass and where her children were baptised, and bears a more local message: 'Please ask your gwalor [cowman] to give me milk after tomorrow (Sunday). 3 seers. I should like half cows & half buffalows. With love Fan.'

Until she was three, Clare Perren was taken with her brother and sister each year to Calcutta. However, in December 1911 there was a coronation durbar in Delhi to acknowledge the new King-Emperor and Queen-Empress. It was the third such durbar to be held and was even bigger than the grand event of 1903. Because of the implications of staging and catering for such an event, most of the families of government staff, including the Perrens, remained in Simla.

The coronation durbar was a dazzling – and a startling – occasion. King George V surprised everyone by announcing that the imperial capital should move from Calcutta to the ancient capital of Delhi. (The decision had in fact been taken on 25th August 1911 by Lord Hardinge of Penshurst, a relatively new viceroy, who argued that as the masses in India still regarded Delhi as the capital, it should also be the capital of British India.) The King went on to announce that a new city would be built and that Bengal would be restored to its former rank as a presidency. As a member of the commander-in-chief's staff, William Perren was involved in the coronation durbar celebrations, which took place on the site of the previous durbars. A marble platform held the thrones of King George V and Queen Mary under a golden cupola, the focal point of two vast concentric amphitheatres, constructed for the enormous gathering of British rulers, princes and other nobles.

Two days after the durbar, William was allocated a seat at the royal review in Delhi at which the new King-Emperor and Queen-Empress, attended by 'His Excellency the Governor General and the Suite of their Imperial Majesties',[37] received the salutes of the armed forces. It was held on the Badli ki Sarai Review Ground and included a royal gun salute, inspection and march-past. Heading the parade was the military élite of army headquarters, a group which was followed by thousands of Indian Army troops including their massed bands, guns, horses, mules and camels. All were under the command of His Excellency General Sir O'Moore Creagh, the commander-in-chief of India. (By this time, Lord Kitchener, commander-in-chief between 1902-1909, was serving in Egypt as His Majesty's agent and consul general.)

The transfer of the capital, and all that this entailed, gave rise to the immediate building of a temporary city north of the old walled Delhi City. This was to serve as accommodation for members of the government and its secretariat during the period that a new city was being constructed to the south and west of old Delhi. It was intended that the city, when finished, would house the largest bureaucracy of the British Empire and reflect its glory. The tract of land on which the temporary city would stand encompassed the durbar site and included the historic hilly north, or Delhi, ridge as well as the old British cantonment.

Early in 1912, from 21st February to 21st May, William was again granted privilege leave, and this coincided with the time that the Perrens left Mount Jakko and moved to Kaithu, one of Simla's northerly outlying hilly regions, overlooking Annandale (where they had previously lived). Typically, as one of Simla's several secondary districts, it sprawled over the flanks of a hill that was connected by unnamed steep lanes and precipitous steps. Their first house here was called West Lynne. Later that year, they went to Delhi as a family for the first time: a card was sent by the Treglowns in December 1912 to 'Mrs Perren, Commander-in-Chief's Office, Delhi' and pictured Simla's Victorian Cecil Hotel with the message: 'Merry Xmas to all from 7, the Mall'.

The visit to Delhi was exciting, particularly for the children. On 23rd December, less than two miles from the site of the previous year's durbar and close to the Flagstaff Tower on the crest of the ridge, they waited together to catch a glimpse of the grand state entry of the viceroy, whose arrival was intended to formally inaugurate the mammoth building project. The place from which they chose to watch was a scrub-covered rocky outcrop that formed the northern extreme of the great Aravalli range. The ridge was the highest point in Delhi, and afforded a panoramic view of the city and the British encampment.

The thrills must have mounted as the Perrens, along with many other families and individuals, waited to catch sight of the parade coming towards them. Then, suddenly, as the viceroy rode through Chandni Chowk, directly opposite Delhi's Red Fort, excitement turned to alarm. At a time of growing unrest and dissatisfaction among Indians, a bomb had been hurled at the procession into the howdah on top of the elephant bearing the viceroy. It exploded, seriously injuring Lord Hardinge and killing his umbrella bearer.

The Perrens had already moved to West Lynne when the last addition to the family was born: Clare's younger brother William Francis, known as Billy or Bill, who arrived on 27th September 1913 at the Military Families Hospital in Jutogh, two stations away. During Mary's period of confinement, her children were fostered out to different families; Clare, for example, went to the Simpsons, who had a son called Arthur.

After two or three years, the Perrens moved across the road to Ivanhoe, on higher ground. This was another wooden bungalow of a type common in the Simla hills, with a number of verandas and eaves and a roof of corrugated iron.

(Common, too, was the sound of monkeys, a local rhesus breed indigenous to and ubiquitous in Simla. They would bound across the corrugated roof tops, making a noise that from within sounded like thunder, but on top of this they were real pests and stole items from rooms, as well as being terribly destructive in gardens.) Next door lived the Bedwells, and the two families became very friendly. For the children, especially Billy and Gertie Bedwell (just four months older than him), this time saw the growth of a bond of friendship which would be renewed many decades later, despite the separation of the intervening years.

Susannah Perren, twice widowed and now in her sixties, came from Calcutta to Ivanhoe to visit the family. She was known affectionately to the Perren children (her grandchildren) as Granny Bensley, and she also came to see her other family: her grandchildren Jack and Lily, her daughter Fanny and her son-in-law Sydney Treglown, who were living above the tailor's shop on the mall in Simla, quite near to the post office. This, however, was to be her last time in Simla, the place to which she and John had come as newly-weds with visions of a long and prosperous life together. Doubtless the long excursion proved a challenge in her old age and the thin air of the mountains was becoming too much for her.

Meanwhile, the Treglowns and the Perrens remained close, to the extent of sharing living space. Sydney Treglown was a Cornishman born in Redruth during the same year that John and Susannah Perren arrived in Simla. He was a first-class tailor whose work included the making of fine garments for a maharajah and members of his family to wear at the third Delhi durbar in 1911. For years, he had been a manager of Harman and Co; and there is evidence that in 1908 and 1909 he and his family were living in Calcutta at 28 Marquis Street, the house also occupied by the Perrens. It seems likely, in fact, that the two families shared this accommodation even earlier: certainly over the cold weather seasons of 1905, 1906 and 1907.

In 1910 and 1911, Sydney was manager at the Simla branch of Harman and Co, on the mall, but in 1912 there is no listing of the shop in Thacker's Directory. It is known that there was a fire, which probably happened before the listing went to press, and which started in the hairdresser's next door late one evening. It was so severe that Clare's brother Jackie, who at the time was staying with the Treglowns in the flat above the tailor's shop, was lucky to get out alive. As it was, some of his clothes were burnt.

With so much timber used for house building, fire in Simla was a real hazard. Back in 1875, fires had gutted a large number of shops, both Indian and European, on an upper road next to Christ Church. The area was

The Ridge, one of the only two flat pieces of ground in Simla, with Christ Church in the distance backed by Mount Jacko, and the grand post office to the near left of the picture.

levelled into a fine open square that concealed a huge, newly constructed reservoir underneath. The Ridge, as it became known, soon came to be enjoyed for its views by inhabitants of the town. On this, practically the only flat piece of ground for miles around, they could stroll; or they might stop and look down over rippling foothills, or across at the jagged white peaks of the great Himalayan ranges 50 miles and beyond to the north, or, on a clear day, south over the hills and valleys to the plains of the Punjab below.

By 1913, although there is no longer any mention of Harman and Co in the lists, Sydney had installed himself in another shop. This time, following in the footsteps of John Perren, it was his own: listed as 'Treglown, S, civil and military tailor, 7 The Mall, Simla'. The shop stood a little further east than that of his previous employer, still on the mall, almost opposite the Gaiety Theatre. Fanny helped with the bookwork. The family at this time, or just a bit later, lived in a house nearby, north of the mall and the theatre, in the Blessington area. It was close to tennis courts which, when they became iced up in winter, were transformed into a skating rink – a particular attraction for the young Perren cousins, who watched the fun.

Clare Perren had started school. She went with her older sister Hester to the Loreto Convent at Tara Hall, an education house that belonged to a teaching order of nuns founded by Mary Ward in Rome, in 1633. It was very near Ivanhoe, though getting there meant a steep climb as the convent was perched high on a hill, as if in surveillance of everything around and below. This convent was principally for girls, although Jackie attended until he was seven, before moving to Christ Church School, which was more central.

Children of school age enjoyed little summer holiday – only about ten days each September – but they enjoyed more than three months off in winter, commencing at the beginning of December and lasting, through the cold weather period in Simla, until the middle of March. During this period, it was common for the town to lie under a thick carpet of snow, though as March approached the days became pleasant, warm and sunny, giving way to chill at night.

In mid-October, the cold weather 'officially' began. The viceroy, government and secretariat made preparations to leave Simla, not for Calcutta this time but for Delhi on the plains, for a period that coincided, at least roughly, with the school holidays. Only a nominal representation of people would be left behind. The transfer occurred over a number of days in mid and late November, with the officers generally travelling ahead of the families, attendants and servants. Such an exodus left the population of Simla greatly reduced, with most of the houses closed and shuttered.

At about midday, the little train left Simla's terminus station, travelling very slowly along the 2ft 6in narrow-gauge that wound all the way down. The scenery was thrilling and magnificent for the whole of the 60-mile journey: travellers would gaze out onto mountains, pine forests and precipitous river valleys during the six-hour journey (it took seven hours to travel up). In fact, as the crow flies, the journey down was just 30 miles in length. For Clare, whether going down or coming up, it was always an amazing adventure.

In contrast to earlier times, no longer were 'the Heads of State and their extensive entourages'[38] obliged to descend and ascend the mountains almost totally exposed to the elements. Nor was their 'precious baggage'[39] shaken on the rickety Indian bullock carts in the manner peculiar to those vehicles and 'left to the mercy of rainstorms and avalanches of mud and stone from the mountainsides',[40] reported Andrew Wilson, a journalist who once beheld it. No longer the dread – whether descending or ascending – of the unpleasant practice of reversing the carts or tongas to negotiate sharp bends until they 'hung perilously over some tremendous precipice'.[41] Only a stone wall edging the track prevented a 'final plunge'[42] and further alarm arose as each bend presented the possibility of meeting some returning tonga or cart.

Edward Buck describes vividly the grand scale of the new railway:

> Through its length of sixty miles it runs in a continuous succession of reverse curves of 120 feet radius, in and out of valleys and spurs, flanking mountains, rising to six and seven thousand feet above sea level, the steep gradients being three feet in a hundred. The works of construction involved are of the first magnitude, comprising 107 tunnels, aggregating five miles in length, numerous lofty arched viaducts, aggregating one and three-quarter miles and innumerable cuts and stone walls.[43]

The railway had been designed to be failsafe. Any train travelling upwards could never meet a train coming downwards on the single-track sections of the railway. Later, after the meal at Kalka, as the main broad gauge left the buffers, passengers on the sleeper-train settled down for the night before arriving at Kingsway Station, in the area of the temporary city, the next morning. Even in those days, it was something of a long haul.

In Delhi, army headquarters occupied part of the temporary secretariat building close to the Alipur Road running north from the old great walled city at Kashmir Gate, an area with ancient houses that had been the scene of brutal murders of Europeans during the 1857 Mutiny. A little further down towards the city, on the main road itself, was the Maiden Hotel (originally a house built in 1900 by a Mr Maiden) that served as the temporary residence of the commander-in-chief.

The Perrens, like other families, were installed under canvas at Kingsway Camp on the site of some of the most significant incidents of the mutineers' siege of Delhi. The camp lay in the shadow of the ridge, from where its occupants could see the historic Flagstaff Tower. The tower was a double-storied circular building that had been used as a lookout post and a shelter for troops during the Mutiny. It was also used as a refuge by terrified women and children one long afternoon in May 1857, though they later took flight when sepoys began to rampage on civil lines in the area of the military station inhabited by British civilians. (From this same ridge some 5,000 British troops, having retaken it in the June, launched their counter attack and all subsequent operations against the mutinous sepoys in the city. In September, they went down, breached the walls of the northern end of the city at Kashmir Gate and, after six days of fighting, retook Delhi itself.)

From the tower, a gun salute resounded so loudly at midday that, as Clare was to remember it, people everywhere could tell the time by its discharge. The daily round in the new encampment here became, more or less, the general pattern of things to come each year. Each family who lived at Kingsway Camp was allotted two or three tents: one contained the dining and living areas; another two bedrooms; and the third and smallest tent, if there was one, housed the commode that was systematically attended to by a mehtar, or sweeper. Besides khansamas (cooks) and ayahs (native nursemaids) and immediate belongings, the families brought cooking utensils and kitchen paraphernalia, bedding, and trunks full of clothes, books and other essential household items.

Mary brought no ayah to Delhi, even then, while Billy was a baby. However, during the cold weather season of 1913-14 she provided him with a regular source of fresh milk by acquiring a couple of goats. In no time at all, one of the females had produced kids that became very tame, and got into the habit of wandering off (on more than one occasion, a member of the family had to go to the police station to retrieve them). It was around this time that a man in a neighbouring tent nearly died. Clare was five: she saw the next-tent-but-one was ablaze. A servant acted astutely by collapsing one side of the adjacent tent to stop the fire from spreading. The man to whom the cause of the fire was attributed (apparently, he had been smoking in bed) suffered severe burns, though he survived.

One highlight of winter was the annual party given by the commander-in-chief for the children of his office staff. Clare Perren, with her siblings, considered the gathering and celebrations to be a marvellous treat: there was a large Christmas tree, and each child was given a present such as a lunch-box or an autograph book. At around this time, too (even the few times when they remained in Simla), Granny Bensley sent Christmas parcels full of homemade goodies (mainly Christmas puddings and mince pies). Clare especially looked forward to the 'mouth-watering mince pies with beautiful flaky pastry'.

Even better were the times when Granny Bensley herself came to Delhi to spend Christmas with the family, though sometimes she came at other times, and not actually at Christmas. Her granddaughter Clare loved seeing her 'sitting up in bed with tears of laughter rolling down her cheeks as she listened to the tales we had to tell her'. Although she considered her granny to be 'quite strict', part of the old lady's appeal must have been her touching willingness to listen to the children, and to enjoy them.

As March wore on, the approach of the blistering hot weather of the north India summer signalled a return for government staff to the cool of the hills, where they would stay for the next eight months. The wives started out first with the children, in time for a new term at school, and the husbands would follow. Soon they were all settled back in the hills.

The custom in India was for the British to engage their own servants and typically there were godowns (the servants' living quarters) set away from the bungalow but within the sahib and memsahib's (man and wife's) domain. There was also a cookhouse in each individual compound or enclosure. The Perren family employed a khansama whose principal duties were in the cookhouse, but who also prepared and cleared away meals, and ran shopping errands. In Simla they had an ayah, too, although probably not a mali (gardener).

They did, however, have a mehtar (sweeper) whose responsibilities were domestic. He would shake down the carpets and do other jobs such as cleaning the bathroom with its tin bath, table with a basin and jug of water and, in the corner, a commode that some people called 'the thunderbox'. The mehtar dealt regularly with the disposal of excrement from this contraption by transferring the used pan to a cane basket with a lid before taking it away to dump the contents into a round tin receptacle or a pit at the back of the compound. There it would remain until a foul-smelling buffalo-cart came to take it away.

A dhobi (washerman) called regularly to collect the dirty washing, which he would clean in primitive fashion by taking it to the brink of a cold stream known as a 'dhobi ghat'. After briefly immersing a garment, the dhobi would rub soap into it quite forcefully, if indeed he had any soap, before flogging or bashing the item against a stone or rock. The idea was to literally knock the dirt out of the clothes, and this process was followed by an amount of rinsing sufficient to render the garment 'clean'. It was little wonder that, time and again, buttons were broken or went missing. Finally, the clothes were laid out on the bank to dry; sometimes items were starched with rice-water. When Clare was a child, ironing was done using large charcoal-filled irons which were later superseded, when she was older, by smaller flat irons: these were heated alternately near a good fire and wiped before use. Clothes were made by a derzi (tailor) who would use either the memsahib's sewing machine or his own. Usually he did it on the veranda floor, where everything necessary was laid out.

For most European families in India, the routine tended to follow a pattern. Upon rising, some would take chota-hazri (little breakfast), which comprised tea, toast and fruit; and this was followed at 11am or 11.30am by a more substantial meal called burra-hazri (big breakfast), which often included curry. Next came tiffin (lunch), relatively light and eaten at 1pm or thereabouts. Afternoon tea, taken at 4pm, was followed later by a full-blown meal. The Perrens, however, had just one breakfast of fruit or eggs, with porridge and tea. On school days, the children took a packed lunch made up of sandwiches and a drink, and returned home in time for tea and cake. After this, the family ate together at night: soup, a main dish, and a pudding.

William, when he was at work, received his lunch in what was known as a tiffin-carrier. An aluminium container, it consisted of two or three compartments, fitted one on top of the other, and holding portions of food – typically curry, rice and dahl The tiffin-carrier sometimes had a section underneath which contained lit charcoal to keep the food warm. The chocra (boy servant) was trusted with the important task of delivering tiffin to army headquarters occupying one of the two large blocks of offices on the steep south-facing Simla hillside, near the railway terminus, but occasionally a hungry youngster committed to this daily pedestrian assignment would give in to temptation. While negotiating the tangle of footpaths and steep lanes into town, he would be overcome by the smell of hot food, and might furtively extract a portion for himself.

The Perrens, like other families, did not believe their servants to be wholly trustworthy and found it necessary to ration out supplies and keep the rest under lock and key. Traders also were treated with suspicion. One of the first callers each day was the gwala (cowman), who came round with milk in churns which would be ladled out according to the family's requirement. Whenever there was a baby in the house, however, Mary Perren shrewdly took precautions: she made the gwala bring his cow to the door to see him milk it, to be sure that the milk she was getting was fresh and undiluted.

Another essential daily caller was the bheesti (native water carrier) who came trundling up the path from the nearby ravine. On his back he carried a mussuck – a leather water bag made from goat or buffalo skin, from which he would empty water into a large vessel, such as a galvanised bath, kept especially for this purpose. Then there was the pedlar known as the box-wallah, a travelling merchant who came periodically with his trunk full of wares. Clare loved the way 'all sorts of clothes and knick-knacks' would come tumbling out onto the veranda floor: 'shawls and cloaks made from the silky hair of the Kashmiri goats; peacock-feather fans, gold and silver embroidered cushions from the bazars of Delhi; painted wooden toys, apricot jams and animal-skin rugs from the people of the hills'.[43a] Lastly and just as excitingly, there was the old man with the beard who would come announcing his presence with his cry: 'Ice-cream, cake-wallah!' Clare was a happy child, and grew up with a sense of unceasing love and care as well an abiding feeling, imparted to her and to her siblings by their parents William and Mary, for what was right and good. There was also a lot of fun in her life. At various times during her childhood there were pet cats, rabbits and once, in Delhi, a white rat that became so tame that it would run up and sit on her shoulder. Nearly always the family owned a dog, usually a spaniel or wire-haired terrier, since William, in particular, loved the companionship.

In his moments of recreation, William also indulged in several hobbies, principally those associated with his love of nature. Like other amateur naturalists of the time, he accumulated a large collection of birds' eggs, preserved beetles and exotic butterflies and moths – many of which he framed. (In those days a love of nature, paradoxically, often went hand-in-hand with an apparent disregard for life.) His latest specimens captured the interest of his children, with their busy little fingers always eager to participate; though sometimes to an extent greater than he was prepared to accept. The Perren children would go out with him on fine nights to trap moths, which were drawn to the sticky sweet gum released when William gouged the bark of trees in the surroundings. Another technique he used, perhaps even to catch butterflies, was to spread a homemade paste directly onto the bark of a tree.

He loved philately too, and photography. The camera he used was a Kodak

Box Brownie launched onto the market in 1900. It was a snapshot camera with celluloid roll film, each frame of which was wound on by hand – all very new at that time. Its simple form and use of the 'point and shoot' system revolutionised popular photography. Now, everyone could take pictures provided they stuck to basic rules about the optimum distance of the image from the lens (seven or eight feet away) and the need for good light. William's model was the second in the series, a Number Two Brownie introduced a year or two later.

It must have been a real novelty when William acquired his camera; probably in 1912, considering the abundance of family pictures taken that year and the relative absence of earlier examples. The novelty was, no doubt, multiplied from the point of view of the children and their cousins by the exhortations of their father to pose and smile wherever they happened to be at the time. The more natural environment and mood shows in marked contrast to earlier family photographs taken in studios, where there would have been great formality and the requirement (uncomfortable for the children, at least) to stay still.

William not only took the photographs; he also developed them. In 1912 he was using a daylight printing technique which was common among amateur photographers at that time, and whose basic chemistry closely followed the process invented in the 1840s by William Henry Fox Talbot. (Fox Talbot, recognised as the father of modern photography, worked at Lacock Abbey in Wiltshire near to Corsham, from where the elder Perrens had set out.) The process for William and others like him was simplified by the use of prepared 'printing-out paper', which was likely to have been gelatine-coated.

The technique was fairly simple. A negative image was produced in the camera and developed chemically. This negative, cut from the roll of film, was placed in a glass frame known as a contact-printing frame, with a sheet of sensitised paper immediately behind it. This was put out in sunlight for between five and 20 minutes, depending on the weather. When she was older, Clare Perren would recall seeing them all lined up in a row and, at the same time, watching her father's movements and critical interactions with these prints. Eagerly, she would await the moment at which, as if by magic, the transposition was made from pose to print. Prints measured 2¼ x 3 ¼ inches, the same size as the negative. Once a strong image had appeared, the paper was removed from the frame and underwent no further development. Lastly, it was treated in fixer and then washed, so the image was permanent.

The images remain well preserved, and the visual family record that William created is remarkable and full of character. Over the years, he took up to a hundred pictures. The majority, it seems, were taken in 1912 in the flush of his enthusiasm. Forty-eight of these are still in the Kodak photograph album specially slotted to take them. They provide an engaging window into the lives of the Perrens on Mount Jakko, with all their activities in the public grounds and gardens and lower slopes of Annandale. The pictures also illustrate their close association with the Treglowns in gatherings and picnics.

However, most pictures William took were of the children at play at Annandale or at home at West Lynne, either out on the lane or seated with their mother on the veranda. The girls were often in hair ribbons, looking cheerful, though it must be said that Clare's smile usually outshone Hester's. Jackie usually seems more intent upon the process of being photographed, but he looks a thoughtful and gentle boy. The few images of William and Mary are not so animated, showing them in less frivolous mood. Perhaps their expressions betray a sense of self-consciousness, or even hint that all might not have been as well as it could be.

FIVE

THE FIRST WORLD WAR

In August 1914, war broke out sparked by Germany's aggressive spirit. At this time, the Indian Army – the force recruited locally and permanently based in India, together with its expatriate British officers - stood at 1.5m men. Previously, its role had been to protect the North-West Frontier and to maintain India's internal security. However, prior to the war, the Committee of Imperial Defence in London had instructed India Command to take responsibility for the garrisoning of the Middle East countries and for operations in Africa. The British government, it was agreed, would reimburse it for the cost of troops employed on such overseas assignments. So now, for the viceroy Lord Hardinge, there was the mammoth task of organising India's war effort. He was to provide four divisions to Britain for overseas service. Three were immediately available; the fourth was held in reserve.

The army's general headquarters, where William Perren worked, was under greater strain than ever before. During his seven-year term as commander-in-chief,

Kitchener had secured for himself and for others who would succeed him in the post a dual role within the government of India: he was not only commander-in-chief, but also the official member of the governor general's council for the army department. However, despite some improvements, his reforms (which had led to a complete reorganisation of the army) were not always good for the staff. Now, with the disappearance of the dual chain of command, these headquarters dealt directly with divisional commanders on matters administrative as well as operations, and shouldered an increased burden of responsibility, while the centralisation of administrative duties caused the workload to rise sharply. All in all, the outfit was not in a good position to tackle the complexities of war. Heathcote remarks that:

> Kitchener's quest for personal aggrandisement had resulted in an administration that was unwieldy, over-centralised, and impossible for one officer to direct. The wretched General Sir Beauchamp Duff (Commander-in-Chief, India 1914-16), an incompetent even when compared with his contemporaries, so far from acting as a commander-in-chief of a great army, in fact lived the life of a hermit clerk. The collapse of the Indian Army's logistical arrangements in the Mesopotamia expedition resulted in a major scandal in which Kitchener's system was completely discredited.[44]

William's superior officer had been promoted and was now Major General Birdwood; he left India for a more immediate involvement in the theatre of war and was put in charge of the Australian and New Zealand contingents then arriving in Egypt for the Dardanelles offensive. He went on to plan the landing at Gallipoli, becoming one of the few British commanders to earn a creditable reputation from that difficult campaign in 1915. (Later, he took his troops to the Western Front, leading them through the appalling battles of the Somme and Ypres in 1916 and 1917.)

The departure must have been a sad one for William, who had worked with Birdwood for 13 years. Birdwood was William's first superior officer and it seems they had developed a long-standing mutual respect. However, in November 1914, three months after Britain's declaration of war (which had been followed closely by Kitchener's appointment as secretary of state for war), William Perren began a new phase in his career and was called upon, intermittently over several years, to work in the army department on temporary promotion.

From the evidence of two postcards, it seems that Mary and the children did not winter in Delhi during the first or second years of the war. One postcard, illustrating a section of Delhi fort, was sent by a friend to Mary at Ivanhoe (Simla) on 25th February 1915. The second was sent later that year (22nd December), showing part of Agra fort, and like the first, it was postmarked Imperial Secretariat, Delhi. The message read:

> From the Simpsons, wishing you and yours a happy Xmas, and a prosperous New Year.
> Delhi 1915, to Mrs Perren, 'Ivanhoe', Kaithu, Simla.

In 1916, events on the world stage looked less hopeful. Kitchener was among those drowned when his ship HMS Hampshire was mined off Orkney on 5th June, but by that time, he had already recruited his great army. In July, William received another promotion: this time it was 'permanent promotion in the Office of the Military Secretary to His Excellency the Commander-in-Chief to the 3rd Grade'.[45]

For the rest of the Perren family, life continued more quietly: Clare was now eight years old, and that year she moved with her family to a house called Northfield, still in Kaithu (close to the neighbouring district of Annandale, to the west) from where they could see Ivanhoe. Four beautifully-coloured cards survive this period, sent by William in Delhi to his loved ones at home in Northfield, and these provide an intriguing glimpse into the Perrens' lives. Each of these cards was date-stamped Imperial Secretariat, Delhi and sent to arrive in Simla the following day.

The first two were sent by William on the same day: 20th November 1916. One, depicting the Kutub Minar, was to his wife and illustrates the pressures he was under:

> My Dearest Mollie, I was very pleased to receive your letter yesterday and to hear that you were all keeping quite well. I intended writing to you today, but have not been able to do so as I am very busy. I will write you a few lines as soon as I can. Fondest love, Yours, Will.

Another card, also of the Kutub Minar but from a different angle, was addressed to his eldest daughter Hester.

> My Dear Hester, I was very pleased to receive your letter and will write to you in a few days when I am less busy. I hope you are all keeping quite well. With fond love to Jack, Clare and Billy and yourself. I am, Your loving Dad.

It seems that Hester wrote on behalf of the children: another card arrived six days later, illustrating the Mutiny Monument, Delhi. It read:

My dear little Hester, I was very pleased to receive your letter. Tell Mummie that I received the shirts quite alright. I am going out shooting with Mr Macdonald and Mr Simpson tomorrow night and will write to mother soon. Fondest love to you all. Your loving Dad.

The last card, dated 18th December 1916, pictured the Taj Mahal, and was also to Hester.

My dear Hester, I received your letter a few days ago and will write you in a day or so. I am very sorry to hear you are not at all well and hope that you will soon be quite yourself again. Fondest love from Daddy.

The family did not live at Northfield for very long. The following year, the Perrens moved back to Annandale, where William and Mary had lived in their first marital home, and settled into a new semi-detached house, Sylverton. There was little in the way of a civil administration in the town, which meant few building controls, and no street naming or numbering. Combined with a widespread nostalgia for an idealised rural Britain, this may explain why every house seems to have had its own name.

Why the family apparently moved house so frequently is a matter for conjecture. There were more of them now, of course, and William had been making progress in his career. Perhaps when a more desirable house with more captivating views became available for rent, William and Mary saw it as an opportunity to be seized; or perhaps the reason lay in the family's great attraction to Annandale, since each one of their moves seems to have brought them progressively nearer to its heart.

Annandale was special and had much to offer the whole family, in particular the children, even though it was a laborious ascent every time they wanted to go up to the town or school. This expansive level area lay deep in a valley 1,200ft below the north side of the Simla ridge, and the valley slopes enjoyed shade from towering chestnuts and eucalyptus trees, as well as from sturdy and beautiful pines and giant deodars. Lovely scarlet rhododendrons grew to a height of 30ft. The slopes were more sheltered and shadier than those of the Simla hills facing south and southwest, which were exposed to the burning sun, hot winds and the pounding torrents of the rainy season. However, the woods between Annandale and another region, Summer Hill, were said to be home to leopards. Some people could recognise the distinct calls of deer and other animals as a signal one was lurking about, but since their numbers had been decimated by the advent of human occupation, they were no longer the threat they had been – even to pet dogs.

It was a delightful place for a growing family. Even when the Perrens lived at Kaithu, they had come here on picnics and outings with the Bedwell family or with Aunt Fanny, Uncle Syd and the Treglown cousins, Jack and Lily. (These occasions offered opportunities for William to put to use his Dodger, a large butterfly net in which he hoped to catch further specimens, and an apparatus that was carted around by a servant.) Annandale had a large green patch of 'table land' on which was a racecourse, and on days when there were no races, local children treated it as a playground and loved to run around the perimeter. Back in 1848, a contemporary writer had commented: 'Rarely does a meeting pass without some serious accident, such as a rider rolling down a precipice, either with or without his horse, into the valley below'[46] but by the time the Perrens were living at Sylverton racing had been made safer – for horses and riders, if not children – 'by enlarging the course and cutting into the side of the hill'.[47]

Indeed, for most Europeans, Annandale was a chief centre of attraction. As well as providing the ideal setting for picnics, fetes, fancy fairs (bazars for the sale of fancy-goods) and fancy dress shows, it played host to gymkhanas, polo, cricket, and football matches which the Perrens loved to watch during the football season. The climax of this was the Durand Cup, a football tournament that originated at the Annandale ground and was named after a military member of the governing council. Different regiments competed for the honour of winning, and both adults and children became very caught up in the excitement of this and other events, the children not least because most of the time they were expected to amuse themselves and make their own entertainments.

The Perrens were lucky: Sylverton, deep in the valley, was just five minutes or so from the playground, so they often played active games. Iiaky (as Clare pronounced it) was a version of hide-and-seek in which the 'it' person counted up, then left base (a tin on the ground) to go and look for the others. When a person was spotted, 'it' called 'I spy you' and ran back to base, aiming to tap the tin three times with the foot in order to catch that person out. Another game was called High Land, Low Land and in this, certain high points (for example steps and mounds) were safe, but on low ground you were likely to be caught by whoever was 'it'. Statues was a further favourite, as was Shadow Kouk, in which 'it' chased and tried to step on other players' shadows.

The children also loved to catch cicadas. These were 'transparent-winged shrill-chirping insects'[48] that lived on the trees and, particularly during periods of bright sunlight, would make a noisy croak, earning them the nickname 'croakers'. The trick was to catch these creatures from the trunks of fruit and forest trees (where they sucked sap) and then let them fly away again. Of course, there were occasions when Clare and her siblings lingered nearer to home: a Swiss couple lived next door and ran a confectionery business, baking delicious cakes which were sold from a tin trunk by a man employed for the purpose. The smells wafted about the neighbourhood and so pervaded the senses that thereafter, for Clare, even their recollection induced a heady nostalgia. In addition to the football tournament, games, and nature watching, there was also the occasional unexpected excitement, such as the time an aeroplane landed in Annandale during a severe hailstorm. 'It was covered in dents,' Clare recalled. 'It was a real novelty to see a plane for the first time – everyone went down to look at it.'

While the family was at Sylverton, William kept pigeons, some of good class. (It fell to the servants to keep the coops clean.) He dreamed that one day he might make them into racers, like those owned by members of the large Muslim community in the old city of Delhi. There, pigeon breeding and flying was one of the oldest and most respected pastimes, and involved training for the racing season. Traditionally, breeders flew pigeons from their roofs and sometimes tried to lure birds from other flocks to join their own.

Meanwhile, he continued up the career ladder. In June 1917, he was promoted from the 3rd grade to the 2nd grade, with a pay rise of 50 rupees per month, working in the office of the military secretary to His Excellency the commander-in-chief. (The post of military secretary was regraded in this year and henceforth was to be held by a major general.) However, all was not well. At around this time, William was forced to take medical leave: he was suffering from a nervous breakdown, and did not work from 18th July until the end of October. Later, though, he did return to the military department (military secretary's branch) and remained there for the remainder of his career.

Clare, as a child, sensed her father's 'worrying nature' – sometimes he would anxiously touch the forehead of one of his children and pronounce: 'That child has a fever, and is going to be ill'. Within the family, it was felt that William was no good in a crisis, although until now he had managed to cope with the many pressures of work, including the yearly commute to Delhi and the exigencies of wartime. It does seem that the promotion – coming during a busy and difficult period at army headquarters, a time of heavy demand – may have tipped the balance for him. India was the base for operations in the Middle East, and William's department bore onerous duties, such as ensuring the replenishment of stocks of war materials and obtaining British recruits to the army. In all likelihood, the extra stresses of the new position were just too much, triggering the onset of neurosis.

Mary decided that the best way to cope with her husband's breakdown was to send the children (except for Billy) away to boarding school. Hester and Clare – aged twelve and eight, respectively – went to live at Jesus and Mary Convent, which they sometimes referred to as Chelsea Convent, a school situated in Simla East at Chota Simla. To get there meant travelling by rickshaw, a common mode of transport that, by the 1890s, had replaced the older jampan. The rickshaw was akin to a bath chair, and had been invented in Japan in about 1870. The journey took them past Christ Church, then on to a higher and more direct road running parallel with the mall, around Mount Jakko.

Clare remembered that she and her best friend were installed at opposite ends of a long dormitory and that she and the other girls used to sing 'the war songs'. However, discipline at the new school was strict, even for the youngest pupils. Girls who wet their beds in the night were put in an annex called The Tower – this was so that they would be near to the toilet in the garret, but it was also perceived by the girls to be nearer to 'all the filthy clothes'. Another punishment was to be obliged to remain on one's knees in the infants' dormitory for a period in the evening. Bath time, once weekly, happened early in the morning and was communal; girls went in three batches, taking their baths in galvanised tubs set in a long row. So that modesty should prevail, every girl was obliged to have two chemises (petticoat-like undergarments), one of which was to be worn in the bath while performing ablutions, the other to be at the ready to put on and cover the body during the drying process. Otherwise, apart from bath time, chemises were not worn; only vests. Being an elder sister, it was Hester's job to see to Clare.

As children, the two girls were often compared. Clare was asked (a lot more than she cared to be): 'Why can't you be like your sister?' She was impish, whereas Hester was rather more correctly behaved. Both of them, however, were equally curious about one delicate matter: the facts of life. In a bid to stem their curiosity, Mary had told them that they had been born in a sweeper's basket. Hester, who had a tendency to take things to heart and was the more literal of the two, believed it and, until she was acquainted with the real facts, felt greatly upset whenever she thought about it. Nor was Clare exempt from anxiety, particularly after she had been naughty and her mother told her that she didn't belong to the Perren family; that she had been swapped at birth, in the hospital. Another time she was told she was discarded, because nobody wanted her. (In those days, before anyone knew much about child psychology, it was probably a common enough admonishment.) But this idea got under Clare's skin. It bothered her, as it was surely intended to – the thought that she didn't belong to this family.

Their brother, Jackie, was taken to a boarding school called St Fidelis' College, which was in the neighbouring hill-station of Mussoorie. (It was in fact 150 miles from Simla through the hills.) His education was provided by the Brothers of the Christian Schools of Ireland, for the college was just one of many set up to educate boys by this worldwide institute, founded in 1802 at Waterford. However, his stay there was curtailed when he contracted paratyphoid (enteric fever) six months after arriving. Mary, to whom this must have been an added emotional burden at a worrying time, made the journey to bring him home. Jackie never entirely recovered from the illness and remained in a rather delicate state thereafter. For the whole of the next year he did not go to school, but was taught privately at the home of a retired schoolmaster at Annandale. Then he returned to his previous school, Christ Church.

The girls, at least, were content despite their more austere conditions. They were boarders for just 18 months in all, and enjoyed a number of memorable times. After they had been at the convent for two months, they were both among a number of children who received their first Holy Communion: the date was 8th September 1917. It was significant that, not long after this at her confirmation, Clare took the saint's name Barbara. Her mother may well have influenced her choice, for if the name was not chosen for a particular affiliation to the said saint, perhaps it was in memory of her former mistress, Barbara Woodroffe.

Both Clare and Hester were chosen – for two successive years – along with pupils from other schools in Simla to attend a children's garden party at the elegant Viceregal Lodge, set in acres of beautiful terraced gardens and trim lawns. Those children who had been selected to attend the party were carried to the lodge, at the western end of Simla's ridge, in a rickshaw. Usually these vehicles had two large wheels, padded seats, an oilskin hood and armrests, and were operated by four Indians: two at the front and two at the back. This time, much to the children's excitement, the operators were dressed in the scarlet livery of the viceroy.

On arrival Clare and Hester, along with the other children, were invited to tuck into 'a great feast', waited upon by servants in similarly splendid livery. On one of these two occasions, in an otherwise magnificent day, there was one blemish for Clare. When the need dictated, she went to make use of one of the chamber pots provided – and to her dismay, having done so, found it was broken. She tried to convince herself that it must have been already cracked, but the anxiety she felt was worsened when the other girls and a teacher suggested she would most probably have to pay for the damage!

SIX

ANNUAL ESCAPES

William Perren had recovered from his breakdown enough to be back at work in the winter of 1917-1918, while the war in Europe raged towards its weary conclusion. In order to be with her husband during the cold weather period, Mary travelled to Delhi with the two boys and probably the cook, although without his family (Clare and Hester, having shorter holidays as boarders, were still at school.) As usual, William had gone ahead with the secretariat staff. The girls travelled to Delhi under school supervision at the end of December and were met by their parents at Delhi station.

In complete contrast to Simla, set in the foothills of the lofty Himalayan area, Delhi stands towards the western end of north India's great Indo-Gangetic Plain, one of nature's wonders. Extending 1,900 miles long and between 90 and 200 miles wide, it is the greatest stretch of alluvial plain in the world. For nearly 1,000 miles of its length, this famous flatland drops less than 700ft in elevation and was formed by the basins of three distinct river systems: the Indus, the

Brahmaputra and the Ganges. In this vast region, the cool weather season begins in December and ends in March.

William had little respite from work, except at weekends. However, for his children, Delhi represented more than three months of holiday time: a profusion of hours stretching out before them, all to be whiled away enjoyably. One of their favourite activities was to go wading in the Jumna, a river that flowed by Delhi and Agra and onwards to feed into the sacred Ganges. Hindus said the river brought purity, wealth and fertility to those who bathed in it; and, believers in reincarnation, they thought those who went there to die would attain higher status in a future life.

The children chose a narrow point of this wide river to paddle across, always on the lookout for crocodiles. These rivers were home to the broad-snouted marsh crocodile or muggur. This animal was more vicious to humans than its cousin the gharial, which had a long slender snout, lived in deeper waters, and ate fish. The appropriately named muggur killed thousands of villagers and townsfolk each year, in particular those who lived on the riverbanks. Fortunately, none of the children ever met one while wading in the water. Presumably, although enjoying the thrill of the crossing, they remained alert and stuck closely together, the regular tragedies making it hard for them to forget the dangers and just to enjoy the sensations of paddling.

During their winter holidays, they also loved to watch the great Indian sport of kite-flying, seen at its best in Delhi. Competitions and rivalry were common. Each kite was personally designed and fashioned by its owner and manipulated by the working of a vast length of twine. It was a colourful spectacle, one that captivated onlookers who watched these 'little specks' dart and dance high in the sky. Some competitors, however, were wilier than others, using rooftops and other vantage points to manoeuvre their kites so as to bring down other kites from the sky. In some contests, ground glass was glued to the twine (moonga) in order to abrade and hopefully to sever the twine of rivals.

Clare and her younger brother Billy had one passion in common: roller-skating at the rink. Hester was 'much too prim and proper' to skate, and Jackie, a typical older brother, 'wasn't that interested'. Clare and Billy, however, were keen, and the soldiers who used the rink encouraged them and taught them to skate. After a while, they were such familiar faces that they didn't even have to pay to get in. Gertie Bedwell, their Simla playmate, recalled the friendliness of the soldiers: she and Billy would walk beside them 'as they marched to church on Sunday mornings and wait outside until they came out, when we would walk back with them'. She remembered a more mischievous activity, too, back at camp – 'sliding down the tents' (having first climbed them) provided hours of fun.

Sometimes families went to the picture house to see the silent American and British films of the day. These soundless films lasted for an hour or more, although the industry was still in its infancy and, before 1912, feature-length films were unknown. (By 1917, however, the United States could boast a yearly total of 687 films; Great Britain produced 66, and India – for the first time – three. The number of cinemas on the subcontinent was growing too, from five in 1910 to 148 just ten years later.)

There were beautiful gardens in which to stroll for hours and restore body and soul, and it was likely that the pretty Kudsia Garden, just outside the historic Kashmir Gate, was home to the brilliant yellow pendants of the Indian laburnum, a tree common in Delhi. Clare, in particular, loved these fragile blossoms that appeared a few weeks before summer started but faded away quickly once the sun became strong. Another place she gave special reference to was the Rochanara Gardens, created by the daughter of Shah Jahan, who lies buried there.

A little further south was the jostle of Old Delhi itself, also known as Shahjahanabad, the 'seventh city' of Delhi built by the fifth Mughal emperor Shah Jahan, the greatest builder of them all. Much of the walling of that city was destroyed throughout the ages, leaving mostly ruins, but imposing gateways remained and it now stood open to all comers. Otherwise, Old Delhi was little changed. Its busiest street, Chandni Chauk, still ran from the Red Fort westward to Fatehpuri Mosque, and its warren of alleys were, as always, thronged with shops and crowded bazaars.

As the historical capital of India, Delhi had been burnished with the glamour of ages. Over many centuries, invaders had swept down to what they saw as the gateway to the rich plain of the Ganges. Over and over again, these newcomers destroyed the city only to re-establish their own capitals on the same site. Hindu and Muslim dynasties came and went until finally the Mughals, the last and the greatest rulers from central Asia, ceded power to the British. Not surprisingly, these invaders left behind them a wealth of monuments, many of them exquisitely ornate and beautiful: mosques, tombs and mausolea, temples, palaces, towers, fortresses and gates. Over the years that the Perren family wintered in Delhi, some of these became familiar landmarks – both from personal visits and through the sending and receiving of picture postcards.

Clare's favourite was the Kutub Minar, eleven miles south of Delhi, which was known as the seventh wonder of Hindustan. The family came here in a tonga – a light, low-seated two-wheeled horse-drawn vehicle – on several occasions. As one of the earliest monuments of the Afghan period, dating from 1199, the Kutub Minar was considered by some to be an outstanding example of tower architecture. The children climbed, with much zeal, the steps to the summit (238ft up from the ground) where they gained a magnificent view, not least of the now-ruined Kuwwat ul Islam Mosque immediately below. This mosque, the first in India, was built in the 12th century on the foundations of a Hindu temple during the first great Muslim invasion.

Also occupying the site of the Hindu temple and standing in front of the central opening to the mosque was the Iron Pillar, a real oddity: a solid shaft of wrought iron, more than 16in in diameter and some 24ft long. In a Gupta inscription, it documents its own history, mentioning King Chandra who was thought to be the Gupta emperor, reigning in around 400AD. The legend goes that anyone who can stand with their back against this pillar and clasp their hands around it will have their wish granted. Needless to say, the Perren children always loved to try their luck. They also liked watching the men and boys who were diving into a large, round well nearby, although there was a moment of panic when the family saw a dog fall in by accident!

Each time the Perrens travelled to and from the Kutab Minar by tonga, they crossed the area on which the new, spacious capital of Delhi was under construction. There, before their very eyes, was history in the making. Edwin Lutyens, said to be the most original and creative English architect of his day, and with a reputation for extravagance, was responsible for the overall design and was also overseeing the new government centre, as well as some monuments and buildings along Kingsway, an immensely broad road about two miles long, bordered by gardens. His aim was to achieve the opposite of a fort: an open, unwalled (garden) city with its radiating roads open to the world. Some 30,000 labourers (both men and women from Agra, Bharatpur and Mirzapur) were working on the construction of grand houses, parliamentary buildings and public offices with bricks and mortar. More than 4,000 flat-topped residences of stuccoed brick were being built, too, ranging from bungalows for senior officers to quarters for menial staff and clerks, as well as hospitals, post offices and other necessary structures. The atmosphere must have been feverish – and dusty.

In contrast to this urban activity, and perhaps as an outlet from it, William had become interested in a country sport: hunting. (This had long been a passion of the maharajahs, as well as the British, and was undoubtedly the cause of the decline of some of India's great beasts: the tiger, the blackbuck, the Asiatic Lion. Even the cheetah's days – as it became clear by the 1920s – were numbered.) To the family, William's activity was known as shikar, a Hindu word meaning hunting and shooting. Shikari described a native expert who accompanied European sportsmen as a guide and aid, or the European sportsman himself. Complete with his double-barrelled shotgun and a copious supply of cartridges in a tin box, he would venture off for the weekend with his hunting companion, Mr Macdonald, setting his sights on an area of dry scrubland forest on the ridge, which was accessible from Kingsway Camp. At other times, they would go by the river tract, along the Jumna.

The pair rode by bullock cart for part of the way to find boars and wild game, and would then go on to the jheels, swampy marshes that were known to yield abundant wildfowl. On Sunday, William would return home, usually with his game-stick laden with the more manageable prizes of the shoot: hare, wild duck, partridge, pheasant and what Clare remembered as 'lovely little quail'. These were served with 'delicious game chips the cook made to go with the game birds'. On one memorable occasion, William returned from the ridge with a wild boar, but his triumph was short-lived after the family cook – a Muslim – refused to prepare, cook or go anywhere near his trophy! Less controversially, in Simla, he brought home two or three bucks' heads, which he hung on the walls of his home. Weary and footsore after any such excursion, he would ease his discomfort by soaking his feet in a mustard bath.

In general, the Perren family's life was comfortable enough, but accidents did happen. William was particularly unfortunate, picking up a leech while drinking stream water in Simla. He took it in through the mouth, and the creature – in shrunken pre-gorging form – managed to lodge itself inside his nose. From then on, steadily, revoltingly, it grew fat on his blood. His daughter, Clare, recalled how he would use a nasal pump to 'sniff up' salt water. 'Sometimes the leech moved down so far, but never far enough to come out,' she remembered. Serious attempts to get rid of it had already been made. Both the hospital and Mary had tried to remove the horrible thing with tweezers but there were fears that the leech's jaw would break off in the skin and cause infection or hemorrhaging (leech saliva contains an anti-coagulant). Eventually though, it did come out and was kept, by William, in a jar.

Another mishap occurred during a year when the family was still under canvas, in Delhi. Winifred Broom, a young mother, was heating milk for her baby son Jimmy in a neighbouring tent. Suddenly, she lost control of her spirit stove, and cried out. Mary came running, and threw a carpet over her burning face and hair; then she concentrated on rescuing the baby, who was crawling inside the tent which, by then, was ablaze. Heroically, she managed to put out the fire with her bare hands, but for the onlookers – particularly Clare, who was ten or eleven – these were terrifying moments.

At a similar time, in the summer and autumn of 1918 as the war drew to a close, a deadly flu virus (Spanish influenza) swept across Europe into Asia. It was a strain that was to become one of the deadliest killers in human history (on a par with the 14th century's Black Death), wiping out more lives than had already been lost in the conflict. Both Indians and Britons died of this influenza in great numbers.

In Britain, a first wave of the epidemic peaked in June and July, but this was followed by an even deadlier outbreak in October and November. It had unusual features in that it killed young healthy adults with haemorrhaging and fluid on their lungs. Across the world, some 40m people died. India had the worst of it, contributing a quarter of the total dead. At boarding school, Hester was struck down with such severity that she was put into the infirmary: she remembered, later, how her illness coincided with the armistice of 11th November. Clare, affected to a lesser degree, remained in the dormitory. Both were then sent home to recuperate.

By this time, the whole of the British Empire was celebrating the end of hostilities, a war in which India had played such a notable part by contributing 800,000 combatant troops. India had sent more forces, and tolerated more demands on its resources, than foreseen: Indians had served on the side of Britain in France, Egypt, Turkey, Palestine, Iran (Persia), Iraq and Greece; and more than 60,000 men were killed in action.

A letter was sent to all by the commander-in-chief. William, of course, received a copy. It read:

Christmas 1914 - 1918.
For the first time for four years we are celebrating Christmas with every prospect of an early peace and I take this opportunity of thanking the staffs of the Army and Military Finance Departments, of the Munitions Board, and of Army Headquarters for the devoted work they have rendered during the war. It has been a record of long hours and ungrudging personal sacrifice. This record is one of which all ranks may well be proud, and of services which I keenly appreciate and will always remember. I offer my hearty good wishes for Christmas and the New Year to all the officers and clerks who have so loyally assisted me.

After the war ended, the army in India was reorganized. Four commands were re-established (after a period of just three), each responsible for its own administration, training and command of forces stationed in its area.

Not long after this, the Perrens moved just across the road even nearer to the Annandale plain, deep in the valley. Their lovely new house was substantial, and was called Clare Dell; they shared it with another family who lived upstairs. By now, Mary's burden was lighter. William was better; and the girls resumed their day-to-day life within the family fold, returning to Loreto Convent as day pupils. Billy, who was five, went with them to the school's kindergarten before he started at Christ Church with Jackie. Using their 'hill legs', they embarked on the daily climb once again. For all of them, going both up and down, it was a rather wearying trek along the steep and winding roads that led to and from the centre of town.

William was not a church-going man, but on Sundays Mary would take the children to mass, usually on foot. There were no cars, of course, but occasionally she would call upon the service of a rickshaw operated by four coolies (as labourers or porters in India and China were called). With two pulling from the front and two pushing from behind, it was an experience at times quite terrifying for anyone unaccustomed to the dramatic tilting of those steep hill paths. (Those riding for the first time would surely have felt some sympathy, too, for the men pushing and pulling.) However, not everyone got to ride: this 'taxi of Simla' could carry only Mary, and perhaps one of the little ones; so the others would follow behind. 'We couldn't afford it on a regular basis,' explained Clare. 'And besides, my mother was a good walker.'

Over the years, a habit grew up for the Perrens to go straight from church to their Aunt Fanny's house for a curry lunch. Clare remembered her as having, typically, 'a chota-peg or burra-peg (a single or double tot) of whisky in one hand and a cigarette in the other'. Cousin Lily, who was ten years older than Clare, would play the piano while the family gathered around to enjoy a singsong. The Treglowns, though, had problems of their own. Uncle Syd, Lily's father, had been committed to the mental hospital at Kanke. This institution was five miles from Ranchi in the state of Bihar, and was the largest of its kind in India, with separate blocks for Europeans and Indians. It was said, and Clare simply believed, that he had 'gone off his head'. The rest of the family moved back down to Calcutta to live with Susannah, Fanny and William's aged mother.

Lily, a young woman of twenty, got married on 2nd November 1918 to William Hayes, a shop assistant at Hall and Anderson, drapers in Chowringhi,

Calcutta. The service took place in St Thomas's Anglican Church, where her father had married her mother. William Hayes was some 18 years older than Lily; he was baptised in July 1880 at the Catholic Church of the Assumption in Ootacamund. (His father, in fact, had been a witness at the wedding of William and Mary in 1904.) Susannah, Lily's grandmother, was a witness to the marriage, and afterwards Lily and William set up house at Suite 7, 54 Free School Street.

Just a month or two after this wedding, Susannah – in her endeavours to see as much of the family while she still could – made the journey from Calcutta to the Perrens' winter quarters in Delhi. She was there when her daughter-in-law Mary was admitted one night to the Dufferin Hospital after suffering a miscarriage at the age of forty-four. It was a trying time for all the family, not least for Hester who had started her first period (an important event in her life) just the day before. As Mary was unwell, Susannah made an attempt to amuse the children, taking it upon herself to 'traipse' them around Delhi. Under the circumstances, the idea was not welcomed!

Granny Bensley did, however, have a talent for delicious baking, as well as for beautiful embroidery and intricate crochet work. Hester remembered the bedspread she had made for Mary, used by her for a long time in Calcutta. To Hester, who had shown some interest, Susannah gave a pattern for one-inch crochet squares which could be joined together but later on, when she tried to master it herself, she found it too complicated to follow. Nevertheless, Granny Bensley had sown in her a desire to learn the art and craft of crochet and to succeed in her own right, and one day her ability would almost reach perfection. Her skill can be seen in the very pretty and functional pieces still used by the family today.

On 26th November Sydney Treglown died at Kanke aged just forty-five, leaving an estate netting nearly 14,000 rupees. This was also the last of seven years in which his civil and military tailoring business in Simla, latterly known as Treglown and Co, was listed in the official Thacker's directory record. Sydney's death meant that the year 1919 ended on a low note for the whole family.

SEVEN

LOSING LOVED ONES

If 1919 had been a difficult year for the Perrens, the cold weather season that began in the following year was to be even worse. Clare was twelve when her brother, two years older than her, contracted typhoid at Kingsway Camp. Jackie was known as 'the brainy one of the family', and he loved playing the mouth organ (particularly his favourite tune *Swanee*) and taking trips to the river. Clare believed it was this that led to him catching the disease, and later recalled: 'The only thing we could put it down to was his swimming in the River Jumna, where sometimes he went on his own.'

Jackie was ill for two weeks, latterly in the hospital. One morning, Clare woke early and found the house unusually quiet. 'I remember waking up and finding my mother had gone; that night she had been called out to the hospital, quite nearby, where my brother died in the early hours of the morning.' The announcement in the daily *Statesman* of Calcutta read:

PERREN – On the 23rd March, of enteric fever, at the Hindu Rao Hospital,

Delhi, John Henry, the dearly loved son of William John and Mary Perren, aged fourteen, five months and twenty-two days. Deeply mourned by his sorrowing parents, sisters and brother – RIP.

The teenager's coffin was transported by horse-drawn carriage to Nicholson Cemetery, named in honour of a prominent British general of the time of the Mutiny. The cemetery lay north of the Nicholson Garden and just to the left of the Kashmir Gate (with the Kudsia Garden on the right). This area was the scene of desperate fighting when the British retook Delhi from the rebels during the Mutiny. Brigadier General John Nicholson, the hero who led the attacks on Delhi when the British were striving to regain the city from the nationalists in the summer of 1857, is buried in plot VIII. Many other Mutiny dead also lie here, British residents killed defending this outpost of the British Empire, their identities evident from the names on headstones. Other graves, like Jackie's, hold the remains of young people struck down by fatal diseases early in the 20th century, before there was a cure.

Losing Jackie was not the only blow for the family. The following year saw William's elderly mother Susannah Perren leave India – her home for nearly 50 years – when she sailed to New Zealand on 11th November 1922 with her daughter Fanny, granddaughter Lily and Lily's husband William Hayes on the BISS (British India Steamship Service) Janus. She was seventy-six years old. Fanny's son Jack was already in New Zealand: he had emigrated there at least two years before, possibly in the shadow of his father Sydney's death, but nevertheless exhibiting a free spirit and a yearning for better opportunities. Perhaps he had had some success by that time, and was confident enough to persuade his family to follow.

It is likely that Fanny's feelings were key in the family's decision to leave India to join him. In addition to maternal sentiments, the fact that she had been widowed and now lacked reliable support may explain her willingness to uproot the rest of the family. The elderly Susannah lived with Fanny, and no doubt relied upon her for some support, but it may still have taken some persuasion to get her to consent to move to another country so late in her life. By all accounts, however, Susannah was a spirited woman, so it may have been that she was just as keen as her daughter to move. Fanny's son-in-law William was a shop assistant and perhaps felt his prospects would be better in a young country, so his enthusiasm for a move might have led him to sympathise with Fanny and persuade Lily, his wife. However it came together, it seems likely that a combination of opportunity, family ties and security, and the prospect of a better climate and less rigid society, put the seal on their joint decision.

How William Perren felt about this, and the degree to which his family considered him, is a matter for conjecture. Perhaps the departure of his mother, sister and niece relatively soon after the death of his own son unsettled him further, and stirred him into thinking that he too should be making plans to be on the move. Indeed, the departure of the Treglown family, to whom he and Mary had once been so close, may well have prompted him to talk seriously about going to New Zealand, conversations later recalled by his daughter. Despite this, it later transpired that his real secret longing was to go not east but west. According to Clare, he had 'a lifelong ambition to go to England'.

There were more problems to come. Hester turned eighteen and, while the family was still living at their house Clare Dell, she contracted dysentery. It was an immense worry for the whole family as they watched and waited and worried while Mary did everything in her power to help her daughter survive this nasty tropical disease of the intestine. It hit her with such severity that the Catholic priest was called to give her the last Sacrament of the Anointing of the Sick. Clare remembered that her sister 'nearly died' and, when she eventually recovered, was so weak that 'she had to learn to walk again'.

While Hester regained her strength, the Perren family was on the move. This time they left Annandale, where the children had so enjoyed playing about in its great pleasure-ground and where the memories of Jackie were so strong, and moved to Summer Hill, another outlying district north of Observatory Hill in the northwest of Simla. This was the last locality in which they would all live together. The coming years would see the remaining Perren children leave the nest and go their separate ways.

The great attraction of Summer Hill may well have been the up-to-date facilities of the new family quarters recently built by the government in a cleared, virgin site, one with a spectacular outlook over precipitous slopes. The family would probably have heard by word-of-mouth about these red brick-built homes, which would have been far nicer than the ramshackle bungalows to which they were accustomed. From these quarters, the family could look out onto the magnificent sub-Himalayan terrain as well as, more locally, Jutogh Hill to the north of Summer Hill.

The Perrens' first house here, like all the others, had 'a proper flush toilet and bath' and was at the end of one of the many new two-storey blocks dedicated for married and for single male government employees. They stayed here only a short time; nevertheless, the walnut tree just outside the house made a great impression on Clare, for not only did her mother make delicious walnut pickle, but the children loved to eat the nuts 'unripened and raw'. The family then moved to number 1, Married Quarters, Summer Hill, which was at the opposite end of another block. These quarters lay on even higher ground immediately above the access road that passed around the side of the hill. For Clare in particular, this was to have great significance a little later on.

Though Summer Hill was linked to the centre of Simla by railway, it was further away from the centre than Annandale. Hester had already left school; now Clare and Billy travelled three miles by train into town, then Clare made the steep ascent up to the mall and began her daily trudge of more than a mile to the Loreto Convent. This journey took a good 75 minutes each way and was, she remembered, 'all up hill and down dale'. Even in bad weather she was expected to make the journey.

Billy had an easier time. From Simla station, he went up the path with Clare to the mall, climbing a steep 300ft, but from there it was only a short walk to Christ Church School, where Jackie had also been a pupil. In 1925, he transferred to St Edward's, a newly opened Catholic school further from the centre, where he was taught by the Christian Brothers. Along with other schools in Simla such as Bishop Cotton, Auckland House and Loreto Convent, this was classed an 'élitist Christian school'.[49] As far as getting to Sunday mass was concerned, sometimes the family was spared the journey into town when the service was held at Summer Hill in somebody's house.

Despite another move, the family had kept with them some of the same servants. Their young cook Nannah, for instance, had moved with them from Annandale and remained with the Perrens for many years. Though he was Hindu, Clare remembered that 'he was not a bit religious' and while he was a good servant 'he drank a lot' – mainly a concoction known as poggle-pani ('fool's water') which was cheap to obtain. Sometimes he would stagger home from town and he regularly beat his meek, delicate-looking wife. 'She had a baby every year and all but two died, either soon after birth or later of rickets,' recalled Clare. 'My mother didn't approve of him getting drunk or hitting his wife, and sometimes she would lose her temper and give him a thump'.

This attitude of chastising the servants was common in India at the time: William, too, 'stood no truck' and would use physical force when necessary, although as the years went on it became less acceptable for the British to mete out such punishments so freely. Although his family experienced William as a 'quiet, lovely man', his tolerance towards the Indians failed to match this characteristic. It was clear to his daughter Clare that, like many others in his position, he felt superior. 'If they trod in his path when we were out walking, he would push them out of the way, elbowing them. I used to feel ashamed of him.'

There were, however, Indians who seemed to secure respect from the British. These included government officials, especially those employees who came from other regions and had no roots in Simla, and who were classified as clerks. (Some were stationed there all year, being paid a meagre salary and usually living in bad conditions.) Another group, by far the largest living in Simla during the time of British rule, were the Indian shopkeepers and businessmen; they also, generally, were respected. However, a third group of Indians were the rickshaw-pullers and other coolie labourers who came to Simla from the neighbouring area and further afield to cater to the needs of the British settlers, and who together made up nearly a third of the summer population of Simla. These Indians were most commonly the victims of British negative attitudes and some of them, it was said, were treated like animals.

Change was afoot in the Simla hills, and the local branch of the Indian National Congress began to make its presence felt, demanding due rights for Indian people. This congress had in fact been conceived in Simla in the 1880s, and its success was largely due to the efforts of Allan Hume, an Englishman who had retired from the Indian Civil Service and who was passionate about the evils of 'begar' or forced labour. The begar system coerced indigenous people, particularly villagers and labourers, 'for arduous jobs or where voluntary labour was not available'.[50]

Before the cart road up to Simla had been built, farmers and coolies were forced to haul up luggage belonging to the Europeans, and this exploitation still prevailed in some instances. Some British sahibs, clearly getting above themselves, even compelled Indians into giving free service as labourers and porters for their shoots (shikars) and picnics. However, in September 1921, 'after a series of meetings and discussions, the government agreed to abolish the system in Shimla Hills'.[51]

Within individual families, however, there were often bonds of affection between the races. Billy, devoid of prejudice, became close to Nannah who, though older, was something of a substitute for the brother he had lost. The two boys enjoyed kite-flying together both in Delhi and in Simla, and when the football season was in full swing, and Annandale became alive with the excitement of the annual Durand Cup Football Tournament, Clare recalled how

'Nannah would hurry to get his work done so that he could come down with Billy and me to watch it'.

For Mary Perren, mother now of just three children, life was not without worries. Though she was renowned in the family for forbearance and fortitude, she was known to lose her patience on occasions, as once when she went into the town centre of Simla and was making her way home with Billy and Clare. The children took a short cut to the station, purchased tickets and waited on the platform, but for some reason – perhaps because she was trying to mend something in her spare moments – Clare managed to swallow a sewing pin.

This was the last thing Mary needed to hear on her arrival at the station and instead of offering her daughter sympathy she gave her 'a clip', which did little to help. Later, an X-ray showed the pin to be 'head first' and Clare was put on a diet of bread to assist its passage through her system and prevent it from becoming lodged on the way. Meanwhile, she was told by a well-meaning friend about someone who had swallowed 'lots of pins'. Happily, nature was kind and Clare survived to tell the tale.

Another incident that caused considerably more anguish and terror happened at Summer Hill the following year, when Clare was fifteen. A puppy belonging to a friend – a 'beautiful fluffy miniature poodle' – turned vicious and began snapping at a group of young people as they played. Some managed to dodge it by climbing a fence, but others, about a dozen in all (including a few adults), were chased. Fearing the dog was rabid, everyone who had been bitten or licked went without delay to Kasauli, the old hill capital of India where the headquarters of the Pasteur Institute of India was based.

Mary and Billy were among those who made a hasty journey to this neighbouring peak, luckily no more than a few stations away. The treatment prescribed for the avoidance of hydrophobia (rabies) was depressing and lengthy: it entailed the washing and immediate cauterisation of each bite site followed by two weeks of daily vaccination. Even the treatment itself carried a risk of brain damage and injections were given in the stomach, with a large syringe delivering its contents to the peritoneum, which was notoriously painful. However, those who had to go through this process counted themselves lucky: such treatment was nothing compared to the horrors and agonies suffered by those who contracted the disease. In the event, it was just as well that they received treatment because when the dog was killed, its brain was analysed and tested positive for rabies.

While her mother and Billy were in hospital, Clare had to cope with her father returning home from having been 'on the binge'. William, something of a worrier by nature but particularly so when members of his family were unwell, may have only gone on such outings when he was highly stressed; even so, Clare and Hester, while fond of their father, had 'very little sympathy for him when he was drunk'. Probably they had picked up this attitude of exasperation from their mother, who had a particular way of dealing with William when he had been on a binge. Clare remembered: 'Sometimes he would prove most difficult to manage and want to go out again and look to fight someone, so the first thing my mother would do would be to take off his boots'.

By now Mary Perren had lived longer in India than she had in her homeland of England. There must have been many times when her thoughts turned to her wider family, whom she had long since left behind. Perhaps when she returned to England in 1903 for her TB treatment she took the opportunity, once she was well enough, to see her mother Lucy and some of her siblings: they may have visited her while she was recovering. However, that visit was long ago and Lucy had passed away in December 1912, at the age of seventy-five, having spent the last 11 years of her life in the care of The Little Sisters of the Poor. This home in Lambeth, London, was run by a congregation of nuns who provided for the spiritual and material needs of the aged poor in homes which entirely depended for their income on charity. (Many years later, Mary herself considered availing herself of such support.)

Though far from them all, Mary found a temporary bridge of this long separation in her cousin Ernest Freed, the son of her mother's brother Thomas, who brought his family to live in India, probably at Naini Tal, before they emigrated to South Africa. The Freeds began to come to Simla for holidays to visit their daughter Marie, Clare's second cousin, who had married Len Marsh, a civilian working at army headquarters, and was living with him and their small daughter Nora at Summer Hill, near the Perrens.

As a teenager, Clare was delighted to get a chance to play mother. Marie was 'always a scatterbrain' but Clare was happy to help. 'At weekends and during holidays I did everything for that baby I idolised: changed nappies, bathed her, made feeds, knitted bonnets and took her for walks,' she recalled. The Marsh family was transferred away from Simla but later returned – by then, sadly, Nora was in 'irons' (leg braces), having been crippled by infantile paralysis, otherwise known as polio. Marie's sister Biddy married a boy from Simla and this couple also made their home in India; but it was Marie's brother for whom Clare looked out on visits. His name was Ernie, and he was one of her first crushes. Clare's interest in boys was widening and soon after, her attention was captured by a handsome banjo-player in a ragtime band performing in the area. The attraction was evidently mutual and he was very likely the first boy she went out with.

Also attached to army headquarters was Dim, a boy from Wolverhampton. Hester knew his friend – the equally unlikely Grog, who like Dim was a sergeant in the Royal Air Force – and the four went around together. The boys regularly came to the house and sometimes for meals. Nearby (west of Viceregal Lodge) there was Prospect Hill, a popular picnic spot with grand views over the plains as well as Kasauli. While wintering in Delhi at that time, they even climbed the Kutub Minar together. It was 'all quite respectable and proper' though in Clare's opinion, Dim was 'the biggest chancer' of anyone she knew.

Photographs taken in 1925 illustrate the fun and frivolity of youth in the relationships between these four, as well as their great ease with one another, and the happiness on the girls' faces is in stark contrast to the solemn expressions in pictures taken in 1922, when it is obvious they were still mourning the death of their brother Jackie (and possibly, too, were sad about the departure of their grandmother, aunt and cousins). However, the friendship of the four lasted only a short while longer before Dim and Grog were posted back to England.

As the girls blossomed into young ladies, it seemed that Simla continued to develop a most liberal and relaxed social scene, one that did not please all observers. A letter to *The Times* in London in 1917 implied it was full of hedonism, calling it the 'regular retreat of a host of avowed pleasure-seekers who go there on leave, and, having no work to occupy them, pass their time in a long round of frivolity and gaiety, in which the idle and the unemployed expect that those who are there on duty shall be as much at leisure as themselves'.[52] The letter went on: 'In ordinary times the station is full of idle military men and civilians, dangling attendance upon the wives and daughters of men absent in the plains, and amusement is the main object and pursuit of all'.[53]

Simla had enjoyed, not without opprobrium, a reputation for frivolity since the 1840s, when ambitious British officers and their equally ambitious female relatives of marriageable age came to the town hoping to secure a match. The years following had seen the town's social life continue to flourish, with an almost endless round of fêtes, picnics, games, tea dances, balls, plays, and sports. In a letter to the *Statesman* in 1913, a 'sojourner' wrote of Simla that 'many of us Simla sojourners are thoroughly "fed up" with its unmitigated frivolities week in, week out'. He continued: 'Play is the rule and not the exception; when day after day shows but a long programme of vanities and inanities, picnics, fêtes, "some lucky bags", and gymkhanas, followed by dances at night…'[54] However, while he charged government officials with indulging in the various festivities and frivolities during their 'jaunt' to Simla in the hot season, this correspondent admitted that some did 'take work seriously' and that there were 'still those who believe that the Government of India is an institution founded and paid for with the one object of administrating the country in an earnest spirit'.[55]

The charges were true, of course. While some dutiful civil servants carried on business as usual, most of Simla's temporary residents were in thrall to the Anglo-Indian social whirl comprising garden parties, formal dinners, high teas, dances and bridge games. This was, after all, the Jazz Age. There were evening promenades for everyone along the mall, the main street that until the First World War had been strictly out-of-bounds to all 'natives' except royalty, rickshaw-wallahs and red-liveried chuprassies (office messengers). Meanwhile, the brown Simla monkeys gamboling around, or sitting by the wayside and watching the promenaders curiously, continued to remain a law unto themselves.

In every way, the mall was the centre of town for all Simla–based Europeans, whether or not they enjoyed a lavish lifestyle. Only the viceroy, the commander-in-chief and the governor of the Punjab were allowed a car or carriage along this road, but everyone else loved to dress up in the latest fashions and to stroll and meet friends or make new acquaintances in the early evenings. Sometimes the viceroy's own band played at the bandstand near that prominent landmark, Christ Church.

This was also the locale of some of the grandest shops in India. It was with sheer delight that Clare was to remember, all her life, the curio shop that Kipling described in his novel *Kim* as being full of wonders – 'all Simla knows it', he wrote. She never once mentioned this place without talking about the collection of small yet intricate silver charms sold there, which obviously fascinated her. (It is easy to imagine her as a young girl making long-pondered purchases of these small enchantments, which she would then attach to her bracelet.) She also loved the mock Tudor library and post office. On the broad road close to the town hall was the new Gaiety Theatre, a pretty little place opened in 1887 by Simla's amateur dramatics club to provide evening entertainment. As a teenager, she saw shows including 'No, No Nanette', Gilbert and Sullivan's 'Mikado' and 'Yeoman of the Guard' and 'Peg O' My Heart', which boasted an appearance by Aunt Fanny's dog Jock.

Spreading immediately down the valley from the mall on the southern slopes of the ridge 'at an angle of forty-five'[56] was Simla's main bazar. It was a 'dense, chaotic mass of corrugated iron roof-tops'[57] which Kipling saw as offering a perfect escape route: 'A man who knows his way there can defy all the police of India's summer capitol, so cunningly does veranda communicate with veranda, alley-way with alley-way, and bolt-hole with bolt-hole.'[58]

Though haphazard and overcrowded, the bazar was full of thrills and exotic aromas. It was 'the only place in Simla that offered any sense of the "real India"'[59] and it was said that in this bazar, 'Tibetans rubbed dirty shoulders with the even more numerous Hindus, who liked nothing better than to squat smoking with their friends'.[60] There were other bazars too, including the Lakkar Bazar on the road north from the ridge leading to Elysium Hill, below Jakko, which offered a vast array of hand-made and carved wooden objets d'art. All in all, there was plenty to see and plenty to do and despite the slightly dangerous exoticism of the bazars and occasional rabid dogs, Simla was a perfect place to grow up – a place too busy enjoying itself to worry about the deeper troubles of life.

EIGHT

A DESIRE FOR ENGLAND

While life in Simla was carefree for some, for others it was more of a struggle. It seems that at work, William was doing well: in March 1924, he received his final promotion within the military secretary's branch of army headquarters, and he had progressed through the ranks to 1ˢᵗ Division Assistant. However, in William and Mary's personal life things were not so easy. The loss of their child must have been difficult to come to terms with, and they were both growing older.

At around this time, Mary received two postcards that hint at disquiet. The first, postmarked 25ᵗʰ May 1924, was sent by Mary's parish priest Father Hickey while he was on a visit to Lourdes and read: 'I have been praying hard at the Grotto for you, your husband, Jackie and all.' The second, postmarked the same day and also from Lourdes, was sent by one of the priest's companions, a Mrs Davies. It read: 'I have been praying much for you and your many needs'.

William was fifty years old, and after 30 years in the service of the Indian government he was still entertaining seriously the desire to emigrate to England.

However, it is apparent from correspondence that his being in a position to do so would depend on certain conditions. A letter he wrote from Simla on 28th July 1924 to the quartermaster general in India read:

> Sir,
>
> I respectfully beg to request that I may be granted "non entitled" passages to the United Kingdom for myself and my family during the ensuing trooping season [September to March and sometimes April if it was a busy year], preferably after next Christmas. I am desirous of proceeding to the United Kingdom on leave, pending retirement, and I trust that this my application will be favourably considered in consideration of my long service of over 33 years in Army Headquarters.
>
> I should be very grateful if second class passages could be granted for my family. As regards myself, I am prepared to accept third class accommodation (with 2nd class messing) should a second class berth not be available for me. I should be glad to receive early intimation of the allotment of passages as it will be necessary for me to obtain the grant of leave ex-India and to vacate Government quarters in which I am residing, etc. I would also point out that I have not taken any leave ex-India during the period of my service.
>
> I am, Sir, Your most obedient servant
>
> W J Perren
>
> Assistant, Mil'y Secy's Branch

This application came 'strongly recommended' by his immediate superiors. The first, one W A Norris (Lieut), testified that William was 'a very deserving and loyal Assistant who has always given his very best to the Branch'.

The second, Major General H O Parr, wrote that 'Mr Perren has always been a very hard working and honest clerk. He is one of the old stamp who perhaps had not the facilities of education of the present day to qualify him for one of the higher appointments. I very strongly recommend his application for the most sympathetic consideration'.

As William had not taken any leave since November 1917, he also applied for four months of privilege leave plus four months of paid furlough 'pending retirement'. He asked for this in another letter of the same date, this time addressed to the military secretary:

> Sir,
>
> I respectfully beg to request that I may be granted four months' privilege leave combined with four months' leave on average salary, with effect from approximately ten days prior to my sailing, in the event of my application for non-entitlement passages being granted to the United Kingdom for myself

and for my family.

My object in taking this leave is to proceed to the United Kingdom, pending retirement, after 30 years' pensionable service in Government employ. I would also point out that I have not taken any leave ex-India during the period of my service.

I am, Sir, Your most obedient servant.

W J Perren

Assistant, Mil'y Secy's Branch

However, it cost money to emigrate and it seems clear from another letter, written on 23rd August, that William's wish to emigrate to England with his family depended very much on his gaining a temporary loan, in the form of an advance on his pay, from the government. This also was addressed to the military secretary, via 'the Officer Supervisor':

Sir,

In the event of my availing myself of 8 months leave ex-India granted to me on the 7th August 1924, I respectfully beg to request that, as a special case, I may be granted an advance of Rs 1000/-/- in order that I may be in a financial position to meet incidental charges such as railway fares for self and family to port of embarkation, messing charges which are to be paid in full prior to embarkation and other additional expenditure which will arise on such an occasion.

I am reluctantly compelled to make this request owing to the fact of my having had a large family to educate and having been in receipt of a small salary. I have consequently also not been in a position to avail myself of the privilege of being a subscriber to the Provident Fund from which source I would ordinarily have obtained financial assistance. If my request be granted I would respectfully request that the advance be recovered from my pay in eight monthly instalments of Rs 125/-/-, the whole amount thus being recovered on expiration of my leave.

I am, Sir, Your most obedient servant.

W J Perren

Assistant, Military Secretary's Branch

Two further letters from his immediate superiors in support of his applications were put forward. One (dated 25th August) from W A Norris read: '... Mr Perren joined this office on the 1st April 1921, but unfortunately his pay is still comparatively small and now towards the end of his service it is only Rs 440/-/- per mensem. He has a wife and 3 children (until 3 years ago he had 4 children) and it will be realised that on this pay (his pay was Rs 225/- only at the commencement of the Great War) it has been somewhat of a struggle for him to carry on and that there has really been little opportunity of putting by for a rainy day'.

The letter continued:

> I have personally known Mr Perren and his family for many years. His wife is one of the hardest working women I know who deserves the greatest credit for the way in which she has brought her family up in spite of hard times. Mr Perren himself has always had the reputation of being an earnest and conscientious worker and I can say without any hesitation that he has always given of his very best to this Branch.
>
> There is no rule under which such an advance as Mr Perren applies for can be granted but I trust in view of Mr Perren's long and faithful service in this office and his necessitous circumstances that Military Secretary will be disposed to recommend strongly this present application for the favourable consideration of Government.

Major General Parr wrote once more on behalf of William, a day later: 'I strongly recommend this application for an advance of Rs 1000/-. After 34 years good service some consideration is merited. The necessity for the advance is dependent on whether Mr Perren obtains indulgence passages.'

In mid-August, while still in optimistic mood, William also wrote to his old superior officer, William Birdwood, who had returned to India after the First World War to command the Northern Army. His career had progressed significantly in the intervening years to the point that he was now Field Marshal Birdwood and commander-in-chief of the whole of India (between 1925 and 1930).

Being responsible for all the armed forces of the Raj and second only to the viceroy himself, surely Birdwood would have the power to help – or so William felt. Even so, his letter to his old senior officer was courteous and restrained. It read:

> Sir,
>
> As one of the old hands of Army Headquarters, I respectfully venture to offer Your Excellency my sincere congratulations on your appointment as Commander-in-Chief and trust that ere long you will be filling the appointment permanently.
>
> I am, Sir, Your Excy's most obedient servant.
>
> W Perren

The following crest-embossed, signed note came back just a day later from the commander-in-chief himself, and the immediacy of the response, combined with the warmness of its tone, demonstrates how fond he was of William:

> My dear Perren, A line to thank you so much for your note, and I am only so sorry not to have seen you up to now. I so much appreciate your good wishes, and much hope that you are yourself keeping well and strong.
> With all good wishes for the future
> Yours sincerely,
> W R Birdwood

It is not hard to understand why William nurtured this desire to go to England, the land of his parents and of all those itinerants who came to Simla so full of talk of the old country. (Many of them, of course, were secure in the knowledge that one day they would be able to return 'home'.) Added to his own secret longing to leave India for the 'home' country were factors including his recent illness, the sad events in the family, his age, and the apparent ceiling he had reached against further progress in his working life.

Furthermore, both of his daughters were about to embark on careers: Hester had left school when she was sixteen in 1921, before the family came to Summer Hill, and she was biding her time at home for four years until July 1925, when she would be old enough to train as a nurse. Clare, on the other hand, was just coming up to sixteen that August, and was about to leave school. Perhaps their father envisaged a better future for them in England, and saw that there would be more opportunities for them to find good husbands.

In the end, however, all the efforts, letters and recommendations came to nothing. Although his case records show that the leave William applied for was granted, it seems he was not so successful in obtaining either Indulgence Passages or the advance of Rs1000/-/- which he had requested.

At first, he evidently believed that an assisted passage to England was possible, having been admitted to the benefit of the European Service Leave Rules with effect from 24th July 1923. However, a year later he was fervently pleading along different lines in the following handwritten letter, sent on 10th September 1925:

> Sir, I beg to submit my application to be brought under the European Servants Leave Rules. I am of pure European descent and in support of this claim attach a certified copy of the Marriage Certificate of my parents who were both English and at the time of their marriage were resident in

England. They were married at Charlcombe, Somerset, England. I attach the necessary certificate for favour of countersignature by the Establishment Officer, Army Department. The delay in my application has been caused by the fact that the accompanying document had to be obtained from my Mother in New Zealand.

I have etc,

W J Perren

It seems he was now trying every door possible. He enclosed a sworn statement with this letter, countersigned by the establishment officer, which read: 'I hereby declare on my honour that at the time of my entering Government service, I had my domicile in England – W J Perren'. This declaration shows William was trying to comply with all the conditions necessary for his ultimate petition to be approved, but it was a desperate measure: all of his family, at least, knew that he had never lived anywhere but India.

None of it worked. Perhaps his application for consideration under European Servants Leave Rules had been received too late, or someone had picked up on his false statement. Whatever the cause, the outcome for William was not good. Over the months and years that followed this disappointment, his depressions worsened and he was ill more often than not.

He was on sick leave from 4th January 1926 for some 18 months, and at first he was paid during his illness (described as furlough, though it was recorded on medical certificates); but in September 1926 his remuneration was cut in half. A year later, he rejoined for duty on 4th October but this was to be a brief spell, lasting only until 21st March 1928. Once again he was committed to sick leave (furlough), initially on full pay and then, from 21st February 1929, on half pay once again. On 16th September 1929 he was formally but prematurely retired, with a pension that remained at the half-pay rate (220 rupees per month), and seems to have been paid in Lahore. He had worked for the government for nearly 40 years.

During these years of William's illness, his daughters were working and living away from home. They returned when they could and were aware of the emotional load that their mother, in particular, had to carry as she strove to nurse him back to health. Over the years, he had become increasingly morose and suffered bouts of severe depression that led to several breakdowns. With no breaks afforded her, Mary had to carry on regardless.

'It was terrible,' Clare remembered later. 'My mother said it nearly drove her mad. She used to try and take his mind off his depressions. Though the family had no wireless in Simla, she would play some records from their collection on the gramophone including those of his favourite singers Harry Lauder (who came to Simla once or twice) and Richard Tauber. But eventually it became too much for her to cope with.' She was as much a prisoner of the situation as her poor husband, at least during this time.

Christmas 1926, in particular, was far from joyous. The news reached the Perrens in India that William's mother Susannah Hester – Granny Bensley, or 'the duchess' – had died on 1st December at Auckland Infirmary, suffering a cerebral haemorrhage at the age of eighty. Soon after this, Mary's friend Mrs Bedwell went into hospital for an operation, contracted septicaemia and died at the end of the month, leaving her two young girls motherless. Gertie Bedwell, who was only thirteen at the time, remembered later that Mary Perren was especially good to them at that 'dreadful time'.

On reaching the age of twenty in August 1925, Hester became a student nurse at the Presidency General Hospital, Calcutta, an institution that was open to European patients of all classes. During the years that followed, she would sometimes stay at 116 Ripon Street where her 'Uncle' Walter Vernieux Bensley (Susannah's stepson) and Aunt Lizzie lived.

Clare had left school at sixteen in 1924, but it may well have only been a matter of weeks or months before she was employed. It seems likely she had started her new job even before Hester began work – a situation that was perhaps trying for the elder sister. Clare took a post as a resident British nanny, the kind of carer employed by rich parents or fathers who held important posts in the Civil Service (those lower down, like her father William, had only the means to afford Indian ayahs). Her first position was with the Newling family, who lived on the mall at the premises of Messrs Whiteaway, Laidlaw & Co, a sizeable emporium. Even if Clare did not know it at the time, this department store was known universally as 'Right away and paid for' because customers were required to pay in ready cash. It was just one of a large number of shops opened by Europeans catering mainly to the needs of European residents in Simla.

Mr Newling was the manager of the shop and seems to have been a sympathetic person: when the shop was closed, for instance, Clare was allowed 'the run of it' and could try on hats and use the toys to amuse her charge, the Newlings' only son, John. The 18 months she spent with the family were very happy. They treated her more like a daughter than a nanny, and while she was working for them, their own second son was born. Not long after, they left Simla.

William John Perren, aged eight months, with an Indian gentleman. Simla, 22 June 1875.

William John Perren and Mary Yates, Calcutta, 19 March 1904.

Three of the Perren Children: Jackie, Hester and Clare at Kingsway Camp, Delhi, c1915.

The Mall, Simla.

A family outing: the Perrens and the Treglowns. Annandale, Simla, c1917.

A rare picture of Mary and her four children after church. Simla, c1917.

Clare with Allan, one of her charges. Simla, c1927.

William John Perren, Simla.

Clare Perren aged 19, c1928.

Then, in 1926, came another job. This time she was asked to look after an infant called Alan Norman, the child of an older Scottish couple. Her employer Mr Norman was Director General of Observations at the Meteorological Office. At first the family was staying at the Elysium Hotel on Elysium Hill on the north side of Mount Jakko; then they moved out further north on the hill to another hotel, Craig Dhu, which had wonderful food, and where Clare was provided with her own room.

Finally, they moved to a more central location, just off the mall near the post office: a house attached to St Andrew's called The Manse which, as its name suggests, was usually occupied by the parish minister of this India-based Scottish kirk. The Normans were lucky enough to own their own rickshaw and the coolies who propelled it wore smart livery with turbans.

Clare was not expected to cope with her charge alone. In common with her time with the Newlings, so here too she had an Indian maty (helper) to assist her. This man wore livery, and was expected to go with Clare whenever she went out with the child. Sometimes she might, by chance, meet up with other British nannies and they would all walk together, each with a maty to push the prams along the mall.

One day she was strolling with Doris Dodd, the guardian of 'a lovely looking child' whose mother was friendly with the Normans (according to Clare, the mothers took afternoon teas together and played whist). A Sikh – one of a sect numerous in this state of Punjab – began to follow in the girls' footsteps, and came close enough to put his hand on Clare's shoulder. Doris, who had her wits about her, told him sharply to go about his business.

This incident frightened Clare and it left her in no doubt that she disliked this group of people. She remembered the Sikhs she encountered in India seemed 'unable to look you straight in the eye'. These were those who came around selling mongooses and white rats, offering to tell fortunes. 'They would say "You got very lucky face memsahib. You got plenty luck memsahib",' she recalled. Often, although she told them she already knew her fortune, she felt pressed to give them money, just to get rid of them.

Usually her day off was during the week, and this was when she went to her parents' home. On one such occasion, a soldier passing by on the road below caught her eye: a handsome young man in cavalry uniform with a black-and-white plumed pith helmet. Whenever she got the chance, Clare would watch out for this soldier passing along the road below on his way from his quarters to Summer Hill Station. An amusing entry in Hester's autograph book from 1925 gives some idea of what those single men, the non-commissioned officers who resided in the blocks below, were like:

In Summer Hill Camp we have some NCOs
Where they obtain stripes from heaven only knows.
They roam round the khud, they talk and they shout
And they speak of things they know nothing about.

A new meeting place for government folk had just been completed at Summer Hill. It was called the Community Centre, though it quickly became known as the clubhouse, and was close to where the Perrens lived. At one stage, when the sprung floor of the dance hall was being laid, sixteen-year-old Clare and one of her friends, Meg Edwards, vowed they would be the very first to dance on it. 'Even though the rest of the building was unfinished, we reckoned we were the first'.

Field Marshal William Birdwood, formerly the superior officer to Clare's father and now the commander-in-chief of India, came to open the centre. With his customary good grace, he took time during this visit to Summer Hill to remember his old but ailing friend William Perren and to honour him with a personal visit to his home overlooking the community centre.

The clubhouse was particularly special to Clare for another reason: it was there that, at the Christmas Eve party in 1926, she came face to face with the handsome dragoon that she had taken pleasure in watching pass by on the road below.

'I chose him in "Kiss in the Ring",' she remembered later, adding – after a pause and a laugh – 'Look where it got me!'

NINE

THE HANDSOME DRAGOON

The man who had caught Clare's eye was Hector Raymond Perks, of the 4th/7th Dragoon Guards, who was attached to army headquarters at Simla. Born on 10th April 1902 at Pound Bank Road, Great Malvern, Worcestershire, he was the second of three sons born to George Henry and Elizabeth Ann Perks (known as Liz or Lizzie, though it seems she also called herself Annie).

George Perks was Malvern born and bred and Lizzie's family came to the district in the late 19th century. George, born in 1875, began his working life at the age of about eleven, as a mason's apprentice to William Hayes & Son, a firm owned by relatives. George was a man of enterprise, and in his twenties began to work for himself, becoming 'Master Monumental Mason, Sculptor and Sub-Contractor' and eventually owning his own stone and marble works.

He had quite a head for business. In addition to his mason business, George invested in property in Barnard's Green in the town and converted part of one of his two houses (one of which he rented) into a sweet and tobacco shop, which was run by his wife Lizzie. For the boys, of course, their mother's new occupation was delightful. 'Boys being boys, we sometimes pinched the sweets and ran!' remembered Gus (Augustus), Lizzie's eldest son.

To his own property George built a small front extension to create another shop he rented and which, according to the 1909 street directory, was the business premises of a milliner by the name of Miss Heap. Five years later, he sold up and made a good profit. He moved his family further down the road into part of a grander half-timbered house that had outbuildings at its rear and sufficient space to store his entire stock and to exhibit and operate his Perks's Stone & Marble Works on site. (Previously, this had been offsite.) Some of the Perks' relatives were admiring of George's success in business and felt that the family enjoyed 'quite a good lifestyle for that day and age'.

Hector was educated, like his father before him, at Mill Lane School in Clarence Road, near Great Malvern Station. As a young boy, he sang in Christ Church choir and was given private lessons by the organist at the latter's home in Church Street. Later he went to a school in this street: Lyttleton Grammar School for Boys, situated in the grounds of the great Priory Church of St Mary and St Michael, a building of great architectural pride in Malvern.

Having won a choir scholarship, Hector became a keen chorister at the priory and often sang solos. He had other talents, too, winning a copy of Charles Kingsley's book The Water Babies for his knowledge of religion. The book is inscribed: '1st Prize Awarded to Hector Raymond Perks for Religious Knowledge, Form IV, Dec 1911. G R Thornton MA [Headmaster]'. George Perks himself, although he liked to see his children go to church on Sundays, wasn't much of a churchman. The wisdom he passed on to Hector was more worldly and businesslike: 'a bad pencil is better than a good memory', for instance, and 'keep your money in your left pocket and your penknife in your right'.

All was going well for the Perks family until 1910, when a series of events changed their fortunes dramatically. Over a period of about 18 months, George was forced into bankruptcy through no fault of his own, and life as the family knew it was devastated, with both George and Lizzie turning to drink to ease their troubles. The trouble appears to have started with the completion of an extension to the rear of Squibb the grocers, a building opposite the Perks' former property. Gus recalled that the owner of this building became insolvent, and was unable to settle his bill of £180. Not long after this setback, George was subcontracted to work on a hall, a separate building that had been commissioned by those of Holy Trinity Church out on the Worcester Road.

A history of the parish states that in 1909, the church was looking to build some kind of additional room, and that in 1910, 'a bazaar raised £300, and in September that year Lady Grey laid the foundation stone'. In readiness, George bought and delivered all the necessary Bath Stone and granite to the site. He committed himself further by taking on two extra masons (besides the three or four regulars he employed that included his half-brother Jack Hayes), as he sometimes did, to work on what was to be a large project. In fact the greater part of it was completed when the main contractor, a builder called A E Allen (of Allen & Co), went bankrupt and absconded, it was said, to America.

Unfortunately for George, a quirk in the law meant that all the stone on site was seized and held to be part of the builder's assets. This meant it was used to pay off Allen's creditors. As a consequence, George lost any claim on the stone and was instead treated as a creditor. Like the other creditors, he was paid the miserly sum of three farthings in the pound, leaving him £300 short – a substantial loss in those days, which ruined him.

Worse was to come. By now a broken man, he loathed the idea of working for his father-in-law Thomas Jones, who had been his great competitor in the town for many years. However, his position was so desperate that he had no alternative. Both men were monumental sculptors and building masons. During the tragic dismantling of George's family home, Thomas Jones bought up much of the price-tagged furniture, which added insult to injury.

Meanwhile, George and his wife and family moved into modest rented accommodation. From now on, Lizzie and her friends regularly put whisky in their tea in the afternoons before George came home. The fall in status which came from bankruptcy affected both parents profoundly, and Gus, their eldest son, remembered being sent to the 'jug and bottle bar' at the Foresters Arms to buy a pint of beer at lunchtimes, when he came home from school.

As his parents could no longer afford to pay the fees at Lyttleton Grammar, Gus decided to join the army, just after the outbreak of the First World War. He had to lie about his age, declaring himself to be seventeen when he was a tender fifteen years and four months old. (Soldiers volunteering for service in the war were not required to produce a birth certificate and many men who enlisted were underage. Their motives may have included patriotism, but often included the wish to escape monotonous jobs or distressing circumstances.) Ralph, the youngest of the Perks boys, remained at home, at least for the time being. The middle brother Hector, with his scholarship at Lyttleton Grammar, was able to continue there for another year or so until April 1915.

Like many people of his generation, Hector did not talk about the problems that beset his family while he was growing up, though when questioned he would mention that his mother lived in poor conditions and had a bad way of life; specifically, that she 'led a pub life'. To have dwelt on these facts would perhaps have been more than he could cope with, so repressing them became the preferred option.

By now, his father George had joined Gus in the army, and his mother was an alcoholic. Although it is recorded that in 1915 the family lived at Need's Cottages, Poolbrook (Malvern) it seems that at some stage Ralph and his mother were driven to sleeping rough in the fields until the boy was taken away into care.

Through his connection with the church, at the age of thirteen Hector got a live-in job as a servant boy with the Reverend Henry Foster, a master of Malvern College who owned a house called Fosmo in Lauderdale Road. Hector continued to sing in the great priory choir and the minister even took him to Wales, on one occasion, to sing with a Welsh choir. The Fosters later recommended him to their son-in-law C H Giles, who was the headmaster of Lyttleton Preparatory School for Boys, another building in the priory grounds. Hector went on to become a servant boy for the school.

'The rest of the staff were servant girls, about ten of them, and a cook supervised the cleaning and so on,' he recalled later. 'My job was to look after the boiler in the cellar, keeping it stoked up to provide hot water for the school. Another of my regular jobs was to clean about 200 pairs of boots and shoes, first with liquid blacking, before I polished them. Mr Giles had lost his wife and he took an interest in me, providing me with a room at the Lodge Gate. No one else lived there. He bought me clothes and saved some of my wages so that when I left he was able to give me a useful sum of money.'

By now Hector was fifteen and Redvers Sandy, the son of friends of his parents, advised him to apply for a better job, one he had heard about. Hector duly met the widowed Lady Martin at her country house, and was accepted into service. As her only servant boy, one of his main duties was to provide Lady Martin with distilled drinking water, which he did 'by boiling water in a vessel so that the steam hit the lid and dripped over'. However, he missed the working environment of the priory school, and did not get on with the housekeeper.

In 1917 he left the 'fair hills' of Malvern, hills he had climbed on countless occasions, and from the top of which one could look over a landscape of 15 counties and spy three cathedrals, six abbeys and priories, and many more historic battlefields. He joined his mother Lizzie in Birmingham, where she had gone in September 1916 to work for a munitions factory at Kynoch. (Gus, returning from the army, had left Malvern at about the same time to join the Royal Marines. He had been in the army for 18 months before the authorities discovered he was underage and discharged him.)

The price of food began to rise steeply, and many women were now working at munitions factories or on farms. It was Lizzie who found her son Hector his next job at Witton, near Aston in Birmingham. The job was in a factory making steel poles (used in the construction of mobile aerials needed during the war), with materials from condemned ships. The business was called Armaduct, and Hector became a 'charge hand packer – conduit etc', a job that involved a great deal of night work. His mother was living with a Mrs Green at Tame Valley Buildings in Brookvale Road, Witton, but Hector himself stayed in lodgings at Aston opposite the Villa football ground.

The war ended 18 months before Hector turned eighteen, but it seems his father's example may have kindled in him a desire to do some soldiering of his own. On 15th April 1920, just days after his birthday, he enlisted at Birmingham recruiting office as a private (army number 394289) with the 4th (Royal Irish) Dragoon Guards. The history of this famous regiment can be traced to 1685, when King James II raised regiments to help him put down a rebellion by the Duke of Monmouth. While not actually Irish in origin, the regiment was awarded the title 'Royal Irish' after serving in Ireland for a total of 42 years. It was among eight or nine British cavalry regiments serving there, firstly to aid the civil powers in law and order, and secondly because it was cheaper for them to live here than in England, with good grazing and plentiful recruitment.

Young men signing up for service in 1920 could ask to be sent to a particular regiment, especially if their fathers had served in the same one (though George had not served in the Dragoon Guards). However, while they were generally granted permission to serve in the regiment of their choice, it did depend on circumstance. Some depot troops, for example, were especially short of men if they were part of regiments serving overseas.

Hector went to Bristol first, for three weeks, to one of a number of training depots where new recruits were kitted out. Here they did square-bashing and were taught to march and salute, and were not allowed to leave the barracks (which meant no 'pass' to go out into the town) until the completion of this training phase. Since regiments did not give any basic training, these young men were sent on to the Cavalry Depot at Canterbury. Hector would have been there for at least six months before joining the Dragoon Guards at Beaumont Barracks in Tidworth, on Salisbury Plain.

At Canterbury, training was more specialist than at Bristol. First recruits had to undergo basic riding and horsemanship and, following this, a period of instruction in 'equitation for application'. This was training in equine care and handling as well as riding in formation in squadron and even regiment-sized groups. Recruits went on to spend a short time at veterinary school and then took a course in learning to drive motorised 'transport wagons'.

The initial six months of riding and equitation training was extended to one year for efficiency instruction and any army educational certificates, and while being posted to a regiment did not mean the end of training, it did mean the end of formal instruction in, for example, riding skills. Hector gained a Third Class certificate on 22nd October 1920 and by 27th January 1921 had reached Second Class: this meant he received 6d (old English pence) proficiency pay per day on top of his wage. Proficiency included skill on the rifle ranges: soldiers were taught how to handle the rifle in varying circumstances, and how to mount and dismount while armed.

During Hector's training at Canterbury, the preferred firearm was the Short Magazine Lee-Enfield Mark III, made by BSA Birmingham – this had proven the very best small weapon during the First World War. Hector may also have been taught to use the lance. He described later competitions in tent-pegging where a lance was deployed. However, lances were more usually restricted to lancer regiments.

In addition, all recruits were taught how to use the cavalry sword, which had a sharp point but no cutting edge. The sabre, an earlier sharp-edged weapon used up until 1908, was a 'cut and slash' sword, but while it was replaced wholesale by the cavalry sword, its use continued in India for a couple of years while the transition occurred. From the very start, it was impressed upon these new soldiers that they were provided with the sword for one purpose only: to kill during combat. The idea was to use it while mounted, and any instruction received on foot aimed to prepare troopers to undertake later training in mounted combat.

The return of peacetime soldiering after the Great War brought most of the 4th Dragoon Guards home from Germany in March 1919. The rest of the regiment returned later for a comparatively brief spell before being posted first to Ireland, and then to Tidworth in July 1919 for two years. By the time Hector joined the regiment, its name had changed slightly: an army order which took effect from 1st January 1921 designated it 4th Royal Irish Dragoon Guards (dropping the brackets), although in ordinary correspondence the regiment was simply referred to as the 4th Dragoon Guards.

During the summer of 1921 the regiment prepared to depart on their next assignment, the men taking embarkation leave in batches during July and August, and receiving the necessary vaccinations. The 4th Dragoon Guards comprised 18 officers and 300 men with six machine guns; on 17th September, the entire regiment set sail for Trimulgherry, one of the Secunderabad cantonments in Hyderabad State on the Deccan of India.

The regiment left Southampton on Huntsgreen, a prize ship captured from the Germans. Hector remembered later how, as they crossed the Mediterranean, a violent storm broke out: 'We were all battened down when we heard that our vessel's sister ship had sunk in Southampton harbour'. On 29th September, after the storm had ended, and having navigated the Suez Canal, the ship called at Port Suez and picked up a draft of 263 other ranks (men) from the 7th Dragoon Guards who were evidently absorbed into the 4th. This regiment was to be reorganised into three sabre squadrons and a fourth D squadron (instituted from 1st October onwards) that included signals, machine-gun troops, the administrative troop and the band. Of this D squadron, 70 men under the command of two lieutenants made up the machine-gun troops. It was to one of these troops that Hector was posted.

When the regiment disembarked at Bombay at about midday on 10th October, it had a total strength of some 27 officers and 591 other ranks. The increase in numbers since leaving England may be explained by the attachment of the contingent from the 7th picked up at Suez. From Bombay, the men travelled by rail to the garrison town of Secunderabad and in the early morning of 12th October, they arrived at Hislop Barracks, Trimulgherry, an entrenched camp some three miles northeast of the town. The very next day, the regiment took over from the 18th Hussars the command of 460 horses (all chestnuts and greys) as well as their bungalows and 309 'native public followers'. All of these followers, or wallahs – nappy-wallahs who shaved the soldiers first thing each morning, chocras ('boys', although some were elderly) who pressed and looked after their uniforms, char-wallahs and dudh-wallahs with milk and butter, plus bheestis and mehtars – were all licensed by the regimental quartermaster.

By January 1922, the 4th Dragoon Guards were well settled in their new, lavishly built barracks, where the 7th had resided ten years before, during a previous stint in India. It was a smart and efficient unit, ready to play its part in the annual celebration of the Garrison's Proclamation Parade on the maidan, a fine stretch of land in Secunderabad. This parade commemorated the crowning and the proclamation of Queen Victoria as Empress of India in 1877, after which all British sovereigns were declared emperors until the time of Indian independence.

More impressively, part of the regiment was also required that month to escort His Royal Highness The Prince of Wales (later crowned Edward VIII) on his Indian tour. They met him on his arrival at Madras, more than 500 miles away, and later when he visited the Nizam of Hyderabad, an independent sovereign within India. During this visit, D Squadron had the honour of forming a bodyguard for The Prince of Wales: two of the squadron's troops (along with eight trumpeters, a captain and a lieutenant) guarded the royal carriage.

After returning to Secunderabad, the regiment awaited the prince's visit to the city of Hyderabad. The train carrying His Royal Highness arrived just after 8.30am on 24th January, from which he rode a horse-drawn carriage. From Hyderabad railway station to Falaknuma Palace, where the Nizam lived, was a good five miles and everyone in the squadron had to 'bump' in their saddles (at the trot) the entire way. Their swords were 'at the carry', a position that denoted the arm was held at an angle with the forearm parallel to the ground and the sword upright. The crowds were enormous and Hector later remembered the magnificent colours of the day, with every variety of uniform and turban on display under the dazzle of India's tropical sun. In the heat of the day, the men endured a gruelling 15-mile ride back to barracks along dusty roads.

A day or two later, another crowd gathered to watch the Prince's Review on the maidan near the racecourse at Secunderabad, which included some 3,000 troops attached to the garrison town. Hector, belonging to the most senior cavalry regiment in the garrison, remembered how the Dragoon Guards galloped past that day, putting on the finest of shows. In the afternoon, the Prince of Wales played polo with the Dragoon Guards officers on the Regimental Polo Ground in Bolarum.

The next day, the regiment took a well-earned rest; but on Saturday the prince attended the Garrison Sports Meeting on the racecourse during the afternoon. In a letter of thanks, he wrote how much he had admired the tandem driving (with two or more horses harnessed one behind another) displayed by some of the warrant officers and non- commissioned officers of the 4th Royal Irish Dragoon Guards.

In the absence of events such as that just described, life in the regiment for a typical soldier was a matter of routine, comprising horse grooming and exercising, guard duty from time to time, and participation in regular Commanding Officer's parades, as well as inspections by officers from brigade or divisional level.

There were also weekly church parades and, on all these occasions, the cavalry sword was carried. On church parade, a rifle party led the regiment behind the band, and a similar party followed at the rear of the column. (The use of these rifle parties stemmed from the time of the Indian Mutiny, when the mutineers at Meerut had fired at a congregation in church.) The Main Guard was generally posted at the main gate of the barracks and swords were carried until 'retreat' at sunset after which a buckshot rifle and five rounds of ammunition were carried through the night. On the other watch, known as Stable Guard, no weapons were carried and trousers were worn instead of breeches, boots and spurs: the sentry was accompanied throughout the watch by a syce (groom).

The Regimental Record of June 1922 featured a fascinating article on how the training arrangements in India compared with those to which the regiment was accustomed at Tidworth.[61] This article argued that India had, possibly, two advantages over Salisbury Plain. Firstly, there was a complete absence of wire and fences, unlike in England. Secondly, water was localised to cultivated land, which was in small patches and easily circumvented. Clearly, wire and fences are hazardous to horses and it is not possible to ride squadrons of horses over crops without damage; furthermore most of these cultivated patches in India enjoyed access to water, which obviously made life more convenient for the troops.

Set against these perceived advantages was the desperate hardness of the 'going', with manoeuvres limited by a lack of water beyond cultivated land, and the rocky terrain making it often impossible to go straight for any distance. The red sand bore witness to the erosion of all the rocky outcrops, and was also evident on the regimental football pitches; those who tore skin on knees and elbows would sometimes have to go for a tetanus injection. Overall, the land was barren, there were not many roads, and those that existed were often in bad repair and pitted by nullahs (gullies) or ditches.

There was, however, one outstanding advantage of India over England. The weather here was wholly predictable, and with the guarantee of no rain or snow for nine months of the year, training programmes could be planned with confidence. This 'amazingly pleasing phenomenon' was tempered by a slight drawback, which was that it was never light before 6am and from March until the monsoon broke in June, it got too hot after 7.30am to walk horses. The unrelenting heat continued until 5pm, and it was dark two hours later.

These considerations meant that the regiment was severely limited during this period, and it was impossible to move far from the barracks. The horses acquired from the 18ᵗʰ Hussars on arrival in India were very similar to the ones the men had left behind in Tidworth, and most of these animals were capable, and could jump. However, it had been said that few of them had 'good mouths' and that 'there were a lot of ugly tempered devils' among them. Hector agreed.

In India, there were fewer opportunities for members of the regiment to take up administrative and other duties, which meant that the majority spent most of their time soldiering. However, compared to England, the pace of change in India was slow and much equipment and facilities were out of date. Like other army establishments in that country, Secunderabad was thousands of miles away from Whitehall and training was hindered by the lack of up-to-date paperwork and equipment.

The only available map of the area was, remembered Hector, little more than 'a good field sketch', and the rifle range was so antiquated that it was the exception rather than the rule for more than four out of the six targets to be working. Moreover, whenever the modern signalling apparatus brought out from England needed repair or reconditioning, the nearest ordnance depot was in Madras, a 24-hour journey even by express train. The regiment had no transport of its own, which meant requisitioning any 'waggon' several days in advance. It was unheard of to see an aeroplane or a tank in that part of India.

The first six months of training in India passed tranquilly enough. Before long, however, the regiment found itself drastically and traumatically reorganised. News came that the British government intended to make cuts of £86m in public expenditure: David Lloyd George, the prime minister, had appointed Sir Eric Geddes to achieve savings in the armed forces. Four British-based cavalry regiments had already been disbanded in order to channel resources into developing a new weapon of war, the armoured fighting vehicle. In India, Hector and his regiment waited uneasily for more news after hearing that the 39 Indian cavalry regiments were to be reconstituted – and thus amalgamated – into just 21 units, to be equipped and maintained by the Indian government.

It wasn't long before the 'Geddes axe' (a common reference to the proposals made by this official) struck again in April 1922, when the issue of Army Order No 133 announced the merging of pairs of regiments of the Cavalry of the Line (the name given to all regiments which took the field in active service). There was to be a pruning of the equivalent of eight regiments, with the senior of each pair to be reduced to two squadrons, and the junior of each to one. For Hector and his colleagues, this meant the 4th Royal Irish Dragoon Guards would merge with the 7th Dragoon Guards to form the 4th/7th Dragoon Guards.

There are hints of some earlier link between these regiments (a detachment of troopers from the 4th in Tidworth to the 7th in Mesopotamia, for instance). This single squadron, absorbed from the 7th, would be known as the 7th Dragoon Guards Squadron, presumably as a sop to those who despaired about the 7th's loss of identity. Both partners of each pair would continue to wear their original badges and carry their former standards and guildons (squadron pennants) on ceremonial parades.

The new combined regiment comprised a regimental headquarters squadron and three sabre squadrons. Headquarters squadron, having absorbed D squadron, included what the others irreverently termed "odds and sods" – the band, the signallers, the machine-gun troop, the administrative troop and orderly room staff. Each sabre squadron was made up of four troops, each troop comprising three sections plus one Hotchkiss-gun section (with two guns). The total strength of the regiment totalled 28 officers, 626 other ranks, 44 chargers (or officers' mounts) and 526 troop horses.

On 24th October 1922, the surviving 7th Dragoon Guards Squadron arrived in Secunderabad from England, ready to start a new life as part of a new regiment. C Squadron (also known as Black Squadron) of the old 4th regiment was required to hand over its black horses to the newly joined men from the 7th regiment. They did so reluctantly but the move was designed to enable the new men to retain another token of their distinction and keep their identity. As part of efforts to make the transition smoother, officials sought to maintain a link with the Princess Royal (the eldest daughter of Edward VII) that had been established by the former 7th Dragoon Guards. It was announced on 20th November 1922 that she was pleased to accept the appointment of Colonel-in-Chief, of the pared down regiment of the 4th/7th Dragoon Guards. Four months later, when the amalgamation of the two regiments was more or less complete, those soldiers who found themselves out of a job embarked for England.

There was, however, one further change. In June 1923, Army Order No 222 changed the designated rank 'private' in the cavalry of the line to 'trooper'. This measure was welcomed by Hector and the other men, almost certainly because the title distinguished them from the more general rank of private in the infantry and elsewhere. Unofficially, the term 'trooper' had been used interchangeably both in the army and among the general public since the term 'private' was first introduced in 1788. Apart from this, the combined regiment remained virtually unchanged in its new configuration for 15 years.

Hector no doubt felt, like others did, that his regimental routine in India provided a good alternation between individual and brigade training (which went on 'ad infinitum'). In spite of the climate, the troops managed to keep very fit. Each January, the entire regiment moved to brigade camp. This annual camp put both men and horses to the test, requiring the latter to manage for hours without water. Hector, being part of the machine-gun troop, saw how complex an operation it was to move the regiment – and particularly his troop – about the country. Eight horses were needed for each machine-gun section during team manoeuvres: four for the men and four pack horses, the latter carrying the guns, tripods and ammunition.

During his five years of service with the regiment in India from 1921 onwards, Hector's tasks as a dragoon guard were wide-ranging. First and foremost he was a machine-gunner, but he also served as a squadron clerk, a remount rider, a scout and a range-taker. (All line cavalry units had to be regularly supplied with fresh horses, remounts to replace sick, lame and dead animals. Similarly, all units designated men as scouts who surveyed the territory ahead of the main body, while range-takers used optical instruments to estimate the distance of targets for the machine gunners.) Generally, Hector would perform his duties as a squadron clerk when he returned from machine-gun training, or the other duties already described: someone else in the squadron would groom his horse, while he attended the squadron office to deal with paperwork.

As a remount rider, Hector's task was to train unschooled horses. The regiment's horses never came from breeding centres in India completely raw: all were used to having a saddle on their backs, but none were trained troop horses and some could prove to be a handful. After they arrived at the stables, horses were trained for a year – a similar period of training to that of the men who joined as recruits - and not all of them passed the final test. It was the remount riders, excellent horsemen and riding instructors such as Hector, whose job it was to train them. This included lunging them on a long rein and teaching them to answer to aids given by a rider. However, as one ex-cavalryman who served at Trimulgherry after Hector pointed out, it took even a good remount rider years to learn how to train a horse well.[62]

In October 1923, a new study group system of educational training was introduced; this was also the month in which Hector passed his coveted First Class army certificate of education. By then, he had already passed his exam in 'ordinary Hindustani' – the language that served as a common tongue between Muslims (descended from India's Mughal conquerors), Hindus and the British military. At first keen, he spent six months studying Hindustani at a higher level, but finding it a struggle, he gave it up.

High-ranking army officers of Southern Command, and commanding officers lower down, oversaw the day-to-day lives of Hector and his fellow cavalrymen. There were various senior officers within the command – inspectors of cavalry, of remounts and of veterinary matters – but the highest officer in the district was one who went by the name of General Officer Commanding-in-Chief. In May 1924 and February 1925, he submitted a favourable report on the 4th/7th Dragoons, saying that in the field and in fitness there was considerable evidence that all units had been well and carefully trained and that there was good co-operation between operators of the various arms.

The most significant officer of them all was His Excellency the Commander-in-Chief, the man responsible for military operations throughout India. In August 1922, this position was held by Lord Rawlinson, who came from Simla to inspect the 5th Indian Cavalry Brigade (of which Hector's regiment was a part). The inspection took place on the open space of Secunderabad maidan and afterwards Lord Rawlinson lunched with the officers of the regiments and went on to look at the barracks and horse lines. His report, which came by letter, was nothing short of glowing. He praised the drill, the precision of movements and most especially the men's turnout. The standard of grooming and the cleanliness of arms and equipment were also lauded.

Standards did not slip. In 1924, the first in a series of reports praised the regiment: the remount officer of Southern Command found that the regiment was 'mounted well', that the standard of horsemanship was excellent, and that the horses were in good condition throughout and were particularly well turned out. Two months later, Major General W B James, director of remounts, came to inspect and commented on the apparent wellbeing of all units and the evidence of good horsemanship throughout. He added that the brigade commander endorsed this opinion and considered that the condition and turnout of the horses reflected credit on all ranks concerned.

Lord Rawlinson's death in Delhi on 28th March 1925 left the position of commander-in-chief vacant. William Birdwood, the longstanding friend of William Perren, took up the post and he too came to inspect Hector's regiment, which was now part of the 4th Indian Cavalry Brigade. He was pleased with what he saw: not only were the turnout of the men and the condition of the horses excellent, but all ranks seemed 'happy and keen'.

Life in the regiment for Hector was routine, punctuated by celebrations and events – such as that early visit of The Prince of Wales in 1922 – which engendered feelings of great pride and joy. Similarly, the annual Garrison's Ceremonial Parade took place each New Year's Day on the maidan at Secunderabad to honour Queen Victoria as Empress of India. A similar event was held each 3rd June to celebrate the birthday of His Majesty the King-Emperor George V.

Nothing, however, could compare with St Patrick's Day. Even after the amalgamations in 1922, Hector's Irish regiment revelled in these celebrations, which probably date back to the year 1788 when the regiment became the 4th (Royal Irish) Dragoon Guards and adopted the Badge of the Order of St Patrick. In peacetime, the day was observed as a regimental holiday with inter-squadron sports and 'officers versus other ranks' competitions. These would be followed by a sergeants' mess dinner and dance.

With early experiences such as these, it was little wonder that Hector, throughout his life, took delight in singing music from the Emerald Isle. During happy singsongs around the piano, or on journeys homeward with his own family later in his life, or simply on his own in relaxed pensive mood, he loved to sing his favourite lilting ballads. As a choir member before and during his early teenage years, he had been trained to sing, and his subsequent renditions were characterised by the melodious and atmospheric qualities of his voice. To more lively reels and similar songs he brought a command of timing and enthusiasm, as well as his fine tenor timbre.

Another excitement during those years of Hector's service with the Dragoon Guards occurred on Christmas Day 1924, when news spread that a 'wireless' receiving set had been installed in the barracks for anyone who cared to use it. Everyone streamed in to try it out: the signal bunk was filled to overflowing and the veranda was packed as people took it in turns to try on the headphones and 'listen in' to the various items of music which came over the airwaves, very clear and distinct.

Garrison and regiment sports tournaments took place during the kindliest nine months of the year. Despite the rather monotonous and enervating climate in southern India, there was a healthy regard for competition within the regiment. Between 1922 and 1926, for example, there were five troop horse competitions, in which cavalrymen tried to gain marks in the categories of condition (70 per cent of final mark), grooming and care of horse (20 per cent), and feet and shoeing (10 per cent).

Sports days were generally held during the slightly cooler months, and often continued for a few days: the mounted sports, for instance, included novelty races that provided a break from routine. Gymnastics were not especially popular, though athletics meetings got more support. However, the best-loved sports were undoubtedly show jumping and all-arms mounted events such as dummy thrusting, 'sword, lance and revolver', jumping and individual tent-pegging with lance (a competition exclusively for members of the sergeants' mess).

Hector and other young cavalrymen took part in individual jumping events, dummy thrusting, a figure-of-eight course, the 'alarm race' and the sword tent-pegging event. Tent-pegging, a sport popular from Victorian times, was traditionally done with a lance and involved competitors galloping towards a peg in the ground, which they pierced with the lance before pointing it through rings suspended from posts. (At the 'point', the arm is straightened and turned so that the edge of the sword is upright and the body from the waist is thrust forward to give the sword a forceful entry.) However, the more tortuous sword tent-pegging involved taking the two rings first, and then the peg. Quite often only the peg got taken; as many as four men abreast would gallop down their lanes and take a peg each. Sometimes there was a 'strike' only, and not a 'lift', though it counted the same. Other times, the pegs split when the sword point penetrated the wood.

During intervals between tournaments, the sports ground – which like the horses had previously been used by the 18th Hussars, and was still in good condition – played host to hockey, tennis and cricket matches. However, football remained the most popular sport, with teams competing in friendly matches and, ultimately, for the Troop Shield. Hector liked boxing but loved football, and played regularly for his regiment. His involvement did not stop there. With a group of friends, he organised a football pool based on English teams, which turned out to be quite a successful venture.

'I used to receive details about the teams from the UK, and I'd work on them,' he explained. 'A friend of mine who'd studied Hindustani at the same time as me, and who was employed at general headquarters, used to print the coupons and these were distributed to regiments in the garrison.' To collect the coupons each week, Hector travelled into Secunderabad on his AJS 500cc motorbike. However, despite the success of the venture, he did have an unlucky moment. On one trip, he passed the commanding officer and his cavalcade and was flagged down for not wearing his 'side hat' – a regulation field service cap. Reprimanded, he had to forfeit his lance corporal stripe.

In March 1926, the regiment was ordered to move from Secunderabad to Sealkot in northern India, during the 1926-27 trooping season. Hector had other plans. He had come upon a newspaper advertisement for 'service clerical personnel' required at government headquarters in Simla. Realising he had the relevant experience as well as his qualifications, he had decided to apply. He got the job.

Appointment to this job meant he was seconded from his regiment. He was to become a clerk in the 1st Division Office, detached from his regiment but remaining on the 'strength' (the depot's appointment list of personnel) until he was finally transferred. This involved a probationary period of six months, during which he continued to wear the badge and uniform of his regiment and was also paid by them. The 1st Division to which he went was the name of the formation of troops in that part of India, and his post was located at the divisional headquarters, and would last for as long as they wished to have him or as long as he wished to stay in it. He had the option to apply for a 'return to unit' to rejoin the regiment. In any event, he was soon pursuing his keenness for football by playing regularly for army headquarters during his probation.

As 1926 went on and Hector settled into the life of the hill-town, he was as yet unaware that his daily excursions from his quarters to Summer Hill were being observed with keen interest. From Clare's recollection of the 'kiss in the ring' game at the Christmas Eve party in Summer Hill that year, it seems the occasion was a golden opportunity for her to come face-to-face with the young man she had admired from a distance. Certainly she seized her chance but the circumstances enabled her do so with decorum, and the fact that she frequently recalled that moment in later years illustrates how crucial it was. Hector never revealed how he felt about their first meeting, but it is clear she caught his eye, and that it was the start of something very special for him, too.

Soon Hector and Clare were courting. Simla provided them with a perfectly romantic setting, where they could walk over the hills and through the dales and spend hours outdoors, time alone that enabled them to get to know one another. Notably, there was Lovers' Lane to which Clare later referred almost as frequently as the 'kiss' game that brought about their meeting. She never failed to draw attention to photographs of the lane when the family photograph album was consulted in later years, usually with a knowing look at her husband. In addition, they would have attended social evenings at the clubhouse. Clare's parents William and Mary welcomed Hector at the house and, in due course, extended invitations for him to join meals with the family.

Within weeks of their first meeting Hector had asked Clare to marry him, although they couldn't marry as quickly as they might have liked: he would have to wait until his twenty-sixth birthday in 1928, when he would be eligible to become part of the 'married strength' of the regiment. At that time there was a quota for married couples, which included those with families who could be allocated married quarters. The families were part of the regiment and travelled to live wherever it was stationed; wives and children received free railway warrants and had all their baggage carried for them.

It was possible for a soldier to marry if he was younger than twenty-six, but there were difficulties: he still had to have permission from the commanding officer (possibly to prevent marriage between soldiers and native girls) and would not qualify for privileges, which meant that when a regiment changed station, he would have to find his own accommodation and apply for a sleeping-out pass to be with his wife. Neither would he receive what was known as 'marriage allowances', which replaced the single soldier's rations. In addition, he would be required to pay for his wife's railway fares and if the regiment went abroad, his wife was left behind and would usually go to stay with her parents. There were considerable disincentives to marrying young.

During this time, Hector put other plans into action. While still on probation at Divisional Headquarters, he applied for entry into the Indian Army Service Corps (IASC) and was accepted. A warrant officer friend advised him also to put in for the Indian Army Ordnance Corps (IAOC), and here again he was successful. The reason for these applications was that he was looking to secure a more permanent way of life in India, still with the army, in order to secure his future with Clare, and he wanted to avoid being uprooted by any movements undertaken by his parent regiment.

Eventually he chose to join the IAOC. The ordnance corps stored and distributed supplies to the troops, primarily arms and other military equipment, obtained from the ordnance factories and other sources, and it was also responsible for the manufacture, storage and issue of clothing, which came from depots. Simply, its charter was to forecast and obtain all stores required for the maintenance of the army and to ensure these were available to units at the right time and in the right place and quantities.

To work for the IAOC meant joining the Indian Army, which comprised all troops recruited and based in India and their European officers. The larger designation of 'the Army in India' referred to all military forces stationed there. Hector fulfilled the necessary requirement, which was to have been attached to a British regiment in India long enough to have become reasonably fluent in at least two of the country's major languages, and on 23rd March 1927 he joined the Ordnance Corps and was posted 130 miles away from Simla at the depot in Ferozepore on the plains of the Punjab. This was a British military station of historical significance. The fort there, rebuilt in 1858 at the time of the Mutiny and greatly strengthened in 1887, contained the principal arsenal of the Punjab – a large ordnance supply centre. Hector was given the rank of temporary sergeant, and six months later he received a permanent appointment to the department.

Following Hector's change of employment, Clare remained as Alan's nanny in the service of the Normans at the Manse. To them, she was a part of the family, and she remembered later how 'they often said how much they would like to take me back with them to Edinburgh when they returned there'. When Hector came to visit, the Normans would sometimes invite him round for a meal. However, when he was away in November 1927, just a day after William and Mary had gone down to Delhi, Clare was overtaken in the late evening by an attack of appendicitis. Mr Norman left his whist game with his wife and friends and arranged for her to be hurriedly carried from the house inside a 'doolie' (he kept pace walking beside her). The bearers dashed down through the Lower Bazar to the Ripon Hospital and an operation was performed in 'the nick of time' that prevented the onset of peritonitis.

After Hector visited her at the Ripon and Clare had sufficiently recovered from the operation, Mrs Norman took her and Alan to stay for a week at Barogh, a little place 5,000ft above sea level. Midway along the Simla to Kalka railway line, it was known as a 'halfway halt' and had a ridge that ran high above a valley. Clare remembered travelling through the tunnel of 3,750ft piercing the hill, 'the longest of all the 103 tunnels on that line'. After this sojourn she travelled on to Delhi alone to continue convalescing. When she boarded the sleeper at Kalka, the guard assured her of seclusion all night and locked her safely into her compartment in the 'women only' section of the train, where she stayed until its arrival in the morning. She spent two weeks with her parents and her brother Bill, and Hector came from Ferozepore to see her. Then she returned to Simla alone to be with the Normans again.

Little time elapsed – it was the beginning of February and 'in the depths of winter' – before Hector too became unwell. He was on four days' leave and staying at the YMCA in Simla, where he developed pneumonia. In a surprising reversal of roles within just three months, he was admitted to the Ripon Hospital, and this time Clare came to visit.

That March, Mrs Norman gave birth to a second son. While she was in hospital, Clare's responsibilities were stepped up: she was now asked to help with orders for the day, including giving orders for meals. However, her own wedding day was approaching and it was soon time for her to leave. As a measure of their gratitude, the Normans bought Clare her wedding dress and gave her an impeccable testimonial, 'a marvellous reference' which she kept safely. It said:

> 5th April 1929 Miss Clare Perren was nurse to my little boy for 18 months and I was extremely sorry to lose her when she left to get married. I found her excellent. She was young and inexperienced when she came to me but she had so much common sense and understanding of the child's mind that for the last year she had complete charge of my little boy. He was very fond of her and her (sic) memory is still fresh. Always quiet and dignified, I never once saw her lose her temper and with a sense of responsibility one seldom meets in one so young. I cannot speak too highly of her own charming personality and of the help she gave me in the house. The jerseys she knitted were the best hand knitted jerseys I ever saw.
> P Norman.

Hector decided to embrace Catholicism, and was received into the Catholic church at Ferozepore. On the morning of 15th August 1928, the day of their wedding, Clare and Hector attended mass together and received Holy Communion at the Catholic Cathedral of St Michael and St Joseph just below the mall, having been there for confession the evening before.

Following this, Clare made her way not to her home but to that of the Freitas family, good friends living close to the Perrens at Summer Hill. A breakfast was set out here and Clare must have tucked in heartily, it being a rule of the church at that time that those who were to receive the Holy Eucharist should fast from midnight in preparation for the rite the following day. The two bridesmaids were Hester and Clare Freitas, a great friend, and the house that morning was full of excitement and bustle.

There was, however, one element of sadness: William was at this point too ill to give Clare away, or even to attend the marriage service and subsequent festivities. Instead, Mr Freitas was going to walk down the aisle with Clare on his arm, while Jesse Bridle, another dependable friend of the Perrens, would serve as Hector's best man.

When the time for the ceremony drew near, the wedding party departed in a small procession of rickshaws operated by coolies, four to each one, trundling up the footpath of the steep hillside onto the mall – a familiar journey for Clare and Hester. Then at the telegraph office, the procession led down south to Ripon Street and arrived at the Cathedral, just opposite army headquarters where the absent William, now sorely missed at such a joyous family occasion, had seen better days.

Clare's mother Mary, brother Billy, and friends of the family on the bride's side had gathered there already for the service at 3pm. For Hector, the groom, there were no family members present. Afterwards the happy couple mounted a special two-seater rickshaw and led the procession (which followed closely on foot) a short distance to H G Wengers, a restaurant on the mall. The wedding party was made up of some 50 people who must have expressed admiration for the exquisitely decorated three-tiered cake ornamented by the emblem of Hector's regiment, on display at the reception. This had received Clare's seal of approval, in Wengers' confectionery shop, the night before.

The celebration over, the newlyweds went to the home of 'Uncle' Tim Maudley and his wife, wedding guests and family friends who lived near the Perrens at Summer Hill. They stayed for a week's honeymoon. After that, it was time to say goodbye to Simla.

TEN

A NEW GENERATION

Now that she was married, Clare's new home was Ferozepore where Hector worked. On leaving Simla after their honeymoon, the couple travelled to this 'very hot station' as she would remember it later. Life on the cantonment (Indian military station) was very different to Simla, although there was still quite a social life, with activities such as club meetings and dances.

Clare had acquired a nickname, 'just a pet name' which Hector had begun using affectionately before they were married: to him she was known as 'Kiddy or Kid', while her own name for him was 'Duck'. In fact, they knew each other by these pet names all their lives, and the only time Hector could be heard to address his wife as Clare was when they were together outside of the family. She, however, often also called him 'Hec'.

Being a married woman, Clare now had her own cook and sweeper. They had also been given a young black Labrador by one of the men at Summer Hill men's quarters in Simla who had left there. Here in Ferozepore, this dog had a habit of wandering down the road from their married quarters to the barracks more than a mile away where Hector had lived until his marriage. Each time, one or another of the men had to bring it back, but eventually Clare realised that it just wasn't happy living with the two of them. 'It was a man's dog,' she remembered.

The couple had another pet, too: a mynah bird – one of a species renowned for their ability to mime the human voice with remarkable verisimilitude. Like most households, they had a crude air-conditioning system comprising a hand-operated arrangement of fans that swung, suspended, from the ceiling, and were made out of cloth stretched on a rectangular frame. An Indian servant, known as a punkah-wallah, operated the contraption and Clare would often have to call out to him if his pulling of the ropes became sluggish. Being constrained in a cage did not prevent this amusing bird from calling out in a manner identical to that of Clare, at regular intervals, 'pull, punkah-wallah, pull!' even when the poor man was working at utmost speed. Clare remembered his clipped Indian accent as he came to her and declared: 'But memsahib, I am pulling!' (He had been discovered previously asleep on the job, several times, and his employer's scolding was memorised by this Indian starling, much to the servant's chagrin.)

Hector and Clare were settling in their new home, and it wasn't long before she was expecting their first baby, although because of a lack of education and awareness which was quite typical of the times, she did not realise for some months that she was pregnant. Hector, meanwhile, went down with malaria and was admitted to the Ferozepore Military Families' Hospital, where he was kept for about ten days. They both had bicycles, so Clare cycled to visit him there.

When he was better, they travelled together over the plains to Lahore, the heart of Kipling's *Kim* country, and the place where the Punjab government had its headquarters. (The headquarters of this military division and district shared the same name.) The train journey took them 70 miles north, and the object was to visit Clare's father William, who was now fifty-five years old and by this time a permanent patient at the Punjab Mental Hospital at Lahore. After giving him many years of daily care, his wife Mary remained living in Simla. Perhaps she was reluctant to give up the government quarters she had been allocated there for a more expensive home in Lahore. Visiting regimes in such institutions may not have been liberal in those days, and she must have felt she was more comfortable living among friends and in familiar circumstances.

William's troubles had worsened since Clare's marriage. As indicated by his service records, apart from a brief spell between October 1927 and March 1928, he was ill for most of the time. He suffered from neurasthenia, which in his case was chronic and severe. This disorder, first named in 1869, was described as a neurosis characterised by symptoms of abnormal fatigue, irritability, headache, depressed mood, insomnia, difficulty in concentrating and lack of enjoyment. At the time of William's own diagnosis, the condition was subdivided into categories: aviator's, post-infectious, traumatic, tropical or war. In William, it seems, depression was brought on by pressure of work, and latterly by the ending of his hopes to see England.

It was fortunate that the Maudleys, whose house Hector and Clare had used for their honeymoon, had in the meantime moved to live in Lahore. This meant that from time to time William could secure a day's respite from the hospital at the Maudleys' new house, and it was here that Hector and Clare came to visit him. The weather was beautiful but William remained depressed, and in hindsight what made this visit so sad was that this was the last time Clare would ever see her father, though he lived on for another seven years within the institution.

Pregnancy did not stop Clare from travelling. In March 1929, when she was nearly seven months pregnant, she and Hector made a trip of about a hundred miles up country to stay with an old army friend and see 'old buddies' from his regiment. In December 1926, soon after Hector's transfer, the 4th/7th Dragoon Guards had left the clammy heat of Secunderabad to take up a new posting some 1,200 miles north at Sialcot, an important garrison which was part of the Northern Command, and not too distant from the troublesome frontier hills.

When Hector and Clare visited Sialcot, it was on a weekend of regimental sports and a miscellany of cavalry events, a familiar display of equestrian theatre which would surely have reminded Hector – keen horseman that he was – of all that he was missing. Even so, although few if any soldiers in the 4th/7th were aware of developments thousands of miles away in Britain, it was at just about this period that strategists were discussing how to mechanise the entire British cavalry.

Like many women of her time and situation, Clare had known little about being pregnant. Some facts of life were too delicate to discuss, hence she had virtually no idea of how babies were made or how they 'got out'. Incredibly, right up until the time when she was actually giving birth to her first baby, she believed that her baby could be born only when her own abdomen was split from top to bottom. Even then, no one had prepared her for the level of pain she might have to endure. The majority of women had no clue where a baby was

Clare (about two months pregnant) and Hector. Taken 11 November 1928, just 3 months after their marriage.

coming out from, which naturally made the experience a dreadful shock.

Clare went through eight months of pregnancy before seeking medical help. The reason she did go to a doctor, in the end, was that she wanted to know whether she could travel to Simla – where her mother was – to have her baby. The doctor scolded her for not having consulted him before, but with his consent she and Hector travelled away from the intolerable heat of Ferozepore by train, to Kalka. Wishing to avoid the discomfort of riding in the smaller train that swayed alarmingly on its 2.6ft gauge lines, they travelled the last 60 miles by motor car, up along the old Cart Road. This was still a tortuous ride, made worse by the fact that one of the other three passengers – the wife of a couple who were travelling with their little boy – was very carsick on the way.

Finally Hector and Clare reached Summer Hill. Mary Perren had moved twice since they had left. The second move was to No 8B Block, an upstairs flat that again was part of government quarters. On 14th May, perhaps just days after their arrival at Summer Hill, Clare's brother Billy had enlisted in the Leicestershire Regiment at Jutogh Cantonment and was posted to the 1st Battalion (part of 11th Indian Division) stationed at Argaum barracks, Kampti, ten miles from Nagpur, the capital of the Central Provinces. (Mary subsequently received a postcard dated 13th June 1929 from her 'ever-loving son Billy', sent from the hill fort at Purandhar near Poona some 120 miles from Bombay. By the 20th of that month he was 'Band Boy Perren'.

Back in Simla, events were moving at a fast pace. Aiming to prevent the trauma of getting to the hospital at the last minute, just before the onset of labour, Clare had been taken by rickshaw to the British Military Families' Hospital at Jutogh, the place where her own mother Mary had given birth to her brother Billy nearly 16 years before. Hector walked alongside the rickshaw. For this and subsequent births, Clare was required to take with her to the hospital two 'binders' for post-natal use: one was to wrap around the baby to protect its severed cord, still attached; and the second was to be pinned around her own stomach 'to restore the body form'.

'It was a lovely little hospital and I was the only patient there,' remembered Clare later. The matron, a Mrs Andrews, was elderly and liked her drink, but she was also a qualified doctor, and – apart from an Indian ayah - the only staff member in the hospital. To try to help speed things up, Mrs Andrews took Clare for walks in the grounds, inquiring intermittently 'Are you feeling all right?' and 'Have you got a backache?' This matron, it transpired, was (according to Clare) something of a 'giddy kipper', for in addition to her duties, she was hastily preparing a costume for a fancy-dress dance that she was planning to go to at the mess in an adjacent building that evening. Still waiting for her labour to begin, Clare stitched countless sequins on to this fancy dress, which depicted stars and moons because Mrs Andrews was to represent 'night' – very aptly.

Perhaps all the stitching was part of a strategy to take Clare's mind off events to come. However, by about 10.30pm her pains had started and the merriment in the distant mess was in full swing. Fortunately, the ayah – who herself had given birth only a few days before – stayed with Clare throughout this and following nights, often sleeping on the floor beside the bed. Clare's labour continued throughout the following day and Hector arrived in the afternoon to find his wife 'in such pain'. Thankfully, the matron was back on duty after her night's revels.

Hector remained with Clare and finally, at 10.25pm on 9th June, their first child made her appearance in the world. The couple named her Patricia Mary Elizabeth Perks and Hector carried Clare from the labour ward back to her hospital bed. It was blowing a gale that night, she recalled. 'Matron gave him some hot soup and a butti (hurricane lamp) to help guide him on his three-mile walk back through the hills.'

In all, Clare's confinement at the hospital lasted for ten days. Her diet was designed to be nourishing, though it was also monotonous with its daily fare of cooked chicken in various forms. Worse still, she had to eat egg custard every day and grew so sick of it that it was a long time before she could face eating egg custard again. As the wife of a soldier who had paid more than 42 weekly contributions before the date of her confinement, Clare was entitled to payments of 'maternity benefit', a fact shown by a slip of paper she signed on receipt of a payment on 28th June 1929.

The infant Patricia was baptised in Simla's cathedral where her parents had been married, although she was baptised in a 'new' part whereas their ceremony had taken place in the 'old' part of the building of 1885 (completed the same year as army headquarters). At the time, Hester was on leave from her nurse's training in Calcutta and she became godmother to her first little niece. Hector returned to Ferozepore alone while Clare stayed with her mother in Summer Hill, but during the weeks that followed he often took leave to be with his wife and new daughter in Simla. By September, Clare was feeling strong enough to travel and to face the heat, and it was then that all three returned to their own home in Ferozepore.

However, their time there was coming to an end. After celebrating their first

Christmas together as a family, they made preparations to leave for their next destination. Hector had achieved that ambition which Clare's father William had once held so close to his own heart: permission to leave for England. He had been promoted to the rank of staff sergeant with effect from 23rd March, and having already accomplished five years of service in India, he had also earned 'home furlough' of one year.

In fact, Hector had been in India not five years but nine, but he later revealed that this first trip back home was delayed by about two years because of fighting on the sensitive North-West Frontier. This was a strategically important mountainous region between Afghanistan and Kashmir inhabited mainly by Pathan tribes and it had been under British control since 1849. More recently, tensions had been mounting against what the tribes felt was discrimination in the reform laws introduced at Delhi in 1919; because the district was judged too sensitive, it was not made a province with its own governor or given rights of regional democracy. The result was a movement (which, surprisingly, included an alliance between anti-British Muslims and Hindus united in their cause) of widespread unrest and civil disobedience aimed at driving the British out, culminating in a wave of dissatisfaction that in 1929-30 was surging through the whole of India.

Towards the end of February 1930, when Patricia was eight months old, Hector and Clare prepared themselves to leave Ferozepore. By a coincidence, the amalgamated dragoon regiment Hector had left in 1926 was now also back in England, based at Shornecliffe Garrison in Canterbury. (Its own Indian tour had ended in October 1929.) For Clare, on the other hand, this was no trip home but her first departure from the only land she knew. It was also her first sight of the sea.

The couple and their baby sailed from Karachi, the chief town in the province of Sind. The date was 21st February and the vessel they travelled on for three-and-a-half weeks was HMT (His Majesty's Troopship) Somersetshire, a ship that exclusively transported troops and their wives and families. Being as yet without a commission, Hector was only permitted 3rd Class travel, and this meant staying in separate (male) quarters at one end of the ship, sleeping in hammocks. The wives and children were in cabins at the other end.

Clare remembered sharing her cabin with another woman and her child, with a sentry posted outside. 'He kept such a close watch that he knew when we were sick and when we went to the lavatory!' At mealtimes, 'ghastly' tea was poured from large vessels that resembled watering cans, while supper consisted of cocoa and 'dog biscuits' (probably ship biscuits, known as 'hard-tack'). A dragoon described, amusingly, what the journey was like:

> I was rather lucky. I was only sick once and that was nearly all the time. The deck rails would come and go again, and the bully beef would go and come again. It's an awful feeling. Take my advice and never be seasick. It is a waste of time, energy and good food. Apart from this, I made the best of life and joined in all the deck sports.[63]

Having left the orient behind, the ship's run across the Arabian Sea ended at the first stopping point: Aden, a British colony known for being 'hot, but healthy'. Here, on the western side of its large inner harbour, was what was considered to be one of the best salvage and coaling stations in the East. Ships were by now, of course, more advanced than when John and Susannah Perren had made their voyage out to India in 1874, and steamers seldom stopped for more than a few hours to take on coal. Ship's boilers were, however, still stoked at 'stoke holes' by men working in conditions of terrible heat.

These few hours provided passengers with the opportunity to visit the bazar in Aden, where could be seen 'wild Arabs from the interior of Arabian Yemen, Egyptians, Swahilis from the coast of the East Africa, untamed shock-headed Somalis, Jews of various sects, Parsis, British soldiers, Bombay Mahrattas, and Jack-Tars'[64], according to the contemporaneous edition of a handbook for travellers by the legendary British publisher John Murray.

On 26th February, the troopship left Aden and travelled through the Strait of Bab-el- Mandeb (The Gate of Tears) into the Red Sea, which extends northwards to the head of the Gulf of Suez for about 1,300 miles, and is about 200 miles across at its widest point. During these winter months, a fresh breeze from the south prevailed during the first third of the voyage up the Red Sea, and an equally strong wind from the north blew the rest of the way.

Proceeding north, only the tops of the distant, bare and arid mountains of Arabia and Africa could be seen from the ship until arrival at the couple's next stop, Port Sudan, lying at the halfway point. On entering the Gulf of Suez, the sea turned a deep blue and the peaks of the Mount Sinai range became visible to the right. Approaching Suez, steamers usually anchored in the 'roads' about a mile from Port Tewfik (the entrance to the canal, which was two and a half miles from the town of Suez).

Opened in November 1869, the canal was 100 'statute' miles long with a gare (station) every few miles, having signal posts to regulate the traffic. This was achieved by allowing a vessel into each block of the waterway in a controlled manner, to avoid congestion or collision. On occasions, two troopships going in opposite directions had to pass each other in a narrow zone. For this to happen, one ship was tied up to the shore, and everyone on both vessels waved and cheered. However, the passage up the canal was slow, lasting – for Hector and Clare – about 15 hours. Finally, they reached another important coaling station, Port Said.

Clare remembered: 'When packing baggage for England during the winter season, it was necessary to pack some winter clothes that were accessible, at a particular stage during the voyage, in cases marked "Wanted on Voyage". Other items not required on the voyage were marked accordingly and secured in wooden crates. All except the accompanying luggage marked "Cabin", was put into the hold of the ship.' The ship's arrival at Port Said, where it was said the East ended, heralded 'baggage day', when passengers were permitted to enter the hold of the ship to exchange their cabin luggage (tropical wear) for 'Wanted on Voyage' luggage, which contained cold weather wear.

Port Said was a modern town, and Clare and Hector went ashore before the ship's departure on 4th March. They also stopped at Malta, and lastly at Gibraltar, going ashore both times (as well as at Aden and Port Sudan, previously – always in the morning, and always leaving Patricia on board in the care of someone they knew and trusted). At Gibraltar, steamers rarely stopped for more than a few hours, and they wouldn't have had time to take more than a quick walk in the town and along the lower fortifications.

On 12th March they left Gibraltar on the last leg of their voyage. The weather had changed and there was a fierce storm at sea as they travelled through the Bay of Biscay. In fact, it was so hair-raising that the men were allowed to remain on the mess decks near the families. Clare was seasick, and developed a curious craving: lying exhausted and famished in her cabin, she could think of nothing she wanted to eat more than herrings in tomato sauce!

Finally, they arrived at Southampton on 17th March 1930. From here, they travelled to Hector's home town of Malvern in Worcestershire, where they found Hector's sister-in-law Emily waiting for them at the station. Hector had known her briefly before she married Gus, and she had found them lodgings in Malvern for their stay.

Emily Perks (known to her family as Em) was a good woman, deeply committed to her wider family. She was born Emily Ellen Harding in Birmingham on 8th October 1904. When she was young, her family had moved to a house on Cowleigh Road in north Malvern, where they remained for many years. She was intelligent, and passed the scholarship exam to go to grammar school, but because her parents had six children there was no money for her to travel to Worcester to school each day. Eventually she took a job at Malvern College for Boys and went to live with her aunt at The Fountain Inn. Here she met Gus – Augustus Stanley Perks, Hector's elder brother – and the couple married on 10th March 1925 at Cowleigh Parish Church.

Since September 1916, Gus had been a Royal Marine in the Plymouth Division. The marines' task was to guard naval vessels and if necessary to fight off boarding parties of enemy forces and sometimes undertake amphibious raids. During his service, Gus had risen from private to corporal, and now he was a gunner. He was an active sportsman and represented the marines in their soccer and rowing team as well as sailing regattas. His job frequently took him away from home, and while he was gone Emily took their two children (Stanley William, born 13th July 1926; and Joan Lillian, born 15th September 1928) to live with her mother. However, when the time came for him to return from a 30- month commission on the China Station (fleet operations in the Western Pacific) there were four people waiting at Hereford Station to meet him: Emily, his son Stanley, his brother Hector and a new sister-in-law: Clare.

While Hector and Clare were staying in Malvern, they went with Gus and Emily to see Al Jolson in a film called *The Singing Fool*. Released in America in October 1928, this was the second sensational screen success in 12 months for Jolson following his appearance in *The Jazz Singer* (1927), a feature film which galvanised a 'talkie' revolution in 'an industry that had been mute all its life'.[65] Previously, films were silent and dialogue came up as subtitles on the screen. Music was provided by a live musician - usually a pianist or violinist – or a house orchestra. For the first time, here was a full- length picture in which the sound had been 'dramatically integrated into the action'.[66]

Creating such a film required a whole new method of production. Jolson's film was made with the Warner Brothers' Vitaphone (sound on disc) system, whose novelty 'lay not in its power to "talk", but to purvey music'.[67] With Vitaphone electrical signals were 'picked up by the microphones on the film set or sound stage' then 'transferred to 17-inch discs by disc-cutting machines that were locked into synch with the film-cameras'.[68]

The changes in production did not stop at the equipment. Jolson, already a renowned musical performer, had spontaneously introduced a 'colloquial ad-libbing'[69] technique which was a first for Hollywood. In the world of silent movies, to have synchronised music and singing, as well as some synchronised speech, made *The Jazz Singer* a breakthrough. Apparently, the snatches of talk were liked well enough to keep them in.

The Singing Fool showed Jolson 'at full throttle'[70] and contained the tear-jerker hit 'Sonny Boy' that was the first to make the transition from the movies into popular consciousness. Sung by a loving father character to a three-year-old son sitting on his knee (with the added pathos that the son is about to die), this song sold 2m records in nine months, with sheet music sales reaching 1.25m[71]. Other songs from the film included 'There's a Rainbow Round My Shoulder' and 'I'm Sitting on Top of the World'. Later in her life, Clare remembered how these songs touched her deeply. The popularity of these new feature-length musical pictures, both in America and England, soon persuaded producers 'that "all-talking, all-singing, all-dancing" pictures were guaranteed box-office successes'.[72]

Gus and Emily got on famously with their guests from India. Clare remembered how the two couples left the three infants (Stanley, Joan and Patricia) with Emily's mother and sisters, and went to Birmingham for the day. There, they walked round the shops and had lunch in Lewis's before they all went on to watch a football match at Aston Villa in the afternoon.

Later, Hector and Gus went off and met with their father who lived nearby with his wife, their mother Lizzie. It is not clear whether they saw their mother; if they did, Hector kept that quiet. Hector maintained that 'Gus and I only saw him [George] at Aston Hotel close to the Villa ground'. However, it appears that George did not want Clare to meet Lizzie at all during their stay, because he was ashamed of her 'poor state of health' – a euphemism for Lizzie's alcoholism. Clare later said that her father-in-law 'would not take Em or me to meet her'. She had met George himself only once, when he accompanied them to the station at the end of that day, and had been impressed by his gentleness and his charm. 'I thought he was a lovely man,' she recalled.

Their brother Ralph, who was as yet unmarried, was working in retail in the area. He had endured a difficult life since the time before both his brothers had enlisted in the services, and had even been taken into care in another county. His father George maintained only intermittent contact, and it seems that on this day out – when time was probably short – they did not see him.

For the rest of their stay in Malvern with Gus and Emily, Hector and Clare made a point of calling on Hector's aunts, uncles and cousins; and no doubt Granny Jones, who still lived at Taynton House in Lower Wilton Road. Her husband Thomas died at the age of sixty-eight on 14th February 1920, ten years before.

Gus was then posted for two months to the divisional headquarters of the Royal Marines at Durnford Street in the area of Stonehouse, Plymouth. He travelled ahead to find lodgings for the four adults and their children, and soon after, both families moved together into one flat in a building in Princess Street, Devonport. Clare recalled that it turned out to be quite unsuitable. 'The place was full of sailors and lasses. Morning, noon and night they played the record "If I had a Talking Picture of You"'. (This was probably the popular version recorded in 1929, sung by Sam Brown and played by Jack Hilton.) She added: 'We went house-hunting every day and were glad to get out of there.'

They stayed at Princess Street a month; then they took lodgings in the same street as the Royal Marine Barracks. Several weeks later the two families split up, with Gus and Emily moving with their children to 56 Emma Place and Hector and Clare taking rooms, firstly, at Caroline Place before moving to a first floor flat at 21 Chapel Street above a greengrocer's, nearly opposite a fish and chip shop. Hector and Clare soon got to know local landmarks, such as Plymouth Hoe, Devil's Point and Devonport Park.

Stonehouse was joined to the centre of Plymouth by Union Street, the longest and straightest street in the city of Plymouth. It was created in the 1820s to connect three towns – Plymouth, Stonehouse and Devonport – and now it was a lively thoroughfare of shops, popular theatres and other places of entertainment. Businesses had benefited greatly from the increased trade brought by the First World War, not least from the influx of soldiers, sailors and marines. It was likely that the smart Savoy picture house in Union Street was where Clare saw *Broadway Melody*, a film that combined drama and musical extravaganza, and was characterised by its chorus line-ups. It was a completely new style of movie, and so exciting for those who flocked to see it. Like the picture house in Malvern, the Savoy was already wired for sound.

Plymouth was where the family bought a very treasured possession, a sewing machine that was used constantly during the years to come. A receipt displaying the Chapel Street address, dated 23rd July 1930, showed that this electric Singer Sewing Machine had been purchased at a discount price of £14 12s. For the lifelong service it was to render the family, it was worth every penny.

In India, Clare could not buy clothes conveniently 'off the peg', so it was little wonder that one of her lasting memories of England was of the strange and overwhelming shops that sold ready-made garments and beautiful furnishings, although even then, early in the 20th century, many of the population still had their clothes made-to-measure. But there were no bazaars, and shopping was, on the whole, more civilised. One of the places she remembered later was F W Woolworth and Co Ltd, the 'sixpenny' store where every item cost 6d or less: a single stocking, for example.

In August, Hector and Clare took a two-week holiday with Patricia to London, where the sights and shops proved 'such a novelty'. They stayed in married quarters at the Union Jack Hostel at Waterloo, which accommodated servicemen and their families. They left the baby in the care of someone at the hostel while they went to the theatre to see a production of *Love's Race*. On 26th August, Clare took the opportunity to meet a few of her maternal relations.

Clare's mother Mary had four brothers and two sisters when she left England. Her brother Thomas had married and had children and there was at least one grandchild, Aileen, who was with Thomas' widow, Sally, at the time of Clare's visit to their Balham address in London. Thomas, a retired railway stationmaster, had died in 1927. A sister, Annie, had married a John Alfred Matthews but had died in 1913 having had six children with him, one of whom, Annie Mary, known as Nancy (Mary's niece), had embarked on a very interesting life and career. Another sister, Emily, who was very sweet and had a cast in one eye, married the widower John Matthews after obtaining the necessary Papal dispensation. However, she too was widowed when John died in 1922.

Clare's cousin Nancy was tall, dark and beautiful, and had initially secured a position as lady's maid to the Belilios family who were wealthy and lived in Piccadilly. She accompanied the family around Europe and to India and Hong Kong but there is no record of any encounter with her Aunt Mary's family. However, there exists a postcard sent to her at the Belilios residence by Susannah Perren's grandson-in-law, William Hayes, in 1908. It refers to a visit that Nancy made to India and may indicate, albeit inconclusively, that she had met some of the family there.

By 1914, Nancy had moved jobs and was with the Countess Elisabeth Baillet-Latour in Sarajevo. The Countess was the niece of Sophie, wife of Archduke Franz Ferdinand, who was heir to the Austrian throne. It was during a state visit by the Archduke to Sarajevo in June 1914 that the fateful events took place which were to plunge the entire world into the horrors of the First World War. The Archduke and pregnant Arch Duchess were assassinated in the bomb outrage perpetrated by the Serbian student Gavrilo Princip. Countess Baillet-Latour took a principal role in the care and repatriation of the Archduke's three children and Nancy became a nanny to these poor royal orphans, looking after them when they were rushed home to Vienna, and when they were greeted by their step-grandmother Archduchess Maria Theresa – all still unaware of the brutal murder of their mother and father.

Subsequently Nancy was appointed (in July 1917) maid to HRH Princess Mary, the daughter of King George V and Queen Mary. According to the archives at Windsor Castle, she was paid £45 per year, and a 'washing allowance' of £14 brought her total wage to £59. These wages were paid by the Privy Purse up until 30th June 1918, when Princess Mary turned twenty-one and took over payment herself. After four years' service with the Princess, Nancy left in October 1921 to get married.

Clare and Hector, with the infant Patricia, visited Aunt Sally's house in Balham. Sally's granddaughter Aileen was there. 'Aunt Sally was very hard but still very much the gentlewoman,' remembered Clare, who met another cousin during her visit: Edith Smoker, one of Sally's daughters. Perhaps the highlight of the visit for Clare was meeting Emily, her mother's dearly loved sister, with a cast in one eye. 'I remember how pleased Aunt Emily was to see us. She thought Patricia, the baby, was so sweet.' This sister had not seen Mary for at least two decades, nor met any of Mary's family.

Back in Plymouth after their August holiday, the close of September marked the return of Gus from nearly six months at sea on the ship Erebus. He was now posted ashore, at Plymouth Headquarters, for five months and during this time his and Emily's second daughter Elizabeth Claire (Betty) was born at the Queen Alexandra Nursing Home, Devonport, on 26th January 1931. It was good timing for all concerned. Hector and Clare were delighted to be able to welcome their new niece into the world before their long voyage, with Patricia, back to India.

The Perks and their young daughter sailed back to India from Southampton Docks on 14th February 1931, on His Majesty's Troopship Dorsetshire. The steamer passed Gibraltar on 18th February and arrived in Port Said a week later. Stopping in Aden, they sailed again on 2nd March and in another week, they arrived in India.

During the voyage Hector wrote, but never sent a postcard to his brother, which read as follows:

Mr & Mrs A S Perks
56 Emma Place
Stonehouse
Plymouth, England.

Dear Gus and Em Very disappointed not to see you at 7.30am. We managed to get away with a rush, but had plenty of time to spare at station. Had nice train journey, taxi to docks, luggage taken by troops to ship and everything went OK. We sailed at 4 pm Sat. All day Sunday very sea sick – everybody. Today, full attendance at meals and very contented. We know 75 per cent of the people on board & so we hope for a companionable journey. We got the cabin with our friends. Clare is writing letters.

Lots of love

Hec

More than five decades later, Clare recalled the voyage as a happy one. She and Hector were in a good frame of mind and were glad to be returning to India, refreshed from their year abroad. Yet for both of them it must have been something of a reverse culture shock coming home to this land of 'bewildering contrasts, where almost everything – whether it was distance, light, darkness, heat or cold – went by extremes'.[73] The impact of this subcontinent, especially initially, was always striking, with its 'ferocious sun, dazzling sunlight, broad shimmering landscapes and intoxicating scents, riots of sound and movement and primary colours'.[74]

They docked at Karachi and took the broad-gauge North-Western Railway to Hyderabad in the province of Sind where a transfer to the narrow-gauge system was necessary. With all their luggage, they boarded the train for the journey along the Jodhpur Railway and travelled 309 miles east through desolate country to Luni Junction for the next stage southeast to Marwar Junction. There they changed again, for now the trains ran on the Bombay, Baroda and Central India Railway (from Delhi) which went south until it met the broad-gauge system at Ahmadabad, which took travellers via Baroda and Surat to the city of Bombay. Though a difficult journey, which took more than 40 hours, this 992-mile route by railway was the most direct. From Bombay, Hector and Clare travelled for another 116 miles overland until they reached Kirkee, nearly four miles from Poona which was the headquarters of Southern Command and Poona District. This was where they were to be stationed for the coming years.

The town's important and historic ordnance establishment, where Hector was to serve, was readily identified by the original and bold lettering emblazoned over the main gate: Kirkee Arsenal. Additionally, the gate was adorned with the pre-1924 crest and motto (Sua Tela Tonanti – 'to the thunderer his arms'). Below, on the ground, were two ancient brass cannons bearing similar inscriptions. Hector started work here on 15th March 1931, and as a staff sergeant his duties included the provision, maintenance and supply of ordnance stores. In his daily round, he accounted for and oversaw the distribution of tools, machinery, timber, oils, paints, chemicals, household and hospital stores, harness and saddlery, tents, guns, arms, ammunition, explosives and ironmongery.

From late September that year to mid April 1932, he was a participant in a course. It was entitled the 8th Ordnance NCO (non-commissioned officer) course and was held at the IAOC's school of instruction, which had been started at Kirkee in 1927 to train officers, warrant officers, non-commissioned officers and military storekeepers. Examinations for the course included knowledge of ordnance duties in arsenals and depots, and of ammunition, guns, carriages, small arms and machine guns. Hector excelled here, as he had done at school, gaining second place out of his intake with an aggregate score of 80 per cent. He was certified as Assistant Ammunition Examiner Class 1, but wrote (in an attempt many years later to describe his career for a family member) that he had 'eventually qualified in all ordnance duties including examiner of ammunition and explosives'.

The ordnance corps was responsible for the storage and distribution of weapons, ammunition and stores and was, in any event, solely responsible for ammunition. Its staff specialised not only in provision and storage but also in inspection, repair and 'proof' – a system of ensuring the safe operation of weapons. On occasions Hector was required to do guard night duty, which meant overseeing this potentially lethal stock, stored along with everything else in the depot. He may well have done similar duties in Ferozepore but here at Kirkee, on the nights he was on duty, a mule was brought to the house to take his camp bed, bedroll and anything else he needed to the arsenal.

Usually he was able to get some sleep because the sentries were also on guard, pacing up and down outside. If the call went up, intermittently, 'No 1 Post, all is well' and 'No 2 Post, all is well', then there was no need for him to be disturbed inside. He also had to do his share of gate duty and here in Kirkee, Clare remembered that sometimes she used to go and keep him company in the guardroom.

The climate at Kirkee was more pleasant than at Ferozepore and Clare began to enjoy the social life. Activities were centred on a huge, well-equipped warrant officers and sergeants' club, which was based in the same ordnance estate where Clare and Hector lived in the married quarters catering for British warrant officers and other ranks. Early in their time there, they applied for and were granted a transfer to better quarters at 15/2 Engine House Road, an end house 'further down on the same street and nearer to the club', which was a distinct advantage. Clare was soon pregnant again, and nearly a year after their arrival, their second daughter was born at the Connaught Military Hospital in Poona on 6th February 1932. They named her Margaret Emily.

At around this time, Clare's mother Mary arrived for a visit. She had not seen her daughter and Hector for nearly three years, since they were last in Simla together after the birth of Patricia, and so she had not yet had the chance to find out much about their recent seafaring experiences. There would have been lots to talk about – news of her distant family, back in England, and the celebration of a new granddaughter as well as the antics of the toddler, Patricia. For all of them, it would have been a very happy stay.

ELEVEN

FAMILY TIES

Although Clare was acquainted by correspondence with major family developments while she and Hector were in Ferozepore, England and then Kirkee, Mary's visit provided the opportunity to receive a more intimate and detailed account. Her mother told them news of Hester, who had completed her nurse's training at the Presidency General Hospital in Calcutta and a fourth year's service in the medical and surgical wards, on 1st October 1929, soon after becoming godmother to baby Patricia. After that, she had returned to Simla to live with Mary, although just after Christmas 1930 she had gone back to the hospital, this time as a patient to have her tonsils removed. Mary, at this juncture, travelled to Lahore to visit her husband William. Three months prior to her visit he had written again to his old friend Birdwood, who responded affectionately in a typewritten letter sent from Simla:

My dear Perren I write to thank you so much for your kind letter which I have just received, and I can assure you I much appreciate the fact that you

127

should have thought of writing to me as you have done – indeed, not only do I appreciate it, but I am delighted to see your hand-writing and to see that it is firm and good – indeed quite unaltered to what it was when you worked with me in the old Military Secretary's Office. I hope this means that you are now fairly well in health, though, of course, I realise how very bad you have been for a long time past. I was so glad to have recently received a nice letter from your wife, to whom I, of course, at once wrote, sending her our best wishes. Hoping that you may yourself be much better as time goes on, and with many thanks to you for good work done for me in years past. Yours sincerely W R Birdwood

For most of 1930, Hester was employed as a private nurse in Simla. As a hill resort, it had long been established as a sanatorium town, catering to prosperous colonials and many of India's wealthier classes. In August and September 1930, while Hector and Clare were in London and Plymouth, Hester was engaged as the nurse to a rajah and rani who were in the hills for their health. The rani, a Hindu queen, was depressed after losing a child; as Hester understood and could speak Hindustani (the main language used between the British in India and the native Indians, closely related to both Hindi and Urdu), she had been the favoured candidate for the job. As that summer drew to a close she went back to Calcutta, a place close to her heart and where her own future lay.

Hester had met the man she was to marry and by 1930 she was already engaged. Since August 1925, when she began her nursing career, she had lived mostly at Lytton House, which provided accommodation for nursing students and was attached to the hospital in Calcutta. Much of her time off, however, was spent at the Bensley house at 116 Ripon Street, the home of Uncle Walter (stepson of her grandmother) and Aunt Lizzie. Another family member lived with them: Frank Leonard Evett-Strange, whose mother was Aunt Lizzie's sister.

Frank was born in Calcutta on 29th July 1900, of mixed blood: he was Eurasian, and an Anglo-Indian; a term coincidentally, adopted by the civil authorities in the year of his birth. An affidavit sworn many years later by his Aunt Lizzie Bensley revealed that Frank's paternal grandfather James Henry Strange was born in London. She declared that he had lived in India, but returned to England before his death in 1900 at the age of sixty-one. Clare met Frank's Aunt Lizzie several times; she was also clearly Anglo-Indian.

Frank plainly had British ancestors somewhere in his lineage. It can be said with some certainty, that at least one of them – most likely a male – married and had children by a native or mixed race woman, but the point at which this occurred is not known. Frank's appearance bore more European characteristics than Indian, which suggests that the incidence of pure native women in his ancestry was far back or infrequent or both. The open discussion of such matters, both in those times and subsequently, were delicate matters.

It was not surprising that both female lines of Frank's family were of mixed race as, before 1830, there were very few European women living in India. Consequently, not only was there a high incidence of intermarriage but also a very high percentage of ancestries with male lines which go back to Britain and female lines which are Indian as in the case of Frank. At ordinary level, the Honourable East India Company encouraged this and at senior level it was entirely acceptable and respectable. The relationship was not casual. Most of the wives were baptized so being called Sarah and Elizabeth doesn't hinder the theory that they were Indian.

Although the affidavit was accepted at the time (having been made in good faith, no doubt), it was subsequently discovered that James Henry Strange was not born in London but in Madras in 1840, although he may well have been British. He was a coffee planter and superintendent of a coffee plantation. His father, Robert Strange, to whom this may also have applied, born in 1804 in Madras, was a writer and an uncovenanted assistant to government, and there is evidence that his father William was in India as far back as the late 1700s. It may have been generations back since the first British forefather of Frank had come to India and had married dark women of Indian and possibly Portuguese extraction.

Frank's father, also born in the south of India in 1869, was William Evett Strange, a merchant seaman at one time before becoming a mechanical engineer with Abcars the shipbuilders in Calcutta. (Evett was William's middle name. When William chose to give his sons Cyril and Frank this name, it was as a double-barrelled surname. There is no apparent source of the name Evett in the family, nor reason why it was used). Frank's mother was Sarah Rebecca Hand, whose father John Charles Hand of Calcutta had been Commander of the Punjab Flotilla. Both of Frank's parents had died in their forties. They were buried at the General Episcopal Cemetary and Frank was left an orphan in his teens.

He was educated, like many British boys in Calcutta, at La Martinière College, and on leaving the school he joined the Calcutta Port Commissioner's Workshops on 28th February 1916. By March 1921 he had completed a five-year engineering apprenticeship. His career continued with various engineering concerns in Calcutta and in line with the city's great maritime tradition, Frank increasingly specialised in marine engineering. He joined the merchant navy as a 4th Engineer on a steamship, then signed on with various shipping lines and was engaged in voyages throughout the Bay of Bengal and the Indian Ocean. At the close of his seafaring career in 1930, he was the proud holder of a colonial certificate of competency as 1st Class Engineer with the British India Steam Navigation Company.

When Hester met Frank, he had a successful career and a position in society. He carried himself confidently and dressed well, showing the trappings of financial security. Even in his late twenties, though, he had the beginnings of portliness and perhaps was rather self indulgent. Clearly he had the means and a large enough personality to sweep any girl off her feet, and Hester fell for him. However, she was collected enough to insist that he leave his seafaring life behind and get a shore job if they were to marry. Family members who encountered Frank in later years told of a man who was somewhat self important, but also generous. His generosity was demonstrated in the beauty and quality of the gifts he gave to his bride to be, tokens of affection that were accompanied by cards describing her, during their courtship, as 'My Darling Girl' and, subsequently, as 'my Sweet beloved' or 'Angel Joy'.

Accordingly, his next and – as it turned out – last job in India was on shore, as a machine shop foreman at the Shalimar Engineering Works. He was to remain here for 25 years until he retired, taking sole charge of the firm's machine, fitting and coppersmith shops, which carried out engine repairs on every launch and inland craft that was docked and surveyed by the company.

Shortly after Frank joined Shalimar, he and Hester tied the knot on 28th January 1931. Hester was now twenty-five, and she had decided she would like the wedding to take place in the Catholic Church of St Thomas, where her parents William and Mary had married some 27 years before. On the day itself, she left the house in Ripon Street and was taken to the church by car. Sadly, her father could not attend.

Relating the details of these events to Clare in Kirkee, Mary must have added in details about the changes in her own circumstances. In October 1930, after many years in Simla – that utopia on top of the world where she and William had raised their little brood – she had decided to leave the town for good. With her husband institutionalised in Lahore, her son away in the army, Clare unlikely to return to Simla and Hester about to marry and settle in Calcutta, it is hardly surprising she was looking to her own future.

The Bensleys were in Calcutta, and so was Hester – and it was to Calcutta that Mary decided to move (after all, the winters in Simla were severe). She came to the city with her dog Jean and, like Hester, she lived as a guest of the Bensleys until her daughter's marriage. However, her departure from Simla severed her family's 60-year link with that place; and she had to leave behind Nannah, her faithful old servant who had once been a companion of her dead son Jackie. After the wedding she moved to live with Hester and Frank in Calcutta, and it was from here that she travelled in February 1932 to Kirkee to visit Clare and Hector and their new daughter Margaret Emily.

Life at Kirkee was very agreeable for the growing Perks family. The River Mula flowed around the cantonment on the north, east and south sides, giving Hector and his soldier friends the chance to do some fishing. Within the village of Kirkee, near the church, lived the Fernandez family, who were Catholic and Eurasian and who ran a chemist's shop. Clare and Hector got to know them – like the others living there, they relished the tasty pickles that the family made, a product so popular that today it is sold around the world under the trade name Ferns.

Two of the servants who stayed with the Perks throughout their five years at Kirkee were the khansama (cook) and his wife Saibi (pronounced 'saybye') who was also the family's ayah. When Clare and Hector's new daughter Margaret was about a year old, these two asked to take leave of their duties for ten days or so, to enable them to return to their village and prepare their fourteen-year-old son to marry a seven-year-old girl. This accomplished, the four of them returned – the parents together with the new couple – to live in the godown, an outhouse near Hector and Clare's quarters.

The tradition of early marriage was common in India. Orthodox Hindu custom demanded that a man have a legitimate son as early as possible, which meant in some cases nine months after his child-wife reached puberty. To ensure the bride stayed pure, the arranged marriage often took place years before. Sometimes the husband was a child or teenager himself; or he might be a widower of fifty or more. Whatever his age, this male became his wife's personal god, and both he and her culture took the view that her one interest in life, and her constant topic of conversation, should be childbirth.

However, bearing children so early and so frequently could weaken a girl's health, and women such as Nannah's wife became increasingly frail. Clare remembered shocking scenes from her childhood, watching young girls running back to their mothers for refuge only to be dragged, screaming and helpless, back to their husbands. In this case, however, the new child-bride was treated well.

'She was a pretty, dear little kid who was still growing her second front teeth'.

At this time, Clare was advised by a doctor to get a change of air, perhaps because of the pressure of looking after two small children. She and Hector decided to travel to Ootacamund, a fashionable hill-station in the Nilgiri Hills in the south of India. Because of its cooler climate, it was home to a flourishing tea industry. Hector and the two little girls accompanied her on the rather arduous 900-mile journey.

The first stage of the journey was taken on the mail train from Poona to Bangalore, for 626 miles. After two further changes of train on this South India Railway they reached Coimbature. Here, they were 1,398ft above sea-level and they travelled on to Mettupalaiyam Station, from where the metre-gauge (3ft 3inch) Nilgiri Railway ascended to Coonoor at 6,100ft, and then a final 12 miles to the mountaintop railway terminus of Ootacamund at 7,220 ft. This last stretch of line, with a central rack rail, enabled it to ascend a gradient of one in 12. As they went up, however, revelling in the glorious scenery, they noticed the temperature plunge to a much cooler level, falling as low as 30°Fahrenheit (minus one degree Celsius), which was the measurement most commonly used in those days.

The Nilgiri Hills were in a region of outstanding natural beauty, dotted with pinnacles and ravines and precipices. Much of the area was densely forested and abounded with game, including herds of elephant and bison, tigers, black panthers, ibex, deer, sloth bears, hyenas, monkeys and wild boar. The last of these was the enemy of the peasants who lived here – especially to their potato crops.

Ootacamund itself was the summer headquarters of the government of Madras. It boasted a lake and 30 square miles of grassy downs, and it was celebrated throughout this part of the world for the opportunities it provided to hunt. Surrounded by lofty hills, it was also the central manufacturing site for quinine, made from the bark of the locally grown cinchona tree. This government industry produced many tons of the medicine, which was distributed yearly to dispensaries throughout India.

The Perks family came to a smaller place called Wellington, nine miles from 'Ooty' and reached along an old road that in parts skirted a precipice of 100ft, though it was well planted with trees including the 'terrific eucalyptus trees' of the region which Clare remembered. This military station town was built on the side of a hill, 6,000ft above sea level, and Hector may already have been here or at least known of this place, since it was where men from the Dragoon Guards, his old cavalry regiment, came on leave or to convalesce (being a mere two-day journey from Secunderabad).

The climate in this part of the hills was said to be very like a perpetual English summer, except that the sun was a little more powerful at midday. On the other hand, the air was much fresher and more invigorating than in the cities down below, so that it was said there was scarcely a soul who did not feel better for a stay. However, compared to the buzz of Kirkee, it was very quiet and Clare remembered feeling lonely during her three months there, even though her children were with her. 'The men used to come up on leave... but there wasn't much doing,' she said.

At the end of their stay, Hector fetched them back to Kirkee and they were all inoculated for plague, as there had been an outbreak in the area, killing several Indians. The sojourn had been so beneficial that on 21ˢᵗ March 1934, Clare gave birth to her first son at the Connaught Military Families' Hospital. This little boy was given an array of names: Peter Raymond Anthony Joseph. 'Peter' was Clare's choice, and the name by which he was to become known; while 'Raymond' was Hector's. Meanwhile the little boy's grandmother Mary Perren, who had come to Kirkee once more to support her daughter at this time, wanted 'Anthony Joseph' – though, if she had had her way, she would have blessed him with 'Bernard' too!

One evening when Peter was in his cot, Clare caught site of a small snake in his room. A friend of hers, who was pregnant, was visiting her at the time, while Hector was on gate duty at the arsenal all night. Thinking fast, she decided to call up the cook to deal with the creature. He caught it and put it in a jar; later it was identified as being very poisonous. Another time, she found a snake in the bathroom. 'The cook wouldn't kill it,' she remembered later. 'They were very fussy about killing creatures, you know.' In Kirkee, there seemed to be more snakes than anywhere else in India, she said. 'I've even seen them crossing the road there. In Ferozepore I never saw one.'

During Peter's early years, Clare found a welcome source of support in the thriving Kirkee Child Welfare Centre. Life was pleasant on the cantonment, and the family was well. Fairly early in 1936, there was another happy event: the arrival of Clare's brother Billy, now Bill, accompanied by her mother Mary. The siblings had not seen each other for more than seven years, since Clare's wedding to Hector, but now he was on leave from his battalion and determined to make up for lost time.

In 1929, when he joined the battalion, it had been based in Kampti. From there it moved north to Ambala, where the hill-station of Kasauli (just 41 miles from Simla) served as its summer retreat. At each of these places, Bill played hockey and basketball in his regiment's teams, and posed with his comrades for photographs. Kasauli was on the crest of a ridge 6,322ft above sea level and enjoyed panoramic views over the Kalka Valley, although for Bill it had less pleasant memories: it was here, as a boy, he had travelled with his mother to receive treatment for his contact with the rabid poodle.

His next move was to the bleak garrison town of Multan, on the Plain of the Indus, a place renowned for oppressive heat with annual rainfall amounting to no more than seven inches. The saying went: 'Dust, heat, beggars and cemeteries – are the four specialities of Multan'. But there was some relief: a Himalayan foothill-station, Dalhousie, provided a cool summer getaway. By June 1935, Bill had gained his army educational proficiency awards and was appointed to the rank of bandsman. His instrument was the clarinet and, like other bandsmen of the regiment, he was attached to its HQ or headquarters wing.

In February the next year, his battalion moved south again to Jubbulpore, an important military and civil station ranking second among cities in the Central Provinces. It was considered the best of the plain stations; and, even better, it gave Bill the opportunity to see his sister, something he had wanted for so long. In Jubbulpore he was roughly halfway between Calcutta and Bombay, within reach of Kirkee.

Conceivably, he joined his mother Mary Perren en route, arriving with her early in March 1936, amid great joy in the Perks family. Mary, energetic and undaunted even at the age of sixty-one, had undertaken once again a gruelling 1,416-mile journey starting at Calcutta's Howrah Station on the right bank of the river, crossing the great width of the Indian peninsula to be with her children, even though her husband was not able to join them. Even so, these were happy days with three out of five Perrens together at last – Clare remembered how she took them on jaunts in a taxicab owned by their friends Harry and Beatrice Fellingham, chauffeured by an Indian who spoke 'beautiful English'.

There was one particular fly in the ointment, though: Hector could not be with them. In September of the previous year, he had been sent to Quetta, a civil and military station 5,500ft above sea-level in Baluchistan; it was also the headquarters of Western Command. India was in a period of exceptional restlessness and it was becoming obvious to some observers that the British Raj was in serious decline.

Quetta had been an important British-Indian military centre from 1880 onwards, when the British acquired the territory on a permanent lease. Prime Minister Benjamin Disraeli and another politician, Lord Salisbury, initiated and oversaw this acquisition, believing it vital for Britain to take control of the westerly route into Afghanistan in the face of Russia's growing influence. Quetta, since it commanded access to the Khojak and Bolan passes and the outpost of Baleli, became a strongly fortified North-West Frontier post.

At the time of Hector's transfer, as throughout its history, there was unrest on the North-West Frontier, with tribal religious leaders provoking conflict against their neighbours inside and outside the region's hilly territory. Upon his arrival, Hector saw disorder of a different kind in the wake of a major earthquake that occurred at 3am on 31st May 1935. The tremor lasted for three minutes, killing 60,000 people in Quetta, which itself was destroyed. Barbed wire was everywhere to prevent looting, and there was an ongoing operation to recover bodies buried under rubble. With no permanent accommodation available Hector, like the others, lived under canvas.

In March 1936, still based at Quetta Arsenal, he was promoted to the rank of sub- conductor, becoming a warrant officer 'on the establishment of His Majesty's Indian Military Forces'. Traditionally most warrant officers in the IAOC were conductors and sub-conductors, and were considered the backbone of the ordnance organisation as well as potential candidates for more senior ranks. The rank of conductor was unique to the IAOC; conductors were the equivalent of plain warrant officers in the rest of the army, and like commissioned officers they were exclusively European. (In the Indian Army Corps as a whole, Indians could only rise to the rank of non-commissioned officer.)

It was the conductor's job to supervise convoys of stores from one place to another, using whatever communication methods were available. Sub-conductors – higher than staff sergeants, lower than conductors – provided an additional link in the chain of command. The relationship between sub-conductor and conductor was the same as that between a company sergeant major and a regimental sergeant major, the former being a Class II warrant officer and the latter a Class I. Interestingly, officers in the IAOC were paid more highly than in the British army.

After Hector had been in Quetta for several months, his baby son Peter – back in Kirkee with the family – developed and sustained a high temperature and a rash, of sufficient concern to warrant his admission to hospital. Hector was granted compassionate leave and returned home to be on hand during the crisis. None of the doctors knew what ailed Peter but he was soon out of danger, and when he had recovered from his mystery illness, Hector took his family back to Quetta with him.

From Bombay harbour, they travelled by boat (a 36-hour run) to Karachi, near the mouth of the great Indus river. From here they went northwards through the province on the North-Western Railway. Finally reaching Quetta, they moved into army quarters. This was where they lived during the day, but when night fell, because earth tremors persisted, families moved into 'wana' huts made of brick walls and canvas roofs, living much as Hector had done previously. It was said euphemistically that Quetta was 'conducive to physical exertion and robust health'. It was not the easiest of times. Here, as in Delhi's tent city, there was the constant fear of intruders. Clare feared someone crawling under the canvas and pinching her family's bedding. Often, a cry of 'chora!' (thief) would ring out in the darkness.

In October 1936 Clare heard that her father, William, had died of a stroke combined with pneumonia at Lahore on the day before his sixty-second birthday. The notice in the newspaper acknowledged his 'years of suffering' and confirmed that he was 'deeply mourned – RIP'. He was buried at Jail Road Cemetery in Lahore in plot VII, at grave number 137. Mary, or those acting for her, employed Dyhan Singh & Sons to deal with the interment. They provided a masonry (platform) grave measuring 8ft by 4ft, with a smaller slab of marble numbered '137' and a name plate which read, in capital letters, 'William John Perren / born 22nd Oct 1874 / died 21st Oct 1936 / RIP'. The bill for the funeral, coffin and hearse came to 180 rupees and was dated 22nd October. It was sent to Mary care of 'Mr and Mrs T Maudley' at 'No 6 Wellington Mall, Lahore Cantt'.

For the last seven years of his life, William had been in the hospital at Lahore under a procedure that provided for 'voluntary admission to mental hospitals'. It seems likely that the hospital was little different from other asylums of those times. Then, it was all about containment and stopping the patients getting into scrapes, as they were seen by most people as little more than wretched nuisances; taking care of them was not necessarily about making a positive difference to their lives. In any case, the care provided often left much to be desired, especially when there was overcrowding and shortage of staff. Little wonder, then, that those who lived within the walls of these places were robbed of a sense of identity and belonging, bereft of hope that their circumstances would change. At worst, these asylums were grim, brutal prisons, filled with fear.

Like other such institutions in most places in India, the Punjab Mental Hospital was maintained under government or municipal management. William's death was one of 37 deaths there that year, most of them due to pneumonia (and pleurisy), tuberculosis and dysentery, illnesses that were the commonest causes of mortality. The frequency of dysentery was attributed to the patients' insanitary habits, but the high incidence of pneumonia was less clear. Other regular causes of death were status epilepticus (a life-threatening condition in which the brain is in a state of persistant seizure), ankylostomiasis (hookworm disease) and debility. At the time of William's incarceration, it was said that the death rate had decreased and the cure rate was on the increase. Suicides and murders were not frequent, and seen as regrettable.

Established in 1840, the hospital was situated south of Lahore and quite remote from the town, near to the Central Jail, the District Jail and the Female Penitentiary. Its first triennial report was published in 1903, when the place was known as the Punjab Lunatic Asylum. The report for the years covering William's care, between 1929 and 1936, show that it had a capacity for 1,008 patients – 826 males and 182 females, including criminals. There were barracks, or wards, for 410 people, but, in addition, there were nearly 600 'cells', taking one patient each, which confined anyone who might pose danger to others.

Of the total number of patients in the hospital on any one night, it seems that the largest number suffered from what was then termed 'mania'. Other illnesses listed in the report included schizophrenia, dementia including dementia praecox ('praecox' implying early onset dementia usually beginning in the late teens or early adulthood as distinct from senile or late onset dementia), mental deficiency, epilepsy and 'epilepsy insanity'. As in former years, the condition of manic-depressive psychosis accounted for the largest number of admissions. For those with this terrible debility, the causes were varied including recurring attacks and abuse of cannabis indica (the powerful Indian hemp infused with water to make an intoxicating drink). The majority of those admitted were Hindu, with a large contingent of Muslims. Only a few patients were European, Anglo-Indians or Christian. Some two or three dozen patients were evidently public and government servants. Meanwhile, the staff establishment of the hospital numbered about 210, including 85 'attendants': a term used for carers or nurses. There was also a matron and four assistant matrons. From January 1933, it was said that another matron and four qualified nurses had substantially improved the efficiency of the staff, when they replaced the unqualified (though dedicated) Franciscan nuns who had supervised the women's section of the hospital for the past 30 years.

The old buildings constituting the male block, William's home for his long term care, were worn and outdated. It stood far inferior to the recently rebuilt female patient facility, considered now to be a real hospital, where the cell and the cage had been eliminated, and there was little to offend the eye and oppress the nervous patient with a feeling of confinement and incarceration. It had all the things the male block lacked: it consisted of pleasant hospital wards, with a few single rooms and excellent ventilation and lighting. The new block was lined throughout with dadoes of white minton tiles, and all the windows were glazed. Although pessimists observed that not a pane of glass would remain a week after its occupation, they were proved wrong. In place of the hard, straight prison bars, typical of the rest of the institution, there were ornamental gratings which provided perfect security without emphasising or even suggesting, the atmosphere of a penal institution. (Not all that was new, however, looked appealing. The so-called criminal section, built on strictly orthodox jail lines, had been completed in 1924).

In stark contrast, the male block was obsolete and very unsatisfactory in many respects. The wards were so badly lit and ventilated that it was impossible satisfactorily to treat the large number of cases of pneumonia and other acute diseases, which carried off so many patients each year. Then there was the perennial problem of an ageing open storm water channel running alongside the block, into which sewage was discharged. This was seen as a continual menace to the health of the staff, as well as the inmates of the hospital; it was responsible for the prevalence of malaria and other sicknesses among them and, even with the greatest supervision, it was not possible to prevent some of the inmates from drinking the effluent.

During all of those years, to add to William's discomfort, there was considerable overcrowding. This was an increasing problem in the institution. (The increase, it was thought at the time, was due either to the general increase in mental disease or to a greater reluctance on the part of people to look after their insane dependents. It could also have been due to an increase in the number of patients belonging to the neighbouring administration, or to the growing confidence in modern methods of treating mental disease.) In just a few years since William's arrival in 1929, the floor space per individual had been reduced from 75 sq ft – considered an irreducible minimum – to 70 sq ft. But since 1929, grave financial stringency had prevailed, and although the hospital authorities had discussed repeatedly the desirability of modernisation and enlargement, their resolutions of that year to acquire additional funding for improvements were frustrated by the financial crisis and increasingly tumultuous world events around that time.

Although the running costs of the institution were inadequately provided for by the government, monies were supplemented to a minor degree by patient fees and the products of the various labours of the inmates. Patients who were suitable and capable of work were employed directly in productive labour. They were encouraged to make textiles (munj matting, weaving of clothing for patients), and trustworthy non-criminal patients were employed in the fields and hospital gardens, growing vegetables. This was considered beneficial for bodily health and mental welfare, and profitable, since the resulting produce was consumed in the institution. There appears to have been a liberal recreational regime for all but unsuitable patients. Best of all, patients appreciated a drive in the motor bus. Attendance at melas, the races and polo tournaments was permitted, which suggests a good deal of freedom. Some 300 patients were permitted, by one account, to sleep in the grounds during the summer months. Given these circumstances, it was extremely difficult to prevent escapes, especially among the groups employed in the fields and gardens but as one commentator said, rather pragmatically, since there were tens of thousands of insane individuals at large in the Punjab, three or four (or even 100) more could make little difference. Patient-upon-patient homicide occurred infrequently; one Afghan pashtun accounted for three brutal murders in as many years.

In the two years leading up to William's death, as financial stringencies continued, accommodation had become so acute that drastic measures were put in place. All patients in the hospital were rediagnosed in an effort to distinguish between mania, melancholia and manic-depressive insanity, but the difference was more theoretical than practical. The great majority, it was found, suffered from manic-depressive insanity. The authorities adopted the policy of refusing a large number of patients who could be treated elsewhere. Strict control was exercised in selecting the most suitable cases for admission and treatment into the institution. Patients were selected according to their curability, so that they could be discharged within a few months to make room for other cases. Those who appeared chronic or hopeless (criminal or non-criminal, male or female), unlike in previous years, were usually refused permission, although in 1936 preference was given for the most part to non-criminal patients and only nine criminal patients were admitted during the year, as against 85 in 1934 and 39 in 1935. This left a large number of them to be accommodated, for the time being, in the various jails in the province, where the provision for their treatment was less satisfactory. To meet this situation and the steady increase generally in numbers seeking admission to the asylum, construction of additional accommodation for 300 male patients was underway. A reduction in numbers admitted was also attributed to the fact that many chronic and harmless patients were handed over to the care of relatives who had agreed to take charge of them. However, while the reduced numbers of patients and the improved conditions in the male block did at last make things somewhat better for the inmates, if only until the next summer's rush, William's struggle with life, during those sorrowful years, had now ended.

William must have suffered greatly during his confinement, far away from the family he loved, undergoing treatment that probably did not improve his underlying condition. Indeed, people with mental health difficulties were often misunderstood and exiled in order to confine their illness and protect others; some patients were seen as dangerous and it was felt that they needed to be restrained for their own sakes, or that of others.

Compared with his outdoor life in Simla – enjoying hunting, catching butterflies and playing with his young children – William's decline within this mental hospital was, as in many similar cases, nothing short of tragic. It was a far cry from the family atmosphere he had known before, and it is tempting to think that had he achieved his one great aspiration to go to England, the slide downwards would never have begun and things might have turned out differently.

Mary also suffered. Because of the great distance from Simla she could not afford to see her husband very often, though she tried to get to Lahore 'at least once a year'. Upon his death, William's pension ceased and she was left without a regular source of income. This provoked her to petition William's former colleague Birdwood, who by now had returned to England and had been, since 1931, the master of Peterhouse College, part of Cambridge University. His reply, on 6th December 1936 to her home at the house of Hester and Frank (12/2 Mominpore Road, Kidderpore, Calcutta) implies she had asked him to encourage the commander-in-chief's office to grant her a pension. He wrote:

> Dear Mrs Perren, I have been so sorry to have just received your letter telling me of your husband's death & write at once to convey the deep sympathy of my wife and myself to you & your children. I well know how much suffering he had for years past & consequently what a very sad time you have had – we do indeed sympathise most deeply. I well remember what a conscientious & hard working man your husband was when in my office & regretted ill health compelled him to retire when he did. Having left India all those years I fear I regrettably am quite unable to help, but I am now writing to the

Military Secretary at Delhi asking him to take the case up to see if anything can be done by the Finance Dept & I am sure he will do so. I wish I could express how sorry I feel for you. With all kind wishes. Yours sincerely W R Birdwood

It seems that Mary replied to this letter on 18th February 1937, but even Birdwood's promised intervention does not seem to have borne any fruit. For the rest of her life she had to struggle on without any outside help, except for that of her own family.

The death of William completed the life cycle of his family's second generation in India. It also marked the passing of the first generation born there. Sixty-two years had gone by since 1874, the year so auspicious for his parents Susannah and John Perren, as they married and set out from England on their voyage to a distant land.

TWELVE

TESTING TIMES

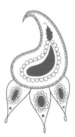

U p in the hills of Quetta, the Perks family endured the bitter winter temperatures that had, once again, set in with a vengeance. Clare was pregnant for a fourth time, and the flimsy fabric of the hut they slept in at night did little to insulate her, the children or Hector against the cold. It was chilly even at the military hospital, severely damaged in the earthquake two years before, yet it was in these conditions that Clare gave birth on 8th February 1937 to her fourth child, named for his grandfathers: George William.

The male doctor, Major Shakespeare, was an Irishman and must have been concerned for Clare's health, for he told her quite explicitly: 'You shouldn't have any more, Mrs Perks – although you're a holy Roman, aren't you?' George was baptised on 27th February at the Church of Our Lady of the Holy Rosary in Quetta. The godparents were his grandmother Mary and his Uncle Bill, though neither was present at the service.

When George was about a month old, a fire broke out at night in the arsenal where Hector worked. Being an armaments establishment, this was a serious business. He was at home when he heard the news and, as fire-master, rushed to the scene. Two regiments of men came to assist moving the ammunition into a safe place. Clare, not wishing to miss anything, characteristically 'bundled the kids in a tonga to see the fire, watched the flames, then bundled them home again'. All hands fought through the night until the fire was quenched and the crisis was over.

Not everything, however, was quite as satisfactory as had been thought. Four of the men who emerged unscathed from the fire came to Clare's hut in the darkness, asking for a complete change of clothes to take to Hector, who had been working hard at the centre of the action. Clare, tickled that it should take four men to convey such a simple request, handed over a pile of garments without quite concentrating on the task. Her lack of concentration became very evident when poor Hector arrived home at 3am, shivering, with his long johns concealed only in part by his overcoat!

The next few months were more trying than ever. About the only bright spot was the fact that they were able to move into one of the newly purpose-built earthquake-proof houses in Quetta. Even this, however, did not prevent George, a 'delicate baby' at four months old, from becoming ill and losing weight; a condition that kept him in hospital for two months. Tragically, while he was there, he developed meningitis and died on 3rd August, aged not quite six months. Hector and Clare were comforted by friends, among them Sam and Lotte Sutton, a couple whose second son was sick in hospital at the same time as George, and whom Hector had known in Ferozepore. However, Clare remembered later that even at that desperate time, 'we weren't especially friendly with the Suttons' (although the friendship was to blossom later on).

The year was shaping up to be a testing one. Later in August, Margaret went down with cerebral malaria and in hospital she became delirious. Clare was told that her daughter wasn't expected to last the night. Fearing she would lose a second child, she prepared herself for the worst. 'Our luck seemed to be so bad,' she recalled, 'but, thank God, she pulled through'. The trials weren't over yet. Hector lost 300 rupees by accident, a whole month's wages. When the family left Quetta at last, on a slow troop train bound for Karachi, Clare felt more than ready to get away: 'I was very glad not to have that eerie feeling of the earthquake, and the worry of never knowing when the next one might be.'

Perhaps the best thing about leaving Quetta was the thought of their next destination. Hector was due for another 12 months' leave and once again the family was intent upon going to England. Patricia, who by this time had become Patsy, was now eight, Margaret five, and Peter three. This time, they set out in mid-October rather than March, departing on HMT Lancashire. Because Hector was now a sub-conductor (at warrant officer level), the whole family was entitled to second-class travel.

In fact, the standards were little different than before, but there were a few privileges. For example, the Perks could enjoy staying in a family cabin with no segregation. Moreover, eating was more civilised, with the adults eating later than the children. This proved a particular blessing for Clare, who remembered Peter as 'a real handful' at the time. Once she found him fishing from the cabin porthole, using a piece of string. Another time, he pushed the bell to summon the steward and then received him at the opened cabin door, stark naked, saying he couldn't find his pyjamas!

On the ship as a whole there were other more depressing incidents. Four servicemen were kept sectioned off at one end of the boat, in a rope cage. They were on view to everyone when they were brought up, heavily guarded, for their daily exercise. Allegedly these were 'mental cases' who were being taken home for treatment, though some or all of them would probably leave the services altogether. However, some passengers were sceptical of this diagnosis, saying that these men were only feigning illness in order to get out of the army. Clare remembered, in particular, one of them regularly kneeling down, with his prayer book, to say his prayers.

On 17th October, five days after setting out, the ship left Aden, calling at Port Said, and departed from there on the 22nd. On 2nd November the ship docked at Southampton. This time, the family made its way straight to Plymouth in good time to spend Christmas with Gus and Emily at their flat at Devil's Point, Stonehouse.

Having left behind the tribulations of the last few months, Hector and Clare and their small son and daughters were glad to be reunited with their extended family. Spurred on by the gaiety of the season, the excitement of gifts under the tree, and the novelty – for the children – of having new cousins to meet and play with, between them the two families created an atmosphere of chatter and excitement. Only little Betty, Gus and Emily's youngest, was disappointed to discover, on appraisal of her three new cousins from India, that they were not, after all, brown or black.

Meanwhile, Auntie Em loved to tease Peter with the words from a song that was popular, 'The Little Boy that Santa Claus Forgot'. She and Gus had bought him a wooden train for Christmas, and she asked him whether he would give his new train away to that little boy in the song. Not sure if she was serious, Peter answered 'yes' the first time, but 'no' the next, clearly in two minds. However, he got his own back when Auntie Em was doing her household chores. Perched on top of the piano, he enquired politely whether she was 'the sweeper'. 'Subsequent to this,' recalled Emily, 'I learnt what the "sweeper" in India was!' The piano was also used for serious practice. Both Joan and Patsy started taking lessons with the same piano tutor. After Christmas, Hector and Clare moved on to 66 Durnford Street, to a second-storey flat almost opposite the Royal Marine Barracks. This, excitingly, had bedrooms in the attic, and was to prove a permanent home during their time in England.

Hector was not the only one to have been promoted. Gus, who was based at the barracks, had risen to colour sergeant in October 1937 – a senior sergeant with special duties and a position originally connected with the regimental colour or flag. However, on 24th April 1938, on the eve of his 39th birthday and after more than 21 years of service with the Royal Marines, he retired.

To his credit, Gus had served for much of his career on board ships of many kinds and classes, both in war and peace. He had served on several great battleships, essentially floating platforms for the heaviest guns. These – among them the Royal Sovereign, the Rodney and the Barham (said to have been the most remarkable of all battleships) – demanded a greater complement of marines to guard them and man one or more of the mighty gun turrets. After leaving the service, he took a civilian job that, although linked to the navy, was more of an educational role assisting with the training of cadets in HMS Ark Royal.

The two young families enjoyed each other's company during that year of 1938, just as they had done eight years before. In the intervening years, Emily had opened a shop at 23 Chapel Street, Stonehouse, two doors down from Hector and Clare's previous upstairs flat. Asked in her old age to recall what she sold, Emily wrote: 'Well, it was "wool and baby linen", we took it empty, we had £100: spent £50 on stock and kept £50 and all profits put into stock...' Clare, always an accomplished knitter, contributed to the shop's stock by making outfits for dolls; these were sold in the shop fully dressed.

Sometimes she and Emily went to the cinema together, having a pick of venues. Many were close by on Union Street, such as the Savoy, the Empire Electric, the Gaiety, the Gaumont Palace and, at the far end next to Derry's Clock, the Royal. The Stonehouse half of Union Street was modest, but when it reached the Plymouth town boundary, the buildings became grander and reflected greater prosperity. The buildings were smarter, and the tram-lined thoroughfare saw a great deal of commercial activity, including dozens of pubs (26 including those on the part properly known as Edgcumbe Street), shops and theatres. The sailors were conspicuous in their dashing uniforms and it was said that Union Street was known, through the men of the Royal Navy, the world over.

On Union Street, too, was the Palace Theatre, a handsome and exquisitely ornate building. Opened in 1898, it was Plymouth's first purpose-built theatre. From the start, the programme was dedicated to a very British type of entertainment – music hall, which had its roots in the Victorian era – although in later years it broadened its repertoire. During Clare's second stay in the 'three towns', the new wave of top musical artists and bands of the day played there. Worth remembering was the show she saw with performing midgets (Fred Roper's Wonderful Midgets) that included a quite dazzling item, 'The China Clock Ballet'.

Usually when they went out together, the two women left their men to look after the children. However, it seems that Gus and Hector couldn't always be depended upon. Emily recalled that once on their return, their husbands 'were out when we got back, all sorts of excuses but I don't remember the details'. Clare remembered quite clearly arriving home with Emily to find the men had slipped out, leaving the children alone in bed. 'We decided to surprise them,' she recalled, 'so we hid behind the furniture when we heard them coming up the stairs. I heard Hector say "Good, they're not in, Gus. They're not in yet". And then we leaped out at them, only to see that they had brought us fish and chips.' She didn't recall another bit of what was probably all one tale. Emily reminded her, in later years, how she, Clare, had hurled this 'peace offering' back at her husband!

In December 1937, Walt Disney had released his wonderful cartoon Snow White and the Seven Dwarfs, which premiered at Los Angeles. It was the first full-length cartoon in the history of cinema, made at vast expense over three years. The film was received with delight all over the world, not least by the Perks children when they were taken to see it at the Gaumont Palace. This was one of the more impressive cinemas in Plymouth and had been built seven years before. It showed the pick of the 'talking picture' hits.

In the early summer of 1938, all three Perks children went down with chicken pox – at exactly the time of a royal visit to Plymouth by the widowed

Queen Mary, on 18th May. Her primary objective was to inaugurate the League of Hospital Friends and thus give royal encouragement to the raising of funds for The Prince of Wales' Hospital in nearby Greenbank.

Plymouthians turned out in their thousands to see what the local press reported as a 'charming and dignified figure' driving through the main streets of the city of Plymouth, past Marine Parade and the Barbican, as well as through Devonport and Stonehouse. The fact that the children were too ill to see the dowager Queen did not prevent Clare herself from joining the excited crowds who were lining the streets to wave and cheer. The Queen, having particularly expressed the wish to see the famous Plymouth Hoe, came with her cavalcade via Lockyer Street to admire the views across Plymouth Sound from the famous promenade.

For Clare and her family, the Hoe was a favourite spot. Among Clare's outstanding memories were the evenings on the elegant Victorian pier on the Hoe, with Hector, Gus and Em, dancing in the ballroom. This special edifice extended from the extensive city foreshore developed by city fathers during the 1890s and the ballroom benefited from its location in the picturesque Sound. The pier, it had been said, was 'one of the gayest spots in England' and it was a place that the children, in particular, loved to visit. On warm days, the two families often picnicked together on the Hoe.

As on their previous stay in England, Hector and Clare took their children to London. A postcard they received at the time from one of Hector's soldiering friends, dated 22nd August 1938, was addressed: 'S/C H Perks, IAOC, Union Jack Hostel (Married Q), Waterloo Rd, Waterloo SE1.' During a two-week holiday there, Clare took her family to revisit her Aunt Sally in Balham, together with her Aunt Emily (who this time had travelled from her home in Newcastle especially to see them). While in London, Hector and Clare went to the Palladium to see the popular Lancashire singer Gracie Fields. For Hector, in particular, Gracie was quite a favourite.

On their return to Plymouth, the Perks' time in England was almost up. However, there was one sad facet to the year. Advised by Gus that it was not a good idea to see either his mother or his father up in Birmingham, Hector had not made the trip. It is not altogether clear why Gus advised Hector in this way, but there are clues. Gus knew through snippets of information from his brother Ralph, and from his own experience years before when he visited Malvern on leave, that his mother was an alcoholic, often destitute and apt to behave in a demeaning and embarrassing manner. Emily told of an occasion when Gus had seen his mother and she had persisted in following him along a street, calling out and making a scene. Emily recalled that they nursed a fear that if Mrs Perks discovered their whereabouts, she would somehow get to Plymouth and make a nuisance of herself and 'show them all up'.

Perhaps Gus saw, first hand, just how pitiful things were. Perhaps he felt it would unsettle Hector and upset him to a point where he would lose focus on his career and the commitments ahead of him including his scheduled return to India. It seems unreasonable, however, to conclude that Gus did not act from the best of motives with his younger brother's best interests at heart. Whatever the reasons for not going to see his parents – and it was his last opportunity – it was something Hector was to regret for the rest of his life. He felt that he should not have allowed his better judgment in this matter to be overruled.

As the Perks family began preparing to embark for India, there was growing political turmoil. Adolf Hitler was making preparations that were to have a huge impact on England and Europe, and destabilise the world. The disturbances and campaigning of Adolf Hitler's National Socialist ('Nazi') party supporters had culminated in the election of Hitler as German Chancellor in 1933. In the ensuing years, Hitler and his party had become powerfully entrenched in German life and had acquired worldwide notoriety. He had dramatically reorganised the German state and gained acceptance of some of his bizarre political and social theories particularly in relation to racial purity. These included the unification of all Teutonic races within the Reich, along with the territories they occupied, and the elimination of the racially 'impure' or 'inferior'.

These aspirations neatly matched Hitler's claim that the German people needed more 'living space' and coincident with his occupation of the previously demilitarised Rhineland in March 1936, he announced that, even at the risk of a major conflict, Germany would find the space its people needed in Eastern Europe. In contemplating war, Hitler recognised the need to confront Britain and France who would strenuously resist the creation of a German super state. He concluded that, taking advantage of his rearmament in defiance of international treaty and the lack of military preparations by the Allies, he should seize the earliest opportunity to wage this necessary war.

In February 1938, during the year the Perks family was in England, Hitler secured command of the German military machine and soon gave orders for the annexation of Austria by military force. Little resistance was expected or encountered since the significant Nazi organisation in that country was sympathetic and the annexation was completed during March of that year.

Austria's capital, Vienna, was the historic hub of the region to its south and east, including the Balkans, and this was an important political and territorial gain. It is not surprising that this act drew so little opposition from the Western powers that Hitler's further territorial ambitions relating to the Sudetenland were encouraged. This part of Czechoslovakia had a largely German population and a Nationalist party sympathetic to joining greater Germany. Hitler had already opened his propaganda campaign in relation to coveted Czech territory in a speech to the Reichstag. He claimed a German duty towards the security and freedom of compatriots across the eastern frontier but left unsaid his desire for access to the oil to be found in Romania and elsewhere.

Hitler's ambitions caused anxiety across Europe and, it has to be said, some disquiet amongst his senior service advisors who were mindful not only of France's pledges to Czech integrity but of the menace of Soviet Russia's Slavic affinity with the Czech people. Anxiety and uncertainty in Britain impacted particularly on members of the armed forces and their families, and acutely on Clare and Hector whose approaching return to India might be significantly affected by the unfolding events they closely followed through radio broadcasts and newsreels at the cinema.

It was of no comfort to anyone that the German chancellor began a programme of propaganda and diplomacy, which only served to confuse things further. He sent representatives to London, claimed to be dismayed by recent British antipathy, and hinted at concessions or delays to the pursuit of his policies. Britain and France agreed to mediate between the Czechs and Germans, the Czechs offered concessions relating to national minorities, and the British Prime Minister Neville Chamberlain met Hitler in Germany on 15th September 1938.

On his return to London, Chamberlain called for the transfer of 'German' districts to Germany – to the consternation of the Czech government, which understandably considered itself completely undermined. Many came to see this as the beginning of Chamberlain's appeasement policy, influenced perhaps by Cabinet perceptions that 'the French had no fight in them'. Extremists among German people in the Sudetenland were, meanwhile, being encouraged to agitate generally and demand frontier changes.

Humiliated by events, the Czech government resigned. Chamberlain returned for a second meeting with Hitler only to have the 'agreed' proposals rejected and others substituted. The Prime Minister merely secured a further delay in Hitler's plans. It was agreed with the French to reject Hitler's proposals but he reiterated his intention to invade the Czech territories on 1ˢᵗ October unless Czech agreement to ethnic cleansing was forthcoming by 28ᵗʰ September. However, he made what was seen as another small concession on the basis of which Chamberlain sought yet another meeting. The Italian dictator Mussolini and the French Prime Minister Daladier, but not the Russians or the Czechs, also attended this.

Evidently, agreement was reached extraordinarily rapidly, and a document was signed on 30ᵗʰ September after only a few hours of discussion. The Sudentenland was to be evacuated by non-Germans in stages, beginning almost immediately and being completed in ten days. An international commission was to determine the exact final frontiers. Czech delegates had been permitted to come to Munich to be shown the decisions reached.

After these astonishing events, Chamberlain spoke privately with Hitler and produced a draft declaration with the following text:

> We, the German Führer and Chancellor, and the British Prime Minister, have had a further meeting to-day and are agreed in recognising that the question of Anglo-German relations is of the first importance for our two countries and for Europe. We regard the agreement signed last night and the Anglo-German Naval Agreement as symbolic of the desire of our two peoples never to go to war with one another again. We are resolved that the method of consultation shall be the method adopted to deal with any other questions that may concern our two countries, and we are determined to continue our efforts to remove possible sources of difference, and thus contribute to assure the peace of Europe.

Hitler read the note and signed it without objection. Chamberlain returned to England and, waving the joint declaration, told the people:

> My good friends, for the second time in our history, a British Prime Minister has returned from Germany bringing peace with honour. I believe it is peace for our time...

The next year was to prove him catastrophically wrong.

THIRTEEN

NEW ORDERS

ews of this appeasement in September 1938 caused many in
Britain to breathe a sigh of relief. By the time Chamberlain arrived
back on British soil, the Perks family was already at sea, having set
off on 16th September and passed Gibraltar on the 20th: they were travelling in
HMT Dorsetshire (the same ship in which Hector and Clare had returned to
India in 1931). When the family arrived at Port Said on 26th September, they
were held for four days while the political storm raged, although stress levels
were alleviated by the fact that passengers were allowed ashore every day and
could make the most of the beach.

It seems a plan had been formulated before the troopship even left
Southampton. Two troopships had left England at about the same time,
although from different ports, and in the event of war breaking out en route – a
very real threat – it was envisaged that one ship would be used, if necessary, to
transport the women and children back to England. Now that Chamberlain had
averted that probability, at least for the time being, both vessels could resume

their colonial expedition. However, at Aden, the last stopping point before the ship embarked on its longest 1,710-mile leg to Bombay on 6th October, Hector received orders from a messenger who came aboard detailing him not to return to Kirkee but to go instead to Dacca in Eastern Bengal.

On 11th October, when the family arrived in Bombay, Hector wired his brother-in-law Frank Evett-Strange in Calcutta to ask whether he and Hester would be able to accommodate Clare and the children for a while. He then wired Dacca, requesting a week's leave to settle his family in a new place, and this was granted. It seems that Hector's redirection in October 1938, to an area where new army formations were being constituted on India's eastern front, may have been linked with the endeavours of Major General Claude Auchinleck, the new Deputy Chief of General Staff in India and part of a special committee for the defence of India.

Following his signing of the declaration in Munich, Chamberlain had ordered an acceleration of the British rearmament programme, and it was the firm opinion of Auchinleck that war in Europe – in particular with Germany and Italy – was inevitable, and would happen sooner rather than later. If this were true, Auchinleck believed that Britain would not be able to fulfill its duty of care and provide India with adequate protection in the event of an attack by a great force. With no motor industry of its own, India imported all of its vehicles and relied upon the Persian Gulf for petrol. Its army was still heavily dependent on animal transport, and could be responsible for no more than the defence of its frontiers.

Two new committees, including one convened by Auchinleck, considered what must be done to equip and prepare the Indian Army for modern warfare. It was concluded that the tasks were five-fold: frontier defence, coastal and anti-aircraft defence, external defence (for example Persia, Iraq and Malaya), internal security, and the provision of a general-purpose reserve. The British government was persuaded to contribute £34m to modernise and train this army, in a lengthy but groundbreaking process that would see the jobs of British officers being taken over by Indians, who would be trained to a comparable standard.

As part of the reorganisation, Hector had been promoted to the position of brigade ordnance warrant officer, and following his week in Calcutta with the family, he arrived in Eastern Bengal, much of which comprised the vast deltaic plains of the lower Ganges and Brahmaputra rivers. The Eastern Bengal Brigade was forming at Dacca, a town some 150 miles northeast of Calcutta; headquarters had been established with a staff, and troops would be accommodated in chitai buildings (matted-roof structures, similar to basha huts), the erection of which was now underway.

The role of the brigade ordnance warrant officers (affectionately known as 'bow-wows') had become more important since 1930. Their appointment to the headquarters of a brigade, in addition to ordnance representatives already functioning at command and district headquarters, provided a closer relationship between the ordnance corps of the army, and the troops. As permanent ordnance representatives with their respective brigades, they were there on the spot to advise on ordnance matters. Through these officers, the ordnance corps became more effectively represented at all formation headquarters throughout the chain: from brigade up to district, to command, to army headquarters. The brigade ordnance warrant officer dealt chiefly with the quartermaster branch of each brigade, and assisted in preparing requisitions of ordnance. (The quartermaster was the regimental officer in charge of quartering or dividing rations, ammunition and so on.) Many units had found this problematic, for if requests were not handled satisfactorily there was sometimes a delay in the supply of stores.

Hector's role was to help quartermasters to make effective requisitions, but he also assisted in stocktaking and identifying stores, disposing of obsolete stores, determining which ordnance was not serviceable, rearranging stores in the storerooms and adjusting discrepancies. There was scarcely an ordnance problem he could not tackle, which made him popular with the 'Q' (quartermaster) branch of the unit.

An important part of the job was liaison. 'During that time,' he recalled later, 'I had to visit all units in the Eastern Bengal Brigade and ensure that they were efficient from an equipment point of view. I travelled mainly by metre-gauge railway and sometimes by river, and in the early days I travelled to Comilla and Chittagong. Later, I went to Mymensingh and to Shillong in Assam. There were two regiments of Gurkhas, the 1/7 and 2/7 at Shillong, plus a headquarters. Eventually a lot of the units forming the brigade moved to Shillong with a view to forming the Eastern Bengal and Assam Brigade. Eventually, Shillong became my headquarters and from there I visited all the units in that area.'

His appointment to Shillong on 3rd April 1939 led to his being reunited with his family when he was able to return to 12/2 Mominpore Road, Kidderpore, in Calcutta. He had left Clare and the children for what had amounted to a pleasurable six-month interlude, as well as providing a rare and much valued opportunity for Clare to be in the constant company of her mother and sister, not forgetting Frank. It had also given her a chance to nurture ties with some more distant non-blood relations there in Calcutta, those of Indian extraction such as Uncle Walter and his wife Auntie Lizzie, as well as May (both sisters to Frank's dead mother).

The intervening Christmas, a few months earlier, had brought Hector back for a brief visit. The pictures taken at the time show large family groups with three generations of relatives, all clearly in a festive mood. The Christmas Day prints show them in novelty hats, smiling broadly, and it is interesting to observe that many of the shots are external, reflecting the clement climate of the location. Up to 12 family members are photographed together, with the various children always in the front row and the men at the rear. In contrast to how Clare looks in photographs taken when she was a girl in Simla, these show her reflective nature, as well as some reluctance to be prominent. Perhaps the losses she had endured and the difficult times she had already overcome had affected her quite deeply, and made her more reticent.

Now that Hector was to be based in Shillong, the family prepared to join him, and soon they were on their way to Assam Province, a region of tropical evergreen forest in the northeast of India. Assam was seen as a paradise, 'as remote and exotic as the Himalayas which border it and the colourful tribes who inhabit it'.[75] At the time of their move, the region had wildlife of all kinds including the one-horned Great Indian rhinoceros, leopards, tigers, black bears and other big game. It could boast a greater diversity of race, language and culture than any other state in India. A report following the census of 1911 stated that it was:

> surrounded by mountainous ranges on three sides... the Himalayas [north], shutting off the table-lands of Bhutan and Tibet... a series of hills [northeast] which form a barrier between the Upper Brahmaputra Valley and the more or less independent Mongolian tribes who live west of the boundary of China... the hills [east and south] which form the limits of the Province of Burma and the State of Hill Tippera...[76]

The report added that on the west lay the Province of Bengal, with huge plains onto which the two river valleys of the Brahmaputra and Surma debouch. These two valleys were separated from each other by the Assam range, which projected westward from the hills on the eastern border. Furthermore, it said that the physical features of the province were 'full of variety' and that from the valley of the great Brahmaputra, otherwise known as the Assam valley (about 450 miles in length and 50 miles in average breadth), 'one never loses sight of the hills on either side' and that 'Mongolian influences were present everywhere, except in the greater part of Sylhet'.[77]

The Assam range, incorporating the Assam (or Shillong) plateau, consisted of the Garo, Jaintia and Khasi hills, which were the home of hill tribes named after the ranges in which they dwelt. The low lying areas were sparsely populated and covered in forest, but on the slopes of the Brahmaputra and Surma river valleys were hundreds of tea gardens forming the main growing areas of Assam's prolific and much prized variety. (Originally, tea had been a local tribal drink.) The opening up of the tea gardens of Assam happened in the early 1860s, made possible when Assam itself was opened up by river paddle steamers of the India General Steam Navigation Company, which operated on the Brahmaputra and its tributaries. The availability of these teas, and the fact that they were cheaper compared to those of China, instantly secured their wide popularity in Britain.

The journey from Calcutta to the Khasi hills took some 26 hours. Clare and Hector, with the children, set out on the Assam mail train which started from Sealdah, the Calcutta terminal on the broad-gauge Eastern Bengal Railway. It was bound for Guahati, 461 miles away. It crossed the Ganges by the Hardinge Bridge, which was then one of the longest bridges in the world and had been named after the viceroy, Lord Hardinge, who opened it. The route followed the course to Darjeeling as far as Santahar junction. Here, the family took the metre-gauge Assam line that branched off and swung east before proceeding to Gauhati.

From Gauhati, an ancient and graceful city, the family travelled the last stretch by the daily motor car (taxi) service, which provided between six and nine seats. Clare remembered this mode of transport as 'a rickety old bus – you wondered how we'd ever get there!' It was a scenic although 'horrible' journey along a one-way road for 63 miles, through tropical forest with steep drops. Gradually, the vehicle twisted and climbed past rolling grassy downs and great pine woods, up to its destination. Shillong was set at an altitude of 4,900ft, with fantastic views of the surrounding hills.

Shillong took its name from the hill. It was the administrative headquarters for the Assam province: the British had acquired Assam in 1826 (taking it from the Burmese who had seized it in 1792) and in 1874 they made Shillong the capital. The town was built on the site of a 1,000-year-old Khasi settlement, but in 1897 it was laid waste by an earthquake; subsequently, it was rebuilt with precautions being taken against a recurrence of the disaster. Thereafter, it grew rapidly as a well laid-out summer hill station nestling amid pinewoods. The surrounding country was not unlike the lowlands of Scotland – in fact, it was known as 'The Scotland of the East'. Later in the twentieth century, this atmosphere, which the Jaintai and Garo tribespeople also shared, was to be captured in the creation of a new state which was their home: Meghalaya or 'Abode of Clouds'.

The three ancient communities living in these hill tracts had enjoyed considerable independence until consolidation by the British in the 19th century. The Garo people lived isolated lives in the thick forests of the Garo hills, but the Jaintia and the Khasi people had more contact with the British. It was thought that the Khasis had their roots in Cambodia or Thailand some centuries previously; before that, their origins can be found in southern China. Together with the Jaintia, they were probably descended from the first Mongolian immigrants to India, speaking a Mon-Khmer language related to those spoken in Burma, Cambodia and even Annam (in Vietnam). In contrast, the Garo people were thought to have descended from a branch of the Tibeto-Burman tribes.

Despite their different origins, all three societies were and remain matrilineal. This meant that the Khasi people were one of very few groups in the world to inherit power and property through the female line. There was no bride price as in other northeastern parts of India, and every child born belonged to the mother and took her name, which meant there was no such thing as illegitimacy. Clare was impressed by this remarkable way of life and by the inheritance given by the mother to the youngest daughter. She firmly declared that 'the women... did all the work' while 'the men were the layabouts'.

Most of the Khasi – as well as the Garo and Jaintia, and the Naga people in the frontier hills of Assam – were and still are Christian. They had been converted by missionaries, notably Presbyterians who established themselves in the 19th century and who managed to persuade the Garo people to end their practice of human sacrifice. There were, however, still traces of tribal belief in animism, evidenced by attempts to appease or placate spirits with offerings. They still celebrated tribal rites and traditional festivals with pageantry and picturesque folk dances. Many of these events were closely associated with the farming year, since as a people they were (and still are) heavily reliant for their income on agriculture. In a good year, there was thanksgiving to God.

Most of the hill people living around Shillong were Khasi. At the Bara (big) Bazar in the hub of the town, they would come in colourful costumes to sell their poultry, meat and produce: they were stocky people, composed and self-reliant. (The Khasi, Jaintia and Garo tribes continue to exist to this day, adding colour to this hilly town. They still celebrate their individual festivals; Christmas,

Easter and Good Friday are important.)

During the dry months the tribes had to travel far in search of water, but from June to September Shillong was a 'washout' as the monsoon drenched the area. Despite this, the plateau on which the town stood had a much smaller rainfall than nearby areas, with an average of 81 inches, and though it was not as dry as hill stations in the northwest of India, such as Simla, it was substantially cooler. At the height of the summer, although it was humid, the temperature rarely reached 80°F (27°C). All in all, the climate was perfect for the beautiful orchids that grew among the trees.

About 33 miles southwest of Shillong, along a spectacular road, was Cherrapunji – a town 'surrounded by hills rent by enormous gorges'.[78] Cherrapunji was famous for being the wettest place on earth, with an average annual rainfall of nearly 40ft. South of the town, awesome waterfalls six times as high as Niagara Falls plummeted down the high escarpments on the edge of the plateau, because this region of the Assam hills, averaging 4,000 to 6,000ft above sea level, lay in the path of the so-called Bengal Sea branch of the summer monsoon airstream. These south-facing slopes received some of the heaviest rainfalls in the world, sheets of water that descended and surged across the flatlands.

Clare and Hector's new home in No 4A Cantonments was a bungalow quite different from the usual regimented barrack-type married quarters. It had a flattish corrugated tin roof, and overlooked some of the gentler slopes of the undulating landscape. Like many of the dwellings scattered about, it was detached. The only encroachment on the Perks family space was by a high-ranking officer from the Assam Regiment who occupied part of the same building at the back. On one occasion, his bull terrier left teeth marks on young Peter's back when he tried, in all innocence, to learn how to ride it.

Foolish and painful though this momentary lapse in his judgement proved at the time, Peter's general awareness of all that was happening around him was acute for a boy of his age. He knew something about the army and it absorbed him to watch, from the sidelines, large groups of native Indian Army recruits being put through their paces at the big training camp and the parade ground not far from the house.

Like their mother before them, both Patsy and Margaret were sent to a Loreto Convent which educated British and Indian boarders and day girls entirely in English. (In one class, Patsy noted that she was the only one who was white.) Peter also attended the convent for two years until transferring, at the age of seven, to St Edmund's College, run by the Irish Christian Brothers. All the children took sandwiches to school each day, since a cooked lunch was provided only for boarders. However, the army authorities assisted in paying for the cost of education and also provided a taxi for the children to be taken to the school, two miles away from their bungalow. The vehicle had a regular driver: Dominic, an Indian and a Christian. The girls also took private piano lessons.

Meanwhile their father Hector was getting into his hobby 'in a big way'. He had become an amateur radio enthusiast, transmitting and receiving messages in the bungalow's innermost room, which was reached by passing one by one through the others – and hence completely out of bounds to his children. He used empty packing crates to accommodate his two-way transmitter and its accessories; and outside he constructed a lofty support system for the aerial, which ran from the ground up to a height of 60ft, supported by an elaborate assembly of bamboo and steel poles. Occasionally, when the transmitter was switched off, he would permit the children to 'have a go' by allowing them to repeatedly press down and release the spring-loaded arm of the Morse key to create a series of clicks and pops. Sometimes they were even able to watch him send a message.

Hector's interest in radio stemmed from their time in Kirkee, when he and Clare had lived next door to a man who transmitted 'in a small way'. So he began by building a wireless in Quetta, and Clare recalled that 'when we were on leave in England he worked, voluntarily, in a wireless shop on Union Street, wanting to learn more and to get things cheaply. He was able to buy a whole lot of components to take back to India'. (At the time, Plymouth's Union Street was home to leading radio, gramophone and record dealers.)

In Shillong, he was sent books from England each month on subjects such as Morse code, the oldest and simplest way of transmitting information using radio. His call sign, which enabled his station to be identified on air, was 'VU2DO'. Morse's characteristic dots and dashes, both of a specified length, were defined by the length of time that the key was depressed, and the call sign was used at the beginning and end of each transmission.

It was a nocturnal hobby: the cooling of the atmospheric layers provided a better, denser blanket from which radio signals could rebound, so his usual time for transmitting was between midnight and 3am. During the day, only transmissions over short distances were possible; at night when the so-called D-layer of the atmosphere disappeared, it was possible to communicate further afield and among those he 'talked' to regularly was a doctor in Ceylon. Like all radio hams, he would scan the frequencies, listening for transmissions and responding to those that interested him. Pat also recalled how during his off duty evenings in Shillong, her father liked to stand under the stars. Sometimes he would identify for his children the great constellations, especially the Plough.

Just before Hector and his family had arrived in Shillong, a garrison commander had been appointed in July 1938: Lieutenant Colonel William J Slim. He was there for a year, in command of the 2/7th Gurkha Rifles. He had been given the job of 'pulling the battalion together', which implied he believed that the battalion had been slackly commanded by his two predecessors, apparently men who just liked a quiet life and hadn't grasped tricky problems. He was also responsible for one other battalion and for providing assistance with local problems. It was said that Lt Colonel Slim considered himself to be 'a cross between the chairman of a Parish Council and a brigadier' and his wider interests evidently extended to the welfare of the children of men in his command – as illustrated when Hector took his son Peter to a Dashera, the most important annual religious Gurkha festival, in the early autumn of 1939.

This festival included a gory spectacle of homage, an ancient Nepalese ritual performed by one carefully chosen Nepalese soldier from each unit. The selected man had to strike and kill with his kukri (a heavy curved knife) an outstretched animal – on this occasion, a buffalo – in a forceful and precise manner, so as to decapitate it in one clean stroke. This action would please the gods and bring their protection to the fighting men; all weapons in the unit would then be blessed with the animal's blood and garlanded with flowers, while the men would receive a blessing in the centre of their foreheads, a place believed by Hindus to be the location of the human spirit.

British officers were supposed to attend this festival and did, but nobody, it was said, liked it very much. Lt Colonel Slim was clearly dismayed to see Hector there with Peter, and reprimanded him for allowing this young boy to see such a distressing sight. However, by the end of September 1939 Slim had left for Jhansi in central India to begin preparing troops for operations in the western desert of North Africa.

At this time, Shillong was the only military station in Assam. Hector's job was to visit every unit in an extensive Eastern Bengal and Assam area to check equipment and to advise and, where possible, to save it from being returned to the arsenals for replacement. In the late summer of 1939, his travels took him to Jorhat, the 'gateway' to North Assam, where brigade headquarters was shortly to relocate. Hector himself returned to Shillong although by then he was aware of the planned move.

It took place on 3rd September and everyone was uneasy: something was going on. 'We stopped at one point,' recalled Hector, 'and at my instigation we got a radio receiver and powered it with motor batteries from the vehicles. We listened to Mr Churchill declaring war'. Britain and France declared war in support of Poland, which had been invaded by Germany on 1st September.

Churchill's declaration meant that India was also at war. The viceroy, Lord Victor John Hope Linlithgow, broadcast to its population of 350m people and told them that they would be 'fighting for the freedom of humanity'. But India was unprepared. While the two committees which were appointed the year before had made many recommendations for the mechanisation and modernisation of the Indian Army, it was too late to implement them. However, although modern equipment was not available,

> the groundwork of modernisation had at least been thought out, agreed in principle, and money made available to pay for it. So cavalry were mechanised only in that their horses were taken from them. For the first year of the war infantry had no carriers, mortars or anti-tank weapons, and no one below brigade had wireless.[79]

One division went from India to the Middle East, but while the Indian government was eager to help Britain, there seemed nothing but the frontiers to defend: the northwest against a possible threat of a German/Russian assault, and the northeast against the more pressing threat of an attack by the Japanese through Malaya and Burma.

Japan had been consolidating its position in the east, beginning in 1931 when – during the world slump – it seized Manchuria in northern China and turned it into a giant industrial estate. After its aggression was condemned, it withdrew from the League of Nations and over the years that followed, Japanese military forces pressed southwards deeper and deeper into Chinese territory, their attacks and atrocities shocking the world. Of Western nations with interests in the Far East, the British had by far the largest stake in China, but Britain's rearmament programme had only started in 1935 and without the support of the Americans, who had a much smaller stake there, it was unwilling to take action against Japan. In November of that year, Japan had announced with typical aggression that, because the nationalist government of China 'had been reduced to a local régime' it would henceforth 'monopolise as much of China's foreign trade'[80] as it liked. It continued to hamper British interests in China and make assaults on Britain's territories.

All this proved an embarrassment and a worry for the British government. Since 1922, its strategy had been to keep a strong fleet at Singapore to protect its dominions in the Far East. However, to keep this fleet at full strength would mean jeopardising Britain's naval strength in the Mediterranean and home waters. Yet, as the world was poised on the brink of war, Britain maintained its intention to send a fleet which was powerful enough to keep sea communications open, prevent Singapore from falling, and avert any major threat to Australia, New Zealand and, most importantly, India.

FOURTEEN

RUMBLINGS OF WAR

D espite the onset of war in Europe in 1939, India was far enough
away for the people who lived there to believe for some time that
'it wouldn't amount to anything'. Social life continued unaffected,
and the only shortages were of military equipment. Perhaps it was not really as
remote from the war as many supposed, but for the time being India was calm
and Clare was pregnant again, for a fifth time.

The new baby, a third daughter, arrived on 18th February 1940 at the 'Ganesh
Das' hospital for civilians. (In Hindu belief, Ganesh is the elephant-headed son
of Shiva and his wife – and the god of good fortune.) Shillong's military hospital
catered only for soldiers, not their families. The army authorities at Calcutta
registered the birth on 16th March in Army Book 112, kept at the headquarters
of the Presidency and Assam District; a copy of the book was later deposited at
Somerset House in London.

For Clare, it was a difficult birth; a 'face presentation' with the baby's chin
leading at the cervix during labour, giving rise to much interest from student

doctors in the hospital. She haemorrhaged so badly afterwards that on returning home from a ten-day stay, she was in bed for a week. Clare's mother Mary did not visit this time because Hector was there, looking after the family. The doctor, this time a civilian, told Clare not to have any more children – the same advice she had received three years before. However, as a devout Catholic, Clare was forbidden to use artificial contraception, and in any event, she considered each child born to her as a gift.

The baby was baptised Barbara Clare on 17th March, at the Cathedral of the Divine Saviour in Shillong, with the child's sponsor being a Catholic friend of Clare's, Dorothy Ashe.

The family now had a Khasi ayah, a young girl who was shy and sweet natured but whose name has, regrettably, been forgotten; servants apart from ayahs were usually known by the name of their task. As the baby grew older, the ayah responded quickly to her cries of 'doodle-oodle-oodle-oodle' ('dudh' meaning milk).

She was trustworthy too, and bore no responsibility for an unfortunate incident that occurred when Barbara was an infant. It arose on a day when Clare and Hector had taken their children to a beauty spot called Crinoline Falls, about a mile to the south of Shillong. In her hasty preparation before setting out, Clare had placed her gold watch, a wedding present from her husband, in the Chinese basket used to carry the new baby, forgetting that there was a hole in the bottom. Predictably the watch fell out, and although the entire family retraced their steps, it was never found.

Relations with other servants were not always so easy. At this time, it was the khansama (cook) who was causing angst, beginning with the fact that the food was less than hot when it was presented at the table. This irritated Hector greatly but was mainly occasioned by the layout of the home. From the veranda on the side of the bungalow ran a long, covered walkway with a corrugated tin roof, a common feature in India where rainfall was frequent; this walkway continued through the garden to the far rear, where it descended to the bawarchi-khana (cookhouse), part of the servants' quarters.

However, this location meant there was a long walk between the kitchen and the dining table. Pat recalled that she, Margaret and Peter would sometimes slink down to the cookhouse where the young ayah could be persuaded to give them hot sweet potatoes; something about which their father voiced his strong disapproval. Things got worse when the khansama became so ill that he lay prostrate in the kitchen between cooking meals. 'He got so bad that I told him to go home to his village,' recalled Clare, 'and the day after he left us we learned that he had come out in a smallpox rash'. About three months later he returned to take up his job, with pockmarks to show for his experience. For little Barbara, such tribulations were of no consequence as she grew to enjoy a carefree infancy within her loving family during that first year of war.

The same could not be said for the rest of the world. Germany had by now invaded and conquered Denmark, Norway, Holland and Belgium. France was overrun and an armistice was signed in June 1940, leaving the country divided: the unoccupied part in the south and southwest was governed from Vichy. Italy had joined Germany, and conquered Greece. Britain stood alone, its army greatly weakened after its forces had been cut off in Belgium and evacuated with difficulty from Dunkirk. It prepared, with some trepidation, to meet a German invasion.

Some believed that India was also threatened by Japanese territorial ambition. At the beginning of the war Japan was stealthy, but by the summer of 1940 it was making bolder plans to acquire an empire in the Far East, with ambitions to extend its sphere of influence to Australia, New Zealand and even India. In September it signed the Tripartite Pact with Germany and Italy, which recognised its leadership in Greater East Asia while ceding authority in Europe to Germany and Italy. All three countries pledged political, economic and military support to each other in the event of the Allies being joined in the war by the United States, a move intended to further deter the Americans from aiding Britain.

However, while the Japanese were working out the preliminaries of their invasion of the Far East, between August and October 1940 the Germans were bombing Britain from the air, in what became known as the Battle of Britain. This was followed by a series of night raids which lasted until May 1941, and severely damaged London and many other cities and ports. Plymouth, with its naval dockyard and thousands of resident servicemen, was a prime target.

In Shillong, remembered Clare, 'we became glued to the wireless'. The family had a Philips set and regularly listened to the war news on All-India Radio everyday, worrying about relatives back in England. Those in Plymouth were having a dreadful time. In July and August 1940 there had been 33 air raids on Plymouth but seven of the most terrible came in the following March and April, causing many thousands to flee nightly to the relative safety of the countryside.

Two of the worst raids came on consecutive nights, the 20th and 21st March. That second night, a force of 168 bomber aircraft dropped an even greater load of bombs and a southwesterly wind fanned the flames through the heart of the city, leaving it totally wrecked. Parts of Union Street were blasted and burnt, and left in ruins. In these two aerial assaults alone, some 20,000 properties were destroyed or damaged. According to one source, nearly 1,000 aircraft dropped 250,000 incendiary devices and high explosive bombs in that spring of 1941, with a simple intention – 'to set Plymouth on fire', as one German bomber pilot recorded.

The wool and baby linen shop on Chapel Street, run by Clare's sister-in-law Emily Perks, was destroyed by a savage night attack. Worse than losing the shop was the nightly experience endured by Em and Gus and their family, living as they did in the thick of it all. Gus had retired from the marines in 1938 with the rank of colour sergeant, until he was recalled to the corps in July 1939. Restored to his previous rank during wartime, he rejoined his old division at the barracks just down the road from where the family lived, not far from Chapel Street.

Clare and Hector were also thinking of Clare's brother Bill, who was now twenty-seven and had just left India for the first time in his life. There had been no opportunity for him to say farewell to his family, and it was five years since he had come to stay at Kirkee when his battalion was at Jubbulpore. In 1938, in recognition of the regiment's service in India and gallant conduct at the Battle of Jubbulpore, the viceroy Lord Linlithgow had arrived in Jubbulpore for its 250th anniversary celebrations, where he presented Bill's battalion with new 'colours' amid scenes of great rejoicing.

The raising of the men's spirits may also have been due to another factor. War had not yet broken out when they heard the news that their next station was to be Razmak in Waziristan, on the North-West Frontier of India. Every soldier in India hoped to see active service, as opposed to the monotony of service on the plains. 'On the Frontier' or 'up the Khyber' were places where hostilities of one kind or another were ongoing. The Khyber Pass, controlled by the British, was a gateway to India in a great wall of mountains forming the frontier, cutting it off from the rest of Asia. The move took place in mid-October 1938 but before this, Bill's battalion had trained in mountain warfare using the few small hills near Jubbulpore.

As a member of the band attached to the HQ wing of the regiment, Bill's duties included toting stretchers and medical kit. He was also a first-aider and sick bay attendant when required. These skills were tested each year. The men in Bill's battalion excelled at various sports including hockey, though it was recognised the bandsmen were the experts at this – due, it was said, to the fact that 'band boys' learned how to use their hockey stick before they were even given an instrument! Bill, a clarinet player, was a fine sportsman.

He was modest, quietly spoken and valiant. Years earlier, his hockey stick once became a valuable weapon, helping him stave off a tribe of fierce monkeys which he unwittingly disturbed near the ridge at Jutogh near Simla, while innocently swinging the stick as he walked over the rugged terrain on his way home. Having beaten them off, he jumped from a high wall and ran for his life, suffering minor injuries in the process; but it was a lucky escape for, as Clare said, 'had the monkeys got hold of him they would have torn him to shreds'.

Razmak had the distinction of being the highest outpost in the British Empire, and the battalion reached it on 1st November 1938. They travelled the last 70 miles through tribal territory along good roads, many with alarming hairpin bends. Razmak itself was a vast garrison camp 6,500ft above sea level, surrounded by a stone-built parapet and barbed wire at its perimeter. There were massive stone towers at strategic points, and by virtue of its position the outpost dominated the turbulent country of the Mahsud and Wazir tribes of Waziristan.

Though there had been great unrest across the frontier since the First World War, in 1936 British troops were involved in some of the 'bloodiest and most serious of conflicts of the 20th century'.[81] It was triggered because the British authorities in India had 'rescued' a Hindu girl, in answer to her parents' plea. She had eloped with and married a young Wazir and had subsequently become a Muslim.

British forces arrested the elopers and returned the girl to her parents, an act which incensed the Wazirs. With (unusually) their neighbours, all of whom needed little excuse to war against each other, they rose against the British in a rebellion. Using their knowledge of the surrounding steep hills, which provided ample cover for snipers and ambushers, they began to wage a highly successful guerrilla campaign against the British, with the intention of ousting the interlopers from the frontier altogether.

The North-West Frontier was a hostile, bleak and mountainous zone; but it was busy. Soldiering duties included being 'on guard' both at the base and in outlying pickets in the hills, together with road protection and snow clearing. Everyone, it appeared, was 'moulding together' to get the jobs done. Early in the new year, Bill's battalion moved out to an independent perimeter camp at Razani, 14 miles away. There the tasks were similar but, owing to very severe weather, less pleasant to perform.

After enduring snow, rain, biting wind and oceans of mud, they were glad to return to comparative comfort in Razmak at the end of April. The base had the benefit of plenty of flat ground and the general climate was now more conducive for sport and competition throughout the day, which meant the men were not limited to activities in the cooler evenings, as in the plains. All in all, it was a successful tour of duty on the frontier, though not without its casualties. At the end of 1939, in the next trooping season, the battalion moved down to Agra. With some pride, it was said that this battalion was as fit as any that had ever served in India.

Then, in the early months of war in Europe, the battalion lost significant numbers of trained and experienced officers, NCOs and other ranks, men who were drafted home. Bill was not selected and this may have been a result of unusual sensitivity on the part of the authorities, recognising the fact that he had been born in India. As a result of the losses, the gaps were filled by drafts of militia men posted to the battalion, and there followed for the stalwarts a period of hard and trying work to train these new recruits.

Spirits fell – the remaining members of the battalion, including Bill, felt they were being 'left out of the war' – but in January 1941 it was announced that they were to move to Calcutta to embark for an unknown destination, and this proved an immediate spur. The battalion was to end up in Penang, Malaya.

Back in Shillong, Hector and Clare had moved to a larger bungalow: No 8A, which was next door to an adult education college. The new home was set a little further down on the gentle slope, closer to the bazar, and it was of a striking design from every aspect. A fine veranda to the front was approached by a long, winding pathway through a large and delightful garden. Elegant cannas bordered the pathway, and there were also arum lilies, rows of fragrant sweet peas, red geraniums and zinnias, as well as Jerusalem artichokes for the kitchen.

The garden benefited from the dedicated efforts of a Hindu mali (gardener), clad in a dhoti (a loose loincloth) and sometimes having a puggaree cloth wrapped around the head. This concealed the mali's long clump of hair, tied at the crown: the shaven head except for the tuft of hair as the pigtail was one of the external symbols that proclaimed a person's adherence to a particular Hindu cult. As a child, Pat was aware of the widely held belief that this attachment would be used to pull him up to heaven!

Little Barbara, meanwhile, never came into the house without a flower in her hand, small love tokens for her mother Clare, to whom as the 'baby of the family' she was extremely close. Clare often reminded her daughter of the great pleasure she took from these offerings for years afterwards.

One small reminder of the ongoing war was the 'slit-trench' air raid shelter that had been dug in the garden of the bungalow at No 8A, before the Perks family arrived. This measured about 4ft by 6ft, and had no overhead cover. In fact it was of little use beyond providing the children with somewhere to play and hide. They also liked to jump across its width, though it was too long to jump over the other way.

There was sadness, however, for Hector. The outbreak of war meant that his transmitter was officially confiscated and put into store at the central ordnance depot in Agra, in a box measuring eight cubic feet. He hardly had time to dwell on this loss. Life at work was busy, although the modernisation of the Indian Army was slow and it still lacked a good supply of up-to-date equipment. New divisions were forming and being trained, but thousands of vehicles were needed, along with additional officers and military technicians. By July 1941, when General Archibald Wavell assumed office as India's new commander-in-chief, more than 100,000 Indian troops were already serving outside the country's borders.

Wavell estimated that 10,000 British officers and 50,000 British other ranks would be needed to form replacement divisions to provide India with strong internal defences, and to make up for deficiencies in existing divisions. Both British and Indian units needed officers and the additional other ranks were required to serve as engineers and in artillery, signals, and other technical corps. However, Britain had no men to spare at this time. Furthermore, the civilian production of cars, village garages and petrol stations in India were non-existent with very few public buses, transport companies and mechanics.

Meanwhile, Bill and his battalion in Malaya were feeling somewhat deflated, their initial excitement at the move from India having turned to dismay at the prospect of little action here in this new place. Others in Burma had the same 'stuck' feeling. These were men in the prime of their lives, full of youth and vigour, ready to defend their country with the utmost bravery. Yet how could any of them have had any idea of all that lay before them? How could they have been prepared? These men were to become some of the outstanding heroes of the war, and they were destined to bear some of its worst horrors, which would haunt those who survived for many years afterwards.

FIFTEEN

A DEAR BROTHER IN PERIL

Malaya was a mountainous country, jungle-clad but with much coastal marshland. Bill's unit, the 1st Battalion of the Leicester Regiment, was 243 men short of its full strength. They arrived on 13th February 1941, bringing with them their newly acquired colours, some of the less valuable 'mess silver' and quite a large weight of personal luggage. Valuable regimental property had been put, with some foresight, into store back in Bombay.

Until 1941, conditions in Malaya had been essentially peaceful: Penang, an island off the west coast, was seen as the place to be, and the British population was kind and made endeavours to entertain the troops. No one could have foreseen how this move would affect the men. The Japanese were closing in and soon their acquisitive plans would cast a deadly shadow over British forces stationed in the country.

The men of the battalion had two immediate tasks. Firstly, they had to set about mastering their new weapons and vehicles, and secondly they had to

169

acclimatise themselves to the humidity, which was oppressive. Over the next few months, there were frequent changes in roles and reconnaissance work, both at Penang and on the mainland. New formations of men and units, all untrained in jungle fighting and few of them fully trained even in armed combat, were arriving all the time. Gradually, their superiors were putting together a plan to defend Malaya.

The story of Bill's life in the months following this deployment is a harrowing one, involving warfare and the extraordinary hardships associated with a jungle campaign against a determined and ruthless enemy. To better illustrate the action and manoeuvres in which he was embroiled, it is useful to briefly describe, in general terms, how a fighting force is organised and deployed. A regiment, led by a colonel, is the basic unit of such a force. Infantry regiments such as the Leicesters comprised between one and (at times) six battalions, each of 500 or 600 men. Only one of the battalions was in the Malayan theatre at this time.

An infantry battalion such as this one usually comprised up to four companies and a 'headquarters' unit, and was commanded by a lieutenant colonel. Individual company commanders were generally captains or majors and each company was made up of a number of platoons commanded by officers of lower rank. Regiments other than infantry had different titles for subordinate units and some ranks. Regiments or battalions were often grouped into brigades that might be wholly specialist: infantry or armoured, for example, or mixed. In large operational theatres of war, brigades were grouped into divisions, and one or more of these made up an army group; brigadiers or generals commanded these larger units.

In June, Bill's battalion was allocated to the newly formed 15th Indian Brigade. They became part of the 11th Division, with divisional and brigade headquarters based at Sungei Patani in Kedah State, on the mainland. Set in a rubber plantation, the wooden-hutted camp was wet and gloomy, and all day long came the unremitting dripping from trees onto the roofs. Headquarters was a depressing place to be.

It was decided to erect a wide defence line in North Malaya, running from east to west just north of Jitra. This would cover the country's two main roads, and control access to the railway into Thailand. The line passed through jungle-covered hills in the east into areas full of flooded rice fields and rubber estates, and through to a mangrove swamp in the west which was affected by the tides. This line would be known as the Jitra Line. Work on it began in June 1941.

Bill and his colleagues were detailed to prepare a vital mile-long stretch of line that passed over the two main roads north of their junction at Jitra. It was slow and uncomfortable work in sodden, leech-infested wetlands and even when the men were not working, conditions were unpleasant. The troops lived in tents, many of which leaked, although the companies were relieved every two or three weeks. In addition to work on the line, the battalion kept up its fitness levels with extra-long excursions on bicycles. This was to get them ready for 'Matador', a secret scheme involving members of the 11th Division with the aim of advancing to forestall a Japanese landing at the port of Singora, 50 miles north in Thailand.

By making incursions into Indo-China, Japan had provided for itself a springboard to the south. It had established new air and sea bases, creating a powerful military force that had a far larger fleet of ships than America. As a precautionary measure, America had already banned all oil sales to Japan, and Britain had restricted the sale of Malaya's rubber goods. Consequently, essential oil and rubber supplies could only be obtained by force, so Japan was gearing itself up for the necessary fight.

On 7th December 1941, the battle for South East Asia began in earnest. Japanese planes bombed Pearl Harbour in Hawaii, sinking or seriously damaging ships of the United States Pacific Fleet that lay anchored in the bay. Their strategy was to neutralise the fleet to prevent its intervention in their territorial ambition. The Japanese then bombed Manila, the capital of the Philippines, and blitzed Singapore, Britain's stronghold in the Far East. In addition, they attacked north Malayan airfields and struck from the air as the Allies tried to make shore landings in Malaya and Thailand, at ports including Singora.

General Yamashita was the man in charge of conquering Malaya and Singapore. His 25th Army comprised three divisions of highly trained and well-supported men. Their aim was to move overland from Indo-China through Thailand. Two days after Pearl Harbour, the British 11th Division responded energetically to the attacks, but it was too late. The division's reluctance to broach Thailand's neutrality (before this was violated so decisively by the Japanese) meant that its advance troops met oncoming columns of Japanese armour at the border, supported by further truckloads of infantry.

Matador, designed as an offensive action, quickly turned defensive and the Leicesters retreated to their positions on the Jitra Line, exasperated and demoralised. Worse was to come: in their absence, the trenches had become waterlogged and useless. In low spirits, they worked without a break for three days and nights to shore up their defensive position. Drenched by the monsoon rains, they had little chance to get their boots, socks and feet really dry, and this gave rise to very debilitating and persisting bacterial and fungal foot infections, which caused their feet and toes to blister. Not only did the conditions make working difficult, but it also undermined the men's capacity to manoeuvre and fight. As the Leicesters were in retreat, the Japanese bombed and sank two of Britain's most powerful warships (the battleship The Prince of Wales, and the battle cruiser Repulse) on 10th December, off the eastern shores. This settled the fate of Malaya and Singapore. The Japanese continued their landings unchecked and started to establish air bases on shore.

Just 24 hours after the start of this campaign, Japanese forces were driving an invasion fork of at least three prongs down into Malaya towards Singapore. The orders of the 5th Japanese Division were to drive south and destroy British forces known to be in position at Jitra, who were covering the Alor Star airfield and several small airfields to the south. This position was vital to both sides.

The Battle of Jitra began on 11th December, but the British – including Bill – were at a severe disadvantage. Owing to the scramble after Matador was abandoned, and to other factors (including the wide dispersal of unit positions, the earlier commitment of divisional reserves and the increasing fatigue and disorganisation of British troops), the Japanese were able to drive a deep wedge right into the centre of the 15th Indian Brigade's position, on the right flank of the Jitra concentration. This was where many of Bill's battalion colleagues held out, displaying great courage and determination in the face of extreme adversity. When they finally received the order to withdraw, the men were isolated and exhausted.

Jitra was undoubtedly the key to Japanese success in its Malayan campaign. With insufficient time to deploy reinforcements, British casualties ran into thousands, while the Japanese lost fewer than 50 men in total. Having abandoned their position, British troops despaired at the loss of guns, equipment and supplies. To the delight of the Japanese, tobacco, bread and tinned food were there for the taking, together with stacks of ammunition for the captured guns and vehicles stocked with petrol.

At 2200 hours on the 11th December, the 11th Division was given the order to retreat south from Alor Star. Troops straggled back in the pouring rain amid much confusion, and mixing of units. Some men decided to avoid the road and to trek cross-country through jungle, swamp and paddy field. Of these, many were never seen again.

At last, two or three days later, British troops began arriving at Gurun, exhausted (although still pursued by the Japanese). Nearly all the men, including the Leicesters – what was left of them – had very bad feet and were in no fit state to fight. On 14th December, men from a detachment at the headquarters in Sungei Patani joined the weakened infantry as they came under renewed enemy attack. But three days later, they were withdrawing again at dawn, using motor transport to get to Taiping.

Enemy aircraft rained fire on the troops during a long halt, and Bill remembered later how, even while the raid was on, he was among those who went out to recover casualties on stretchers. At dusk on 17th December, the brigade reached Taiping. Bill and his fellow Leicesters counted themselves lucky to be accommodated in a jail, where they could bathe, change their clothes and – except for the few unfortunates among them who were on anti-looting picket duty in the town – get a much-needed rest the following day. However, the nearness of the enemy was a constant pressure, and the losses of many of their friends and colleagues en route to Gurun and Taiping were still raw. They would hardly have been in a mood to rejoice, and they had little idea of what lay ahead for them.

The next night, Bill and others belonging to the 1st Battalion of the Leicestershire Regiment arrived at Ipoh. Here they were amalgamated, for the rest of the campaign, with the remainder of the 2nd Battalion East Surrey Regiment. This battalion had also suffered heavy casualties at Gurun but, combined with the Leicesters, the new formation pulled together strongly in the last weeks of the campaign, recovering quickly from their losses to forge a good reputation as the British Battalion (which was still part of the 11th Division). There were 790 men in the new battalion, though a further 120 men – most of them sick – were evacuated.

At Ipoh the battalion stayed at a large school for three days, re-equipping and reorganising while enemy planes flew overhead. Some men who had gone astray in retreat or had been in hospital rejoined the battalion here, and the religious fathers at a home nearby helped to tend injuries, including many cases of very sore and infected feet. On 23rd December, the British Battalion moved by road and rail to Kampar and started work on a new position. From 24th to 30th December, the men were hard at work digging, clearing and wiring. Enemy planes flew over most days to view the work.

There was little time for Christmas that year, but on the day itself everyone got a ration of beer as well as a ration of turkey or meat from other livestock. The battalion chaplain held a short service. Many of the men were too unwell to enjoy the few festivities; they were suffering and dying from malaria due to long exposure to the elements during the battles of Jitra and Gurun. More than 100 men with fever were evacuated.

The pressure started again on New Year's Eve, although this time, during the Battle of Kampar, there were heavy losses on the Japanese side. The brunt of the attack was borne by the British Battalion, which sustained 100 casualties while performing feats of outstanding bravery. Large numbers of Japanese forces had landed on the west coast south of the Kampar position, and were threatening to cut off all troops in the area, so the battalion retreated to Tapah. Early on 4th January the men got underway by motor vehicle on a very long, slow journey down to their new rendezvous, but as the humiliating British retreat continued, the Japanese pressed relentlessly their advantage down the west coast of Malaya.

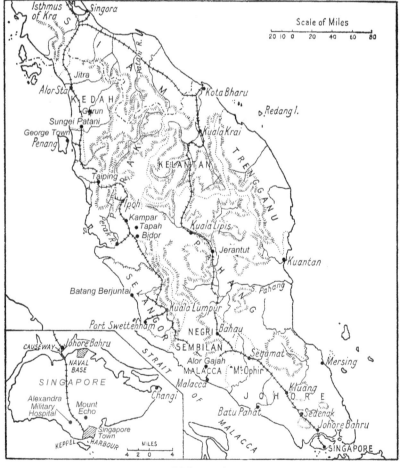

Malaya 1942

For the men, it was a frustrating reversal. Having sought action, they now had no choice but to run from it. Time after time, the same thing happened: wherever a stand was taken, the enemy would land on the west coast behind the position, as at Kampar. Whenever the Japanese threatened the flanks and rear of the 11th Division, the British troops would be forced to blow up the bridge they were holding, and withdraw.

Meanwhile, a disastrous defeat of other British troops on 7th January, on the Slim river, meant that central Malaya lay open to the Japanese. Gaining momentum, and with increasing strength on the ground, enemy forces could bomb and machine-gun the British from the air, which meant that it was only 'safe' to withdraw and dig new defensive positions at night. Working without sleep had a seriously debilitating effect.

Overall, Japanese control of the sea and air, as well as superior strength on land in armoured fighting vehicles, meant that Britain was severely outclassed, though not in inner qualities such as courage and determination. However, even on the ground at the most basic level, the Japanese troops had another secret weapon – the bicycle. Cycling along jungle paths and roads, and across bridges, they overtook and disposed of many wounded or exhausted British soldiers.

Bill was among those who had survived, and on 13th January he heard the news that there was to be a general withdrawal into the region of Johore in the south. It was hoped that they could prevent further advance of the enemy by establishing a really strong line of defence across the 90-mile front of Mersing, Kluang and Batu Pahat.

Since leaving Kampar, the British Battalion had been forced into defensive positions at several places in succession: Bidor, Tapah, Sungkei, Batang Berguntai, Batu Arang, Sungei Buloh, Kuala Lumpur and Labu. From Alor Gajah the battalion was withdrawn into the brigade reserve and ordered on a long march south to Kluang, where the plan was to rest the men in preparation for further action. However, relentless Japanese pressure and outflanking movements forced them to withdraw even further south.

By 16th January the unit had reached Batu Pahat, 30 miles to the west, where a considerable number of Japanese landings were taking place. For the next few days the British Battalion tried hard to prop up existing forces on the west coast, and especially to hold Batu Pahat and keep the coast road open. The 15th Brigade, still serving with the 11th Division, was ordered to accept the risk of encirclement in that endeavour – a very real risk that arose from the ability of the Japanese to land forces from the sea or undertake rapid outflanking movements.

However, the situation was quickly deteriorating and when the Japanese forces managed to cut off the majority of British forces, it became critical. Finally, on 25th January, the order was given to abandon the planned 90-mile front and to evacuate the mainland of Malaya. That night, the army started out on the last stage of its retreat to Singapore. The British Battalion followed the rest of the 15th brigade from Batu Pahat on a tricky trek in the darkness, which included transporting nearly 100 recently wounded men. They were covered by offshore gunfire from the Royal Navy, which was presumably directed by radio signals from the signals units ashore. Bill's battalion reached Sengarang at 1000 hours the next day. From here onwards, however, the journey was severely hampered by Japanese roadblocks and the troops were forced to abandon their guns and vehicles and to leave their wounded in the care of the Red Cross. (On this occasion, the Japanese respected international law and did not massacre the wounded, as they did elsewhere.)

That night, a group of about 1,000 British and Indian soldiers escaped by going inland from the coastal road and making their way cross-country through mud, swamp and prickly undergrowth. These men arrived at Benut late the next day, ready to drop with weariness, their only remaining duty being to retire towards the town of Johore Bahru, from where they would cross to Singapore.

Bill was not with these men. Instead, he joined another group of soldiers, perhaps twice as large, who decided to move along the shore side of the road. Coming up against a jungle river that was clearly too deep to ford, they were forced to turn downstream to part of the shore that was fringed by mangrove swamps. It must have been a terrifying ordeal for Bill, already exhausted from several long marches. Wading along in the darkness, the men did not know whether they would be shot by the Japanese, preyed upon by wild creatures, or separated from the others and left to wander alone, or drown.

Fortunately, most of them were met at the shore by the crew of two naval gunboats and a few small craft, who rescued the remnants of the 15th Brigade, including the British Battalion, and took them the short distance to Singapore Docks. For four successive nights, these vessels put to sea to save British troops, about 2,700 men in all. Considering the proximity of the Japanese and the difficulties of nighttime navigation, it was a remarkable feat.

By 0530 hours on 31st January, all British forces based in Malaya had been evacuated to the British garrison of Singapore Island – except the 22nd Brigade, who had been cut off by the Japanese. Furthermore, the plan to blow up the causeway linking Singapore to Malaya, in order to deter the Japanese, was accomplished on that same day. General Percival assumed operational command of British troops, estimated to stand at a total of 85,000 men (including recent arrivals from India and Australia who had not yet seen combat). Morale throughout the garrison was very low. Most members of the British Battalion were, understandably, in a very bad way, although at least here they got a few days of rest and were able to reorganise and re-equip before their next challenge.

This came on 8th February, when the Japanese began their crossing of the 1,000-yard wide Strait of Johore using the armoured landing craft that they had managed, somehow, to drag with them through the jungle especially for this purpose. They landed without too much difficulty on the northern shore of Singapore Island. By dawn the next day, the whole of the 5th and 18th Divisions of the Japanese army, and part of their artillery, had followed the British across the water and landed on the island.

Singapore was a huge naval base for Britain, defended by enormous guns pointing out to sea – the direction from which it had always assumed the enemy would come. Now, however, the island itself became a battlefield for domination of the Far East. The Japanese pressed forward to the southeast, pushing the British back towards Singapore city. In the city itself, more than a million civilians were living with almost constant air attacks and were greatly anxious about their supplies of food and water.

By 13th February, Bill's battalion – by now attached to the 44th Indian Brigade – had become so split and weakened in numbers that it was not considered an effective fighting unit, and was put into 'brigade reserve'. The Japanese had penned the British troops into a 28-mile perimeter around the city, and as the line shrank, units and formations became hopelessly mixed up. Late that night, the 44th Brigade arrived at the Queen Alexandra Military Hospital area west of Singapore city, the site of the main British ammunition and ordnance depots. At 0100 hours on 14th February, the brigade was ordered to a hill known as Mount Echo. This would be its last stand.

In fact, by this stage, the Japanese troops were almost out of ammunition themselves, and were thinking of withdrawing to the mainland of Malaya. General Yamashita had not prepared any plans in the event of a British surrender. However, the morale of the British had collapsed. On 15th February, the British surrendered to the Japanese who agreed in writing to guarantee the lives of all civilians, and Australian and British troops. General Percival, the commander of Malaya, marched with British officers bearing the Union Jack and a white flag of truce to Bukit Timah village where, at the headquarters of their Japanese conqueror, Commander Yamashita, they signed the deed of surrender.

Thus ended one of the most disastrous campaigns in Britain's military history. For half of the campaign, the 11th Division had borne the brunt of Japanese attack, and Bill and his fellow Leicesters were in the thick of the fighting from start to finish, often being part of the last unit to be withdrawn from a position. In less than two months, they had covered 400 miles in painful retreat as the Japanese conquered Malaya.

Fundamentally, the campaign failed because Britain was stretched to the limit in its war with Germany, and there were not enough spare troops to defend the wider empire. When the Japanese invaded Thailand and Malaya in December 1941, two-thirds of the forces defending British territories in the Far East were Indian. In the jungle of Malaya, British troops were utterly unprepared for the harsh conditions, and – because it was a low priority – suffered a shortage of arms and equipment. They had no tanks or mobile AA guns, and very few two-pounder anti-tank guns. While they did have motor transport, this confined them to travelling on the roads.

In the end, there were just not enough trained men on the ground, and nor was there sufficient airborne or naval backing to beat off fierce and sustained Japanese attacks. Their casualties totalled nearly 10,000 men, of whom about 3,000 were killed. Of the British, Australian and Indian soldiers fighting in Malaya and Singapore, some 9,000 men were killed or wounded. More ominously, however, 130,000 were captured.

When Singapore fell, Bill was at the Alexandra Military Hospital, where British troops were treated, though it is not clear whether he was sick himself, or whether he was helping out. Like the Tyersall Park Hospital, which treated Indian troops, this hospital had been overrun in the past weeks with thousands of sick and wounded men who were systematically evacuated to Singapore from the Malayan mainland. Like most of the soldiers who had endured the toll of the jungle environment, they were utterly exhausted, both physically and mentally, and malnourishment was widespread. Some had been rendered lame from foot sores and fungal infections, while others suffered from dysentery and malaria.

The need for treatment was so great that other establishments in the city (including official service and government quarters, clubs, schools and churches) were converted to try to accommodate patients. Meanwhile, hospitals such as the General Hospital and many smaller ones were filled to capacity and beyond with thousands of civilian casualties.

Bill was there that terrible evening before the British surrender, when

Japanese troops entered the Alexandra Military Hospital and used their bayonets to murder medical officers, orderlies and even some of the patients. Nearly 200 others were rounded up in the morning, then taken outside and shot in the grounds. Even after General Yamashita put his name to the terms of surrender, his guarantees for the safety of soldiers and civilians were not observed by his troops, who were renowned for their brutality and lack of compassion.

Out of the 130,000 troops taken prisoner, 60,000 Indian troops were sent by the Japanese to separate camps away from the leadership of their British commanding officers. Of these, some 25,000 were persuaded to join the traitorous Indian National Army, sponsored by the Japanese, which fought against the British. These soldiers were breaking their oath to the British Crown.

On 17th February, Bill was among the British and Australian prisoners who were marched out of Singapore City to the Changi cantonment in the northeast of the island. Each carried rations for ten days and a small amount of equipment. A perimeter fence was erected around this cantonment, and prisoners of war (POWs) were left to themselves within it, responsible for forming their own administrative systems.

Bill's battalion had shrunk in numbers. At Ipoh on 20th December, its strength was 786 men all ranks, but at Mount Echo on 15th February two months later, it was only 265 men. In the days that followed, however, the battalion grew to about 800 men as many Leicestershire and East Surrey soldiers who had been in hospital rejoined the others. Some also came from parties who had been cut off from other troops since their arrival on the island.

Bill and his fellow soldiers arrived at Changi late in the day, tired and defeated. The barracks were already overflowing with British and Australian soldiers, and they were sent on to the 'coolie lines' – huts in the camp. Living conditions in these huts, it was said, made the British Battalion the envy of many, though not for very long. After the first fortnight or so, conditions at Changi started to deteriorate rapidly, and once the rations were exhausted the men were forced to exist on a monotonous and meagre rice-based diet. This reduced intake, lacking in any protein, weakened the men and had dire consequences for their health.

However, there was one advantage of being at Changi. In the early days at least, many prisoners who stayed in the barracks saw very little of their captors, although all had to sign a statement promising not to try to escape. Others were forced to go out and work: the British officers in charge of the new administration system in the camp had to provide working parties for tasks on various parts of the island, such as clearing up war damage, disposing of mines, building roads and working at the docks. Many of these parties went by lorry to work each day, but primitive camps were set up for the others.

It was hard, relentless labour and even those men who were sick had to continue to work until they dropped. Few drugs were provided to relieve infection or pain, and any man who failed to obey orders was beaten. After his ordeal, Bill remembered the Japanese contempt for the British. 'They considered us inferior beings, to be scorned since we had "accepted" defeat and submission. This was something they had been taught never to do themselves.'

Despite the periods of separation and the injuries sustained, the solidarity of the British Battalion set an example for other troops in the camp. Nevertheless, many of the tens of thousands of POWs in camps scattered throughout Singapore, Malaya and the Dutch East Indies were suffering from sickness, injury or disease, and were unfit for the prolonged and heavy work planned for them by the Japanese over the next two years. These soldiers – Australian, American, Dutch and British – were to become the military labour force that built the Thailand-Burma Railway.

Eventually, it would become clear that while the plans prepared by the Japanese Imperial General Headquarters in 1941 were undoubtedly for aggressive expansion, they did not include the taking of India. Even British-held Burma seems to have been an afterthought, added to the Japanese list of targets because of this country's resources of timber, oil, tungsten ore and rice, and because of the protection it offered to the flank of Japan's 'southern offensive zone'. Burma's three great rivers ran north to south, each one flanked by long, parallel mountain ranges. The great Irrawaddy river on the west, navigable by steamship for 900 miles, emptied itself into the sea through a great delta, on the eastern edge of which is Rangoon.

On 23rd December 1941, at around the time Bill and his fellow soldiers were on the retreat after the catastrophe of Matador, General Iida's 15th Army – which had already gained control of the airfields and railways of neutral Thailand – was directing a campaign of air attacks against near-defenceless Burma. The Japanese seized British airfields in southern Burma as bases for their attacks and on 20th January 1942 their forces moved across the Thailand border in a major thrust towards Rangoon, Burma's capital and major port.

The man in charge of the defence of Malaya and Burma was General Archibald Wavell, who was appointed Commander-in-Chief South-West Asia Command (though, following the fall of Singapore, he became simply Commander-in-Chief, India, again). When the Japanese struck Burma in early 1942, he was promised substantial reinforcement. He sent his chief of staff Lieutenant General Sir Thomas Hutton to army headquarters in Burma, in order to reorganise the brigades there into the 1st Burma Division and the 17th Indian Division. Hutton's task was also to protect the Tenasserim Airfields, three of which were on the reinforcement route to Singapore. In addition, he had to watch for a possible attack of the Japanese from Thailand, along Burma's mountainous jungle border on the east, though it was almost impenetrable.

Burma was well provided with airfields but extremely short of aircraft. The American Volunteer Group, which had been formed to give aid to China (at war with Japan since 1931), had three fighter squadrons in Burma. One of these defended the Burma Road, the only land-based connection China had with its Western allies running from Kunming in China to Mandalay in Burma. Under the new formation, this squadron was diverted to an airfield near Rangoon, where it proved extremely valuable. As it was very much in his interest to do so, the Chinese leader Chiang Kai-shek also agreed that two of his armies (whose total strength equalled roughly that of a western division) should serve under British command, with a third army joining them in April 1942.

Much depended on the British holding Rangoon for as long as possible. There was no road from India along Burma's 700-mile western front, only a few connecting hill trails. Rangoon was the only base from which reinforcements and supplies could reach the entire country; this was why the Japanese were so keen to take it. Fortunately, the British held the capital until reinforcements arrived on 8th March and disembarked. These included the 7th Armoured Division. Without the help of these additional troops, the likelihood was that the two divisions already in Burma would never have been able, eventually, to withdraw to India.

The Japanese advance proceeded as fiercely as before. On 19th March 1942, Major General Slim (formerly Lt Colonel Slim, who more than two years before had reprimanded Hector Perks for allowing his young son to see the gruesome rituals at Dashera) arrived to command Burcorps, a newly formed body of British troops. Also under his command, were the rather weak Chinese armies. However, as Charles Chevenix Trench put it, both he and Alexander (commander of the forces in Burma), 'were handicapped by lack of instructions about the overall plan. Were they supposed to try to hold any part of Burma, or to fight a rearguard action back to India?'[82]

In the event, the Japanese march north forced retreat upon them. The Japanese, skilled in jungle warfare and fresh from their conquest of Singapore, left a trail of chaos and destruction the length of Burma. They also managed to cut China's vital supply line. In the growing confusion, many wounded men were abandoned and left to die along the roadside. In addition, thousands of Indian settlers in Burma (who, like the Eurasians and Chinese, were now refugees) clogged the roads and tracks as they made their way back up to the frontier of India, hoping to find refuge in their old homeland.

In Assam, Hector and the men under Eastern Command were at the receiving end of this flight. Now, as well as preparing to defend the frontier against a possible Japanese invasion, they had to face the problem of assisting and dealing with this great influx of refugees. The Japanese had mounted their invasion of Burma on 20th January 1942, even before they had captured Malaya and Singapore, and India Command felt itself obliged to acknowledge the distinct necessity of having to deal with an issue not previously envisaged; to defend the North-East Frontier between the Assam area of India and Burma. This was a wild and mountainous 200-mile front that presented soldiers with difficulties including a high risk of malaria and torrential monsoon rains.

'From my base headquarters at Jorhat,' Hector recalled, 'I had to visit all units as far as Imphal, travelling through Kohima which was a hospital station'. This meant a 60-mile journey as far south as Manipur Road Station (Dimapur), after which he would take the fair-weather Manipur Road for about 110 miles to Imphal (the Manipur State capital and base) close to the border of Burma. At Imphal, the road ended.

Hector had been to Imphal several times between 1939 and early 1942 and had also journeyed further east along jungle track into Burma itself, as far as the Chindwin river, a tributary of the north-south Irrawaddy. He came to check that all was well for the forward units; like them, he had to sleep in the jungle at night. Daily life was not easy in that inhospitable tropical terrain, full of ridges and valleys. One problem was rations: there were no local supplies of food to provide the men with a fresh or even adequate diet.

Supplies of meat, vegetables and milk sent up to Jorhat were already in poor condition, and by the time they reached the front they were further contaminated. Tinned food was of limited variety. Even the tinned bully beef liquefied in the heat.

At that time, the standards of hygiene were poor and sickness from dysentery, jaundice, jungle sores and malaria was common. This led to further shortages of troops when the men affected were evacuated. The situation was not helped, Hector remembered later, by the fact that the river water upon which British troops depended for everyday needs was being fouled, inadvertently, by the thousands of half-starved and diseased evacuees fleeing Burma, who were aided in their flight by tea plantation workers. While the local hill tribes were generally pro-British and proved useful allies, the situation was chaotic.

Hector's health also started to fail, though at this early stage he was unaware of it. Later on he became convinced that it all started when he was on his way to one of his field units. Hungry for meat, he bought some rashers of bacon locally, though these must have been imported. Just that one act of eating was to lead to great problems lasting for quite some time afterwards – even though, as he performed his duties, there were at first no noticeable symptoms of anything wrong.

The British authorities faced further difficulties relating to the deployment and maintenance of a much larger military force to and within the frontier area.

Frontier region of North-East India and North-West Burma

While an all-weather road system existed for local needs, there was no reliable through-road to Assam from the rest of India. The fast-flowing Brahmaputra river running through the province was broad and unbridgeable, and there was another problem: the railways systems did not match. The main railways west of the region ran on the 5ft 6in broad-gauge, while those railways east and south of it used the 3ft 3in metre-gauge. This meant a succession of changes, including the need to unload and reload equipment and stores at the river ports, as well as men and animals. The single-track, low-capacity, metre-gauge railway to Dimapur could not supply more than two divisions of men near the anticipated front. A new specification of rail locomotive, powerful enough to haul heavier loads without exceeding the relatively low axle load restrictions of the metre-gauge line, was needed.

In early 1942, an advanced base depot was established at Dimapur to hold 30 days' supplies for three divisions, and to be capable of handling 1,000 tonnes of stores per day. Work to improve the road linking this depot with Tamu on the Indian border, and eventually with the west bank of the Irrawaddy at Kalewa in Burma, was underway. This was a main line of communication, and a better, all-weather road would allow the rapid transfers of equipment and reinforcements.

This region of the frontier was known as the Naga Hills. The men of the Naga tribes were warriors: some of them, like the Garo people, had been fierce headhunters until just a few generations before. Hector noticed how it was the women of the tribe who came together to form a labour force to build new roads, and later he remarked on how this ambitious roadwork programme advanced at a pace hitherto unknown in India. Working in the ordnance services, he was concerned with sourcing and supplying arms and military stores during wartime, with the responsibility of ensuring that equipment reached the right place at the right time. He was, therefore, keenly interested in the success of these plans.

As Heathcote describes in his book *The Indian Army*, during times of peace:

all heavy equipment, siege trains, engineer stores and ordnance parks were kept in store at the arsenals. On mobilisation, equipment was issued to units requiring it, and the ordnance field parks were sent out to join the troops on service. Supply was then from the field parks to units, and the parks in turn were resupplied from the depots and arsenals further back.[83]

Effectiveness of the ordnance supply chain was further improved by the attachment, to operational divisions, of ordnance corps officers in the newly created role of Deputy Assistant Directors of Ordnance Services (DADOS).

There was another major change taking place in the Indian Army Ordnance Corps (IAOC), too. To meet the critical demands generated by the expanding corps workload, more experienced officers were desperately needed. It became inevitable, therefore, that senior non-commissioned officers and warrant officers would be considered for promotion.

A man called Williams, the Deputy Assistant Director of Ordnance Services (DADOS) at the headquarters of Bengal and Assam District Eastern Command, was instrumental in securing a promotion for Hector. Though he was transferred away to another post in August 1941, Williams had become friendly with both Hector and Clare, and on his departure he left a handwritten letter attached to a document entitled: 'Recommendations for Promotion of a Warrant Officer of the Indian Army Ordnance Corps to Commissioned Rank'. In it, Williams expressed his opinion that Hector, with whom he had been working, was a suitable candidate for a commission, and he invited more senior officers to endorse this view.

The accompanying letter opened with the lines:

Dear Perks,
This is to wish you and Clare goodbye. I'm off on Friday to take over DADOS 17th Ind Div and later for somewhere unknown. I want to thank you very much for all your most valuable help whilst I've been DADOS. It has been a pleasure to have you working under me...

Williams' proposal was approved some months later by an 'OC [Officer Commanding] an Ordnance Field Company' who wrote that he had known 'S/Condr H R Perks' on paper since August 1941 but had only met him once on a short liaison visit to his (the OC's) office. In view of this lack of personal knowledge, he requested 'EB & A Area to remark underneath', a request with which the commander and staff captain complied. Their comments confirmed that Hector was above average in his ability to take the initiative, and in administration; his power to command was rated average. In addition, he was described as an extremely conscientious and efficient warrant officer who had the gift of making himself very popular with the units with which he worked.

The commander and staff captain concluded that he would be suitable to officiate as Deputy Assistant Director of Ordnance Services if the need should arise, or as a departmental officer at army headquarters, and that he would be able to officiate successfully as officer commanding any ordnance field company for any length of time. He was considered fit in every respect for promotion to commissioned rank, and on 19th March 1942 he became Lieutenant Hector Perks, Assistant Commissary.

To have been selected as commissary, Hector had met several requirements: he was a man of some experience with detailed knowledge of the accounting, receipt, issue and repair procedures relating to ordnance stores, and also had the technical know-how to evaluate whether stores (particularly arms and accoutrements, guns and projectiles) should be condemned. He had a deep knowledge of the different kinds of ammunition used in all types of weapons, both heavy and light. Most importantly, he had the combination of administrative abilities and personal charm needed to turn a group of subordinates into a team.

In fact, Hector was in Jorhat when he received the good news of his promotion. However, before he could take up his new position, there was the small matter of a hard-earned rest of a week or more that he was owed – while the Japanese continued to make inroads to achieve their objectives. With Rangoon in their hands, they could now supply and sustain an army sufficient to occupy the whole of Burma. They wanted to be able to enter the country by rail, using their planned Thailand-Burma Railway, rather than taking the long, dangerous and costly route by sea. With this in mind, they saw their newly acquired POWs in the Far East as little more than machines to drive into the ground, in order to produce the results they wanted. It was a line that would become notorious as the Death Railway.

In April, in order to safeguard their position, the Japanese carried out operations at sea, attacking and severely damaging the British Eastern Fleet in the Indian Ocean and the British naval base at Ceylon. Another Japanese force was instructed to disrupt Allied shipping in the Bay of Bengal and to launch air raids upon Indian ports, and this caused heavy shipping losses and brought havoc to sea traffic. Following attacks on 5th and 6th April, the normally bustling port of Calcutta and other east coast ports were brought to a virtual standstill for the next three weeks. It was at this time that Hector took his long awaited leave with his family.

SIXTEEN

HOME AND AWAY ON THE NORTH-EAST FRONTIER

Calcutta had never before been brought to a halt in quite the same way. The docks at Kidderpore, close to where Hester lived with her husband Frank and her mother Mary, were a particular target for Japanese air raids, although there were also bombings on the city of Calcutta itself.

The whole of the Perks family arrived in Calcutta in early 1942 for a short holiday. They came at about four o'clock in the afternoon just after the raids that same day. Peter later recalled that the train on which they travelled was halted about one hour short of Calcutta without explanation. It eventually drew into Sealdah station, which was quite deserted. Indian stations were normally chaotic, and Hector and Clare were unaware of what had happened until some Indians explained.

They realised no one was there to meet them, and that they would have to find their own way by taxi to Hester's house. Peter further recalled seeing, en

187

route, a truckload of cheering Indians triumphantly waving fragments of shot down enemy aircraft. On another occasion, upon passing Dum Dum aerodrome, he spotted what he thought were Spitfire or Hurricane fighters on the 'apron'. At the house they found Clare's mother and sister still reeling from the dreadful news they had received on 15th February: that their beloved Bill had been taken prisoner at the fall of Singapore.

The house Hester and Frank lived in was the elegant and roomy 32/2 Mominpore Road, Kidderpore. Mary lived at one end of the house, but gave up space when her other daughter Clare arrived with her family to stay. The house's grace was enhanced by dozens of pot plants close to the building and a lovely garden beyond. Among other exotic and prolific flora, there were several trees: a mango (from a seed Mary had planted), bananas, two guavas, a papaya, a custard apple, a lime, and three coconuts. A large and gloriously scented shrub bore pure white gardenia flowers.

The grounds were home to a number of dogs, waifs and strays taken in by dog-loving Hester since her marriage. Coincidentally, they provided an effective intruder warning system. At one time there were eight dogs living in and around the house, answering to names such as Sally, Judy, Togo (the name of the Japanese Foreign Minister at that time), Bhunda, Rin Tin Tin (Rinny), Susie and Peggy.

For Hester, who had grown up with a family dog, these creatures may have become a substitute for the children she could not have. (In those days before a more enlightened view supported by medical advances suggested otherwise, childlessness was usually attributed to the woman's infertility; it was just 'something that happened'.) She wanted to adopt children but Frank would not agree, fearing the possibility that a stranger's child might have genetic characteristics that would be unwelcome. This state of affairs upset Hester greatly. The visit in 1942 must have roused her emotions once again, for not only was she presented with her newest niece, Barbara; but she and everyone else could see that her sister was pregnant for a sixth time.

Despite her own childlessness, Hester was affectionate towards her nephew and nieces, but to those outside the family her husband Frank could be an intimidating man. He had become exceedingly portly, and had an imposing demeanour and an irascible temper. He also spoke gruffly, had a tendency to grouse and was generally a difficult man to please. Clare remembered: 'If anyone got in his way whenever he took us out on the road for a ride in his car, or out to tea, or for a slap-up Chinese meal, the air was blue. He would sound his horn at other people and shout and swear at them, to make sure that they understood'.

One of his favourite expressions was 'Sewhar kaa bachchaa', which was an insult meaning 'child of a pig'. Hester, aware of his hot temper, would reprimand him with 'Frank, watch your language in front of the children'.

In fact a tragedy had occurred many years earlier when a child had accidentally got in his way while he was driving. He was courting Hester at the time; it was before they were married. Clare recalled later that the collision with his car had killed this child. 'I think it was a little girl,' she said. 'The child ran right into the car. It was all hushed up. Hester wanted him to report the incident to the police, but he wouldn't. He was a very hotheaded man.'

Sometimes his sense of humour verged on the unkind: he might, for example, describe himself as having 'no mother, no father, only a gor-blimey wife'. During their stay, the Perks children became the butt of his humorous expressions, although sometimes they sensed that his 'jokes' were close to the bone. Frank's name for them and other children was 'reptiles' and to his sister-in-law he would often say, 'Why don't you dump them Clare, and pull the flush?' Some listeners then and thereafter suspected that, although declaimed in an apparently humorous tone, these remarks represented shades of his real feelings on these topics, or perhaps masked a deeper sadness.

However, despite these traits and the fact many Indians incurred the verbal wrath of this typical 'burra-sahib' (important man), whether justly or unjustly, there was another side to Frank that was generous and amiable, shown in his keenness to take high-quality photographs of Hester's relatives. In addition, he frequently plied Clare, Hector and the children with delicious sweetmeats, such as jelebis, gulab jamuns, rasgullas and kulfi.

Here in Calcutta, among the middle classes – and there was a large and affluent mercantile community in that city – a ready market existed for the sweets that were traditionally bought by Indians for festive occasions. Frank's weakness for these rich morsels is likely to have contributed to his own rotundity. While obesity was also seen in India's affluent, sweet-toothed Bengali citizens, it was widely acknowledged that 'the British ate too much'. Two breakfasts, tiffin, tea and dinner every day were, apparently, quite standard throughout these privileged sections of India's society, and the same ritual, with the exception of tiffin, was followed at Frank and Hester's house.

Calcutta provided a pleasant climate from November to March and the means for this class of people to sustain a decent life but in this city, second only in the British Empire to London in terms of population, there was also terrible overcrowding and human suffering. Appallingly, millions of homeless were living, sleeping and dying on the streets, but the fortunate, including Frank and Hester in those days, were living the life of true colonials. Frank's portly appearance marked him out as being someone from one of Calcutta's pockets of wealth.

For Hector, the trip to Calcutta provided a welcome though short break, as well as a diversion from the increasing intensity of activity at his station in Eastern Bengal and Assam. With effect from 14th April 1942 Hector, the new lieutenant, was sent back up (albeit briefly) to the war headquarters of the Assam Division, in the Eastern Hills region that divided India and Burma. Having ensconced the family safely in Shillong, and readied himself in his usual attire and kit, he returned via Gauhati up to brigade headquarters on the metre-gauge railway that threaded along the valley of the Brahmaputra almost to its northeastern extremity. Although Jorhat was not that far away, it was well up beyond Manipur Road (Dimapur) station, and reached by a short branch off the main line. The journey of about 300 miles was a slow one. None of the families joined the men at Jorhat: the place was too remote.

For the brief time remaining here, he was given his own room within the headquarters, and a wide-ranging remit. He recalled later the visit he made to Tinsukia up at the far end of the railway line, when he had met some members of an American oil expedition among whom he encountered a man he knew: 'He had been in communication with me when I had my radio transmitter'. Even in the far reaches of the jungle, in the days before mass media, it could occasionally be a 'small world'. He said that from there he was ordered to visit another unit which was preparing to advance into Burma and, in order to do so, he had first to travel on a branch line to Sadiya, and from there journey on a trail by elephant.

On 28th April 1942, just two weeks after Hector had returned to Jorhat in his new capacity, Major General Slim was finally given orders to withdraw his troops from Burma to India along the sole escape route, through the jungle-covered mountains from Kalewa (on the west bank of the Chindwin river) via Tamu to Imphal. This was the route of the new road being built at such a pace, and getting the men to relative safety in India was a race against time. Many thousands of men didn't survive the Burma campaign, but at last the remaining British, Indian and Gurkha troops who made up Slim's Burcorps completed the longest retreat (900 miles) in British military history.

By the time the monsoon broke on 20th May, thousands of soldiers and refugees were assembled in northeast India. Fortunately, although the Japanese were poised on the frontier, the weather ruled out any immediate threat. Many of the Allied units not needed in the forward area were sent away to rest, reorganise and re-equip. America had now joined the war and was sending fighter, bomber and transport squadrons to India, though it had made clear it would not sustain British imperialism. New airfields were being built, and a huge building programme of roads, railways and pipelines had begun.

Back in Shillong, Clare was often anxious during the periods while Hector was away. She was worried that 'the Japanese were getting nearer'. Pregnant and in charge of four young children, she was often unable to contact her husband, particularly when he was sent to remote destinations across the northern expanse of the country. Away from the front line in Assam, the few divisions of India's expanding army were still mainly under-trained and ill-equipped. With so many of the best troops overseas, there was a strong political feeling in India that the Indian Army should instead be reserved for home defence. However, some things were improving. The fall of Singapore meant that consignments from Britain and America intended for the Far East were diverted to India. At long last, after months of struggling on small amounts of equipment, the infantry got carriers, mortars, anti-tank guns and even wireless sets. Anti-aircraft artillery expansion was rapid.

Hector and the men of the IAOC had never been busier. With the added responsibilities of maintaining all mechanical vehicles used by the Indian Army in the field, and of providing, storing and issuing spares, it was a hectic time. However, the authorities felt that the existing ordnance establishments were unlikely to be able to sustain a modern war effort effectively, and an extensive development programme of new establishments and depots had already begun.

In 1942, a central armoured fighting vehicle depot was set up at Kirkee. These sorts of vehicles had only recently been introduced into the service. Four years earlier, the 'horse-soldiers' of Hector's old cavalry regiment had been ordered by the British government to mechanise their operations, and with much sadness had surrendered and bidden farewell to the horses they loved. In exchange, they were given the armoured fighting vehicle. The regiment itself, renamed the 4th/7th *Royal* Dragoon Guards in 1936, became part of the new Royal Armoured Corps three years later; this comprised all 18 mechanised cavalry regiments plus the Royal Tank Corps, which was renamed the Royal Tank Regiment. The 4th/7th had been the third most senior cavalry regiment, but only the two most senior (the Royal Dragoons and the Royal Scots Greys) were allowed to keep their horses.

On his final departure from Jorhat and from the Assam front, Hector was posted to a succession of ordnance establishments still distant from Shillong and at places – some now familiar to him – over the northern expanse of the country. For example, on 24th April 1942 his record of service shows him back at 'Arsenal Ferozepore', at an incredible distance of 1,300 miles, for just six days, acting as 'AC [Assistant Commissary]. On relief.' Between 1st and 29th May, he was AC at 'No 4 OSC Reinforcement Camp, Ferozepore'.

For most of June, he was AC at Ranchi in Bihar State, closer to home but still (at 262 miles from Calcutta) nearly 800 miles away from Shillong. Living here at '25 Ord Railhead Detachment', his health was troubling him due to the suspect bacon he had bought and eaten in Assam a couple of months before. His handwritten memorandum headed 'Hospital' records the barest information: 'Admitted CMH [Civil Medical Hospital] Ranchi. June 1942. Tapeworm.' The creature growing in length in his gut had by now made its presence known through the excretion of broken end or tail segments. It is not hard to imagine how unhappy Hector, coping with this horrible creature living off him night and day, together with all the new challenges of work and travel so far from home, must have been feeling at this time.

From the end of June to the end of July he was at station '212 IAOD Jamalpur', again in Bihar. Here he was acting up: his job title was acting captain (deputy commissary). Then, in August and at the start of September 1942, he was at '51 Ord Field Park' in Delhi, and reverted to being simply lieutenant (assistant commissary). It was at precisely this time Mahatma Gandhi started his Quit India campaign in Delhi against the British, causing disorder and bloodshed and putting further pressure on the already beleaguered Indian Army.

Between April and September 1942, Clare herself was not having an easy time. Although her mother and sister visited from Calcutta to lend support during her pregnancy, another family member was causing concern. Peter, now aged eight, was playing truant. This matter first came to her attention when he arrived home early one day, quite wet. His siblings Pat and Margaret later confirmed their mother's suspicions by reporting that when they had called at his school in their taxi, to pick him up, he wasn't there.

By this time Clare had already bathed and dried Peter. When he finally admitted that he had not been at school at all that day, her response was to threaten him with a walloping, but he was too quick for her and ran off, whereupon one of the servants was sent to catch him and bring him to his mother. However, Peter was no pushover and fought back, biting the ear of the servant and scratching him, which created further havoc by alarming the servant, who feared getting rabies and wanted to know whether he should have injections!

The fact that he had arrived home wet was a clue to what he had been doing on his 'day off'. It emerged soon after that he had already played truant three or four times, and liked to go to a lake opposite the school where hill-trout and carp were bred. From here, taking his sandwiches with him, he would wander into the countryside. One occasion he even visited European confectioners De la Nougerie (long remembered by Clare for their delicious sponge cakes) at their farm bakery, a short stroll away from home, and accepted their offer of a cup of tea.

The reason for his truancy also became clear: one of his masters had taken to caning him with the edge of a ruler. Clare went in to the school and managed to resolve the matter, but Peter's intense dislike for both teachers and discipline went way back to his days in Calcutta as a little boy. There, he had often been carried screaming onto the school bus that took him, along with his older sisters Pat and Margaret, to Loreto Convent in Middleton Row. When the family came to Shillong and he transferred to the Loreto Convent in this town, his fears about school were confirmed on one particularly humiliating occasion when the nuns made him stand on the stage in front of the other children as a punishment for wetting his pants.

Hester and Frank had travelled to Shillong with their dogs Peggy and Judy and stayed with the Perks family for two or three weeks. While they were there, an Indian woman was raped and murdered, particularly brutally, then left on the roadside beside the rock that had been used as a weapon against her. Word about the killing soon got out, and the incident inevitably caused much concern in the neighbourhood. Frank went to see the body before it was taken away, and a photograph he took then shows a pitiful and unsightly scene.

This contrasted with other pictures he took on his visit that reveal the attractive environment of Shillong. These show the hill station nestling amid the trees, as well as views of the elegant and capacious bungalow that was the family home. Away from the town's centre, there are views of tranquil neighbourhoods containing Victorian bungalows and houses with Tudor-style frameworks. The heavy, cloudy and threatening skies also show the approach and perhaps the onset of the monsoon.

Other shots capture the Perks children with Hester's dogs and wearing topi (cork or pith) helmets; some were taken at the large and bustling bazar, where

Clare is shown purchasing heaps of fruit that are being weighed on hand scales by a pretty Khasi woman. This woman is dressed typically in the traditional jain kyrshahs (woven woollen shawls worn slantwise from one shoulder over a blouse and skirt); others wore colourfully chequered tartans. Some of the prints portray smiling children, together with Barbara's ayah and 'Auntie Hester with her knitting'. Shillong had been neatly laid out after the earthquake of the 19th century, and appears to have been a restful and pleasing family environment. For those fortunate enough to live there, like the Perks family, it remained a fond memory.

By the time they returned to Calcutta, Clare was nearing the time of her delivery. Soon her mother Mary arrived, just as the servants were becoming troublesome again. Working relations between the khansama (who had suffered smallpox) and the bearer (who was supposed to wait at table and ensure that food was hot) had turned bad, and they disagreed bitterly over a woman that each claimed as his wife. The matter worsened from time to time when the families of these servants turned up at the bungalow to bicker and fight.

Clare's condition had weakened her ability to take a firm stance, although she had sacked the khansama before Mary arrived and took the situation in hand. During the following day, which coincided with Clare's confinement and labour, she saw to the needs of her grandchildren and employed herself interviewing several Indians until she found a replacement cook for her daughter.

On 11th July, Hector and Clare's fourth daughter was born at the Ganesh Das hospital. Her name was Mary Veronica Perks, and her namesake – her grandmother – acted as godmother by proxy in the stead of Hester, who could not be there. The older Mary stayed for the baby's baptism on 5th August, and for the rest of the month. A surviving army form relating to the birth of this new baby shows that Clare, as a wife of a soldier serving in India, was able to claim maternity benefit from the Navy, Army and Air Force Insurance Fund.

At the end of August came the biggest treat of all. The entire family was overjoyed when Hector returned home and was able to meet his new daughter for the first time.

SEVENTEEN

ONCE UPON A TIME

Hector was home, but soon the whole family was to be on the move again. Only days later, the entire Perks family was packing with the help of Mary Perren (who, as she had travelled widely as a lady's maid, was something of an expert). The next posting was at Agra, and this time – because of the disruptions of war, including a massive rescue effort that was underway – the family travelled to Calcutta on a more tortuous southerly route through Eastern Bengal, one Hector had discovered during his recent assignments. Clare, who was breast-feeding and coping with all the other tiring demands of a two-month-old baby in some awkward situations, later remembered the journey as 'terribly disjointed' and found it arduous.

Clare also remembered that in every long haul journey from one area of India to another, all the family's 'worldly goods' travelled with them. There was no furniture to transport, as the army-owned houses they occupied usually came equipped with essential items such as beds, table and chairs. Extras such as cupboards, couches and suites could be hired from a local company on a monthly basis. Nevertheless, as Clare now had a family of seven people, a fair amount of paraphernalia accumulated in boxes, cases and trunks. Each person had a bedroll, carried on their long train journeys, and used specifically for setting down on the bare bunks. Each one comprised a pillow, blankets and sheets from the household bedding and a light narrow kapok-filled mattress, the whole arranged to roll up inside a waterproof canvas covering secured by straps. Mary was to travel with the family back to her home, with Hester, in Calcutta.

The first 86-mile stage of the journey was by bus from Shillong along a road that made a gradual descent (albeit covering thousands of feet) down the southern aspect of the Khasi Hills. These hills rose very steeply out of the hot plains below and presented a huge obstacle to the sodden air mass of the monsoon, leading to rapid cooling and the precipitation of staggering amounts of rain each year. Reaching Sylhet on the lower valley of the Surma river at the foot of the Khasi hills, the family embarked upon the second stage of the journey, for Kulaura, boarding a train on a branch line of what had become the Bengal and Assam Railway.

Now the Perks and Mary Perren were leaving behind the pleasantly cool hills. They journeyed for 186 miles southwest, passing out of Assam and into Eastern Bengal to reach Akhaura station, through the flat, wide sub-region comprising the Surma Valley and the eastern part of the great tidal Ganges delta, the largest in the world. Near the end of August, the heavy monsoon rains persisted and the country they travelled through was intensely humid, and still inundated with floodwaters. There was also a 5 per cent chance of a cyclone!

When the family reached the end of the metre-gauge line at Chandpur, they beheld the swollen course of the mighty Ganges-Brahmaputra river system, which was shortly to discharge into the Bay of Bengal. This massive body of water originated with the summer rains and melting snows from as far away as the Himalayas. It was an awesome and, for some, fearful sight. At Chandpur, they connected with the next regular steamship service and, for the next seven hours, travelled upstream and across a body of water so wide that, from the middle, the low shores were scarcely visible. They disembarked at Gaulando, just ten miles south of the junction of the two great rivers.

However, owing to the unreliable nature of the riverbanks at this point, there were no permanent buildings. Some soldiers helped to carry the five children across a stretch of deep, muddy floodwater between the quay (if there was one) and the station in order to board a train, though Hector, Clare, Mary and the other passengers had to 'manage somehow' by themselves. From the terminal station there, the site of which was frequently shifted, they took the broad-gauge railway for another 155 miles to the terminus of the Bengal and Assam railway at Sealdah Station in Calcutta.

Despite having arrived in Shillong at a time when she could provide such greatly- needed help to Clare, Mary Perren may have been heartily relieved to get back, finally, to Hester's house – her home – at Mominpore Road. In fact, Hester provided the entire family with a warm welcome and comfortable beds, so that everyone was able to get a good night's sleep before the next day's journey.

The following evening, the seven remaining travellers set out again and travelled across the famous Pontoon Bridge. The bridge crossed the Hooghly river, part of the system of the Ganges delta and there at Calcutta, 121 miles from the sea, at its narrowest point although still 1,700ft wide. This bridge was constructed in 1874 with a middle section that opened to allow vessels to pass. It was the only road link between the two parts of this huge city carrying a constant multitude of people, and vehicles of every kind, in both directions. The vehicles jolted disturbingly over the joints between the bridge sections. Because of the high and fast tides of the river in rainy season, combined with the unpredictability of the Ganges, there was no rail crossing.

On the west bank was the great station of Howrah from where mail trains bound for Bombay, Delhi and Madras started their journey. They took the Eastern Indian Railway to reach their distant goal, Agra, 790 miles further west, and among the places they passed en route were Patna, Mirzapur and Allahabad, where the Ganges receives its chief tributary, the Jumna. Proceeding further on their journey, through Cawnpore, the family finally reached Tundla Junction, 127 miles short of Delhi. Then they transferred to a branch line for the last 15 miles across the Jumna Bridge and into Agra Fort Station.

The family's accommodation was actually to be within Agra's fort, quite a contrast with the character of their previous homes. 'There aren't many who can say they've lived at Agra fort,' Clare told her children proudly. The Perks were among a small élite who were privileged to stay at a section of the fort – the British military part of it – that, prior to the war, was a small ordnance depot. The area occupied comprised about 12 acres and, in the Mughal era, had been an elephant stable.

One possible explanation for the chance to live here was Hector's friendship with Harry Fellingham, from the days of Kirkee. Harry (a captain) and his wife Beatrice already lived within the curtilage of the fort, together with a handful of other officers and their wives who lodged, although officially there were no married quarters. Two dirty rooms, part-filled with stores, had caught Harry's eye and he organised the clearing of them to make a home for the Perks family. On their arrival, there was basic furniture ready to use and the Fellinghams and others helped everyone to settle in. What luck to be at the hub of such an awesome and historic site! They set down their bags with sighs of both exhaustion and incredulity.

Like Delhi, the city lay on the west bank of the Jumna. This river flowed past the city from north to south but changed direction for a while opposite the fort, in a great loop, before resuming its southerly course. The fort itself was in the shape of an irregular triangle, with a strong base on the riverfront and two sides joining at the Delhi Gate, and with a perimeter wall over a mile long. With its forbidding double walls and flanking defences of red sandstone nearly 70ft high, coupled with a ditch 35ft deep and nearly as wide, the fort presented an imposing appearance.

The edifice had been built by the two greatest Mughal emperors, members of the fierce and powerful Mughal dynasty from Central Asia that ruled in northern India from the establishment of its empire by Babur in 1526 until the demise forced upon it by the British in 1857. The building of the walls and the other red sandstone constructions in the southeast corner were attributed to the emperor Akbar (1542–1605), who chose Agra as his capitol.

Later, the emperor Shah Jahan (1614-66) constructed most of the magnificent buildings within the fort and, in doing so, rendered it one of the two greatest Mughal legacies in a city so richly endowed. In 1638, the emperor transferred his capital from Agra to Delhi, over 100 miles away, and there laid out the new city of Shahjahanabad. With the end of Shah Jahan's reign, the so-called golden age of the great Mughals, lasting more than a century in this region, came to an end.

Later, in 1764, an army of Jats (Indo-Aryan people widely distributed in northwest India) sacked Agra, but six years afterwards a Hindu warrior race known as the Mahrattas recovered and occupied it until 1803, when the British seized it. The fort was to play a key role some 50 years later, during the Indian Mutiny, when it offered refuge to soldiers as well as thousands of men, women and children (including Indians) who would otherwise have been killed by the rebels burning the cantonments and murdering all Europeans they found outside.

The Mughal architectural legacy, characterised by great arches and domes, included lavish mosques, palaces, squares and halls, each one immensely ornate in design and often inlaid exquisitely with marbles. Shah Jahan's hallmark was shimmering white marble. However, in 1658 he was deposed by his son Aurangzeb, who proclaimed himself emperor of Delhi and kept his father a state prisoner for seven years. Shah Jahan was held at Agra fort in the southeast corner of the Anguri Bagh (Grape Garden) in three fresco-embellished rooms comprising his private apartments. According to tradition, he died in the one nearest the river, an octagonal pavilion, while gazing across at his superb creation, the Taj Mahal.

Close to where the families lived in the fort, sepoys (Indian soldiers) were billeted at the barracks. During the daytime the children could see them drilling up and down, and hear them calling on the ramparts. At sun-up there was reveillé, a word that later, upon discussion of that time, conjured up for Clare a memory of a catchy little song: 'Fall in A, fall in B, fall in every Company. Soldiers all big and small, listen to the bugle call.' Peter remembered the sound of reveillé in Shillong each morning, coming from the army camp near to the family home at No 4A.

Living at the fort meant heightened security. When approaching the fort through the giant, exquisitely finished Delhi Gate, anyone who wished to enter had to produce a security pass to show the sepoy standing guard at this Mughal gateway. (Beyond here, there was an inner entrance through the Elephant Gate.) Pat, then thirteen and the eldest of Hector and Clare's daughters, remembered how the school bus would pick them up and drop them off near this monumental gate. In the morning family rush, she or Margaret or Peter would sometimes pick up the wrong security pass, but fortunately, as the sepoys couldn't read English properly, they were none the wiser. The fun was in fooling them!

Hector's job was at the new central ordnance depot. Agra had long associations with ordnance, but, by 1941, because accommodation deficiencies inside the fort had become so acute, the authorities decided to build a central ordnance depot in the city. Each day he cycled to work in the south of the city, beyond the cantonment. The central ordnance depot had opened in April 1942 and was of a type new to India. It was constructed rapidly on 271 acres of land and was one component of the huge expansion programme that was necessitated by the outbreak of war. Despite the commissioning of many such facilities, the ordnance corps was still grossly overstretched and its officers severely burdened. Not only were new types of equipment coming out of production facilities, room had to be found for shiploads diverted from Malaya and Singapore. Hector was in the thick of efforts needed to cope with the storage, maintenance and eventual re-issue of this plethora.

Hector (back left) with his family in England prior to his service. 1916 or 1917.

Hector, a cavalryman of the 4th/7th Dragoon Guards in India. Taken while on secondment at Army Headquarters in Simla, c1926.

Hector & Clare in their first home together in Ferozepore. 27 December 1928.

Uncle Walter and Aunt Lizzie. Calcutta, Christmas 1938.

Billy with his nephew Peter in the Fellingham's car. Kirkee, c1936.

Mary Perren with son Billy before his posting to the Far East.

George William Perks, a very sick infant. Quetta, 1937.

Hector, the amateur radio enthusiast. Shillong, 1938-39.

Hector on the Assam metre-gauge railway. 1939-42.

Barbara with her ayah. Shillong, c1941

Clare buying fruit at the Bara Bazar in Shillong. 1942

The Fort in Agra where the Perks family lived from September 1942 until February 1943.

The Perks family at Hester and Frank's house while in transit from
Agra to Shillong in 1943.

Back at the fort, a bullock-cart brought army food supplies. Because of the war, basic provisions such as flour, rice, tea and sugar were rationed. The family also got limited amounts of butter, beef and corned beef, and 'army' bread. A water tanker organised by the army delivered purified water that the family stored in chatties (earthenware pots), while the ice for the icebox came separately. All of these had to be paid for.

Packs of brown monkeys roamed the fort and, living at such close quarters, it was hard to ignore their social – and anti-social – behaviour. They made a real impact on Clare, who watched with interest the fights between males in the group, when challenged to retain dominance over females. She saw couplings between monkeys, and later a mother nursing her newborn baby, much as she was doing herself. These stocky rhesus macaque monkeys had pink faces, short tails, and grey-brown fur tending to reddish at the rump. They were inquisitive and intrusive, but they also had tempers. 'Generally they were not aggressive, but they were to be avoided,' said Clare, remembering that she never left baby Mary out in her pram.

One particular pack in the fort she thought of as a troop or gang. 'They were quite a family,' she recalled, 'with a leader who was a great big ugly creature. One day one of these brown monkeys came into the house and started to remove systematically, one item at a time, clothes from the Chinese basket. I was terrified. Then the monkey got up onto the table and found some fruit and sat there eating it. Finally, it picked up a large jar of pearl barley, jumped down and made off with it, dropping the jar just as it was going over the step. There was pearl barley everywhere.'

The stagnant, green waters of the defensive ditch and the nearby river, close to their accommodation, presented a more serious threat to the family's health and wellbeing. Their quarters were infested with mosquitoes and it was only a matter of time before Pat, Margaret and Peter all came down with malaria, one of India's great and deadly curses. Pat and Peter suffered particularly badly, and were admitted into the military hospital just as Margaret was beginning to recover from this terrible 'shivering' disease.

The younger girls escaped the infection, and while the others were in hospital the family moved into better and more private quarters, not more than 100 yards away. Their new abode was a fairly old, single-storied, semi-detached house that came with servants. It was in an area of the fort where several other officers' families occupied houses in small rows. Perhaps the most striking thing about the location was the view it afforded of the Taj Mahal, the seventh wonder of the world. Looking out from the rear veranda, the children could see the magnificent sight of the sun rising above it each day. For Pat and Peter, brought home from hospital by their father in a tonga, it must have been quite a sight.

They were both better, though still in their pyjamas and dressing gowns. Just as everyone thought the storm had passed, Clare came down with malaria herself – on Christmas Eve. Fortunately the doctor who attended her, a civilian, was a man who inspired confidence. 'He was smashing,' she recalled, 'and he played balloon games with the children'. Thankfully, it was a mild case and she was in bed only for a couple of days.

Hector, however, was suffering in a different way. From the second day of his service in Agra, he had sought medical help for the ill health that had been plaguing him ever since his field visit in March or thereabouts. A hospital memorandum makes clear the frequency of his visits:

Admitted Agra Combined IMH 4.9.1942 Tapeworm
Admitted CMH Agra 28.10.42
Discharged CMH Agra 2.11.42 Common Cold
Admitted ditto ditto 14.11.42
Admitted ditto ditto 17.11.42 Tapeworm

The tapeworm was a monster. Every two months it grew so large inside his gut that it would protrude externally from the rectum, and for many months it seemed the only treatment available was Epsom salts, a laxative. Hector followed instructions from various army doctors, but continued to find long curly sections of the worm's body in his faeces (which he would bury in the ground). The long, segmented worm, between 6ft and 12ft long, continued to absorb nutrients and grow inside him.

During these few months in Agra, Hector and Clare became close to the Fellinghams. Childless themselves, this couple felt fondly towards the Perks children and were glad to look after them whenever Clare wanted to go shopping in the city bazar. Barbara, however, who by now was two years old, was going through a phase of aversion to men. 'She wouldn't go anywhere near Mr Fellingham,' recalled her mother. 'He was such a nice man and tried to win her over by coaxing her with sweets, but she'd just turn away. Mary was the opposite; she was anybody's child!' Harry Fellingham's assiduity paid off and eventually Barbara became 'quite fond' of him.

After five months in Agra, Hector was sent to Eastern Army Ordnance, the 215 and 220 Indian Advance Ordnance Depot in Mymensingh, Eastern Bengal, which meant that the entire family would be heading back to Shillong. Barbara turned three on his last day in Agra – it was also around the first anniversary of the fall of Singapore – and, as before, they decided to break their long journey by staying with Hester and Frank in Calcutta.

As they had done on two previous occasions, they took the railway line (which was of great strategic significance at this time) from Sealdah terminus in Calcutta via Santahar Junction to Gauhati, in the region of Assam. Then the family transferred to a taxi, which took them up the north-facing slopes to Shillong along the very winding and precipitous route they had used twice before. Along the way and familiar to them, they passed native travellers making their way on foot.

Clare recalled how these people would make a friendly greeting call of 'khublei', whereas elsewhere in India, the cry was mostly 'salaam'. Furthermore, she and other members of the family remembered this road as a narrow road with a one-lane system, when the only thing they passed for much of the way were these people. Vehicles journeying in opposite directions in a single lane, made their way to a wider passing point roughly midway along its length, which could be reached by a given time. During the wait, there was the opportunity for everyone to have a sandwich and a cup of tea at what was known as the 'halfway house' until the oncoming vehicles had passed. When this was accomplished, it meant that the passengers could once again board the bus and continue the second stage of about 30 miles, which would take them up among the familiar, tall, rustling pine trees. However, because of the war, the road may well have been widened.

The fall of Burma had occurred during the Perks family's previous stay in Shillong, and brought with it a huge influx of fleeing refugees across the frontier into Assam. Hector had witnessed the start of this upheaval when at the frontier the previous spring. In the intervening months, thousands of people had passed through the region: Anglo-Indians, native Indians, Burmese and Chinese, many of them in a very poor state.

Large numbers of the sick and otherwise distressed had been aided and sustained in casualty clearing stations established in the many tea plantations of the area. For others there had been emergency hospitals and welfare centres, set up and run mostly by women. This extraordinary effort had shattered the usual tranquillity of the districts, especially when to that activity was added the efforts of the authorities to improve the transport infrastructure in preparation for troop deployments. In addition, the people who were fit enough were given blankets and some food and dispatched to Calcutta on the trains that were to return with troops and equipment for the defensive effort.

In fact, in Calcutta Hester had been at the receiving end of the stream of casualties of the war in Burma. She was one of the British women, working alongside Indian women, who played their part as nurses and workers in the auxiliary services: she was a voluntary worker at Mayurbhanj Palace, the fine residence situated diagonally opposite where she lived. This had been the home of the maharajah of Mayurbhanj, whose state occupied more than 4,000sq miles of territory in Orissa, Eastern India, but the young maharajah had died in 1928 (without issue, it seems) and his father had died some 16 years before that. Hester only ever remembered the palace housing 'the old rani' – the Dowager Maharani, the father's elderly widow. During the war, the palace had become 'Mayurbhanj Hostel' after being given over to the use of the convalescing Indian troops.

At times, the camps outside Shillong had caused the food supply for the town to run short. The electricity and water supplies had also been affected. Ambulances operated up and down the hills and when Japanese planes flew over – the targets of anti-aircraft batteries positioned throughout the tea estates – the air raid sirens went off. Unblemished, however, were the marvellous views which greeted the family on their return to the familiar heights of Shillong, the capital of Assam. In 1850 a British naturalist had noted that, from a local hilltop, in one direction one could scan the distant Ganges plain, and in the other, 'the whole Assam valley... the dark range of the Lower Himalaya crested by peaks of frosted silver'.[84]

This time, the family moved into the ground floor of a black-and-white timbered house called 'Our Home'. Clare employed a new ayah called Matilda, a Christian Khasi girl whose aunt felt it her duty to come and walk her home from work (Matilda was afraid to go alone because of the American soldiers whose units had by now been posted to the vicinity.) This area of Shillong was called Laitumkhrah, and had a strong military presence: it lay east of the town and was situated conveniently close to the schools.

Pat and Margaret returned to a much-depleted Loreto Convent, as most of the boarders had moved out and much of the main building had been taken over to provide accommodation for soldiers. Peter went back to St Edmund's College, which now displayed large red crosses as it was doubling up as a military hospital for soldiers. These included casualties of the defeated army who, together with the civilian refugees, had poured across the border of Burma and India, into

Assam. Assam remained on a war footing like neighbouring Bengal, which was to be Hector's next destination.

By 22nd February 1943, Hector had hauled himself off again – this time to Mymensingh. He took with him the usual items of kit essential for his creature comforts: a canvas camp bed and camp chair, and a camp washstand and basin. Having travelled down from the Khasi hills of Assam to Sylhet, he went on over the plains of Eastern Bengal, using bus, rail and river. Once again it was rather a tortuous journey, covering part of the route taken by the family less than six months earlier. As a captain and deputy commissary, he was back in the region of the frontier where a limited offensive for the recapture of Burma was in progress.

When Hector had left the Assam frontier a year before in April 1942, Slim had all but lost the battle to save Burma from the Japanese. All the forces withdrawn came under Indian Command, but within weeks of that retreat there were plans to recapture Burma, using India as a base. Clearly much had to be done before control could be regained. Japanese communication lines in Burma were, for example, far better than the abominable British communication lines from forward positions in far-flung Assam to the main centres of India. General Iida's army benefited from using the great rivers of Burma as supply lines, navigable from the port of Rangoon in the south up to the jungles in the north, together with a main railway line running parallel to the rivers through the country's central corridor.

In contrast, the Indian Army's main artery in the east was totally inadequate and susceptible to weather damage: a railway that was mostly metre-gauge was inferior, having lower axle loads and less stability, leading to lower capacity on the route. Furthermore, the line to the central front stopped 110 miles short of the base of Imphal. Going south, the front in the Arakan (a province separated from the rest of Burma by wide rivers and densely forested mountains) could only be accessed from Eastern Bengal by a variety of railways, river steamers and country boats. Now that the Japanese had achieved their objective, they were determined to hold Burma along the line of the Chindwin river and to reinforce this front as quickly as they could. For beyond it lay the main eastern base of the Allies: British India, which for centuries had provided a foundation for British influence throughout the Far East.

Although Rangoon had been the key city in the Japanese victory in Burma, its supply route was still very vulnerable just east of the Bay of Bengal, where the Allies could attack them on the last leg of a long sea voyage. Because of this,

Imperial General Headquarters in Tokyo decided to switch the terminus for its sea traffic from Rangoon to Bangkok in Thailand, a much shorter route by sea. Their plan was to build a railway to link the Thai rail system with the Burmese railway, providing an alternative route along which supplies and reinforcements from Bangkok could pass to the Burma front. In addition, this would save them an immense amount of time and fuel, and would also provide direct overland communication with forces in Singapore, Malaya and Thailand.

This plan involved the construction of a 260-mile stretch of single-line metre-gauge track. The Japanese wanted it completed by November 1943, and had amassed its labour force to work on the railway. This comprised some 61,000 Allied prisoners of war, half of them British, rather fewer than a quarter Australian, and most of the rest Dutch, except for 700 Americans. These men were already severely weakened by previous ordeals such as the Malayan campaign, and debilitating internment in POW camps such as Changi.

While the tropical rainforest, fast-flowing rivers and mountainous terrain over which the railway was to run was impenetrable enough to ease the security problem for the Japanese (the nearest Allied forces were 1,000 miles away through dense jungle, making escape an impossibility), the engineering task presented by the region was formidable. The job would be immense and excruciating, and it would cost more than 16,000 prisoners their lives.

EIGHTEEN

FORTUNES OF WAR

The Japanese chose for their railway a route that followed an old British survey line, one that was abandoned before the war because of the difficulties it presented. Work was to start at both ends of the route simultaneously, from the base camps of Bang Pong at the Thai end and in Burma from a place called Thanbyuzayat. At Ban Pong, the line would connect with the existing Thai State Railway, which ran directly to Singapore, Bangkok and Singora where large merchant ships could unload their cargo onto trains that would be able to run into Burma and join up, at the far end, with the existing Burma State Railway.

The first POW labour forces from Java, Sumatra and Singapore (the camp of Changi) were dispatched north in the months of April and May 1942, just as the southwest monsoon was beginning to break. They had been told to 'volunteer' to go to better camps and living conditions. For these and for greater numbers of men who went later, it was an appalling 1,000-mile railway journey from Singapore, across the causeway and up through the Malayan and Tenasserim peninsulas. The men were packed into scorching, cramped steel box cars that were normally used to transport rice, or in cattle trucks, taking it in turns to lie down. Dysentery and malaria were already rife among these men; the tropical heat could only make it worse.

For several nights and days, the trains rattled over the narrow-gauge rails, along a route that, for much of the way, followed the road from south to north up the Malay peninsula. In doing so, they partly retraced a path that had already caused Bill and his comrades much pain and frustration. They passed places where their friends had died at the hands of the aggressors who were now herding them back. It was a harrowing experience for them, knowing that their own fates were likely to be little better. Many of them were still only in their early or mid twenties.

They went through places where they had fought hard, such as Kampar and Ipoh. There the British Battalion had been formed on 18th December the year before, from the remnants of Bill's Leicestershire regiment and those of the 2nd East Surreys. Then they travelled on up to Taiping, another battle zone, and passed close to the idyllic Penang Island, which Bill and the other men had so enjoyed when they first reached Malaya, at a time when they had no vision of the trials that lay ahead. Beyond here was Jitra, where the nightmare first began.

Their destination was Ban Pong, 50 miles from the Thai capital of Bangkok. Thailand ('The Land of the Free') had become a reluctant ally of Japan, though a few opposition groups operated underground. At Ban Pong they found their first camp, a place with flimsy jungle-style dwellings and bunks made of bamboo. The huts were thatched with attap leaves (from a type of palm) and lashings were made from the stringy underbark of trees. Untypically, in contrast to other locations, the camp was 'ready-made' for them and in a flat, richly agricultural southern plain, near a village. Here, some of the prisoners, seldom closely guarded until later in the war, would be able to barter with the villagers and exchange their few remaining valuables (including clothing and mosquito nets) for food.

However, the advance parties at Ban Pong were soon moved up country to build fresh camps. They also had to hack a path for the engineers and surveyors, and for telephone lines. For the first 20 miles or so, the ground was flattish, and skirted the east bank of a river. This was the wide, meandering Mae Khlaung that flowed south from Kanchanaburi, a junction where its two constituent tributaries, the Kwae Yai from the north and the Kwae Noi from the northwest joined to form the main stream. At Tamarkan, just north of the confluence, the track was to cross the Kwai Yai over a wooden bridge that had yet to be built, the infamous 'Bridge over the River Kwai'. POWs often modified local names while the Japanese simply applied their own pronunciation to Thai words. For example, Ban Pong was 'Banponmai', Kanchanaburi was 'Kanburi' and Tha Makham was 'Tamarkan'. The track would continue a few miles further upstream to the tented camp of Chungkai.

At Chungkai, the task of the advance parties was to erect wooden huts to house a much larger labour force. The place was destined to become a busy staging centre and a major base, with a big although crude hospital comprising a motley collection of bamboo and attap huts. Men who were working the section

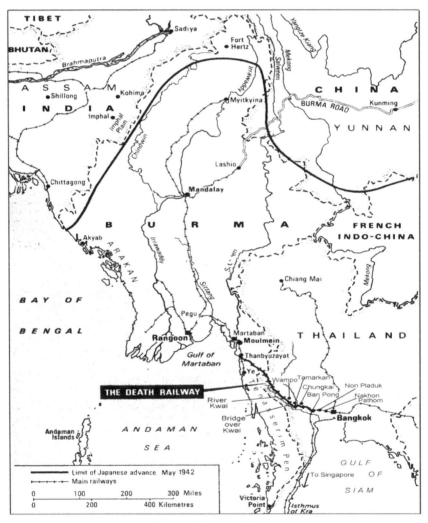

The Death Railway, Thailand

of the railway operations controlled from the Thai end came to this hospital. In his book *Death Railway*, Clifford Kinvig writes:

> As the weeks went by, activity extended northwards along the riverbank as more spaces were cleared and huts erected. The work became steadily more difficult as the vegetation changed from the dreary expanses of paddy to the bamboo thickets and forest covered hills across the Mae Khlong, and then to the jungle clad mountains further up country.[85]

In that region where Ban Pong and Chungkai lay, some 12 inches of rain fell in September, and a further 8 inches in October. As the end of the monsoon season approached, most of the remaining men left their camps in Singapore (Changi) and Java and were brought north to the Ban Pong railhead. From there, they were drafted to camps stretching northwards along the east bank of the River Kwai, following the route of the proposed track, well up beyond the river's source. Some fell by the wayside even then, too sick and exhausted to carry on. Those who were sent later had to march further northwards and were even more poorly supplied with rations. Consequently they endured even greater deprivation and hardship.

Kinvig found that battalions that had been kept together after the surrender of the British forces generally attempted to make the trip as a complete group. However,

> the trains were not designed to transport whole units and many had to leave part of their complement behind, sometimes to rejoin them later on, but frequently never to see them again until the Japanese surrendered.[86]

A report on troop movement to the railway indicates that between 18th and 26th June 1942, some 3,000 British prisoners, destined to become Work Party No 1 Group of the Japanese Prisoner of War Command in Thailand, were moved up. The next troop movement was between 9th and 15th October, and again solely concerned British prisoners – 3,250 of them this time. This batch was moved up to the camp of Chungkai, now the headquarters of this Work Party No 2 Group. With it came the core of the British Battalion, including Bill and many officers and senior warrant officers.

At Chungkai, the battalion was merged and reformed into No 6 Battalion: at the base, there were eight 'battalions' in all, with 600 men in each. Bill's new battalion consisted of 30 officers and about 350 members of the British Battalion (with almost equal numbers of Leicesters and East Surreys). In addition, it had 200 members of the Royal Army Ordnance Corps (RAOC), along with 30 officers each from the RAOC and the Royal Army Service Corps (RASC).

In fact, most of these officers were later removed and formed into new, officer-only 'working battalions'. The disciplinary standard of No 6 Battalion, combined with the abilities and efforts of its medical officers (and probably too its stretcher-bearers and first aid and sick bay attendants, including Bill), was to help greatly in the dim days to come, as everyone strove to keep body and soul together.

Eventually there would be six numbered POW groups along the Kwai railway. Four were in Thailand, while numbers one and five were in Burma. Each was under a different Japanese command (for example, No 2 Group) and consisted of a headquarters or base camp with other smaller camps in the area. The memoirs written by one former prisoner of war, Geoffrey Pharaoh Adams,[87] record the early arrival of companies of Leicesters and East Surreys.

Men from other regiments provided reinforcements at Tamarkan – a camp in the area of Chungkai – where work was already underway on the famous wooden bridge and on part of the embankments along which tracks would be laid in the run-up to the bridge. (Later, a permanent steel bridge of 11 spans was built almost 100 yards further upstream from the wooden bridge.) From Chungkai, the land rose steadily and became more rugged and isolated. The jungle here was heavy and dense, with towering hardwood trees and stubborn bamboo clumps. Clearing it for the railway track became increasingly backbreaking and difficult work.

The system for building the railway was for two or three or more battalions to move up the river, 10 miles beyond the last camp. These men would work first to raze the jungle, and then build the railway in two directions, five miles each way. Sometimes, if the ground was level, this took only three or four weeks. Other sections took three months of work, especially if bridges needed to be built or if there was rock to blast. On completion of a section, the working groups were moved up progressively through the camps until they reached the next area of virgin jungle. Here, huts of bamboo were constructed and the process of building the track was repeated.

The food rations supplied by the Japanese through the base camps were meagre and irregular, and the diet was always rice-based and of poor quality, often ridden with weevils and maggots. It included little salt, other than what was found (along with tiny amounts of protein) in small portions of salted meat or fish. Sometimes there were a few vegetables, tea and a little sugar. Astonishingly, the men were paid a daily rate for their work (delivered monthly) but, with inflation, it was still a pittance. The sick received no pay, though often their needs for extra resources were greater. In some camps there was an opportunity to buy other food, through the Japanese. Duck eggs, brought in by merchants who came upriver in barges, were a commodity that provided some of the prisoners with much-needed protein, and helped to save many lives.

However, virtually all the men became malnourished. This, combined with continuously heavy work and overcrowded, primitive conditions, lowered the men's resistance to diseases and led to the rapid spread of malaria, jungle fevers and sores, dysentery and other intestinal conditions. The fact that the Japanese supplied medical stores both infrequently and inadequately meant that these diseases could not be controlled, and the men saw them as unavoidable. Added to this suffering were the frightful beatings inflicted by the Japanese soldiers upon their prisoners to make them work. Bill, for example, was made to stand out in the blazing sun (in an episode reminiscent of the events in the film *Bridge over the River Kwai*) just for taking a bar of soap. Often, incidents arose over misunderstandings of language, or over small insubordinations such as a prisoner's failure to salute a soldier in Japanese uniform.

Christmas 1942 was the men's first in captivity. At this stage, the track had not advanced very far and the difficulties of the engineering task remained daunting. Almost invariably, the track had to be laid down on an embankment, cut along the side of a mountain, or across or through solid rock. The primitive tools they were given to use, manufactured locally, made little impression. The most irksome job was to break rock into pieces in order to make ballast for the track. This itself, for the near part of the route, had been ripped up and brought from Malaya. As the war continued and the Allies grew in strength, the Japanese became more anxious to make fast progress and drove their prisoners ever harder.

In India, the monsoon of 1942 had given the British sufficient time to construct new airfields in Assam and to deploy and prepare fresh squadrons. Although they were not yet numerous enough to take command of the airspace, British forces were conducting raids from Calcutta on railways and air bases in Burma from September and October onwards. The Americans made a series of persistently heavy bombing attacks on Rangoon, which seriously retarded Japanese preparations for combat.

In September, General Wavell ordered Lieutenant General Irwin, the commander of the Eastern Army (with ground forces based in Assam, Bengal, Bihar and Orissa, and headquarters in Calcutta) – to secure the Bay of Bengal. The aim was to reoccupy upper Arakan and to capture Akyab Island, which had a valuable airfield. If successful, this would put the Allied air forces within easier striking distance of Rangoon and at the same time, as John Connell has pointed out, 'deprive the Japanese of an advanced refuelling base for raids on Calcutta, the focal point of all communications to the North-East Frontier and the heart of the only great industrial area in the whole of India'.[88]

The Allies had planned an assault by sea to capture Akyab Island, but this did not materialise and the Japanese took the opportunity to seize the island instead. As a counter-measure, the 14th Indian Division was given the task of making an overland advance down the coast of North Arakan to try and retake the island. This division was the only one available, though it was under-trained and ill-equipped: it comprised two brigades in the Chittagong area reinforced by a third recently formed.

When Hector arrived in Eastern Bengal in late February of 1943, as the ordnance provider for the forward units on the Calcutta Front (the front from which the Arakan Campaign was being launched), things had begun to go very badly. Heavy rains in December meant a delayed start, and since then the troops had gone south, covering a difficult terrain – one almost entirely without roads – between the port of Chittagong and the base of the Mayu peninsula, just short of Akyab Island itself.

In spite of repeated attacks carried out by the Indian Infantry Brigade on Japanese positions, strong opposition from the Japanese had forced them, by March, into a fighting retreat. On 15th April, Major General William Slim assumed command of all forces south of Chittagong. In the middle of May, in a dispiriting defeat, the men withdrew to the line from which they had started five months earlier. Such an unsuccessful and limited assault, with great cost in terms of human life, further demoralised the spirits of those serving in the Indian Army.

Emergency directives and dispersals due to various military crises elsewhere in the British Empire had already weakened the army's strength. Yet Japan was feeling the pressure, too. The Japanese might have been in possession of Akyab Island, but India presented a growing menace and the Allies had re-established mastery in the air and at sea, in both the Indian and Pacific Ocean. By the end of 1942, more than 240 merchant ships belonging to the Japanese had been sunk, and for this aggressor nation there was now a new sense of urgency. The

Americans had also initiated a series of (sometimes risky) airlifts, transferring from India across the Himalayan foothills a steady flow of war equipment to Chiang Kai–Shek's army in China.

These pressures upon Japan had a direct impact on Bill and his comrades, working on the Thai-Burma railway route. In February 1943, just as Hector was arriving to serve the Calcutta Front, his brother-in-law heard the Japanese announce a new and much earlier target date for the completion of the railway. They wanted it finished by August, before the end of the monsoon, after which the Allies were sure to begin a wave of fresh attacks.

The force of 50,000 Allied prisoners who had until now been deployed along the pathway of the line was not numerous enough to complete the project by the revised deadline. In April and May, some 10,000 more men were selected from the 16,000 who remained at the camp in Changi, Singapore. These soldiers were dispatched by train to Ban Pong, the first transit camp, and forced to walk for 180 miles to a jungle destination deep in the interior of Thailand. These men carried out some of the line's most gruelling work, in the most challenging terrain, with dire consequences. At the same time, more than 250,000 Tamil, Chinese and Burmese coolies (labourers) were either cajoled or pressed into the labour force.

No one on the outside knew what was happening to these troops. The Allied forces had no information about how many prisoners were working in the camps along the railway, nor about their conditions. This phase became known as the Speedo period because the men were so grossly overworked. The level of sadistic beatings and punishments inflicted by the Japanese now rose sharply. Many sick and exhausted men were forced to go on working until they dropped: it was a desperate struggle for life. Some groups had to march as much as eight miles each day to their work sites, and longer working hours were enforced so that many didn't see their camp in daylight for up to 15 days at a stretch. Their oppressors provided no lights.

Bill was among those who suffered this ordeal. After the war, he spoke very little about his experiences in camps and terrain 'from Ban Pong to a point 150 kilometres further north', and declined to record his experiences or the details of his days of work, or to describe life in the camps. He did, however, mention that the men – and even the Japanese themselves – were driven by grave shortages of food to eat birds, monkeys, cats (which he called 'Changi rabbits'), lizards, snakes and any other kind of animal they could trap and cook. He also remembered finding numerous scorpions, centipedes and tarantula spiders. The other thing that became apparent was that throughout his time there, Bill was sustained by his deep and abiding trust in God. This fortitude was boldstered by the small cloth wallet, with religious medals attached, that his mother had made to house the small printed card with prayers and a notice that a Catholic priest should be called should a near death situation arise. Against all the the odds, he managed to keep, not only this safe and close to him, but also a few small treasured photos he had of the the family and one of a group of his army pals. Each of these had been veted by the Japanese authorities and stamped.

It is possible that by this stage, he had already become separated from the others in his battalion. A few members of the British Battalion had been left behind in camps along the way, and from the little Bill revealed of his experiences it was unclear whether he was among many of his battalion who eventually moved up the river to Takanun with headquarters at Tarso. The distance he spoke of above indicates that this was probable. The traditions and close ties of the regiment had been so fragmented by the numerous transitions and transfers that many of the men must have felt isolated, knowing that they were likely to face death, and all its harbingers, alone.

The Japanese had found the task of providing the prisoners with food to be increasingly onerous. They experienced numerous difficulties in administration, exacerbated by trying conditions, including insects, heat and rain. The floods and swamps created by the five-month monsoon – the second one endured by those who were first to arrive – made things even worse for the prisoners. Soon more men were in the grip of sickness and disease.

In May there was an outbreak of cholera, a hideous disease that attacks the bowels, causing them to empty painfully and uncontrollably, and through diarrhoea and loss of fluids and salts can lead to death. This disease spread rapidly south through the camps in Thailand, perhaps because some of the jungle streams in the north (from Burma) were already contaminated. It could also spread through infected food, flies and clothing, and was highly contagious. It ravaged the large camp of Chungkai.

Perhaps Bill's greatest sorrow during that final relentless summer was the death of his best pal Avroe James Wood, one of the remaining Leicestershires. 'Rosie' Wood ('because of his rosy complexion', according to Headley Evans, the best mate of Bill's and a fellow bandsman) died following a bout of amoebic dysentery. Like cholera, this disease – causing inflammation of the intestines, resulting in severe diarrhoea with blood and mucous – often led to death through a process of withering and wasting. Headley recalled the particular comradeship that existed between Bill (whose nickname was Jock) and his pal Rosie. 'They used to go on outings with all the rest of the band but they were always together and one could see the friendship between them,' said Headley. 'This I saw and know between 1937 and 1942.'

Headley and Bill made contact again, much later on, after both had come out of the war. After Bill died, Headley spoke of him as 'a jewel of a man'. He added: 'I valued his friendship very much. He was quiet, always willing to help, always in the background ready for anything. He was a man amongst men'. Headley had been lucky to escape from Singapore just as it was falling. After escaping death during that gruelling period, he committed himself to return to Thailand in later life in order to visit that infamous jungle railway and pay his respects to less fortunate comrades. At Kanchanaburi Allied War Cemetery, one of the two graveyards built by the Commonwealth War Graves Commission for prisoners of war, he took a photograph of Rosie's grave and sent a copy to Bill. The headstone read: '4857005 L Cpl AJ Wood, The Leicestershire Regt. 26th July 1943. Age 25.'

The Speedo period lasted for six months, and claimed the lives of thousands of men. In India, people were also dying at a rapid rate, but from a different cause: the terrible Bengal Famine of 1943, which brought starvation and a rash of epidemics. It seems that the food crisis had begun in 1942, with the spread of fears and rumours. There had been a shortfall in the crop of rice that year but nothing of great impact since there had been no serious failure of the monsoon. Normally, a below average harvest would have been supplemented with rice from elsewhere. In the case of Calcutta, it was Burma that provided a reserve, but because of the war its supply was cut off and the people knew it. With ships on the sea being lost and the bombing of Calcutta, there were fears of acute shortages. In this climate of uncertainty, it seemed a good thing to buy rice. Those who could afford it, and there were many, began to buy earlier and this increasing demand caused prices to rise.

As more rushed to buy, what little grain there was in the markets of Bengal became unattainable for others such as the casual labourers who bought day by day, and the landless village labourers who flocked to the towns. Industrial workers, on the other hand, had grain supplied to them by their factories and many were both protected and fed by their employers. In the last months of 1942 and the first half of 1943, Indian newspapers carried shocking photographs of some of the victims lying in the streets of Calcutta, dying of hunger for all to see. It was an urban famine.

Rationing may have provided a solution, since there was almost certainly enough in the province to go round. However, distribution at that time was not as efficient as usual due to the fact that boats and wheeled vehicles had been removed from the coastal areas in case of a Japanese invasion. Transport had been disrupted as a result of the primary needs of the war effort. Above all, the catastrophe resulted from the government of India's inability to break down regional barriers in order to free movement of food, and to organise distribution efficiently and fairly.

In Mymensingh, Hector was living in a basha hut constructed with bamboo lathes over a hardened mud (or cement) floor, with a roof made of fronds. It got rather damp in the monsoon season, though inside it was cool. The Arakan campaign was in its most advanced stages, and he remembered going 'down along the coast towards Burma, then to Comilla, and further down to the advance ordnance depot at Chittagong, at the southern limit of the metre-gauge railway which ran northwards through Eastern Bengal and Assam. We stayed there for a while, living under canvas in the heavy rains. They were terrible conditions. The Japanese were approaching'.

He shared his hut with another officer who died of cholera while they were there together. It must have been an unnerving and unpleasant experience, though there is some evidence Hector was vaccinated against this highly contagious disease. There were other problems to contend with, too. Mymensingh was part of the Meghna Depression, an unstable area of the great Ganges delta plain, which was exposed to floods for weeks or months during the wet monsoon season. Fortunately, Hector had a good sense of humour and later related how he would sit on the commode and watch fish as they swam in the water all around him!

The floods that swept across the delta during this monsoon season of 1943 – in part a cause of the Bengal famine that killed well over one million and perhaps two million people – washed away roads and railways to the northwest of Calcutta, further exacerbating the situation by hampering relief efforts for the famine. The floods also brought chaos to military operations, delaying construction works vital to Wavell's plans for a full-scale offensive across the Assam frontier and the Bay of Bengal. Added to this frustration was the fact that the deteriorating European situation had led, since December 1942, to a sharp fall in the delivery of army stores from Britain and America. Within India itself, political unrest was increasing all the time.

The British prime minister, Winston Churchill, voiced his concern about what was happening. In particular, he was worried by the poor outcomes from a series of limited and under-manned offensives. There had been one notable success in March, when Orde C Wingate's 77th Indian Infantry Brigade (a newly formed special long-range penetration force of British and Gurkha troops known as The Chindits) set out from Imphal in Assam and managed to get behind enemy lines beyond the Chindwin; this had harassed the Japanese and raised the morale of British troops. On the whole, though, Churchill knew that while Britain's own land forces serving in India had increased substantially over the past two years, there was still a shortage of trained troops and modern equipment, and he feared the men could grow demoralised.

In order to try to close down the threat to India and to regain territories and protectorates in Burma, Malaya and elsewhere, he liaised with others to make changes at the top. In June 1943, Wavell (now a field marshal) became Linlithgow's successor as viceroy of India. General Sir Claude Auchinleck was appointed Commander-in-Chief, India, and it was announced that a new South East Asia Command (SEAC) would relieve India Command of responsibility for operations against the Japanese in Burma, Thailand, Malaya and Sumatra, as well as for the defence of Ceylon and the North-East Frontier of India.

The Allies agreed that the new SEAC should come under the control of a British Supreme Allied Commander, and Lord Mountbatten was selected for the job. He was the great-grandson of Queen Victoria and an acting vice admiral, and would be assisted by an American deputy and an integrated staff of British and American officers. This change meant that, although India Command still had to train and supply the majority of fighting troops in South East Asia (as well as providing administration for those Indian units serving overseas), it was free to get on with the job of transforming its army into a first-rate organisation. It also had spare capacity to deal with issues of internal security and the defence of the North-West Frontier of the country.

Exactly a month after the formation of SEAC on 24th August 1943, the Thai-Burma railway met in the middle, joined from north to south. In an incredible feat of engineering – albeit one the long-suffering POWs could take no pride in – the Japanese had come near to meeting the deadline. Japan could now send its troops and stores by train to Burma, and on towards India. The cost in human life had been massive, though no one in the outside world knew about the suffering incurred. Over 100,000 men had died building this railway. Some 16,000 Allied servicemen were among the victims, but the biggest cost was in Asian lives. Tens of thousands of leaderless labourers, deprived of basic human dignity and kept in camps isolated from the British and Japanese, died as they worked on the railway. In many ways, their conditions were even more terrible than for others.

In Calcutta and Shillong, Hester, Mary and Clare begged God for Bill's life. They knew he had gone missing in Malaya and did not know whether he would ever return, though they knew nothing of his hardships over the past two years. Closer to home, there was some cause for cheer. Hector had at last got rid of his parasite; one that had sapped his strength viciously for more than a year. However, it had been a long process. His hospital memorandum reveals that in May 1943 he was 'treated for tapeworm in Unit lines Mymensingh by Unit Doctor' and his record reads:

Admitted CMH Mymensingh 29.8.43. Tapeworm. No treatment
Discharged ditto ditto 2.9.43. Ditto. Ditto.
Admitted Welsh Mission Hospital [Shillong] 11.9.43. Tapeworm
Discharged Welsh Mission Hospital [Shillong] 18.9.43. Tapeworm

The pork tapeworm was sometimes called the armed tapeworm – for a good reason. Its head has a ring of hooks as well as four suckers with which to attach itself to the wall of the intestine. If, after treatment for expulsion, the head is left behind, the worm will grow again. Even more gruesome is the fact that the patient will often have not just one but several worms. Hector had lost weight, a symptom of this affliction. Regrettably, the Epsom Salts he was taking would have done nothing other than to promote weight loss.

In September 1943, when Hector had been back with his family for a short break, he went along to the Welsh Mission Hospital in Shillong. (This was a hospital where Peter, during the first family stay in Shillong, had had his tonsils and adenoids out – a normal practice in those days – and had been circumcised at the same time. He would have been eight or nine.) Hector himself was admitted to the hospital the following morning, but did not let on that he was a soldier. When they found out this fact the next day, the staff were furious: this was a civil hospital and, as such, not for military personnel. However, despite telling him he should not have come, they could hardly throw him out, as he had already started treatment to remove the tapeworm.

This time, he was forbidden food for several days. The only thing he took in orally, except for water, was a substance that would prove poisonous to the tapeworm. The aim was to release the grip of its mouth on the lining of Hector's intestine, and the treatment worked – much to his relief. Finally, the doctor brought in a tray and showed him various curled sections of the evacuated worm, including (under a magnifying glass) the head. This vital part, as Hector later told his daughter Barbara, was tiny, about the same size as a link in the fine silver chain she was wearing.

The Perks family was in Shillong for nine months while Hector was based at Mymensingh. One night, at Our Home, the children woke up suddenly. It was five minutes past midnight, and a terrific earthquake was taking place. At the time, officers were billeted on the first floor of the house, and came charging down the stairs and out of the door. 'I was terrified,' remembered Clare, 'but the first thing I had to do was to get my children out'. Only later did she realise how rudely the soldiers had abandoned her; they came back much later, when the earthquake had ended and the ground had settled, to ask whether she was all right. 'Talk about women and children first,' she would say, 'but no, for in this case, it was everyone for themselves and God for us all!' Shillong was in an earthquake district, but the tremors of this particular quake were felt as far away as Mymensingh, where Hector was playing cards at the time.

The children all had their own reminiscences of their times in Shillong. Pat remembered the 'delicious' large rose bed and the path that led around it, along which she would trudge while beating cream, skimmed from scalded milk, to make butter. One of her saddest memories concerns her adopted dog Lady, a collie-cross who was probably left at the house by the people who occupied it before her family. When Lady gave birth to a litter of pups, Peter was instructed by his father Hector to drown them. Years later he expressed dismay about the instruction. Sometimes the children passed by that spacious family bungalow with its classic façade in which they had first lived in Shillong – No 8 Cantonments. It was here that Hester and Frank, and the children's grandmother Mary, had all come to visit. This, too, was where Peter's truancy had been discovered; where the servants had fallen out, and the khansama had been sacked; and where Pat had admired the mali's pig-tail as he tended the garden, and little Barbara had plucked love-tokens from the grounds to take in to her mother.

This, their former home, was also part occupied by soldiers, one of whom returned late at night and noticed the bright flickering light of flames coming from a room occupied by Mrs Jackson and her children. This woman's husband was in the Royal Army Ordnance Corps and was away serving in the Middle East. Fortunately, the soldier reached the room in time and rescued the children in their pyjamas, though the bungalow itself burned to the ground. While Mrs

Jackson was not a special friend of Clare's (in fact, Pat positively disliked her daughter, Joy), she came and begged for refuge: she had already packed up in readiness to leave for England, and now she had lost everything. Clare agreed, others rallied around to provide clothes, and about ten days later, the family went on its way.

Clare and Hector and the children were very sad to see the remains of their old home in such a sorry state. However, soon it was time for them to leave, too. They would not return to Shillong and the ayah, Matilda, wept torrents as she said goodbye to baby Mary, her number one charge. Family members later reflected that it would have been nice, during one of their stays in Shillong, to have visited nearby Cherrapunji, the place where the world's greatest rainfall was recorded.

They were leaving Shillong, the celebrated Khasi hill station, for the last time. In contrast to their last journey to Calcutta, when they had taken a tortuous route to avoid the chaos arising from the Burma evacuation, this time the trip was more straightforward. Avoiding the watery plains of Eastern Bengal, they descended by bus to Gauhati and thence westwards by train down the valley of the Brahmaputra, that mighty river cutting through the length of Assam. Then they turned southwards to the sea. More than a day later, they reached Calcutta – having left exotic Assam far behind.

The family was surprised to find that a new bridge, wide enough for eight lanes, had just been erected at Howrah (the main approach to Calcutta from the west), replacing the pontoon bridge and providing Allied troops with better access to the Burmese front. It was a huge cantilever bridge spanning the river, and was, at the time, the largest of its kind in the world. To the children, crossing it was quite an event. Barbara remembered 'its web of steel girders, not unlike those in a child's Meccano set'. These rose almost 100m from the ground and she remembered them 'resounding loudly' under the very heavy load of slow-moving two-way streams of jostling pedestrians and the clanking axles of tongas, rickshaws, trucks and lumbering ox-carts 'grinding past each other'.

Out in the world of war, the city ordnance depot at Fort William was growing rapidly to cope with the heavy supply of equipment to forces in frontier regions of Assam and Bengal. The children themselves, having left behind the relative safety of Shillong, were growing more aware of the catastrophe that had been unfolding in India and in the east over the past three years. On a different level, on arrival at Hester's house on Mominpore Road, Barbara noticed for the first time the wondrous display cabinet assembled by her Uncle Frank, full of amazing model soldiers and a cannon on wheels. This, however, fired nothing more fearsome than matchsticks.

NINETEEN

A FORTRESS CITY

By the time the Perks family moved back to Agra, their friends Beatrice and Harry Fellingham had moved on. This time, the family would not be living in the majestic fort but at 100 Grand Parade Road. They arrived early one morning, and had to wait at the cantonment station for some time until their new house was vacated later in the day. During these hours, the older children – Patsy (now also answering to the name Pat), Margaret and Peter – were 'farmed out' to the Blairs, another army couple whom Hector and Clare knew from Shillong and who were Scottish.

100 Grand Parade Road was an army property in the British cantonment to the south of the city where, during the Mutiny, there had been violent skirmishes. With its wide avenues and elegant bungalows set in gardens or 'compounds' and shaded by verandas, the spacious and stately cantonment was typical of those that the British, at the height of their influence in India at the end of the 18th century, had laid out around the edges of the main cities. Agra cantonment was a self-sufficient community, with its own post office, lending library, churches, club

THE BUNGALOW, Nº 100 GRAND PARADE ROAD, IN THE CANTONMENT AREA SOUTH OF THE CITY AND SITUATED ON IT'S OWN SMALL HILLOCK.

Site Plan

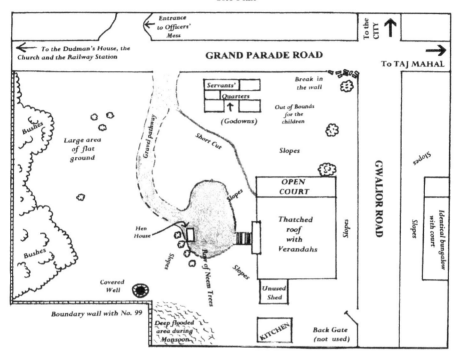

Floor Plan

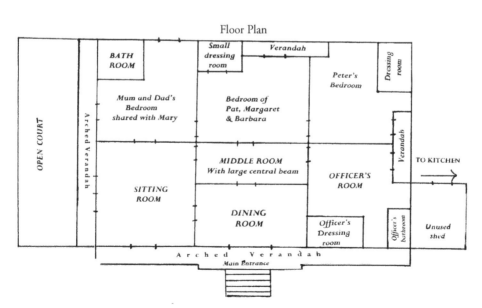

and whist parties. This meant those who lived there could easily cut themselves off from local life and doggedly create their own evocation of 'home'.

Perched on the crest of a hillock, 100 Grand Parade Road was a grand white stuccoed brick bungalow with a thatched roof. The thick outer walls of the veranda provided solid protection against the elements. Like other such bungalows, it was set within its own large compound inside a low wall that encompassed both the house and the servants' quarters. At the lower fringes of the compound, this wall separated the bungalow on two sides from crossroads, where a road running from east to west, Grand Parade Road, intersected with the Gwalior Road, running north into the city of Agra. Across the Gwalior Road at the corner was an identical bungalow, also elevated slightly on a hillock. Here Hector and Clare's kilted Scottish neighbour played his bagpipes and could be seen stepping up and down in time to the music in his little outdoor 'court'. The children liked to watch, but if he was playing out of sight they were content to hear the pipes.

Contrary to convention, the front of the bungalow did not face either the Grand Parade Road or the Gwalior Road. Indeed, it had been built side-on, which offered the family some privacy in their comings and goings. At the front, outside the dining room, the long veranda gave onto a staircase that descended to a flat gravelled area. From here, the main path curved gently downwards as the land dropped away to the left and right. Close to the entrance of the grounds (on Grand Parade Road), were one or two U-shaped outhouses – known as godowns – in which two of the family's servants lived with their own families, goats and chickens. The bungalow was well located: opposite the entrance, across the Grand Parade Road, was the officer's mess. On the side overlooking the mess, there was a sitting room and a veranda, as well as an open 'court' space where the family spent many hours outside. Two or three steps led off on the left, down a well-worn shortcut to the main path. The bungalow also contained an inner chamber, a windowless middle room above which ran a sturdy beam. This served as a perch, safely out of reach, for the green parrots (or, more precisely, rose-ringed parakeets) that Pat and Margaret periodically managed to lure from their natural surroundings and keep inside, at least until such time as their patience in trying to recapture them evaporated.

This room was an obvious storage place for all the empty cases, trunks and bedrolls that belonged to various family members, as well as for Hector's army camping gear and other paraphernalia. Over time, though, the nooks and crannies between these things became a perfect shelter for rats that had found their way in. Young Peter wielded a stout stick quite lethally, and would usually be able to get rid of them.

There was little time for the family to settle into their new home before the first in a series of new medical problems arose. First of all, Margaret developed an infection in her thumb. It rapidly became poisoned and led to a swelling under her arm, necessitating a lancing of the infection and a stay in hospital. Not long after, Peter, who was still only nine, caught a fever and was taken to the same Military Families' Hospital, where he was kept under observation for a whole month while being treated with a full course of quinine. (This treatment, used against malaria, was also helpful in dispersing the fevers Peter intermittently developed in his childhood. Clare remembered it was also 'a tonic' and was given to her in the last month of her pregnancies 'to boost the uterus'.) Meanwhile Clare herself had 'fallen' for a baby again, for the sixth time. Hector had arrived at the central ordnance depot in Agra on the 16th November 1943, where he was as fit as the next man. Despite the deprivations he had been through, he was rated in the A1 medical category just a week later. Nevertheless, for the time being, he remained rather lean.

From both the temporary and substantive promotions that Hector had secured, it would appear that he was well regarded. He had also gained much valuable experience supporting operational forces on the North-East Frontier and must have acquired a good appreciation of their needs. Given that the whole Indian Army was undergoing reorganisation to meet the challenge of the Japanese in South East Asia, the Ordnance Corps was required to reflect these changes by improving its own performance.

It is against this background that Hector's withdrawal from Eastern Bengal to what had become a major central ordnance depot in Agra, should perhaps be viewed. He was, no doubt, qualified to play a part in ensuring that new methods of working met the needs of the changing circumstances at the front and satisfied the demands of the new commanders who were being appointed to front line units. India was now functioning as the main base for the offensive against Japan in South East Asia. Since August, all ground forces east of Calcutta were directed in Delhi from the new HQ South East Asia Command (SEAC) rather than from General Headquarters, India. In December 1943, General William Slim had been given command of the newly-formed 14th Army comprising two-thirds Indian troops and including divisions in the Arakan and in the Imphal area (and the new Chindit force when it entered the operational area), and he had begun his second attempt that year to recover the Arakan region.

Although Auchinleck, the new commander-in-chief in India, no longer enjoyed operational control powers or field command (having ceded this to SEAC), he had great influence over administrative backup within India itself. His responsibility was to supply the needs of SEAC and he started by asking the British government to return Indian units in the Middle East to their home country, pointing out that India urgently needed their experience in order to train new divisions for the campaign in Burma. Although on paper the Indian Army comprised some two million men, in fact less than a quarter of this total was available for deployment on the North-West frontier and in Burma. During the cold weather season of 1943-1944, the Allies suspected that the Japanese were building their divisions in preparation for 'a major offensive aimed at capturing Imphal, and Kohima in Assam. They could then cut the railway supplying the whole central front, and [make] a breakthrough into Bengal'.[89]

The central ordnance depot at Agra was burdened by heavy receipts of supplies exacerbated by a lack of proper storage, but by the time Hector arrived there at the end of 1943, the situation was gradually improving. Ammunition holdings in the country were increasing at a rapid rate and he remembered having charge of more than five acres of stock. General stores and clothes were in the process of being transferred to a newly built depot at nearby Mathura and the following June, the Fatehpur Sikri sub-depot (with its stocks of motor transport vehicles) was handed over, appropriately, to the Indian Army Service Corps, which was responsible for mechanical vehicles. The sub-depot at Jhansi was also made separate. These measures ensured that, by the middle of 1944, the Agra depot could assume its intended role as the central ordnance depot for highly sophisticated electronic and scientific stores.

Having left the tranquil atmosphere of the Shillong hill station to come back and live in Agra for a second time, the Perks family was, once more, in the heart of chaotic India. Like Delhi, Agra was in north India on the upper Ganges plain, part of the Plain of Hindustan, the lowland east of the Punjab as far as the state of Bihar. As with Calcutta, this was a city where the great majority of people lived at subsistence level. Every day the children saw people who were overwhelmingly poor, hungry and illiterate, sitting here, there and everywhere in the heat, the dust and the dirt. Young children like themselves had sore eyes and skin ailments, and were plagued by pestilent flies. All of the Perks children were well aware of the hardships suffered by the aged, the blind, the crippled, the palsied and the diseased.

They were beginning to understand, albeit at a simple level, that fatalism and indifference were part of the Indian way of life. It may be unfashionable these days to generalise about a particular race, but – because of life circumstances – the main trait that characterised this type of Indian was inertia: a lack of enthusiasm, vigour, stamina and commitment. To look at it in another way, most people did not complain about their underprivileged condition because they lived under the powerful philosophy of Hinduism. This was far more than a mere religion: it was a complete rule of life, noble but for certain primitive social customs (including child marriage, the caste system and the concept of untouchability).

The caste system, which condemned tens of millions of people to perpetual social immobility, was the frame of Hindu society. It defined four divisions (themselves subdivided) headed by the Brahmans, or 'earthly gods'. Beneath them were the Kshattryas ('fighting men'); and lower still, the Vaisyas ('cultivators'). The bottom division was the Sudra, a caste of people born solely to be servants of the other three.

A person's caste was the outward sign of the history of his soul. Outside the system and far beneath the other four caste divisions were the Untouchables, whose disgrace was signalled by this description. They lived under the scorn of everyone else, a condemnation supposedly earned by the sins of former existences, meaning that Untouchables were fated to grovel forever. Fellow Indians regarded these people as sub-human and reserved for them the most unpleasant of tasks. Others knew deeper misery because they were not permitted to work at all; all they could do was beg. In desperation, some Untouchables would even maim or blind their own children to incur sympathy and get money.

Beggars were a ubiquitous feature of India at that time and Agra had its share. The orthodox Hindu rule relating to Untouchables as late as 1926 stated that, when they begged, they should not use the road but stand far off, unseen, and cry out for alms from passers-by. Despite this, they tended to congregate, where permitted, at particular vantage points – in city centres, and outside churches, railway stations and other places where more fortunate people such as the British (and those of the fortunate who were charitable) might take pity on them.

Some beggars came into the cantonment where the Perks family was living, crying plaintively for a few pice (the smallest Indian monetary unit). To passers-by, they would point to their mouths and stomachs to demonstrate hunger, calling 'bucksheesh, bucksheesh' – a slang word for 'tip'. The children liked to run and give money to one beggar in particular, a man who came along the Gwalior Road beneath the bungalow and was so deformed that he could only

100 Grand Parade Road, home to the Perks family between 1943 and 1947. (Note the presence of Barbara, Hector's bicycle and the salamander hot water heater).

shuffle along on his buttocks.

Daily activity out-and-about in Agra was a chaotic conglomeration of pedestrians, handcarts, bullock-carts, donkeys, camels and wandering pariah-dogs, and various horse-drawn vehicles providing transport in varying degrees of comfort. There were undoubtedly those for whom life was not so demoralising or abject. The merchants at Agra's fine bazars (shopkeeping everywhere in India was a major occupation) as well as the snake charmers, monkey-wallahs and other touters were all proof and a constant reminder that it was possible to rise above life's difficulties. They were living evidence that amid the poverty, it was possible to ignore the squalor and develop a spirit that could rise above it. In some individuals it was even possible to sense a personal discipline at work, a determination to make the best of one's god-appointed destiny.

Despite such large-scale suffering, India was a beautiful country to those with eyes to see it that way. Pat and Margaret and Barbara, in particular, admired the more fortunate women, who looked so feminine in their saris and skirts: they were vibrant in their bright violets, lime greens and vibrant fuchsias, their hems sparkling with gold and silver threads, metal bracelets jangling about their wrists and ankles. These women rimmed their eyes with black pigment and wore a caste mark on the forehead, along with a jewel in the nose. Deftly, on their heads, they carried baskets or pots of water from the wells, and their calm, stately walk seemed to confirm to the children their eternal serenity – although the truth of it was that despite their grace, most Indian women worked hard, were subordinate to men and enjoyed few freedoms or luxuries.

In Agra, the family had new servants. Previously their khansama (cook) had also been the table servant, as was the case when Clare was a child. Here, however, and also for a short time in Shillong, they employed another servant, a bearer whose wife became the children's part-time ayah, because she was so conveniently situated at the godowns. Both husband and wife belonged to the Sudra caste, and it became a family affair when Hector and Clare took on their young son as a chocra (boy) to work alongside the khansama and the bearer by doing odd jobs and washing up. The bearer's job was to superintend the table and give notice when meals were ready, and this he did, especially when the children were outside playing, by banging a small gong. (The gong had been given to Clare by her mother since Hester – with whom Mary lived – had a gong of her own at 12/2 Mominpore Road. Mary had been given the gong by her great friend Minnie Talbot, a woman Clare had met in Calcutta, and whom she considered was 'aptly named', being 'just a slip of a thing'.) The bearer's other duties, previously done by the various cooks, were to look after the furniture and dust the rooms, although Clare herself made all the beds. In keeping with the usual garb of household servants in India, he dressed in white with a puggaree on top – the traditional Indian head-wrap.

Again in Agra, the Perks family had a mehtar, the lowest caste servant, who performed the most menial of tasks. The mehtars were the worst paid and they dressed in whatever attire they had. Ironically the word initially meant 'great personage' or 'prince', but this etymology had been long buried by the time Clare came to use it. To her, a mehtar was a sweeper, and that was that! Generally, these servants were known to be responsible, kindly, long-suffering and indispensable individuals and Clare remembers this teenage boy as being no different. He was responsive to the point of obsequiousness when she or indeed any other member of the Perks household bid him 'idhar aao' (come here) and 'jao' (go). To her, the mehtar was 'the most important servant of the lot'.

The mehtar shook out the carpets and swept the rooms, veranda and pathways, but his most important responsibility was the gussal khana (bathroom). Throughout the Raj, this room typically had simple but primitive facilities set on a slightly raised floor strip that bordered the sink area, where the family performed its ablutions. A drainage hole led through to the outside, and provided access to the house for occasional visits from unwelcome creatures. (Clare remembered how a snake once entered through such an aperture.)

The family was fortunate enough to have a water supply in the bathroom as well as one outside, despite the fact that Agra was plagued by a yearly drought. The supply was cut off during the day so, early every morning, a tin bath and other containers were filled to provide a reserve. Family members were thus able to indulge themselves by standing in the gussal khana to refresh and cool themselves with cold water. For safety's sake, water for drinking had to be boiled.

The mehtar would organise hot water for baths and ablutions with the use of the Salamander, a kind of water heater that Hector and Clare had used in most places they lived and kept outside as a rule. Here in Agra, it was kept close to a second cold-water tap on the flat piece of ground fronting the bungalow immediately below the staircase. The apparatus comprised a lower section for the hot charcoals and one above with a tap from which the mehtar drew hot water into empty kerosene oil tins and carried to the tin bath in the gussal khana.

(It was here, on the flat ground, that a hen house was erected for the chickens Hector acquired at some stage. Subsequent to this acquisition, he also brought in a smaller number of turkeys. It was the mehtar's job to clean out their pen as necessary, during the daytime, when the creatures were allowed to run around in the open.)

More crucially, it was the mehtar's job to be ever vigilant for the sound that told him it was time to empty the commode. Pat remembered later how she used to open the door of the bathroom and shout to the godowns 'gussal khana sapha kur doh'. This meant, literally, 'bathroom clean do it'. Perhaps a dozen times a day, the mehtar would come and put the pot into a covered basket, which he would take away to the open cesspit in the compound before returning it, cleansed, with a solution at the bottom (commonly creosol) ready for the next visit. Early each morning before dawn, an Untouchable (otherwise permitted only to scavenge or to beg) came round in a bullock cart to take this sewage away to septic tanks elsewhere.

Not everyone was Hindu in India, of course, though roughly three-quarters of the population, including tens of millions of Untouchables, were. The family's khansama in Agra was a Muslim, whom Clare remembered as 'a lovely old man – I would have trusted him with my life'. He was a devout believer, and didn't live in the godowns but was based further out near the Sadr Bazar.

'Our khansama was most religious and at five set times in the day, including sunrise and sunset, no matter what he was doing, he would put everything down, unroll his prayer mat and pray – bowing down towards Mecca,' remembered Clare. Like the other servants, he dressed in white and wore a turban, and sometimes he would lift little Mary Perks up in his arms and say 'khuda khatm gaa' meaning, in Urdu, 'God's will be done'. He was loyal beyond the call of duty, and slept on the veranda outside to keep guard over the family whenever Hector had to stay late at the depot or travel away from home, as when he went 23 miles to the Agra sub-depot at Fatehpur Sikri (probably in June 1944 when it was handed over to the Indian Army Service Corps). Like other servants, the khansama was keen to stay in employ for as long as possible.

Having been born in India, Clare was accustomed to its ways. However, she spoke vehemently against the behaviour of some British officers (particularly from the Royal Army Ordnance Corps) and their wives, who were posted to India for a tour of military duty. She hated the way these officers treated native people, calling them 'wogs' and using them 'like skivvies' or 'like dirt'. She felt that they were ignorant and unappreciative of the qualities of gentleness and courteousness to be found in many Indian people, and that they focused instead on the vulgarity of common Indian habits such as loudly clearing the throat, spitting, or blowing the nose with the fingers and flicking the product on the ground (ignoring the fact that it is possibly more disgusting to blow into a handkerchief and put it back into the pocket!).

The wives 'thought themselves a cut above everyone else' and wouldn't deign to speak to their servants except, in a limited way, to their cooks. Civilian and Indian Army wives like Clare, who had been brought up in the country, treated servants quite differently, handling them firmly, fairly, respectfully and with compassion. But she did, of course, have the advantage of understanding a fair amount of Hindustani, and could conduct conversations in this tongue about a variety of matters. Hector, though he fitted well enough into Indian ways, found the language more difficult, having learned it later in life 'by the book'.

For the servants here in Agra, the cooking and serving of food was made easier by the fact that a kitchen was installed, albeit inconspicuously, close at the side of the bungalow furthest from the adjoining roads. It was more usual for food to be prepared in the servants' quarters in the compounds. Clare consulted with her khansana each day and gave him orders for the purchases to be made for the following day's menu. He would set off early to the bazar to purchase vegetables, fruit and spices and the like, whereas he went to an establishment supervised by the army authorities for meat whenever Clare considered it necessary to supplement that which they regularly delivered. She would provide him with rupees and annas and check his purchases against the expenditure when he returned. Then she would dole out precisely what was needed for the day from her own store, kept under lock and key: this included bread, salt, sugar, rice and flour, which was usually ridden with weevils and had to be strained before use since 'there was nothing better', said Clare. The tea was invariably Orange Pekoe, a high quality tea made from the downy tips of the young buds of the tea plant.

Where appropriate she would weigh out ingredients in parts of a seer, a unit of measurement equalling two pounds that was commonly used and which her khansama understood. After that, what was left was returned to the store and and locked away. Despite her good relationships with some of the servants, Clare felt that no matter how scrupulously honest they were to her personally, they would commonly steal food or misrepresent costs in order to try to make a bit of profit from the excursion to the bazar. 'I think they all used to do it if they had the chance,' she remembered later. However, in Agra as elsewhere, she followed her rule of giving leftovers to the mehtar, along with discarded items such as woollen clothing for his children.

She also had the greatest respect for Indian cooking. Often the khansamas used Anglo-Indian recipes handed down by word of mouth from their fathers and grandfathers. The Perks family day-to-day menu would include chops, stews, curries and roasts as well as one particularly memorable dessert called mango fool. Pat later remembered some of the food prepared by the Muslim khansama using dechsies – handle-less saucepans placed over the holes of a primitive, rectangular, mud-brick stove fired by charcoal. 'Pretty well everywhere', she said, these were a standard cooking utensil.

The servants maintained a generally good standard of personal hygiene: Clare thought they were 'very clean, especially the women'. Though none of them shared the family's facilities, whenever they used the toilet they would always take a bowl of water with them. However, although Clare herself was careful to make regular inspections, the state of the bawarchi khana (kitchen) always left much to be desired.

'I'd go to the kitchen and find it filthy,' she remembered. 'The first thing I would do would be to rub my fingers around the dishes for grease and examine the utensils. The servants were not very fussy. You had to shut your eyes to a lot of things – you couldn't afford to be too particular or you'd have been on to them all the time, and then they might have left. But sometimes I would feel as though I had to give it all a good clean. On one occasion I disposed of a bowl full of chicken feet and when the khansama returned, he wanted to know where they had gone. He told me he used them for turning the pancakes and fritters!'

Whenever the khansama, bearer or mehtar had his day off each week, ('and they did if they wanted to', remembered Clare) she simply 'had to make do'. It was no easy task with a family of seven and another on the way, combined with the enervating weather. Finally, the family invested in a Rippingale Blue Flame Stove with three burners that worked on kerosene. Clare bought it especially for the days when the khansama was off or when he went sick. Even if he was there, she would use it to make cakes, scones or pastries, which – by her own admission – was not that often, but she would never allow the khansama himself to use it.

The climate of Agra brought problems of its own. In the sweltering heat of the plains, food went off in no time at all, although the family did have an icebox: a square, zinc-lined container with an outer chamber. The iceman was an Indian employed by the army who came around with a daily quota of ice, sold at a charge, which helped to preserve the meat supplied and delivered by the army. There was also a military dairy van that came with milk and butter. Clare had to pay a deposit on every milk bottle, a system she had been familiar with since

Ferozepore when she was first married. In the event of breakage, the cost of the bottle had to be paid in full.

As the Perks family passed the next couple of years in Agra, the older children were stretching their wings. Pat and Margaret enjoyed each other's company. Margaret was not yet twelve but, with the onset of menstruation, had already begun the journey towards young womanhood. She was developing at a faster pace than Pat, who was fourteen and who must have wanted so much to be like her sister, as well as those of her school friends now on that path. With each passing day, Pat must have hoped that her time would come.

Peter had Bruce Blair and his other school friends, and increasingly pursued boyish interests away from the predominantly female environment of a home with four sisters. Mary, the youngest, was growing in mischief, while Barbara – though fun-loving – was perhaps the most shy and pensive of the four, observing keenly all the features of Indian life going on around her. Since they were both still of pre-school age, Barbara and Mary had to play together when Pat and Margaret were not there on weekdays to amuse them or to mother them, which the older girls loved to do. In all cases, and at whatever time of the week, Clare, a devoted mother to them all, was around and at their beck and call.

TWENTY

PEACE AND WAR

1944 was the family's first full year in Agra. January and February in India were known as the cold weather season, although the level of coolness was relative to the rest of the year. This time of year was characterised by rather feeble high pressure over the northwest area of the subcontinent; consequently cool, dry, and generally light winds blew along the Ganges valley. Sheltered by the Himalayas from the cold winds that swept down from Siberia (particularly between October and the end of March), India was effectively insulated from severe winter cold. In fact, it was said that January temperatures were on a par with West European summer temperatures, although it could be significantly warmer in the southern subcontinent: most days were dry, and the sun shone from a nearly cloudless sky.

At night, the story was different and it could be positively chilly, particularly in parts of the Punjab. February saw a slight rise in temperatures, especially in the northwest, but the weather generally remained calm and pleasant. In Agra, the mornings and evenings were cool and fresh (50°F or 10°C) and the days were warm and sunny (65°F or 18°C). For as far back as Clare could remember, this was the time of year at which the viceroy, the commander-in-chief and their secretariats ensconced themselves at their headquarters at Delhi, near Agra and enjoyed a similar climate away from the Himalayan winter snows. This tradition, of which the Perren family was once a part, dated back to the 1860s.

With basically three seasons in India, there was no spring as such. The arrival of early March heralded the beginning of the hot weather season. Temperatures began to rise rapidly, well above 80°F (27°C), and this was the signal for habitual migrants (as so many British people were) to start moving back up to the cooler, very English hill-stations that they and their forebears had built: places such as Mussoorie, Naini Tal and Darjeeling. For the retinue of the government and for Clare herself, the most enchanting place had been Simla. Now, for the majority of government and military personnel and their wartime accoutrements, there was no more retreating to high altitude. The war had changed everything, and it was essential for the government of India to waste no time in elaborate rituals of moving location. Instead it must be on the spot and in touch with the developing situation.

In 1944 the Perks family had to remain in the plains, where Hector was based. As April and May approached, there was no escaping from Agra up to pleasant Shillong or to Simla. With an average daily temperature of around 104°F (40°C), these months together with June, were the hottest of the year and for some nine or ten weeks, as the sun blazed down, the air was very dry and everything became parched.

Like thousands of other British people, the five Perks children became accustomed to sleeping outside at night, on the side court, to avoid the stuffiness of the overheated bungalow. Lying there in the dark in the open air, though it was still hot, it was peaceful except for the occasional eerie howls of jackals. The children could look up at the stars through their mosquito nets before drifting slowly off to sleep; Clare remembered, once, seeing a total eclipse of the moon. Her thoughts on those nights, however, tended to focus on the trials and triumphs of the past day and perhaps on some of the problems she had overcome, coupled with her hopes for the future. She thought about her pregnancy and worried about her dear younger brother Bill and other members of her dispersed family, praying for all of them.

What Clare did not know, as she lay under the stars, was that her brother was now working deep in the jungles of Thailand in conditions that remained difficult and punishing. Later on, like everyone else, she learned about the horrors of the Death Railway and its completion after the dreadful Speedo period of September 1943, but for the time being she had to endure a disturbing absence of any news relevant to her brother.

In fact, the Japanese were already exploiting their new mode of transport to carry an increasing number of steam trains full of their troops, horses, guns and other supplies; and some prisoners were engaged in ongoing maintenance of the track. Working in the jungle of Thailand, Bill's health had deteriorated so markedly that in January 1944 he had been evacuated 'down river', conceivably by train from Takanun, to the base camp at Chungkai. The enormous prison camp was still there, together with a large 'hospital' facility, albeit one that could only offer very limited treatment. As Bill later recalled, he had become 'very ill'.

The men of Bill's No 6 Battalion at Takanun who were sent back down by rail to Chungkai at this time were each given a postcard 'for sending off' (as one prisoner vaguely recorded) and were instructed to give their address as 'No 2 POW Camp, Thailand': perhaps these were distributed by the Red Cross. An officer of Bill's battalion said later that he had been delighted to find alive in hospital at Chungkai a number of the battalion's men who had been evacuated down river from various camps.[90]

This apparent major relocation of prisoners to larger camps was the precursor to a major reorganisation by the Japanese and redeployment of their 'slave labour' force. By now, many of the men were wasted by disease and malnutrition, some beyond hope because of the harsh treatment meted out combined with the gruelling labour they had endured. The movements began early in 1944 and involved sending men to major camps at the southern end of the new railway line and also to Singapore. It was said that the Europeans were concentrated in greatest numbers within a series of large camps on the plains between Chungkai and Nakhon Pathom, a few miles east of Ban Pong.

A number of the fittest remaining Europeans, including a few from No 6 Battalion, were sent from Thailand by ship to work in mines in Japan itself – but many were to perish when these ships were sunk by Allied action during the voyage. However, because of the serious nature of his condition at this time, Bill, who had arrived at Chungkai in advance of his battalion, was soon admitted to another hospital. An entry in his soldier's service book reveals that between 2nd February and 2nd May, he was in the new Nong Pladuk POW hospital near Nakhon Pathom and not far from Bangkok.

It had been the idea of the Japanese, the occupiers of Thailand, to create 'a general base hospital' and the Nong Pladuk POW hospital – whose primitive nearest thing they could come up with. By the end of January 1944, hospital staff members of various nationalities (including a consultant surgeon from civil life and thirty-four doctors) had been despatched from all the other camps to open and run this hospital. It was intended to take in up to 5,000 patients (although it stretched to accommodate 8,000), including all the chronically sick and injured men from the various groups employed on the railway. Despite its shortcomings, including great shortages of appropriate hospital supplies, it was to achieve incredible results in treating many of the worst cases. Among the conditions from which Bill suffered upon his admission were a leg ulcer, oedema, malaria, anaemia and general debility, all of which were common among his comrades.

Tropical ulceration of the leg was a common scourge endured by prisoners in these conditions because their resistance had been so badly lowered. It was particularly insidious and spread steadily from the slightest wound or scratch – often from a sharp piece of bamboo – before it became a large, open, sloughing sore which ate deeply into the flesh until it exposed the bone. Drugs and dressings were in desperately short supply and, in efforts to avoid amputation of the limb, prisoners were forced to endure a frequent scraping away of the festering tissue. This was done with instruments improvised from spoons or scrap metal: it was a painful business.

Where possible, the wounds were covered to prevent bluebottles laying eggs in them, although sometimes the coverings failed to prevent incursion. There were instances in which prisoners were horrified to see maggots crawling about their leg ulcers. In some camps, however, 'maggot therapy' was said to have been used under medical supervision, apparently 'with great success'. Maggots would be planted deep into the ulcers to crawl about and eat the necrotic flesh and clean the wound. Invariably, when they had done their work, the fattened creatures were scraped out, or flushed out with a saline solution (possibly a brand known as Eusol), leaving sound tissue with a good blood supply. It was said that many legs were amputated where maggots were not used.

Bill had maggots in his ulcer but it was never clear whether they were there by accident or design. His lifelong friend, Gertie Bedwell, whom he had known from his childhood in Simla, later remembered him saying that his leg had started to heal after a doctor tried a new ointment. He was lucky not to suffer the same fate as a fellow patient who had travelled down river with him and who endured amputation and then, sadly, died.

Bill's service book records that he was in Nong Pladuk hospital for three months, but he later recalled that he 'was treated and looked after for six months or more'. By whom and where this happened is not known. While his sister Clare and her family were spending the hot and eventually wet months between May and August in Agra, had Bill perhaps been returned to the even more primitive hospital at Chungkai? If that were so, he might have had some convalescence and an opportunity to recover his health and some strength. He may also have been able to buy a variety of food sold there in what was described as a canteen. An exercise path ran within the one-and-a-quarter mile bamboo-fenced camp perimeter, for those who were able to use it. Whatever had happened to him, the fact is that he was eventually ordered back to work.

A letter from Mary Perren dated 24th March 1944 is the oldest of several surviving and treasured letters that Bill had received from his mother: it thanks him for his postcard, which she had received. His mother's letters were brief, as they had to be, but this is the only one that acknowledges any contact from him. Up until this point, none of the Perrens, including Clare, had known anything of Bill's ordeal since the fall of Singapore. Despite the hazy disquiet of the days that followed, the news – at long last – that he was still alive must have excited them all and instilled a lighter spirit and fresh hope. In May and June 1944, Mary wrote again to her son, assuring him they were all well, and thinking of and praying for him. She invoked God's blessings and safekeeping and encouraged him to keep up his spirits and his courage. As always, she sent everyone's fondest love.

Following his time in hospital and recuperation, Bill had been left with a massively deep scar on his savaged right leg, which ran from below his knee down to his foot. His estimated 'six months and more' of illness meant he would have suffered throughout the monsoon period. In his own words, he 'never properly recovered' from that ordeal of illness. However, his leg had healed enough for him to be 'moved on' as he put it later, rather vaguely, to another arduous labour project. At around this time, the Japanese took him and some others far away from Chungkai, separating him from many if not most of his British Battalion comrades. For these men, it was said, 'work was now not so hard, but deaths still continued'.[91]

Bill was sent to Ubon (Ubonrajthani), a province in the Korat Plateau, East Thailand, close to the border with French Indo-China. A town of the same name lay some 310 miles northeast of Bangkok on the railroad. From the base camp at Ubon, where he remained until Allied liberation, he and the others were forced to march into the jungle to begin work, constructing an aerodrome.

exactly having an easy time. Six months into her pregnancy, she was struck down with a particularly horrible complaint: amoebic dysentery. This she had no doubt contracted from eating raw fruit or vegetables that had been contaminated. At the Military Families Hospital, she received a course of injections over a number of days but was moved out of isolation and into the general ward so that her bed could be given to a British nurse from the Queen's Alexander's Royal Army Nursing Corps, who – as it happened – died soon after of poliomyelitis, having contracted it from a soldier she had nursed.

Clare was still feeling 'pretty bad' when the news came that her eldest daughter, Pat, who was almost fifteen, had broken her arm. It was now the school summer holidays, and the two eldest Perks girls had been left to fend for themselves and look after the younger children while their father was at work and their mother was recovering in hospital.

The accident happened in an empty godown, when Pat was attempting to stand on the shoulders of her friend Christine in order to locate a squirrel's nest, high in the wall where a brick was missing. These were no ordinary squirrels but five-striped palm squirrels, endearing and rather tame little animals with grey and white back stripes, who would frisk about on the ground or scamper in trees, gardens or houses. They could be quite bold: sometimes, when Clare had washed fruit and put it out to dry on a tray in readiness for making cakes, they would make off with it. Pat, however, had tamed a baby squirrel and considered it her own pet. In her bedroom, one of her favourite tricks was to give the creature a bit of cotton wool that it would carry off to one spot or another, and which it would shape into a hollow, then climb in. Now she was looking for another little squirrel for her friend.

As she was standing on Christine's shoulders, however, she fell, breaking her arm in two places – a compound fracture that ruptured the skin and made the arm bleed. Her friend rushed off on her bicycle to the hospital, bringing back with her a military ambulance, and eventually the limb was set in a plaster cast. Poor Pat had a terrible night of pain, and the following day her father Hector took her to have her arm reset. By this time, Clare had arrived home but there was no respite for Pat – only another sleepless night of agony (it emerged later that the doctors had set her arm too tightly). The next day, Hector took his eldest daughter all the way to Delhi from the nearby cantonment station, a journey of 122 miles north on the Great Indian Peninsular Railway. The pair of them stayed for about three days while the arm was reset twice more, and Pat finally got some relief.

The month of June in India, as in Thailand, heralded a season of rains and a reversal of wind conditions. The southwest monsoon dominated the climate as warm, moisture-laden air began to flow in from the Southern Indian Ocean. As this warm air reached the Indian landmass, it rose over exposed highland areas and then cooled quickly and rain burst upon the parched landscape. The rain arrived around the start of June in the extreme south and steadily swept north to cover the whole country by early July. As mid-June approached, the humidity felt in Agra added to the oppressiveness of the heat, but soon the skies darkened and became sullen and there was a great sense of expectancy as everyone waited for the monsoon to burst. Finally it arrived, with violent thunderstorms, torrential rainfall and the steady winds that were to persist for several weeks.

At the same time, shallow depressions moved westwards up the Ganges valley from the Bay of Bengal. The rains were heavy but usually they were intermittent, occurring in most areas of India between mid-June and mid-September. In Agra, for example, a whole year's supply of rain – 30 inches or so – came in just three summer months. Even though conditions remained close and hot (82°F or 28°C on average), the rain did at least help to lower the temperature. By the middle of September, the rains began to slacken off. Now the period of the 'retreating monsoon' began, lasting until December, and entailed the gradual replacement of moist maritime air from the southwest and the southeast by the dry continental air from the northwest.

Relief came too late for Clare. After several trying months, she gave birth to her fifth daughter at about 1am on 14th September. This little girl was born with defective nasal organs and other complications, possibly due to her mother's bout of dysentery in June. Owing to the baby's critical condition, Father Bonaventure the parish priest was called urgently to baptise her right away and he did so, giving her the names Marie Céline. She lived for fewer than four hours. Her tiny body was placed in a padded coffin and buried in a grave with a memorial stone in No 6, Plot 1 of the Roman Catholic section of the cantonment cemetery. (This cemetery was located on Grand Parade Road, past the family bungalow, on the right after the intersection with Gwalior Road.) Father Bonaventure recorded the little girl's birth in the register kept at the Church of St Patrick, in Agra cantonment.

Later in her life, Clare's daughter Barbara wondered why the name Marie Céline had been chosen for this child. She was intrigued to come across the same combination of French names in an old Indian newspaper that had been used to line one of the old trunks she inherited. The name came up again in another cutting, kept by Mary Perren, about the death by drowning in February 1946 of a seventeen-year-old named Patricia Marie Célene. The most likely explanation is that this was a daughter of someone she knew from her local church in Calcutta.

Then, in correspondence on another matter with a nun whose name was also Marie Céline, Barbara asked about where the name came from, and was told that Marie Céline was a sister of Marie Françoise Thérèse Martin of Lisieux, the Carmelite nun canonised by Pope Pius X1 in 1925. Sister Thérèse, also known as 'the Little Flower', wrote in her autobiography about this younger sister, who entered the same Carmelite Convent and to whom she was very close. After the death of St Thérèse, interest in her spread and in the 1930s and 1940s, the names of her family – including Marie Céline – became widely known.

While Clare sought to recover from her physical and emotional stresses and come to terms with the shock of losing the baby she had carried for nine months, the season of the life-giving monsoon rains had abated. In October the skies cleared and the sun shone, but the heat and humidity made this an unpleasant month to some extent. It was the time of year for tropical cyclones to brew up in the Bay of Bengal and hit the coast, notably that of the Ganges delta area, which Hector, Clare and the children together with their grandmother Mary Perren had crossed in 1942. November, however, was cooler and refreshing, and while most of India was practically rainless, the southeast parts of the peninsula received heavy rainfall.

On a wider political scale, 1944 had been a turning point in the Second World War. It was the year in which Japanese ascendancy was finally halted. As early as 7th January, Tokyo had authorised an attack on Imphal (India) to be carried out by Japan's 15th Army led by Lieutenant General Renya Mutagachi. The Japanese needed to stop British preparations in Assam for another offensive in Burma, though ultimately they aimed to conquer India itself. This ambition was bolstered by an alliance with Subhas Chandra Bose, a Bengali nationalist who had built the Indian National Army (INA) from Indian prisoners-of-war held by the Japanese. Not realising the Japanese intended to use his army simply as an initial thrust to exhaust British resources, Bose sided with the Axis Powers. Mutagachi, for his part, was convinced that once the Japanese entered India, the Indian people would rise against the British.

A week after Tokyo's authorisation, Lord Mountbatten approved the Allies' final plan for offensive operations against the Japanese in Burma, for which India was the main base. By the end of that month, General William Slim's 14th Army had successfully withstood a Japanese offensive in the Arakan that was designed to deflect British attention from the north. On 26th February, the Japanese ceased their attacks, providing British and Indian troops with their first major triumph in this region. Although the Japanese were still intent on invading India, the Allies now began to take offensive initiatives of their own.

The timing was fortunate. The Japanese launched their invasion of India on exactly the same date – March 6th – with their so-called March on Delhi. Advancing into northwest Burma, they moved through the jungle hills using their habitual tactic of envelopment, and succeeded in dislodging Allied forces from Tamu on the frontier line to Imphal. They surrounded the garrison at Kohima: a strategic point, since 30 miles further on was Dimapur, a big supply station on the metre-gauge railway and one of Slim's bases for his proposed offensive into Burma. The loss of Dimapur would undoubtedly have been a disaster. However, the Chindits disrupted the Japanese move and by the end of March managed to block enemy communications almost entirely, although their leader Orde Wingate was killed in an air crash in mountainous country near Imphal on the 24th March and did not live to see this first success or reap the fruits of the expedition.

Kohima was a hill-town in Assam, some 5,000ft above sea level in the Naga Hills, which was to become the location for one of the Second World War's most bitterly fought battles. The fighting was part of a larger Japanese offensive named U-go. Slim, foresightedly, realised Kohima would need to be reinforced, and he moved the 5th and 7th Indian divisions by air to the region as well as activating other troops to relieve the Kohima garrison and open the road to Imphal. By early April, the 161st Indian Brigade was creating defensive positions in and around the village. Together with the Assam Rifles and 1st Assam Regiment, they contained the Japanese advance. Slim's enemy counterpart was unaware that the British and Indian troops based in Assam were now properly trained, unlike their predecessors in 1942.

The Japanese were forced into a battle of attrition. During two weeks in April, the little hill-station was obliterated in a desperate battle that included fierce hand-to-hand combat in the garden of the deputy commissioner's bungalow and around the tennis court. Although some 60,000 British and Indian soldiers were based in the Imphal plain, in the event Kohima's Garrison Hill – together with a long wooded spur west of the village – was held by just one battalion, the 4th Royal West Kents. Other units were sent forward to provide support. Altogether, they withstood 13 days of siege and heavy fighting and managed to clear the

Japanese 31st division from the area and to open the Kohima-Imphal road from the middle of April until 22nd June. The climax came in May. By the end of June, Japan's invasion of India had collapsed.

On 11th July Japanese forces finally received the order to call off the offensive. By this time, many battered survivors had already retreated from the Assam front along jungle tracks, trying to reach and cross the Chindwin river. The monsoon conditions left them bedraggled and starving, and their army had sustained catastrophic losses. This was also the month in which the Allied nations received the first authentic accounts of the conditions of prisoners-of-war held in Burma and Thailand, given by Allied troops rescued when a Japanese prisoner ship transporting them in a convoy from Singapore to mainland Japan was captured by American submarines.

The information provided by these former prisoners caused the Allies to step up attacks on the Thai-Burma railway, which the Japanese was using to transport supplies to fight the British in Burma. From November 1944, after the monsoon had ended, the railway came under heavy bombardment, much to the terror of remaining Allied prisoners-of-war who were still repairing and maintaining the railway under the Japanese. Repeated poundings of vital bridges (including the big steel and concrete bridge over the Kwae Yai at Tamarkan) and other tactical targets had their effect.

Together with this and other problems – ships sunk at sea, problems within the Burmese domestic railway system, and the inadequacies of the new railway itself as a result of hasty construction and prisoner-of-war sabotage efforts – the line never achieved its objective. There were so many breakdowns, derailments and bridge faults along the 260 miles of makeshift track that, even when it was fully operational, only 600 tons of equipment per day could be transported towards the Burma front. The Japanese had hoped for 3,000 tons per day.

By the end of 1944, there was good reason to think that the danger of an invasion by the Japanese Burma Army had passed. Following a directive issued to Mountbatten by the chiefs of staff for the recapture of Burma, Slim's 14th Army – as a preliminary – moved forward to its new headquarters at Imphal, and by December had reached the Chindwin.

The clearance of Burma was set for 1945 and as the new year rolled in, the Allied advance in the Far East seemed more and more likely. Bill and others like him continued to labour right up until the Japanese surrender, but around the world many others were hoping that this, at long last, would be a better year – one that would finally bring some peace.

TWENTY-ONE

A TIME TO GROW

Back in Agra, the effects of the war seemed distant as the weeks drew on towards Christmas. The cool weather season was bracing and stimulating for the British in India (with the exception of those living in the Ganges Valley, where night fogs occurred) and the excitement reached its peak during the week after Christmas, when the New Year's Eve Ball at the European Club in Agra was the social event of the year. Clare attended the ball with Hector once or twice but didn't especially enjoy the experience, one reason being that it was 'where all the big knobs went'.

The club was a particularly British institution, and was to be found in all but the very smallest of stations in India. It was the social centre of every civil and military station, the so-called hub of society, but principally of senior civil and military officials. In fact Clare and Hector felt more at home in the mess, which had a congenial atmosphere, was exclusive to army officers and was situated just across the road from their bungalow. Although women were permitted to go there on guest nights only, they all enjoyed the company of the service friends

245

with whom they met up, and the regular social dances. These were often held outside and accompanied by music from recordings played on a gramophone.

For officers and NCOs, both married and single, the mess was the centre of regimental life. Presumably other ranks had to find their amusement where they could or remain in quarters or barracks. Certainly, the officer's mess was a place that Hector liked to be. All his life he was partial to good company and a few drinks, and the fact that the building was only across the road meant he spent more time in there than, perhaps, he should have done. For example, he was in the mess drinking until 10.30pm on the night before the birth of his daughter Marie Céline, a fact that grieved his wife for many years after the event. The fact that the mess had become his second home was a bone of contention between them and sometimes, irritated that he was not home, Clare would lock up and go to bed, though Hector devised a technique for entry through the front double-door entrance which involved twisting (beneath the lock) the lower end of one door inwards and the other door outwards, enabling him to squeeze between the two.

Another feature of the family bungalow was a room at the rear side that had an independent entrance door and veranda. It was sometimes agreed that officer colleagues who were friends of Hector could occupy this room when, for various reasons, a need arose. At one time, by coincidence, the family had a Captain Ken Perks (no relation) to stay, who developed a particular fondness for five-year-old Barbara, often choosing her as his little guest for tea. Clare remembered later how shy her daughter was of men as a child – but perhaps that was part of her appeal.

Each day, after a breakfast of porridge oats and sujee (semolina) or sagoo (sago) or rice cakes – 'round balls made from ground rice,' remembered Pat – the four oldest Perks children would pack their sandwiches and board the school bus to travel along the Muttra Road to St Patrick's School. There, in the north of the city, the girls' section (otherwise known as the Convent of Jesus and Mary) took British and Indian female boarders and day pupils.

Next door was the college which Peter attended. The two schools were separated by a high wall, which the boys would clamber up to show themselves off and take a good look at the girls. Later Pat remembered that as a teenager, she was indifferent to their attentions, especially after she and Margaret began to move in the same circles as young army officers. This school was where Barbara, the youngest of the four, learned by heart the nursery rhyme 'The House That Jack Built' from an illustrated book, and where the nuns gave the children lollipops on their birthdays.

Adjacent to the schools was the Catholic cathedral where the family had attended mass when they lived in Agra fort. (It is said the Christian mission here was founded in the sixteenth century in the time of Akbar and 'that it has long been celebrated for its school, where the children of soldiers and others are educated'.[92]) They used to take a regular Sunday door-to-door trip to the cathedral by tonga, including Hector when he wasn't working; sometimes the children would hold their breath as the horse's hooves slipped perilously over the cobbles at the entrance of the fort's mighty gate. The conveyance at that time was a standing order and subsequently at Grand Parade Road, to Barbara's great delight, her parents had the same arrangement to get to St Patrick's Church in the cantonment.

Latterly, however, the horse was a wretched animal that chose to halt and gibe as the tonga passed the stable – so much so that the driver was forced to hit it, usually in vain. Then he would climb down and drag the horse along by the bridle. But Barbara remembered it as a magical ride, sitting behind in the back-to-back seats, her feet perched on the wooden foot rest close to the dusty road, listening to the rhythmic trot of hooves and the jingling of the bells on the horse's harness, watching all and sundry fall away into the distance as the vehicle moved along the metalled roads. During the rainy season roads often flooded but the ride was exhilarating in the freshness of the frequent, often intense downpours when all underneath their feet and all around was awash.

The church was quite large and during mass, the space was organised so as to lessen the oppressive heat. A row of electric fans ran down the middle of the ceiling, and two long poles hung parallel, one on either side. These supported sails along their length and at the back of the building two punkah-wallahs were employed to pull cords attached to the poles, causing the sails to swing and convey a cooling breeze over the gathered worshippers. The congregation was mixed and included some service people, though it was mostly Indian or Anglo-Indian, and the services (including feast days) were the usual mix of Catholic homage.

After the service, the family would sometimes go further afield. Several army families would get together and borrow a large army truck to see one or other of the impressive Mughal sights dotted around Agra, for this was the city – more than any other – associated with the Mughal emperors. One of the most interesting places of all, 23 miles west by a dusty road, was the long-deserted city of Fatehpur Sikri, the creation of the great Emperor Akbar. On its completion in 1574, Akbar had moved his seat of government there from Agra. The city was nearly seven miles in circumference and was surrounded on three sides by a wall, and on the northwest side by a large artificial lake, now dry. Its buildings, cut and skilfully chiselled from the local red sandstone, were palatial and elegant.

Inside the city was a giant courtyard with a large and very beautiful mosque said to be a copy of that at Mecca. In the south wall was the Gate of Victory, which towered to an incredible height of 130ft. Outside this gate, a flight of steps led down to the surrounding ground, from which standpoint the imposing gate reached 172ft skywards. From the steps, the children could see for miles around, towards the villages of Sikri and Fatehpur and beyond to barren country. What captured Barbara's attention, though, was the spectacle of villagers – men and boys – launching themselves off the city walls and diving into the algae-covered water of the large sandstone well below, west of the steps. Some dived from heights of up to 80ft (doing so, of course, for money) while many onlookers watched and held their breath.

Fatehpur Sikri was perfectly preserved from the days of the great Mughal's court. In fact, it was something of a ghost town: in 1584, just ten years after its inauguration, this brilliant new city was abandoned because of a shortage of water, and the court returned to Agra. There, Akbar started building his tomb at Sikandra. Having ruled northern India for 49 years, he died in 1605 and was buried there, although he did not rest in peace because Jat villagers pillaged the tomb and burnt his bones. (The Jats were rebelling against the powerful Mughal empire, whose forces had conquered the area of their kingdom, near Gwalior, and eventually subdued the Jats themselves. Later, Jats established a reputation for being determined, sturdy and fierce fighters and were recruited by the British in large numbers into the army.)

Sikandra itself was another popular destination for a day trip. It was a five-mile drive from the cantonment along the main Muttra road running northeast from Agra, and on arrival, a broad road linked a beautiful marble-inlaid gateway to the main building. This, of course, was Akbar's mausoleum, situated at the centre of a 150-acre garden and enclosed by a high outer wall. Standing on a 320sq ft white marble platform, the structure had four tiers: the first three storeys of red sandstone, and the fourth of marble. This top floor was open to the sky, and held a cenotaph hewn out of a single block of faultless white marble, placed in exact position over the real tombstone in the crypt well below.

Inside, the mausoleum was dark and hushed, and it was possible to walk along the massive cloister running around the lowest storey, and then upwards to explore the arcades on each floor. In this way, the children and their parents could climb the narrow staircases until they came to the open terraces and the platform above, with its louring cenotaph. For the children of the families with whom the Perks mixed on those day trips, Sikandra was an exciting place. Barbara recalled how the older, daring ones among them, like Pat and Margaret, would climb up and stand on the platform at the top of the site gateway and take in the views, before climbing one or more of the four white minarets at each corner, each of them three storeys high.

Sometimes the families picnicked *en masse* in the garden enclosure, which may have reduced the risk of being pestered, either by any of the bold kite-hawks of India, always hovering in places and ready to suddenly swoop down and steal food from right out of the hand, or by the langur monkeys that could get vicious if they decided to take food. A favourite tactic was to hang about on the edge of the party trying to get lucky by waiting to be given a snack – then run off with it. These creatures were pale grey with black faces, hands and feet, and though they were slender in build, they were larger and more aggressive than their rhesus macaque cousins (whom they tended to intimidate). Like them, though, they were to be found in large troops in woods, ruins and even in towns.

Under construction at Dayal Bagh, some five miles out of Agra towards Delhi, was another important building, which ultimately one day would be a tall and beautiful temple. During their time in Agra, the family observed at close quarters the skill of the devotees of the Radha Swami religious sect (founded in 1861 with headquarters at Dayal Bagh), who worked intricate shapes into white marble, and lined the exquisitely carved pillars and panels with precious stones and mother-of-pearl. Incredibly, to this day, the temple has not yet been finished, though construction first started in 1902 and continues under the aegis of The Radha Swami Trust. It is said that when the temple is complete, one day in the 21st century, it may even rival the awesome splendour of the Taj Mahal which, by comparison, was built in just 22 years.

For Hector and Clare and their family, there were other excursions nearer at hand, such as Ram Bagh (The Garden of Leisure and Rest) about three miles up river from Agra on the opposite bank. It was the earliest Mughal garden in India, and the water gardens here were based on a rectangular system developed in Persia, and laid out in 1526 by the founder of the Mughal Empire, Babur. His great grandson Jahangir (Akbar's eldest son) continued the tradition of using it as a place of recreation, as did his wife Nur Jehan who eventually – because of her husband's addiction to alcohol – became the power behind the throne.

To make a day of it there, the Perks family would go down to the river bank and paddle in the abundant waters of the 300-yard wide Jumna, a tributary of the 'life-giving Mother Ganges'. Clare, however, was wary of it – in 1921, upstream in Delhi, her teenage brother Jackie had died of enteric fever after swimming in this very same river. However, for her children, the river held other interesting diversions. There were turtles, for instance, some very large, which would bask on the sunny riverbanks. The younger children loved to try to approach them, as stealthily as possible, but each time the turtle would somehow sense a human presence and would retreat, as hurriedly as a turtle could, into the water. Sometimes, though, the children would be delighted to sense one of these creatures passing closely in the water as they paddled.

A safer place to take a cooling dip was at the indoor swimming pool in Agra's fort, close to the barracks of the ordnance sub-depot (somewhere Hector had never actually worked). The pool was a new addition, built for the benefit of Agra's army officers and their families, and a place to enjoy the company of friends and indulge in some aquatic frolicking. Clare was content to watch the fun from the side of the pool, never having the courage to venture into water deeper than paddling depth in the shallows of the Jumna.

The fort was just two miles from Grand Parade Road and visitors could enter and explore the historical part through the southern Amar Singh Gate. As time went by, the Perks family got to know well the fort's numerous white marble palaces, courts, mosques (including the lovely Pearl Mosque), baths, gardens and pleasure pavilions, many of these constructed according to the architectural genius of the greatest Mughal builder, Shah Jahan. From its broad ramparts in the southeast, they could look out over the course of the river and this was usually the time for a break from exploring, when family members would take the weight off their feet and sit for a while on the top of the lofty ramparts to soak up the splendour of the surroundings – a balm to the spirit.

From here it was possible to see the Taj Mahal standing majestically against the blue sky. The same view could be obtained from the terrace of the Machichi Bhawan and along to the Palace of Akbar, and from the roof of the Mirror Palace. (This contained the bathing facilities of Shah Jahan's private palace and the dressing room of the harem, above which were the remains of reservoirs and water-ducts.) There was also a view from the octagonal tower in which Shah Jahan was imprisoned, by his son Aurangzeb, for the last seven years of his life; from here visitors could gaze across at the emperor's noblest creation just as he did himself, though in the end he was hampered by failing sight. The Perks children were used to this view, even blasé about it, because for several months, when they lived at the fort, they had looked out upon this wonder of the world from their rear veranda each morning.

The Taj Mahal was set rather more than a mile due east of the south end of the fort and stood 243ft high. No cost was spared to make it the most beautiful, alluring and irresistible monument the world had ever seen – an 'exquisite example of that system of inlaying with precious stones which became the great characteristic of the style of the Mughals after the death of Akbar'[93]. It was fashioned from white marble and red sandstone; silver and gold; carnelian and jasper; moonstone and jade; lapis lazuli and coral. Most importantly, and movingly, it was a labour of love from start to finish – built by Shah Jahan to commemorate his favourite wife Mumtaz-y-Mahal (Elect of the Palace) who died giving birth to their 14th child.

Like Sikandra, it was a holy place and a shrine of Islam, which meant that everyone had to remove their shoes and go barefoot or to put on special canvas over shoes before entering (over the years, the family did both). Inside, the mysterious smells of joss sticks wafted through the air. The bodies of Shah Jahan and his wife rested in a vault at ground level, beneath plain gravestones placed exactly in the centre of the Taj monument but not visible or accessible to the general visitor.

Above the basement room, visitors were admitted to an upper octagonal chamber where light percolated through the exquisite and finely cut marble screens. In this room, under the peak of the great central dome, 'false tombs' or cenotaphs were to be found placed directly above the burial vault below. They were much more ornate, and that of Mumtaz was inlaid with jewels and offset a little to one side – the only asymmetric feature in the building. The emperor's monument was slightly smaller but richly decorated.

The calm waters of the Jumna mirrored the perfect splendour of the Taj Mahal's form, rising on its huge marble terrace and surmounted by a magnificent dome. Its walls and recesses were delicately sculptured in low relief, the dome flanked by four tapering minarets, dark up through their stepped interiors (though this did not deter some of the Perks children from trying – and sometimes succeeding – to reach the summit). The watercourses along the walkways of the formal Persian garden also reflected the building, which stood at the north end. These gardens were where the family relaxed and admired the setting of their surroundings later in the day.

The Taj became a favourite place to visit. It was virtually on the doorstep, a simple tonga ride away and just as easy to get to by bicycle with friends, as Peter often did. By the time they left Agra, the family knew the Taj intimately in all its stunning moods, from the soft pink glow at dawn to the fiery tints reflected at sunset. At night, under a full moon, its pure white marble turned to shimmering silver, though the youngest members of the officers' mess crowd (Barbara and her younger sister Mary, for example) never got to see this in person, as they were left behind when others went on occasional organised night-picnics in the grounds. Peter, however, did glimpse the Taj in its moonlit glory together with his friend Bruce, when some American servicemen they had befriended at an American ammunition dump took them along.

Family and army life in Agra continued in this vein as 1944 drew to a close. With the new year about to begin, there was a perception that in Europe and elsewhere, the war was also coming to its conclusion. Meanwhile, it was reported that Clare's erstwhile home of Simla had experienced the heaviest February snows of the century with coverings of nearly 8ft. However, this was the end of the cold weather season and soon the temperature started to climb again. With heat building up across the plains, Agra was once more a hot place to be and this meant, from soon after the Easter holidays until the long summer break (as always), an alteration to the school hours: 7am to midday, with no school in the afternoons.

In their free time, the children (Pat and Margaret were now teenagers) were usually to be found somewhere in the open spaces of the grassy compound which sloped away from the bungalow crowning the hillock. In places, lower down and away from where Grand Parade Road met Gwalior Road, there was a dense growth of bushes. In their pursuit of adventure, Pat and Peter tried to cut a passage through the undergrowth. Despite their determination, demonstrated by their persistence and the long hours they spent at the task, the exercise was doomed from the beginning since they had nothing more effective at their disposal than one pair of scissors!

Nearby was a disused well with a fitted lid that the children would lift in order to throw stones down into it. It was situated quite close to the broad boundary wall, and another favourite activity was to climb this wall and walk along it, round the garden of a neighbouring Indian. No matter how much this Indian gentleman looked up at the children disapprovingly, and bade them come down in order to have words with him, they never did. (Later Pat realised that the reason he stood under the wall was to look up the girls' dresses.) There was never any sign of a wife or children and when he wasn't around, Pat and the older children occasionally raided the man's fruit trees, though it was more a feat of daring to alight on the ground than to pinch the blemished and under-sized plums.

Among the trees that dotted the compound and sketchily bordered a grassy bank near the flat gravelled area close to the bungalow, were the common neems of India. Since ancient times, the neem had been a celebrated medicinal tree. It was known as the 'village pharmacy' because of its outstanding qualities as a source of healing and revitilisation. In towns and villages, Indians used trimmed twigs of the neem to cleanse their teeth, as did Clare's servants and herself from time to time. (When there were no neem trees at hand, Indians had to resort to rubbing their teeth with their fingers – which they always appeared to be good at – and, if they were lucky, to then rinsing their mouths with water from the river or a well.)

A particular neem tree at the back was favoured as a night shelter by hundreds of noisy rose-ringed parakeets, all fighting for space while emitting a cycle of screeching crescendos. This green bird, a smaller variety of parrot with a long tail, was famed in Indian culture as a symbol of love. Other trees here and there offered relief from the heat of the day, and goats belonging to the servants also used the trees for shade. One overstepped its liberties by venturing further, into the house, and later in life Clare was always tickled to recall the sight of this goat's bemusement upon confronting its own reflection in a mirror!

Sometimes the teenage mehtar and a few of his friends (known as chocras) would play football with the children, but Peter had developed another love – kites. He became just as scheming as any Indian in his careful preparation of the lengthy moonga (twine) attached to the kite he had made. The idea was to bring down the kite of any opposing enthusiast who dared to launch one, and so to engage in a battle of the air. The way to do this was to make the moonga sharp, a result achieved by first boiling rice and then mixing it with glass crushed as finely as possible before coating the gluey substance onto the twine.

Under the devoted guardianship of Clare and Hector, the children passed long, tranquil days in India. In the warm sunshine, they revelled in the amount of space they had in which to play and in the freedom to wander and delight in the sights and sounds intrinsic to this exotic land. There was plenty to occupy them, not just the daily comings and goings of the bearer, khansama and mehtar (and their families) at the godowns, but also the activities of regular and not-so-regular callers. Anyone living in India in those days was familiar with these sorts of visitors.

The dhobi (washerman) made his weekly round to collect the family's dirty clothes to wash. From time to time, Clare employed a derzi (tailor) who, typically, brought and used his own manually operated sewing machine. Her machine was electrically powered although it did have a (as far as she was concerned) less favoured manual option. Generally, throughout her married days in India, she made curtains, pyjamas, knickers and muslin nappies but she preferred to employ the professional for particular tasks.

The derzi was capable of making up literally anything that was asked, and usually made the dresses. (With four girls in the family, however, there were a lot of hand-me-downs.) Typically, he would work all day squatting on his haunches, or would sit cross-legged on the veranda floor laying the fabric out and cutting it there. Patterns could be bought from a shop in Agra – Clare also remembered Weldons in Simla – but often, in common with his kind throughout India, he took inspiration from a picture in a magazine, or copied one garment from another, producing items at a very low cost.

Sometimes Clare needed to visit one of the bazars in order to buy things over and above those that were delivered by the army or purchased by the khansama. To visit the streets of India's bazars was to see Indian life in many of its facets. The bazars were alive with human activity, pungent smells and captivating sights, and were characterised by myriad colour and the huge variety of what was on offer: spices, Indian tea, exotic fruits, Indian sweets – less tempting because they were usually covered in flies – and other local foodstuffs.

There was usually an abundance of fine silks and cottons, jewellery, pottery and canework. Agra's market was renowned for its carpets, and particularly for its exquisite marble inlay work depicting, for example, images of the Taj Mahal which could also be found engraved on trinkets and cigarette boxes. Wooden carvings and brassware featured, as did beautiful handcrafted ivory pieces. Quality leatherwork included open sandals, called chapplis, which were favoured by Hector. Some merchants, hardly worthy of the description, presided over nothing more than a few spices, for example. Amid all of this or around the perimeter, it would not be unusual to see the odd stray animal – a cow or a dog (the latter known to the British as 'pariahs') – wandering aimlessly or looking for food. Sometimes there would be a camel with its owner.

In Agra there were two markets known to Clare. The Sadr Bazar was the preferred place to shop, while the city bazar lay beyond in the old part of the city. The former lay within the vicinity of the cantonment, an area known as 'town' and one that incorporated, among other things, the picture house. Unlike the city bazar, which was typical of a market place where much of the produce was displayed in rows of stalls, the Sadr Bazar seemed more fitting to the British system: it was made up, to a great extent, of small streets of little shops. Generally the Indians ran these, but among them was a 'Chinaman shoe shop', as it was called. The Chinese had quite a reputation in India as makers of good shoes to measure, though there was also a Bata shoe shop run by the company that had originated in Czecheslovakia. Pat later recalled a refreshment shop, selling ice cream and soft drinks. Nearby, too, was a shop that sold fabric for dresses, including gingham for school uniforms. Clare would buy this and have the dresses made up by the derzi, who performed the task to a high standard.

Sometimes Clare bought other fabric or shoes at the bazar, a place where prices were endlessly haggled over, with a seller asking for more than he expected, a buyer offering less than he was willing to pay. Of course, she spoke good Hindustani and became skilled at saying, in that language, 'That's too expensive. I'm going to another shop'. Even so, it was hard to beat the sellers down; understandably so when most of them were so poor that they could scarcely afford to reduce their margins. Poverty was very conspicuous in the bazars, and to go there was to be hounded by beggars. Pat recalled how she hated going into the city bazar, because she was petrified of catching leprosy from the lepers who hung around there.

The towels and sheets that the family bought in India, sometimes directly from the cotton mills, were the finest and most durable they ever had. In addition, over the years, Clare knitted dozens of garments for her family from wool including socks for her husband and matching sets of pleated skirts and jumpers in pink and blue for Pat and Margaret, when they lived up in Shillong. The quality of her work had been recognised by her former employer, Mrs Norman, when Clare had been a young nanny; she had written that Clare's hand-knitted jerseys were the best she had ever seen, and it was true that her ability with wool was quite remarkable. (Later in her life, Clare knitted for Pringles, one of Scotland's most famous houses, producing garments for the Aran hand-knitwear brand. This was a type with traditional patterns, involving in particular a raised cable stitch and large diamond designs.) She had picked up the love of wool from her mother Mary Perren, who also worked to order for a shop in Calcutta, as well as knitting for her friends. However, considering Clare's skills, the financial rewards were meagre.

It appears that Clare was prepared to shop in the bazars and other local outlets to a greater extent than other army wives who had been born in Britain.

According to her, many of these women chose to try to live as if they were in England, hardly venturing outside the cantonments and consequently failing to get to know anything of India and its people. But Clare felt she had the best of both worlds, having grown up in the country and being at home with its ways and customs despite her English ancestral background and marital status. While Clare may not have contemplated life away from India in her early years, as the years passed and the clamour for the independence of India increased, she, like many others, began to recognise that going 'home' was a more likely outcome than staying in the country of her birth. At the time, however, towards the end of the war, she may not have viewed it as an entirely welcome prospect.

In contrast to the embattled families in wartime Britain, she had few hardships in relation to feeding and clothing her family, or concerns over healthcare. The army provided a life of great security with the assurance that Hector would work until the moment of his anticipated retirement. Pay rises came as a matter of course as he rose in rank, and there was an added benefit of a generous family allowance, a sum that appeared on all his old pay chits.

If family members were sick, the charges for hospitalisation, catering and medical attention were low, freeing Clare and her family from the dreadful and frequent worry, endured by their counterparts in England, of how to raise a few shillings to pay for a visit from a 'panel' doctor in those days before a nationalised health service. Attention was paid to the dangers of smallpox and typhoid, and vaccinations were now administered as a matter of course. Even during the war, there were no serious cuts in food supplies and Clare could order as much meat for her family as she wanted. In addition, fresh and often exotic produce was available locally: papayas, mangos, lychees, custard apples and guavas. The only limitation was money, in terms of feeding and clothing a family of seven and paying the servants.

Another occasional caller to the bungalow was an itinerant waste-collector, the bikri- wallah, who came on foot to collect bottles, tins and newspapers, which families would save for him. Then there were the 'John Chinamen', so-called after a caricature drawn by Thomas Nast that was sympathetic to the Chinese. (John Chinaman represented, in Western society, the stereotypical Chinese man). These men were vendors who offered small wares for sale, including tusser silk – silk from Indian or Chinese silkworms – by the yard, as well as made-up garments, embroidered shawls and semi-precious stones. These were carried around in wicker baskets that were stacked one on top of the other and strapped together. Many of these callers struggled to make a living.

Possibly of greater nuisance value than the Johns were those who brought animals. These included snake charmers, monkey men and a bear man who turned up at the door at different times to give 'a show'. Each prompted the antics of their animals using noisy instruments: a gourd pipe in the case of the snake charmer; a tin rattle or hand drum in the case of the monkey man (who dressed up his performers, and would ask for 'bucksheesh').

Perhaps the saddest sight was that of the shaggy black sloth bear, an ugly creature with elongated mussel and lower lips, long and powerful claws and short legs. With his thick coat, even in the fierce heat of the summer he was regularly cajoled into 'dancing' and mock-fighting with his owner, the madari, a form of torment which drew much sympathy from Clare, who wished he was back in his natural habitat, deep in the forest.

Sometimes, the odd cow strayed into the compound and grazed on what it could find up the gentle rise. Hindus had a remarkable respect for all life, which extended to the smallest of the earth's creatures. Bulls, elephants, snakes, birds and monkeys were among the animals most popularly venerated in India, and although many were not especially well treated, they were at least protected from being slaughtered. (Apart from rats, which were among revered animals although they carried the plague, monkeys were the most commonly seen mammals in India.)

Unhealthy and unwanted cows ambled sleepily through towns and villages, mingling with the traffic. Frequently hungry, they roamed the countryside and foraged for what they could from the sparse natural vegetation of this upper Ganges plain. They did have one use, though: their dung was collected and dried into cakes to be used as fuel. Some of the bullocks fared worse. They were essential draft animals, many of them looking grossly underfed but forced to pull heavy carts and wagons of grain and cotton. By the end of the hot season, when every scrap of vegetation was burnt up, these creatures usually looked no more than tottering skeletons.

Overlooking the crossroads from their bungalow, the children loved to watch whatever passed in or out of Agra along the Gwalior Road. In fact, this road – running from Delhi to Bombay – was a long arm of the historic Grand Trunk Road, once described by Rudyard Kipling as a truly wonderful spectacle, 'such a river of life as nowhere else exists in the world'.[94] Like much of the long stretch he wrote of between Calcutta and Peshawar, the section from Agra up to Delhi was one of many roads made up by the East India Company in the final 30 years of its rule in India. (Before the British came, there were few good roads.)

From Agra, this great artery continued 70 miles south to Gwalior, an ancient and renowned stronghold with a 300ft fortress built into the rock, and with a history dating back through several dynasties: the Mahrattas, the Mughals, and the Tomars. Emperors, princes, maharajahs and great armies all passed this way and one record even tells of an army sent from Agra in 1516 to conquer Gwalior with 30,000 horses, as well as 300 elephants and other formations.

More than four centuries later, the traffic was somewhat less exciting. Along the road crawled bullock-carts hauling crops such as cotton, sugar cane or Indian corn (bhootas – a favourite food for the Perks children). Tongas and the like passed by, as did poor little overburdened donkeys, camels, old buses and bicycles. During the war years, the increased volume of motorised vehicles reminded everyone of the significant military presence in Agra. But along the side of the road came those on foot, too, from various poverty-stricken backgrounds. Some had chatties (earthen pots) and baskets skilfully balanced on their heads. Among the throng were some of the thousands upon thousands of people who wandered homeless throughout India, many toting small bundles that constituted the sum total of their worldly possessions.

The children particularly enjoyed watching festivals and fairs come into town. These marked events of regional significance, as well as rituals and traditions of the Hindu and Muslim faiths. The older children knew that all aspects of Hindu life, in particular, were regulated by ritual, even relatively simple activities such as rising in the morning, eating and praying. Death had rituals of its own, and every so often, they would see a human corpse being carried through the streets on a bier, its face exposed. Mourners were clothed in white, and along with drums and noisy instruments, they headed for the cremation fires at the Jumna ghats (similar to others along the course of the Ganges). This was something to which every good Hindu aspired: having one's ashes cast on holy waters was a way to ensure a happy future life.

In Agra as elsewhere, Diwali and Holi (festivals of light and colour) as well as Dussehra (the harvest festival) were more apparent in the city itself than on its outskirts. Nevertheless, colourful and lively processions passed by the bungalow at certain times of the year. Of these, one stood out. On this day, even before dawn, a great stream of pilgrims would begin to pass by on bullock carts, as well as on foot, carrying empty vessels to collect holy water and moving along the Gwalior Road as far as the eye could see. It seems that they were on their way to gather at the spot where the River Jumna meets the River Ganges, known as the Sangram, at Allahabad – an ancient and sacred site. Several days later, discord reigned as the pilgrims returned to Agra beating gongs, blowing horns, ringing small hand bells and chanting. As a young child in Agra, Barbara had no idea what this festival was about, but later in life she met an Indian who grew up in the city, and asked him for more details. He had the facts at his fingertips and agreed to write an account of the significance of it.

It emerged from his explanation that the Hindu festival, honouring the god Shiva, the destroyer and reproducer, was part of that of Kanwar Puga in the month of August. Although it was very popular throughout Uttar Pradesh (once the United Provinces), in Agra it was a very holy festival. Only males were allowed to get the holy water from the River Ganges. They went in a large group by vehicle or on foot. After collecting this water, the pilgrims had to return only on foot, carrying the water in a traditional pot called a kanwar. This was decorated with colourful cloth, or bells, streamers and balloons. The person carrying holy water in the kanwar was not allowed to sit down but if he wished to take a rest, he could give the kanwar to another person to carry on foot. Those carrying a kanwar by themselves could hang it on a tree in order to rest.

On the way back into Agra, all members of pilgrim groups would sing loudly 'for their enjoyment' – and no one could stop them, or even touch them, because of their perceived holiness in carrying out this task. It seemed the climax of this festival occurred on what they called the '2nd Monday of Sawan' (August) when the group, or groups, went to the four Shiva temples in various parts of Agra city to pour the holy water in the Kanwar over the Shiva Ling, the solid symbol or image representing fire. (The ling or Shiv Ling made the worship of Agni – otherwise known as Shiv or Shiva – possible anywhere, anytime, by using it in place of fire and pouring oblations over it.) Though the main events were over, the festival didn't end there but continued with a fair held at these four temple areas on the next four successive Mondays.

Five-year-old Barbara was intrigued and enraptured by these sights and sounds, though it was only later in life that she learned that there was a precise symbolic meaning to each of the formalised movements and gestures of the swaying girls (professional dancers were known as nautch-girls) who danced at the festivals. Ablaze with colour, the sight of these dancers endowed with rhythmic grace and epitomising femininity must have been quite thrilling. Years later, the sound of a traditional instrument could evoke powerful memories and emotions from her childhood, and the haunting beauty of vocal Indian music could bring back, in an instant, the excitement of those hot, sultry Agra days.

TWENTY-TWO

MEANWHILE IN ENGLAND...

Back in England, life had become severe. There were shortages on a wide scale and rationing was in force to provide fair shares for all. Ever since the German air raids that had showered explosives and incendiary bombs on towns and cities during the Blitz of 1940 and 1941, the country had suffered depression and gloom as a result of five years of nightly blackouts. (Auntie Em's shop in Plymouth had been destroyed in the blasts.)

In 1944 civilians bore the brunt of another assault, this one lasting some months, from flying bombs and rocket bombs projected from the European mainland. More than a thousand of these made it over the Channel, falling mainly in the London area. At Christmas that year, however, one fell short and landed on the Protestant church of St Mary, a mile from the village of Little Chart in rural Kent where Mary Perren had spent some of her childhood. The bomb so badly damaged the church that even the ruins – the pieces of wall and part of the tower – had to be abandoned.

In total, some 60,000 British civilians were killed by enemy action, and

Birmingham was one of the many war-torn cities to have suffered severely in the bombings of 1940/41. Both of Hector's parents – George and Elizabeth Perks (Lizzie or Annie, as she was known) – died during the war years, though neither as a result of these bombardments. Lizzie's death could not be attributed to natural causes, either, although their eldest son was reluctant to deliver the exact details of what he saw as a 'sordid story'.

Gus, when pressed, wrote to his niece Barbara: 'I am very reluctant to help you owing to the unsavoury story it would unfold, revealing the havoc affecting our young lives and the sad endings which befell them caused through excess drinking of alcohol. I am sure your father knows all the facts, he being younger than I, but perhaps he too is avoiding the issue.'

It is true that Hector had been living with his parents during the terrible times of the family's bankruptcy, and would have seen the way that alcohol took over his mother's life, and how it demeaned and discredited her. But having been away in India for more than 20 years, since 1921, it is difficult to see how he could have known much about the downward spiral of his parents' lives unless his older brother had filled him in. Of course, Hector himself had been in England on leave between October 1937 and September 1938 – and he had taken Gus's advice *not* to visit them then. It is not even certain that he saw his mother on his first return to his home country, years earlier. Like his visit to his father at that same time, it would probably only have been brief, if it occurred at all.

Clare knew even fewer of the facts, though Hector shared with her the news that his father George had died on 10th June 1942 at the age of 67. He had been living in Bracebridge Street, an address in the heart of the city of Birmingham that was 'a very small house in a very poor district' and had 'only a table and chairs'. This information came from Gladys, the second wife of Hector's younger brother Ralph, whom he was courting at the time. Gladys herself never met George, and only met her husband's mother for the first time at the funeral.

It appeared that George had recovered from the blow of bankruptcy to some degree, working since the end of the Great War for Roddis & Nourse, a firm of architectural and monumental sculptors based in Birmingham – although it is pitiful that on 15th June 1942, he was buried in a common grave in Quinton Cemetery, five or six miles west from the house in the Aston area of Birmingham. No stone or marble memorial of any kind was made to mark his resting place, though in his lifetime he had fashioned hundreds and perhaps thousands of such pieces for other people. Only grass covers the single-sized plot where he and nine others were laid to rest that year between 3rd June and 26th November, including a baby six days old and three stillborn children.

The registers at that time indicate that roughly one fifth of interments were in communal or public graves. This simply meant that, as no family member had purchased a grave, the local authorities retained ownership. Typically, it was dug deeper than a purchased grave space to provide for a number of interments. However, a service was performed for George at the time of his interment, and the grave itself lies in a consecrated Church of England section within the cemetery.

The marriage between Ralph and Gladys spanned more than 30 years, and in all this time Ralph's love for his father George was very evident to Gladys. But it was a different story when it came to his mother, Lizzie Perks. The youngest son's resentment towards his 'alcoholic mother' as 'the cause of all the trouble' was just as clear, though he spoke of her very little and Gladys concluded that her husband was probably trying to forget the hurt of that part of his life when he had been taken into care.

However bleak the old couple's life had been up until George's passing, it was clear that alcoholism had taken its toll and, after her loss, Lizzie had collapsed mentally. At some point in 1942 or 1943, she jumped into the Birmingham Canal in an attempt to take her own life, fracturing her leg. Shortly after, she was admitted to Highcroft Hall mental hospital in Erdington. Ralph and Gladys visited her until she was discharged to her home in Aston, where Gladys continued to visit her mother-in-law to take her the food and postal orders which Gus's wife Emily was sending from Plymouth. The visits were fairly awkward and short, however, and they talked little about the family.

With the war on, Gus was not able to get away but Emily 'struggled' to get up from Plymouth to Birmingham on one occasion while Lizzie was still in hospital. Not surprisingly, her husband's mother didn't know her at all when she finally arrived: they had only met a handful of times in the 1920s and there was no friendship between them.

Emily had never forgotten the first time she had met Lizzie, back in the days when she was still courting Gus, a Royal Marine. When on leave, he had made his home with his half-Uncle Jack and Aunt Hannah who lived in Court Road, Malvern, as Hector himself had done at times while he was working as a servant boy for the Fosters after he left school. Jack's house was opposite the Fountain Inn, on the corner of St Andrew's Road (near to where George had once had his own stone and marble works at the railway siding, just below where the lines converge, and where he had employed his half-brother Jack as a stonemason). At the same time, Emily was living at the inn with her aunt, and this had been where she had met Gus and, subsequently, his mother when she came in and introduced herself. According to Emily, she was unkempt, dirty and drunk and asked for a drink even though she was not old enough to serve her.

Later, years after they were married, Emily and Gus had seen Lizzie in Birmingham 'living in one room, very degraded in all ways'. Gus gave her the money to get them something to eat, but she didn't return so they went back to Malvern. It was apparent to Emily that the bankruptcy in 1913 and its repercussions had robbed her mother-in-law of all of her dignity, making her 'pretty grim, almost derelict, entirely irresponsible with regard to money and her personal appearance'.

In fact, the family kept Lizzie at a distance on purpose. 'Mrs Perks never came to Plymouth,' remembered Emily. 'One couldn't possibly allow her to know where one was as she would have got here and showed us all up. Even in Malvern, when Gus was on leave, she would follow him and call after him in the street. Maybe I was wrong, and Gus too, but we vowed she should never see our three children – her grandchildren.' It was an issue about which Stanley, the youngest of their three, grew very bitter in his later life; he was angry that his parents, feeling this way, had prevented him and his sisters from knowing their grandparents.

According to Hector, who reflected on these matters later in his life, his own grandfather Thomas had tired of his daughter's 'wayward' behaviour and after that had had very little time for her. Hector had heard (through his brother Gus) the details of his grandfather's will, which was proved in 1920 after his death. Knowing the destructive effects of his daughter Lizzie's addiction, Thomas had granted her a legacy in the 'sum of five pounds in the purchase of mourning' along with 'the sum of fifteen pounds' to be paid 'namely five pounds' initially, 'and the balance at the rate of four shillings per week until such legacy be exhausted'.

The clause applied only to Lizzie's legacy and prevented her from squandering the lot in one go, but it was a meagre amount compared with what he left to other relatives. Her mother was 'left very comfortably off' and some of Lizzie's own siblings even got houses and gardens. Thomas died a comparatively wealthy man, owning nine properties, six of which (1-6 St Peter's Cottages at Belmont Road, Malvern Link) were adjacent to each other. The eldest son, Tom, inherited his father's stonemasonry business. His brothers were already working for it, and Thomas hoped they would all continue in the firm for their mutual benefit.

It appears that they did and were doing so at the time Lizzie was widowed in 1942.

After her hospitalisation following the suicide attempt, Lizzie had returned to Aston. 'She ended her stay in Birmingham living on a bomb site in the city,' recalled Emily later. 'I know that is true because Joan, my daughter, was staying with Uncle Ralph for a day or so while she was evacuated to Malvern and he took her to see the old lady... terrible, I believe, and we were very annoyed with Ralph for taking Joan as she was at a very impressionable age.'

Not long after, the 'old lady' was taken back to Malvern by her brother Albert and installed at 5 St Peter's Cottages on Belmont Road. He himself lived at number 1, a property his father had left him, but number 5 was one of four houses (3-6) which Thomas Jones, in his will, had charged his trustees to sell by public auction or private contract. It is unclear how long she lived at that cottage, but it was to be her last home.

On Friday 19th November 1943, Lizzie went into the house of her sister-in-law Kate Jones, married to Albert, and said she felt 'worried to death' that she had to pay 16/- a week rent – and that she couldn't afford it. Kate told her this was 'rot' and that she would not have to pay 16/-, but Lizzie burst out crying and left the house.

Another married couple occupied rooms at 5 St Peter's Cottages, and the husband reported that he had seen Lizzie on Sunday night, when she seemed to be in good spirits. The next morning, as he left for work at 6.45am, he called upstairs: 'Good morning' and Lizzie replied, saying she would be down shortly for a cup of tea. She had been drinking rather heavily lately, he reported, and when he had spoken about getting a fowl for Christmas, she had replied: 'Maybe none of us will be here for Christmas'.

At 10.30am the same morning, the next-door neighbour living at 4 St Peter's Cottages called at the house and, on opening the front door, smelled gas. She went into the back kitchen and got a brief glimpse of Lizzie lying on the floor; then, obviously much distressed, she ran back to the house belonging to Albert. His wife Kate was in, and came running to find Lizzie with her head in the gas oven. She testified later that she had immediately turned off the gas and tried to pull her sister-in-law out of the oven, but she was already dead. It appeared that Lizzie had taken her own life.

Evidence given at an inquest held by the coroner on the 24th November, two days later, indicated that although Lizzie had an old age pension and 'a son' (Gus) who sent her money, she had worried over money matters. A verdict was recorded of 'carbon monoxide poisoning due to inhaling coal gas, and suicide whilst the balance of the mind was disturbed'. With a touch of gallows humour, in retrospect, the coroner advised the neighbour who had called at Lizzie's door that if ever such a thing should occur again, the correct thing was to turn off the gas at once. (The neighbour replied that when she saw what had happened, she was too afraid to do so.)

On 27th November, Lizzie Perks was laid to rest in the graveyard of St Peter's Church, near the cottage where she had lived. Much later her son Hector (who took no pleasure in seeing any one of his four daughters consuming alcohol) considered wistfully that: 'At one time she was quite the lady'.

TWENTY-THREE

PRAYERS ARE ANSWERED

May 1945 heralded the end of German domination of Europe. Hitler committed suicide, acknowledging he had failed to realise his dream of making the Third Reich into the greatest power in the world. With the surrender of all German forces to the Supreme Allied Commander General Eisenhower, the 8th of May was declared Victory in Europe (VE) Day, although the exhilaration was not confined to that continent but spread throughout the world and to India.

At the central ordnance depot in Agra, Hector had been in the administrative branch since November. As finance and establishment officer, his responsibility lay in matters of pay, staff, welfare, and the feeding and clothing of military and civilian personnel. With increases in personnel and frequency of transfers to meet needs in the field or at new depots, his role had become enormously complex. Perhaps reflecting his new status, he was given a 40-gallon barrel of rum to celebrate the VE occasion. He shared this with his British, Indian and other ordnance troops, offering them 'as much as they liked'. Anyone else in the depot (such as the civilian labour officers overseeing the expanded force) could buy rum from him at three annas a pint. According to Hector, everyone was 'rolling about as drunk as coots'. It was, of course, a holiday!

It had been a hard fight. All of Europe had been involved in the war except for Portugal, Spain, Sweden and Switzerland. In Britain, every capable man had been compelled to join the fighting force, unless in a reserved occupation or engaged in 'essential' work such as farming, nursing, mining, or the manufacture of armaments and munitions. Other civilians were drafted into these and similar occupations. America had supplied massive amounts of materials and equipment to the Allied nations, and some, including Britain, incurred a formal debt. German forces had succeeded in occupying Poland, Norway, Denmark, the Netherlands, Belgium, France, Yugoslavia and Greece; and in all these places, as well as in Russia and Germany itself, they had terrorised, tortured and massacred millions of people. In the end, though, they could not resist the combined power of America, Canada, Russia and the British Empire, together with troops from countries including France, Poland, Norway and Belgium.

However, the war was not over for those in Asia and the Pacific. While India continued to support operations in Burma and other Far Eastern theatres, the Allies could now concentrate on crushing the Japanese. The offensive in Burma that year had made good progress in regaining control of the Burma Road – that land-link between China and her Western allies. In addition, the prized Akyab Island had also been retaken and could now provide an excellent air base for transporting supplies into central Burma. William Slim remained the dominant figure in South East Asia as far as operations on land were concerned; he now had control of the great administrative centre of Meiktila and the city of Mandalay – the twin keys of central Burma.

By May 1945, he was ready to recapture Rangoon. By 4th August the conquest of Burma – undertaken increasingly by Indian units, as British regiments dwindled through lack of reinforcements and repatriation – was complete. Slim, who was to be promoted to Commander-in-Chief of the Allied Land Forces, South East Asia, was said to be the best British commander of the Second World War, perhaps even the best of the Allied commanders. He paid close attention to detail, illustrated by his personal criticism of Hector for taking young Peter to that Gurkha ceremony when the family lived in Shillong.

Meanwhile, American forces captured one Pacific island after another and prepared to invade Japan. However, an invasion would be incredibly costly in terms of loss of life. On 27th July 1945, Japan refused to surrender and America decided to shorten the war by using its newly developed atomic bomb. On 6th August, an American bomber nick-named the Enola Gay (after its pilot's mother) launched a weapon codenamed 'Little Boy' on the Japanese city of Hiroshima, producing an explosion equivalent to the detonation of 20,000 tons of TNT. It killed tens of thousands of civilians. Three days later, America dropped another atomic bomb on the city of Nagasaki, killing another 70,000 people. The Japanese surrendered shortly afterwards.

On 15th August, India celebrated Victory over Japan (VJ) along with the rest of the Allied nations. Much of the praise for India's great war effort went to General Auchinleck, the Commander-in-Chief who since 1943 had been transforming inexperienced divisions into capable and competent fighting units. He had been responsible for all training of the Army in India (both the Indian Army and the British Army units on tour of duty in India) and had boosted the number of troops in his 'new model Indian Army'[95] from 150,000 men to 1.8m. He had also made the Indian Army more self-reliant by increasing the number of Indians commissioned as officers to serve alongside the British, and now some senior Indian officers were commanding battalions, regiments and brigades with equal courage and efficiency.

The new-look Indian Army – every man in it a volunteer – had adapted itself with remarkable speed. In earlier times, warfare had been based on proficiency with horses, mules and camels, but now everything was mechanised. In addition, thousands of Indians had trained as technicians. (The Indian air force and navy, also demanding technical skills, had developed in similar ways.) All in all, it was clear that India had played a most honourable part in defeating the combined forces of Germany, Japan and Italy.

With the celebration of VJ Day came a second barrel of rum for Hector. He was as generous with this one as he had been with the first and, he recalled, its widespread distribution had the same effect upon the conduct of the men. A holiday was declared, and the Perks family went on a celebratory excursion to Agra fort, where the children climbed the ramparts.

Crowds of army people gathered for the gun salutes and fireworks that commemorated the end of the Second World War, and the smallest children – Barbara and Mary – participated joyfully, though they had little understanding that the world had just come through the most dreadful and destructive conflict in its history, and that many areas would lie devastated for months and years to come. Some 50 million people had lost their lives, but the Perks family pinned their hopes on the fact that their dear Uncle Bill had managed to cling onto life, and would soon be coming home.

The task of rescuing prisoners-of-war from camps in various locations, covering a vast part of South East Asia, was not simple. Before it was known that the Japanese would surrender, the organisation set up for prisoner rescue had planned to undertake a gradual operation. Now they recognised that this operation would have to be undertaken simultaneously with American action, and with the utmost urgency, since not only had it been discovered that thousands of men were close to death from starvation and neglect, but in the face of Japanese defeat these prisoners-of-war might be massacred.

Even today, the Japanese prisoner-of-war camps are not very well documented. Their locations were not always known at the time and the constant movement of prisoners, together with problems regarding the translation of names, means that anyone trying to work out where the camps were, exactly, comes up against various inconsistencies. What is known *is* that, with the coming of VJ Day, the initial phase of the task had begun with the Allies dropping leaflets by air, giving the Japanese guards, prisoners and local civilians notice of the surrender. Then more leaflets were dropped, instructing prisoners to stay in their camps so that food and medical supplies could be delivered by air. (Since about the end of 1944, the prisoners had been kept securely in their camps anyway.) The second phase of recovery started with the actual drop of food and supplies, and the parachuting of Red Cross relief teams into known camps.

On 16th August, the Japanese authorities in each of the 11 Thai prison camps informed their captive senior Allied officers that the war was over. Thousands of letters that had been withheld for many months were given to the men, together with stocks of Red Cross parcels. Early in September, a formal surrender ceremony – albeit delayed – was held in Rangoon. Then the urgent release of ex-prisoner survivors into Allied hands began in great earnest.

In Thailand, where Bill was, the release was executed hurriedly because the Allies knew the desperate plight of the prisoners there. The rescue parties contacted some 29,000 prisoners in all 11 Thai camps. Much to their benefit was the fact that the Thai government was by now very much on the side of the Allies (unlike the local governments in Malaya, Java and elsewhere), and these Thai camps were also nearer to a collection centre hosted by the British base in Rangoon.

Having received food and medical aid, those from Thailand came forward to be transported home. A more exhausting task, still to be carried out, was that of identifying graves and cataloguing reports written in the camps by British and other officers.

It is clear that Mary Perren was full of hope and anticipation that her son had survived until the end. He kept the letters she sent from Calcutta at this time, and the phrases she wrote (the repetition of the words 'speedy return', for example) reveal both extreme anxiety and hopeful longing. The first was dated 6th September 1945.

Ex Prisoner-of-War Mail No 4855446
Bdsn WF Perren, 1st Leicestershire Regiment
No 1 Prisoner-of-War Camp Thailand
C/o South East Asia Base, Post Office, Calcutta

My Darling Son,
I am daily looking out & hoping for news of you, that you are safe & well. You are in my thoughts & prayers constantly. We have had no news of you for so many months. How thankful we all are that this war is over at last & we are so looking forward to having you home once again. We are all well here thank God. All old friends send their love to you & looking out for your speedy return. I cannot give you much news in this letter I will reserve all that until you are with us again which I hope & pray will be very soon now. Frank and Hester send their fond love. With my fondest love & God's blessings & prayers for your speedy return.
Your fond loving Mother, M Perren.

The second letter was written on 2nd October and was addressed: 4855446 Bdsn WF Perren, 1st Leicestershire Regiment, No 1 POW Camp Thailand, C/o Recovered POW Mail Centre, Bombay, India Command. In retrospect, it seems quite incredible that Bill should have received either of her letters, given the exhaustion of the region and the dilapidated state of communications. But he must have read her words avidly. This letter reveals that, by this time, Mary had heard from her son for she refers to a cable and letters from him. She must have been relieved beyond imagination, although her joy is still tempered with anxiety over his continued absence:

My Darling Son,
We have been eagerly looking out for some indication of your arrival home daily & each day we are so disappointed. I did not reply to your cabel (sic) as it had been delayed on the way, having arrived after your letters, & the trams and buses being on strike too I could not get out, & in the meantime we were hoping for your arrival. We can get no information as to your present

movements. I don't know if you will get this letter dear boy. I hope for your return or some news of you <u>very soon</u>. We are all so happy to know that you are safe but we are also longing to have you with us. Frank is on holiday this month & is hoping to go with Hester on a visit to Clare in Agra, but they are waiting for your arrival. We are all well here also at Ripon St & all send their fond love & longing to see you safe back. Auntie Lizzie & May [Frank's aunt] have been over this evening. <u>All</u> send their fond love to you my darling. Mrs Talbot will be over tomorrow & will expect to see you home. All my fond love dear Son & I am so longing to see you. All God's Blessings
Your ever loving <u>Mother</u>, M Perren

Meanwhile Clare and Hector, living in Agra, had a different worry with which to contend. Clare had found herself in a dreadful predicament: she was pregnant again, for the eighth time. The conception had evidently taken place soon after the celebrations of VE Day, and three months of torment followed. Later she remembered only her fear at hearing the news: 'I was so afraid the baby would be deformed, like last time'.

Clare was a woman of godliness and Christian values, one who had an affinity for and dedication to motherhood that was abundantly clear in her tenderness and nurture of her children from infancy into adulthood. All of her instincts centred on family life and she saw a child as a sacred gift. The strength of her feelings and love bonded members of her family throughout their lives. With these feelings in mind, it must have been agonising to appraise the current situation. Nevertheless, with her husband's support, and in great distress, Clare took the decision to terminate the pregnancy.

She described how she went to an Indian doctor in the back room of a chemist shop. 'I lay on the bed and was "put out" while he performed the abortion'. When the doctor had finished, Hector took her home in a taxi but more pain and anxiety followed because the procedure had induced severe haemorrhaging and Clare was confined to bed.

Hester and Frank could not have timed more badly their visit to Agra. Usually Clare was a most genial host, but it was the worst possible time for a visit from her childless sister. Hester and Frank, wholly unsuspecting, arrived in Agra accompanied by Frank's brother Cyril and his wife Vicky. Clare was still in bed and could not receive them with her customary enthusiasm, although no one told Hester the cause of her sister's illness.

In fact, the bleeding persisted and eventually Clare was admitted into the Women's Indian Hospital and given a transfusion. The blood she received came from Sandy Spencer, one of Hector's Royal Ordnance friends and an amiable man who was residing, at that time, in the rear apartment of the Perks family bungalow. Much later on in her life, Clare would reveal that she had Scotch blood in her veins from a transfusion, but she disclosed to no one the reason for it until an intimate and very special series of conversations occurred.

Barbara had embarked upon a study of the family's life in India, and it was during one of the personal conversations that Barbara had with her mother on the subject that Clare revealed her secret. Since this tragic event had occurred, Clare had mentioned it to no one outside of the confessional box, except one very special friend. Having disclosed the details to Barbara, Clare brought up the subject of the abortion on more than one occasion. She had not confided in any of her other daughters, but it was obvious that she wanted now to take this daughter into her confidence; subsequently she displayed no regret about her initial decision because she spoke freely to her about it several times. Barbara felt privileged to be told the secret and tried hard, at those times, to allay her mother's feelings of guilt and her fears that God might not have forgiven her.

It was a desperate trial for Clare. The risk to her own life was great – abortion was illegal then, of course – and many women in similar positions suffered badly from ingesting concoctions of pills or taking potions or receiving injections of dubious solutions. Others used knitting needles or crochet hooks to try to terminate their pregnancies. The complications that arose, such as shock, haemorrhage and infection, could be fatal. Instruments used by back-street abortionists were not usually sterile, and often the uterus was perforated or its contents were not completely removed.

Fortunately (in some ways) this was a more innocent age and both Clare and Hector were unaware of these dangers at the time. All they felt was the gravity of the impending situation, and the desire to avert it.

However, the remorse for what she had done was never to relinquish its hold on Clare. Over the years, she admonished herself greatly, especially as the issue gained increasing exposure in the media. 'You can imagine how I feel,' she once told Barbara, 'when talk of abortion comes up'. Quietly, and in agony, she asked herself again and again whether God had really forgiven her for ending this child's life.

Hester was equally pitiable, though in another way. Perhaps, had she known her sister's situation, she might have grieved again over the injustice of her own childlessness. Throughout their marriage, she and Frank had an underlying fondness for and lifelong commitment to each other, though resentment about the lack of a child may well have lain at the root of their frequent marital arguments. Nevertheless she filled her life in other ways, developing the emotional, pleasure-loving side of her nature and looking after her mother Mary Perren, her dogs and the garden. There was also fine crochet work to make, and friends to visit and entertain.

By now the processes were underway which would liberate Bill and send him home to India, and five weeks after the celebrations of VJ Day, he was taken by train from his camp at Ubon to the capital of Thailand: Bangkok. There, British troops that had been flown in were operating a programme at what was known as POW HQ to manage the numbers of prisoners expected from 'up country', in preparation for the RAF to fly them out to Rangoon. Bill flew to Rangoon and ended up in what he later remembered as a 'big hospital camp'.

From Rangoon, most men were evacuated by ship. Those bound for England included many of the survivors of the British Battalion – about three hundred men – from the two constituent regiments: namely the 1st Battalion Royal Leicestershires and the East Surreys. (It seems that most, if not all, had remained in Chungkai after the completion of the railway.) However, Bill did not go with his old comrades. After a month in Rangoon, he was flown back to Calcutta, arriving on 28th October 1945. It was more than four years since he had left that port, strong and fit, heading east. Now he was emaciated (6st 7lb), just a shadow of his former self. For him and so many like him, having suffered for nearly four years in the jungle, half-starved, debilitated, diseased and ever at the mercy of the Japanese, life had been preserved by only a narrow margin.

Throughout it all, he did not lose the will to live, and was spared the fate of those who died of the strain of the experience. It is possible that his love of sport and his healthy upbringing in the Simla hills had stood him in good stead for this punishing experience that he had been forced to endure. For many, the war ended too late; thousands of those that did survive had to bear the burden of ruined health for the rest of their lives. It is hard to know how significant it must have felt to those men to hear of the trial in December 1945 of General Tomoyuki Yamashita, known as the 'Tiger of Malaya and the proud conqueror of Singapore'. He was hanged for his crimes on 23rd February 1946.

Nevertheless, Bill himself was home and reunited with his mother Mary, sister Hester and brother-in-law Frank. It was the homecoming of all homecomings. A week after he arrived, he wrote to his brother-in-law on 7th November asking about the pay and allowances that were owed him. Hector, usefully in a position to know these things, wrote back from the central ordnance depot at Agra on 28th November, providing a list of Bill's entitlements since his capture at Singapore. He sent the letter care of Mary Perren and added:

> We will be glad to see you any time. What do you propose to do – are you signing on or deferring release? It seems a pity to waste 14 years towards a pension. All are well here. Hoping to hear from you soon. Your loving brother, Hector.

It seems that Bill was of the same mind. After one month's leave, he was ordered to report either to the nearest local military unit or to military headquarters at Fort William, Calcutta, and appears to have done so on 29th November. The following day's medical exam classified him into the B2 service grade. The B category meant he was free from serious organic diseases, able to stand service on Lines of Communication in Europe or in garrisons in the tropics; the B2 subcategory passed him as being able to walk five miles and able to see and hear sufficiently for ordinary purposes. He was granted 28 days' compassionate leave until 17th January 1946.

After that, 4855446 Bandsman Perren of the Leicestershire Regiment, was posted to the British reinforcement camp at Kalyan, some 34 miles from Bombay, and was to serve there until the following November. He was one of approximately 246 so posted. This was at a time when 'the transition from war to peace was in full swing. All units were in a constant state of change, suffering heavily from repatriation and post-war demobilisation'.[96]

By 16th March, his health had improved to the extent that he was certified as A1 service grade. The A category defined him as being able to march, see to shoot, hear well and stand active service conditions, while the 1 subcategory meant he was fit to despatch overseas (as regards his physical and mental health) for training. The rapid improvement illustrated his powers of rehabilitation as well as his greatness of spirit. He had enrolled to study Pelmanism, promoted as 'a system of mental training' to help develop 'sure, clear, quick thinking'.

Pelmanism was billed as a scientific development of mind, memory and personality, and it was said to have been studied by admirals, generals and other leaders, as well as thousands of officers and servicemen, and those in responsible civil work. The War Office offered concessions on this correspondence course of 15 lessons (inclusive of text books, instruction, progress-tests and correction of exercises) to members of the armed services. The time taken to complete the course varied from three to six months, but could be extended for one reason or another. Perhaps he felt this training in personal efficiency would help him to sharpen his capacity to concentrate and allow him to focus his mind, so that he could once again be on top of things, express himself in the outside world, and make good decisions. These diversions may have helped to restore him and lessen any tendency to dwell on the tortures of the past.

In May 1946, Bill finally came to Agra. The city was sweltering in the heat of another summer, with typical highs of 120°F in the shade, so that even under their sola-topees (Indian sun-helmets made from the pithy-stemmed east Indian swamp plant), the Perks children couldn't stay cool. Nevertheless, they waited eagerly at the station for their uncle. He was to stay for a week, at the end of 26 days of 'war' leave. Snapshots taken in the compound at Grand Parade Road show that he had regained some of his former weight and substance, compared with a picture taken in Calcutta soon after his release (perhaps his aptitude for sports had helped him recover muscle tone), though he was still diminished and it appeared he had some way to go to regain his pre-war stature.

Even so, there was much joy all round not least because of his first encounter with his two youngest nieces, Barbara and Mary. He was only in Agra a week, but had the art to give Pat and Barbara the confidence to learn to swim when they all went to the pool at the fort, and to the walled open-air pool at Laurie's Hotel, a charming establishment just north of the cantonment. He might have been through a terrible ordeal, but underneath he was the same man: gentle, unassuming, a loving uncle.

TWENTY-FOUR

THE WAKE OF WAR

As May 1946 wore on, and the land became scorched by months of drought, there was another cause for expectancy. The cold air masses that accumulated over central Asia during the winter were warming up and ready to rise sufficiently to pull the wet winds and rains of the monsoon up over India from the Bay of Bengal and the Arabian Sea.

This was the time of year for short, violent and unpleasant dust storms to sweep across the plains. The first sign of one approaching was a sky that grew red. Since it was undesirable to be out in such a storm, this was the signal to retreat inside quickly and tightly shut all doors and windows. The rusty-red cloud, from the sand of the Thar desert in Rajputana to the west mixed with red dirt from other parts of this area, would grow thicker, eventually obliterating everything outside and turning day into a virtual night as winds full of sand particles slammed against the bungalow at speeds of up to 44mph. When it had 'all blown over' it was safe to go outside again, though the storm usually managed to leave its detritus inside, too, with a fine layer of dust coating everything.

These prevailing 'hot-winds' – dry, westerly forces – could almost be regarded as a season in their own right in upper India alongside the three primary seasons (cold weather, hot weather and monsoon).[97] Typically, they came in the month of May. They blew day and night over the vast open plain until, in mid-June, thunderclouds began to bank up. As the family sat out chatting in the dark on the court, with their drinks, they would watch and hear the distant storms approaching with sheet and forked lightening that brightened the sky. Between them, they felt an overwhelming sensation of wonder and anticipation of the inevitable. There was an unbearable feeling of pressure until the sudden onset of the monsoon. With this came instant relief.

Barbara and Mary, still little children, loved to run out of the bungalow with next to nothing on, and to dance and jump about with delight in the refreshing rain which fell with a tremendous force. Although the rain came in heavy daily downpours that filled the streets with water and brought some aspects of life to a halt, it didn't rain solidly all day. The water tended to come down in torrents for a while, after which the sun would come out and it was all quite pleasant.

The earth smelled beautiful. Any unpleasant odours and dustiness in the air seemed to be washed away and the pleasant smells associated with vegetation and even masonry took on a fresh and beguiling character. With every breath came an uncontrollable urge to inhale deeply and feel a new purity and freshness in the cooler air, which was almost intoxicating. It was a smell the whole family loved.

The rate of run-off down the slopes was high, so the ground absorbed relatively small amounts of water, but each year it did build up in the lower area of the compound, enough for a small flood. This delighted the girls even more, since they and their older sisters and Peter could spend hours wading about in their gum boots, though all of them avoided two deep areas which shelved down too far.

Soon a heavy humidity settled in, and for many, the sticky air of the rains was more difficult to endure even than the hot dry weather. Such was the life-giving power of water that, within a few days, the whole area had turned green. The wet conditions also stirred into activity beautiful little velvety creatures known to the children as lal bahutis, which, like ants, were driven out from the parched ground in large numbers during monsoons. In places, because of their vivid colour, they formed a beautiful red carpet.

To the Perks children, as to Indian children, these creatures were hugely fascinating. In fact, they were neither spiders nor beetles but giant red mites (dinothrombium) found mainly in desert and semi-desert areas and also in some humid parts of the tropics. Each measured about a centimetre long and had the exact texture of velvet. After heavy rains they covered the ground and could be counted in their thousands, and on at least one occasion the sisters collected them and brought them into the home where, much to Clare's dismay, they escaped.

The rain also coaxed out snakes, cockroaches, mosquitoes, huge iridescent dragonflies and multitudes of insects. These were an extreme nuisance: hundreds of them found their way into the bungalow through open doors and windows, and would later bang noisily and incessantly against the lights and fly madly about the rooms. (The small black 'stink bugs' in particular, when squashed, smelled repulsively.) Electric fans in several of the rooms proved to be effective deathtraps, but it was impossible to get rid of every insect. Clare remembered that in all the years she lived in India, she could never get used to the 'creepy crawlies'. It was, she said, 'the only thing' she hated about the country.

At dinner, whenever soup was on the menu, the light was switched off until everyone was served with a portion and ready to start. Even then, when all the flying insects were on the move again, it was often someone's bad luck to lift a spoonful of soup into the mouth just as a bug landed. Most were foul tasting but, with luck, could be spat out in time! To deter climbing insects from getting into her store cupboards and the icebox, Clare kept saucers of water permanently under the legs of the cupboards. However, this did not prevent weevils from making regular raids, and contaminating the flour. 'It was full of them,' she remembered later. 'There was nothing you could do about it – you just had to sieve it and use it.'

She remembered, too, the proliferation of little house lizards (or geckos). Unlike the insects, these would emerge from cracks in the walls and other hiding places as soon as the lights were turned out, and at night would climb about and run upside-down on the ceiling, chasing their insect supper. They chose all manner of odd places in which to lay their eggs, including her dressing table, but they were slippery customers, and easily thwarted attempts to get rid of them by releasing all or part of their tails and dropping away free. Having slipped to safety, they could regenerate – though the original tail was always the longest.

In addition to the geckos, 'lots of destructive little cricket-like creatures got into the clothes and made holes all over them,' Clare remembered. Once she lay in bed in the darkness, trying to work out what was fluttering about the room before it was hit by the fan and knocked down. Reaching out for the torch she kept by her pillow, she inadvertently put her hand directly on the cause of her alarm – a bat – which, like the geckos, was quite harmless!

However, in and around Agra there were other risks from more harmful creatures that were lurking to prey on the big insects and lizards. Biting centipedes were to be avoided, in particular. These were ground-loving creatures measuring up to eight inches long with a painful, venomous bite inflicted not by the jaws but by the front legs. These legs were in fact poisonous claws that could break off into the flesh if this invertebrate was disturbed in mid-attack.

There were scorpions, too. By day these flat-bodied creatures are solitary, hostile even to other scorpions, and usually hide away from human dwellings in cracks or holes or under rocks; but by night, like geckos, they hunt – and this is when they come into houses and crawl into beds, shoes, furniture and under carpets. Perhaps worst of all for Clare were the spiders; 'especially the spiders,' she remembered later. She might have been exposed to them all her life, but she always especially hated and feared these creatures. (In close second place came the 'huge' cockroaches that she described as measuring 'a couple of inches long'. In the confined spaces of train compartments, these tended to proliferate and Clare found them 'disgusting'.)

Inevitably, living in such a climate, there were times when her fears were realised. On several occasions while she was making up the beds after a night's sleep, she found a scorpion lurking. 'It was always Barbara's bed,' she remembered. It was fortunate she never came to any harm for in each case, Clare noticed, these creatures were of the dark brown, less common and more poisonous type; they were likely to have been spider-scorpions of the buthus species. Even 'ordinary' scorpions were capable of inflicting an intensely painful sting, if provoked, which might last anything from a few minutes up to a few hours, though it left no after-effects.

There were threats outside as well as inside the bungalow. Like everyone living in the tropics, over the years the family learned to deal with the dangers of their environment. Clare had encountered several types of poisonous snakes in Kirkee. In all her travels, she reiterated, she had come across more there than anywhere else. The reality was that tens of thousands of unfortunate local Indians were killed each year by contact with poisonous snakes, insects and wild animals, but none of the Perks family succumbed to this fate. One small factor was that the servants were very reluctant to kill creatures; another was that members of the family rarely, if ever, went barefoot unlike so many of the Indians.

The children and their parents often slept out on the court beside the bungalow on midsummer nights, though the weather was so changeable that often the little ones would be awakened from sleep under the night sky by a sudden disturbance. This was caused by the hurried efforts of Clare and Hector and the older children to carry them inside – while still in their beds – along with all the other beds and the chatty (earthenware pot) filled with drinking water, before the onset of a dust storm or torrential rain.

Early one morning, when the family was sleeping out as usual, Barbara awakened at dawn (which in the tropics, like dusk, was brief) and looked up through the mosquito net onto the low, thatched roof of the bungalow. In the increasing light she could see a number of monkeys moving about. Petrified, she lay for a while too scared to move: there was no doubt in her mind, from the evidence of their intimidating glances, that these monkeys were just as aware of her as she was of them.

Once or twice they went over the top of the roof, out of sight, which made it worse, but even then she didn't dare move or wake her siblings or her parents for fear of drawing attention. Fortunately, at last, they came down from the building and scampered off. Clare was scared of monkeys too – when she was a patient in hospital, one trespassed in the ward and stole food from the top of the lockers. Later she remembered that she had covered her head with the bedclothes until it went away.

As the hot and humid days continued, Hector's efforts and achievements in his post were recognised. On 18th June he was designated acting major in administration (since 1943, this had been one of the three main functions of a depot). Three months later, his status was further advanced when he was made temporary major in the depot's security section, and put in charge of the new sub-depot of engineering and fire control stores which operated within Agra's central ordnance depot.

During the war, India had been a vital source of war supplies for the Middle East – as in the First World War – and for the Burma campaign. Commander-in-Chief Auchinleck, in his rhetorical exchanges with the British government (whom he criticised on more than one occasion for its attitude towards India), referred constantly to the enormous debt owed by SEAC (South East Asia Command) to India Command. With ever-increasing commitments, the ordnance services in particular had worked under enormous strain to handle heavy receipts and issues. Wartime expansion (from ten ordnance installations in peacetime to some 77 by VJ Day on 15th August 1945, as well as enlargements to existing establishments) made the task for ordnance forces all the more difficult because there were few proper facilities for storage.

This meant that, in the aftermath of hostilities, while other services were enjoying a well-deserved rest, the Indian Army Ordnance Corps engaged in another phase of hectic activity. For some ordnance installations and units, the immediate post-war period posed no less a challenge than wartime itself. They had to cope with a flood of equipment and stocks coming back as units and depots disbanded across India and South East Asia.

After the war, a formidable mass of stores of all descriptions, including those captured from the enemy, were sent back to the returned stores sub-depots at various installations. Some had been rendered unserviceable; others were repairable. All of them had to be sorted out with a view to either conditioning and reissue, or disposal. Luckily, a contingency plan had been prepared to deal with this vast surplus, and the system never broke down. Nevertheless, with a considerable reduction in staff of ordnance depots due to the abolition of some categories of personnel, it was said that the increased workload in the wake of the biggest war in history stretched the ordnance corps to its limits. At Agra there was a steep rise in receipts of goods. Typical categories were survey, drawing, opticals, electrics, electrical and fire control instruments, watches, radar, generating sets, signal and wireless equipment.

Hector's hectic work schedule was demanding. To revive body and soul, he had many diversions to pursue in this historic city of the Mughals, as well as agreeable options within the social calendar for company with his officer-friends. Later Hector's old friend Harry Rowlands, who hailed from Halifax in Yorkshire, a lean and fit fellow officer with a cheerful disposition, wrote in a letter to him and Clare of those 'unforgotten days'. He remembered 'the dinners, the private parties, the gathering on Sunday mornings', but above all else, 'the people'. Hector enjoyed all of that but nothing, it seemed, could compare to the jolly evenings around the piano at home.

Hector liked nothing better than to invite his officer-friends around, along with other young and possibly homesick British Army officers, for a lively soirée. Some of the men were housed in the mess across the road, and sometimes he would bring them back for a drink and a singsong. Paddy O'Mara, a contemporary, was invariably called upon to play the piano, summoning up a stirring run of tunes. These included a range of Irish songs that Hector particularly loved to sing, recalling them fondly from his days with the 4th (Royal Irish) Dragoon Guards and their historic association with Ireland.

Some of them were: *MacNamara's Band, When Irish Eyes Are Smiling, Mother*

Machree, Mountains of Mourne, Danny Boy, The Rose of Tralee, and *Cockles and Mussels.* There were many others, too, among which were: *If You Were the Only Girl in the World, With Someone Like You, I Love a Lassie, On Ilkley Moor Bar T'at, Clementine, There is a Tavern in the Town, She'll be Comin' Round the Mountain, Goodnight Ladies, There's Something About a Soldier, She was One of the Early Birds, Oh, Oh Antonio, Daisy! Daisy!* and *I've Got Sixpence.* Some of the great songs of those war years included *Bless' em All, Hey, Little Hen, The Quartermaster's Stores, Run Rabbit Run, I'll Be with You in Apple Blossom Time* and *Shine on Harvest Moon.* Paddy was a good pianist, although amusingly, according to Clare, 'the more he drank, the better he played'.

Continuing his letter, Harry Rowlands summarised: 'They truly were the good old days, by and large, good people, good living, good quarters, good food and overall a "togetherness" that one does not find these days. We never heard the tune MacNamara's Band [without thinking of] Paddy O'Mara... and all the Perks family'. One popular song of Scottish origin was called *Will Ye No Come Back Again?* and it became particularly pertinent when Hector and Clare's friend Sandy Spencer, who had stayed with them, and donated blood to Clare, went home to England to see his family and fiancée (only to find out she was carrying on with someone else). From the moment of Sandy's temporary absence, this Scottish song took on a new slant with new words. Instead of the introductory lines 'Bonnie Chairlie's noo awa, Will ye no come back again?' they sang 'Sandy Spencer's gone awa, Will ye no come back again?' This rendition, like many of the others Paddy played, became a perennial favourite around the piano in the Perks household.

When Hector and Clare entertained friends for dinner, and sometimes when they were alone as a family, they played records on the gramophone. This plugged into the wireless for amplification and had been ingeniously put together for the first time by Hector in Shillong. It comprised a wooden box into which he had screwed a wind-up clockwork motor-operated turntable and an electric pick-up arm. Needless to say, the pick-up required an endless supply of needles. Subsequently, before and after each long haul journey, he had dismantled and reassembled it for safekeeping. The chances are that he had learned how to build it – and had bought all the individual pieces to enable him to do this – in the radio shop in Plymouth, where he had worked during the family's year in England between 1937 and 1938.

Musically, though, he found his elder daughters something of a disappointment. He had paid for years of private piano tuition and examinations (set by Trinity College of Music in London) at their convent schools, and although they were relatively accomplished and could play beautiful, haunting pieces by Chopin, Liszt, Schubert and Beethoven, Pat and Margaret usually declined his invitations to entertain his friends at the piano. Their intransigence seems to have been the key factor in his decision that Barbara and Mary should not be taught the piano at all.

Looking back, however, the girls' reticence seems entirely understandable. After all, they were sensitive young adolescents (Pat was seventeen, Margaret fourteen) and the last thing they wanted to do just then was to put themselves under the scrutiny of a circle of men, not least the two young officers of the Royal Army Ordnance Corps (RAOC) with whom they had started to go out as a foursome. Jack Stacey, a lieutenant, was courting Pat, while Margaret spent time with Ronnie Lord, a captain (though she knew he had already promised himself to another girl in England). Opportunities to meet and mix with young officers came occasionally on Friday nights, when Pat and Margaret were permitted to go with their parents to the mess dances. In turn, such a late night provided an ideal reason to be excused from Saturday morning school, which had become compulsory. At the time, both of them were preparing to take the Junior Cambridge Examinations.

However, now that the war was well and truly over, the time had come for Ronnie Lord to return to England. Margaret was tearful as she liked this young man very much, but Pat had little opinion of him (and he knew it). She felt he wanted to split them up as sisters, and disliked the way he tended to order her about. Once, she remembered, he even told her to 'hurry up'! Before Ronnie left for England, he gave Margaret his dog, a cocker spaniel called Sally. She became a companion to Lassie, the stray mongrel puppy that Pat had found whimpering on the khud-side, the incline of the compound above the Gwalior Road.

These two dogs were much loved by the girls, though having heard about their mother's experiences in Simla with the rabid poodle they knew enough to be careful about any contact with strange dogs. Their Aunt Hester had taken many strays into her home in Calcutta over the years and these had become much loved as pets as well as guard dogs, but she had experience and obviously knew what she was doing. In India, it was one thing to adopt a stray and keep it as a pet, but it was another thing to protect it from contact with certain other animals. Rabies was quite widespread.

Jackals were often infected. These normally timid, dog-like creatures were common in many parts of India and around Agra they lived everywhere, feeding on lizards, rodents, carrion and small mammals, and sometimes preying on livestock. They came into the compound too, making their home in the dense bushes close to where the children would play. In daytime they appeared rarely, but at night they would howl to each other, a signal that enabled them to form into packs.

One day, however, a pair of these reticent creatures emerged from the bushes and started scrapping in full view of the front veranda. Clare and her family immediately took notice, unsure if they were mating or if it was something more sinister – jackals were, after all, nocturnal animals and this was broad daylight. Unfortunately, the activities of the jackals also caught the attention of the two dogs, Lassie and Sally, who by this stage had only been living with the family for a matter of weeks or perhaps months. In just a few seconds, these two dogs had both bolted, but not to the table as they usually did when answering the call of the gong at mealtimes (so that they often reached it before any of the children). This time they were defending their territory, confronting these brazen jackals in a rough and tumble.

At last the jackals ran off, but when the dogs came back to the veranda they were quickly caught and tethered. Hector was contacted at the depot, possibly after Clare gained assistance from the officers' mess, and he arranged for a sepoy to come and deal with the unfortunate pair. In Hector's absence, Peter was in charge of ensuring that the soldier carried out the necessary but grisly task. There was a good chance the jackals had been rabid, so it was too risky to leave the dogs alive: they might have been bitten or wounded, though there were no visible marks. All Pat and Margaret could do was to wait for the penetrating sound of gunshots. There were at least three – clearly the marksman was less than perfect. Afterwards they remembered it as a 'horrible day'.

Another upsetting incident occurred at about this same time. A chora (thief, known in slang as a chewer, or rat) managed to gain access to the main bedroom of the bungalow through one of the open windows above the Gwalior Road, and among items he took were Hector's bush-shirt, which he had left hanging on one of the bed poles that held up the mosquito net. In the pockets were the keys to the depot together with some Mars bars and other chocolate he had bought to give out, as he occasionally did, to his family. (In fact, he discovered the burglary when he went to the bedroom to get the chocolate, after the evening meal.) Also missing from the dressing table was Clare's gold engagement ring (embellished with a diamond and a ruby) and, equally distressing, a valuable brooch given to her by her mother Mary. These two pieces comprised most of the little good jewellery she owned, but she never saw them again. The burglar may have been a stranger, although at one stage Clare suspected the young mehtar, whom she felt was not to be trusted. Whatever the case, he left not long after the incident.

Earlier, Clare had also lost her wedding ring when she cast away the shell of a monkey-nut while sitting out on the court. Being loose, the ring had slipped off her finger and flew somewhere across the sloping ground but despite repeated intensive searches, it could not be found. The servants, perhaps hoping for some reward, spent hours digging and sieving the soil but even they could not find it. This story, however, did have a happy ending six months later when hopes had dwindled and Barbara, out playing one day, unearthed the lost ring. As a mark of her mother's relief and delight, Barbara received a colouring book and crayons which, at the time, to the little girl, far outweighed the significance of what she had found.

TWENTY-FIVE

TROUBLE BREWING

Anew tide of Asian nationalism was rising in 1946, and winds of change were about to sweep through India. In Delhi, British staff officers planning how to reduce the army to its peacetime establishment were confronted with a situation in which most British soldiers wanted to get back to Britain as soon as possible, while most Indian soldiers wanted to remain in their posts.

In the British general election of 1945, the Labour government took power and the viceroy, Lord Wavell, was summoned and advised that the new government was favourably disposed to Indian self-rule. On his return, Wavell announced elections for provincial and central assemblies as well as the establishment of a constitution-making body. Subsequent voting in these contests confirmed the desire of Indian people to rule themselves.

How and when independence would be granted had been the preoccupation of educated Indians since 1885, the year of the formation of the Indian National Congress, a political movement that would put forward their claims. That was the year John Perren had died. The strength of the Congress continued to grow until the start of the First World War, at which time one particular champion arose to lead the way: Mahatma or 'Great Soul' Gandhi.

In 1918 William Perren was suffering one of his deep depressions and Clare and Hester were away boarding at school. That same year Gandhi, an articulate and principled man of low Hindu caste, committed himself to the campaign for independence and went on to win the hearts of millions through his dedication to the poor and lowly.

He came to prominence during a period of post-war restlessness. After the First World War ended, Indian leaders were promised a greater measure of self-government, but although there was an outburst of loyal enthusiasm over India's role in the war (contributing a significant number of combatants in France and other theatres), India's political leaders considered the reforms granted to be inadequate. There seemed to be little let-up by the British of the wartime restriction on political freedom.

In 1919, racial hatred was engendered after a number of Europeans were murdered in Amritsar town, causing the subsequently notorious General Dyer to order his troops to fire on a packed crowd of Indians who had assembled in defiance of his ban on public meetings. Some 400 unarmed people were killed, and more than 1,000 were wounded. This incident horrified and alarmed Indians of all classes, who felt that all their wartime efforts to help the British over the past four years had been betrayed.

Convinced that the British would never willingly give India the status it wanted for itself, namely home rule, Gandhi, who was now leading the Congress, called for a campaign of non-violent opposition, which would manifest itself in a strike on the part of officials and professional workers, as well as a boycott of British goods to force further reforms. Despite his teaching, however, the campaigns of passive resistance he advocated led to frequent disorders. Passions erupted among his followers as differences developed between Hindus and Muslims in the nationalist movement. Perhaps for the first time, Hindus began to think not only of how to rid themselves of the British, but of how they might control India after the British had gone.

In 1935, the year Hector was in Quetta following the massive earthquake, the British parliament passed an act that gave a bigger share of the government of India to the Indians. This was not enough for the Congress, which consisted mostly of Hindus headed by Gandhi and Jawaharlal Nehru (both these men had graduated in law from London universities). The Congress had now become a political party, and went on to win majorities in seven of the eleven provinces in the elections in 1937.

In 1939 the party demanded immediate independence and continued to agitate, opposing moves to join the war in Europe. Despite this focus on non-participation, however, thousands of Indians ignored the nationalists and flocked to recruiting stations, even though the conditions and pay for Indian soldiers was far inferior to that of their British counterparts. Perhaps they felt that it was more important to be active – to protect their country, and prove themselves worthy of gaining what they felt was their birthright – than to simply protest.

The Congress claimed to speak for the Muslims, but the divisions widened irreparably after the Muslim League, founded in 1906, detached itself. Under the leadership of another British-educated lawyer, Mohammed Ali Jinnah (a man said to be both brilliant and arrogant and, like Nehru, extremely Westernised), the League argued that, if India secured the home rule for which it was agitating, Muslims would not receive fair treatment from the far more populous Hindus. In 1940, the year Barbara Perks was born in Assam, the Muslim League demanded not only independence but also the creation of a separate Muslim state.

Two years later, the British rejected a further demand by the Congress for immediate independence, offering instead an interim government until the end of the war. In response, the Congress initiated a programme of civil disobedience. The result of this was widespread agitation and disturbance, costing about 1,000 lives when militant elements launched the Gandhi-backed Quit India movement that August, all of which put a strain on the Indian Army, even as India itself was in danger of being invaded by the Japanese. The British responded firmly, jailing Gandhi, Nehru and the other Congress leaders along with some 60,000 of their followers. Army recruitment, however, was not seriously affected, and Indian troops in Burma and Europe fought with continuing gallantry.

When the Second World War ended and all the political agitators were released, it seemed inevitable that waves of renewed agitation among Indians would follow. In June 1945 the viceroy met Hindu and Muslim leaders at an all-party conference in order to draw up a mutually agreeable constitution. In Britain, the Labour Government under Clement Attlee favoured Indian independence at the earliest date, though it was anxious to avoid partition for reasons including future prosperity and matters of defence.

In February 1946, however, events turned nastier. There was a very ugly mutiny in Bombay that involved members of the Indian Navy attacking officers and British soldiers. Following missions by three British cabinet ministers (including Sir Stafford Cripps in April) to try to bring the parties together, the rift became wider than ever. Each suspected the British of favouring the rival group. Jinnah and his Muslim League had supported the war and gained strength, a fact shown by their striking success in winning almost every seat in Muslim areas in the Indian general elections of 1945-46. Jinnah insisted that there must be a separate state of Pakistan, comprising Baluchistan, Sind, the Punjab, Bengal, Assam and the North-West Frontier. He rejected proposals for a Pakistan that did not include most of Assam, the Punjab and Bengal, claiming this would be a 'maimed and moth-eaten' country.

The leaders of the Congress, still the largest and most popular party, were equally determined India should *not* be split, and it seemed that in the face of this mounting distrust, the country might be facing a civil war. In May 1946, Wavell and Auchinleck broadcast to the nation an explanation of a hurried compromise that proposed an interim government as a prelude to independence. This would give leaders the experience of joint administration until such time as a transfer of power took place. They appealed for patience, cooperation and efforts towards stability. However, after an initial acceptance, within weeks Jinnah rejected the proposals as unsatisfactory for Muslims. Once again there was a deadlock although by July, Auchinleck (now also a Field Marshal) was still cherishing the hope that partition could be avoided and that his Indian Army could remain the guardian of stability, as well as providing the country with strong defences.

Meanwhile Nehru, the president of the Congress, got on with planning an interim all- India government. Jinnah's Direct Action Day on 16th August, designed to express dissatisfaction with and rejection of the Cabinet Mission's proposals, caused severe rioting between Muslims and Hindus, notably in the United Provinces (UP) of which Agra was a part, and in East Bengal. In Calcutta some 6,000 people died and thousands of others were wounded in several days of unrestrained communal riots. In addition, immense damage was caused to property by arson and looting. The time came to be known as the Great Calcutta Killing, because the streets were strewn with corpses.

Photographs still in the possession of the family, probably taken by Hester's husband Frank Evett-Strange, depict the gory street scenes in the aftermath of the violence. Mutilated bodies are depicted, as well as the preparation of funeral pyres for their disposal. One photograph even displays how vultures scavenged the corpses. How could Indians behave this way when, for so long, they had lived and worked together peaceably? The pictures are a graphic reminder of the atrocities perpetrated on so many innocent people. During those days, Hester remembered later, a 'little Hindu family' came over the wall of her house begging for protection, and the couple agreed to shelter them in the godowns within their compound for one night.

The Indian Army, which included members of both religions working side by side, joined the British regiments to clear the corpses off the streets and to help restore order. However, fearing that civil disobedience could develop further, the military had already, it seems, begun to take steps to safeguard British lives and interests. Hector, for example, was told he should no longer cycle to the central ordnance depot, and instead was conveyed in an army truck fitted with a rope net across the open back to prevent injury from stone-throwing. Clare sensed the increase in antipathy towards the British from many, though not all, Indians. 'When you went into a shop,' she said, 'they would serve the Indians first, even when you had come in before them'.

In December, the family was still at 100 Grand Parade Road. Pat and Margaret took their Junior Cambridge Examinations, although the situation had deteriorated sufficiently for Clare and Hector to decide that they should stay at school as boarders for about ten days during the exam period, a precaution which would avoid any disruption to their routine, such as disturbances en route to school, at this important time in their education.

Their spirits were borne up by fruitcake made by their mother; they secreted it in their desks, allowing themselves one slice a day. When the time came to collect her daughters, Clare was taken through the city in an army truck, but the congestion was such that at one point, it scraped another vehicle. This almost sparked a fight when the vehicle's irate Indian occupants, egged on by the crowd, accosted Clare's driver and demanded that he get out of the truck. Terrified, she urged him not to argue but to do as they said. Her advice turned out to be effective. Tempers soon cooled and he was told they could go on their way.

Still fresh in Pat's mind decades later was another occasion upon which the homeward-bound school bus was forced to turn back and take a diversion to avoid a large and noisy mob in the city. Frighteningly, this mob started to bang the bus, reducing one of the girls – Pat remembered – to a state just short of hysteria. Whether or not the British in general realised it, the writing was clearly on the wall for British rule in India. Hector and Clare knew they would have to leave India as soon as a political settlement was reached. Great changes were about to occur in the Indian Army and it was unsettling for Hector to know that the day was coming when he and all his British fellow officer members would have to go. However, even independence, when it came, would not provide a neat solution or an orderly dismantling of the army and of other long- established British institutions. For the time being, many British troops – including Clare's brother Bill – were staying on in India, although there was to be lengthy debate between Auchinleck and His Majesty's Government as to how long they should remain, in view of the unrest, and many realised that the use of these troops in support of the civil power in India would almost certainly be controversial.

On 18th November 1946, Bill was posted from the British reinforcement camp at Kalyan to the barracks at Colaba, Bombay. Having been born in India, and always associated with the 1st Battalion Leicestershire Regiment in his military career, he now joined the 2nd Battalion. This battalion had been released from its 'unpleasant' internal security duties assisting the Bombay Police in severe communal rioting rioting in September, and its men had begun a training programme. As Brigadier WE Underhill later commented in his history of the regiment,[98] the purpose of this programme was to make the men fit and to take their minds off matters of internal security, repatriation and demobilisation.

In December, the men heard that King George VI had conferred the title 'Royal' upon the regiment. They took great pride and delight in their new title, which was felt to be richly deserved by both the dead and surviving members of battalions. This, after all, was the regiment that for nearly 150 years had served in India through war and peace. One or another of its battalions had provided an almost continuous presence in the country since 1804, and the exemplary conduct of its men had been recognised early, from the start of their service there that year to 1823. In lasting honour of this, the regimental badge (the Royal Tiger) with the word 'Hindoostan' was authorised in 1829.

By Christmas 1946, however, some British Army personnel were starting to leave. The Blairs, Ronnie Lord and Sandy Spencer had all gone – and that was only to mention a few. For Pat and Margaret, the degree to which they could revel in any Christmas festivities depended very much upon the detailed reports that gave the results of their Cambridge Examinations. Despite nearly two and a half years' difference in age, the girls had taken these same exams together; Margaret suggested later that she had been 'pushed forward'. The requirement was nothing less than a pass in ten subjects including Urdu (Hindustani), which was studied only here in Agra. However, disappointingly, success eluded both of them and there was no chance of a retake.

By the time Christmas actually arrived that year, it seems the family had acted upon good counsel and may have already left their little hillock bungalow with its views over the crossroads. The children, as usual, had busied themselves in the days approaching 25th December making paper chains, but Pat's recollection was that, for the cooler nights of late December, the family had gathered around a new hearth. For greater security, they were moved to the ordnance officers' quarters further south on the Gwalior Road. These were situated near the meteorological base, which periodically sent up balloons to gather data, and incidentally provided a diversion for young Peter. The family was allocated rooms at No 3 Quarters, one of a number of detached but closely set single-storey units occupying a flat stretch of land, from where it was possible to walk up to a pig farm. On site there was a sergeants' mess, which had a canteen where Clare could buy provisions additional to those purchased in the market.

For the Perks children during these politically troubled times, day-to-day life continued to be relatively peaceful. Though they were aware of the disturbances going on around them, they remained confident that their parents, to say nothing of the authorities, would take whatever steps were necessary for their wellbeing. When Barbara asked Clare later in life how aware she had been of the increasing tension, she answered: 'It didn't seem to bother me that much, though I suppose it did up to a point.' The older children, of course, began to avoid trips into the city where anti-British feelings were on the rise – they were prudent enough to avoid any brush with any risky or potentially volatile situation there, and tended now to keep to the cantonment area there in the south of the city and to the more local Sadr Bazar area. As it turned out, there was nothing to worry about.

Amid India's growing turmoil, not everyone was anti-British. Hundreds of thousands of the country's people had benefited from the presence of the British in India, and hundreds of thousands of others, living in filth, hunger, disease and squalor had not the time, energy or capacity to think much beyond their lot.

However ruffled and differing the political convictions of the family's faithful Muslim cook and loyal Hindu bearer, both servants still wanted Clare to keep them on. But there were no godowns at the officers' quarters, which meant that the bearer and the family's new mehtar had to find somewhere else to live, and had to travel further. The cook, of course, had never lived at the godowns. Now the Perks family had to travel along the Gwalior Road in order to reach the officer's mess, church and hospital, as well as Laurie's Hotel, the picture-house and the shops, which were all in 'town' in the Sadr Bazar area. Whether they went on foot, by tonga or on the school bus, they always had to pass 100 Grand Parade Road, which stood above on the left as they reached the crossroads. Each of the children, as well as Hector and Clare, felt a sense of loss at having had to leave their old home so suddenly, for it had meant much to them.

By comparison, Clare felt, the officers' quarters forced the family to live cheek by jowl and gave everyone a cooped up feeling. Each one realised, however, that they had to make the best of it. They were safer here, gathered in with other families they already knew, such as the Miles, the Macks and the Freemantles. Sometimes Clare used to meet with the other wives for elevenses and afternoon tea, and there were plenty of opportunities for their children to mix casually and make friends.

There was, however, one special family with whom Hector and Clare had established a close relationship even though, for one reason or another, they did not move from where they were to the officers' quarters. Hector had known Major 'Badgy' Dudman since his Kirkee (Poona) days. In Agra, his wife Kitty became a close friend of Clare; their four daughters – April, Christine, Georgie and Gerry (twins) – attended the same convent school as the Perks girls.

The Dudmans were staying on in the cantonment area in their lovely big bungalow at 91 Drummond Road, opposite the colonel's bungalow and 'not too far from the Anglican Church', only a short walk away from what had been the Perks family's bungalow. Half a century later, Kitty Dudman recalled the years when she and her family used to come round to 100 Grand Parade Road for a singsong at the piano. Hector and Clare were very sociable, she remembered. 'I used to pay visits for morning tea and a chat! You were all so cheerful. Sometimes you all came to my place, and my children loved that.' Though the Dudmans did not move to the same quarters as the Perks family, the regularity with which the two families socialised together, if anything, increased.

On New Year's Day 1947, officers and families took a day trip to Fatehpur Sikri. While the younger children spent a lovely day roaming about and picnicking, the adults would surely have discussed the political situation and the possibility of leaving India. However, it wasn't long after this pleasant outing that Barbara became ill with what turned out to be a severe bout of whooping cough, reflecting her mother's maxim that 'whatever she got, she got badly'. It proved a long drawn out and debilitating business, filling the last few months in Agra with frustration and putting a dampener for Barbara on what would otherwise later seem a sublime chapter of her eventful childhood, living in that city.

Despite their move, the family still managed to sit outside a lot, and on their new plot they continued to keep poultry. Before they left 100 Grand Parade Road, Hector and Clare had dispensed with the chickens and the turkeys by giving some of them away to their special friends and selling the rest to someone who came to buy. Now Hector bought a new lot of birds, including chicks. The new mehtar would clean out the henhouse but there was another person who had long held a keen interest in the chickens' welfare – Mary, the youngest of the Perks children. These creatures were a source of continual fascination to her, and the unwitting victims of several experiments.

First of all, innocent of what might happen, she lifted up and swapped the eggs underneath several broody hens. On another occasion, with a child's love of creativity, she removed several eggs and placed them in a row along the middle of the henhouse. (Clare, when she discovered this, had to reinstate the eggs at random and hope for the best when they hatched.) But Mary's mischief didn't stop there. Once she boldly carried the cock bird to the cook and, on her own authority, instructed him to kill it. However, being suspicious of this order, he was old enough and wise enough to check with the memsahib first if the order had come from her. It had not! Another time, she drowned one of the turkeys while attempting to bathe the poor creature in a bucket of water. The rest of the birds, usually, were readily disposed of between friends in a more traditional manner!

The family had 48 birds in total at their new quarters, including turkeys. Rhode Island Reds, free during the day to wander around, would sometimes saunter into the house though the open doors and windows. They went into the bedrooms and even onto the beds, so that it was not unusual to find one or another of them sitting on a pillow. Pat, however, described the chickens as 'pests' and objected strongly to this habit. One chicken even had a policy of settling on top of the cupboard. However, whenever Pat or any of her siblings chased the birds out of the house, Hector remonstrated with them for disturbing the birds when they might, at any time or any place, want to lay an egg. It was he who had acquired them, together with a henhouse, and he was convinced that any emotional or physical disturbance would upset this process! As dusk fell each day, Hector or someone else would account for every bird. Then he would pen them in to keep them from becoming prey to a predator, such as the commonly found mongoose.

Meanwhile, the older girls – having both failed their exams – were beginning to think of their future. Margaret was growing in self-awareness and, for the first half of 1947, kept a diary. She was meticulous in maintaining a neat daily record. The diary itself was fairly small, with two days per page, while her accounts of the days often spilled over to fill the top margins.

Although Ronnie Lord, the light of her life, had gone back to England, another ray of light had appeared for Margaret. This was evident from day one of her diary, New Year's Day, when the Perks family travelled with others on the truck to Fatehpur Sikri. She recorded that she had spent the day there with another officer and, as she put it, 'had one of the loveliest days for a long time'. The officer was Peter Emerson, a handsome but (again) two-timing officer who fancied his chances with women.

Pat had observed his behaviour, knowing that while he had a girlfriend up in the hills, he was also more than just friendly with a half-Burmese girl from their school. Even so, whenever Peter danced or sat with Margaret at the officers' mess dances and socials, including one she wrote about on 13th January, she came alive (although she and Pat were always escorted by their parents).

She recorded in her diary a 'List of Records Lent to the Mess', which included *That Lovely Weekend, In the Mood, When Irish Eyes are Smiling, Green Eyes, Saturday Night and You Can't Black Out the Moon,* as well as *My Melancholy Baby, Marie Elana, I Used to Love You, It's a Happy Day, Remembrance, Jealousy, Elmers Tune and The Velite.*

The diary made constant references to the way she took care of Mary and Barbara – 'the babies' – by giving them supper, bathing them and putting them to bed. Almost on a daily basis, she, Pat or Peter played games of table-tennis at the mess or badminton 'over at the Miles', but soon they realised they had the remains of an old court of their own at the side of No 3, their new home. With typical energy and togetherness, they set about restoring it with newly drawn lines and a net. Ken Miles was the same age as Margaret. He had a bicycle, which was put to great use when he gave the girls rides. Pat bore her sister a grievance, reminding Margaret in later years that she was always the one he chose to sit on the front while she (Pat) had to sit at the back. 'We used to career around the streets of Agra', Margaret later recalled.

Another frequent activity for Pat and Margaret was to keep company with two lieutenant-officer friends, Jack Stacey and a boy called Norman, whose surname has been forgotten. Margaret was rather indifferent to Norman at first, agreeable to associate herself purely to make up the foursome. However, it seems that when they weren't playing tennis in their twosomes or foursomes at the officers' mess, the four of them were at the family's house, sitting either inside or out, chatting and drinking. Jack and Norman were billeted at the mess and were called upon from time to time to do duty there as orderly officer. The usual drinks at the house were thirst-quenching Coca-Cola or a long orange juice, or sometimes sherry with card games or Monopoly. (The girls were allowed an occasional sherry at home, but forbidden to drink anything stronger.)

Margaret also wrote about going to school in the same old bus (by her own admission, it frequently had to wait for her to arrive at the stop in the weeks after she started school again, on 20th January, following the Christmas holidays). On Monday 27th January she wrote: 'Got up at quarter past 7. Bus came early. Was not ready. Came home played the piano before tea. After tea started the badminton court. Did this until dark. Came in washed & tidied myself then sat down to do some homework. Had dinner of roast peafowl. After dinner read till bedtime. Went to bed at 10.' (The following day she recorded, among other things, that there was peacock for dinner.)

The school retreat in February included religious exercises intended to benefit the soul, but Margaret found at least part of this period of seclusion for prayer and meditation depressing, as when she recorded Tuesday 4th as having been 'a very miserable day'. She was, however, enthusiastic about her regular piano lessons, and practised after school with much vigour; sometimes two or even three times in the hours between arriving home and tea, between dinner and bedtime, and between social activities and individual activities such as homework, reading, knitting, sewing and bathing. Often on a weekend or during holidays, she would get down to a session of cake-baking, though she was just as likely to be found watering the grass or 'walking up and down' within the bounds of the site with her older sister Pat. For both of them, the pressure was over and no big examinations loomed on the horizon for which to study.

Early on Sundays, there was church. The family travelled either by tonga (operated by the same man who picked them up from 100 Grand Parade Road, though not necessarily with the same troublesome horse) or, if it failed to arrive, as it sometimes did, they went on foot. As before, there were Sunday outings, with army friends taking a truck to the Taj Mahal, to Sikandra (where, on 26th January, Margaret recorded that she 'went up the minarets') and occasionally to the jeel (lake) close by. Most frequently they went to the beautiful Mughal gardens at Ram Bagh. Sometimes there would be picnic lunch or tea.

That same week as the retreat, it seems there was a day or two when school was out. On one of them, Thursday 6th February, Margaret turned fifteen and recorded: 'Got up late, washed my hair, had breakfast, curled my hair & then Mum, Pat & I went to Mrs Dudman's. Came home, had lunch then played the piano. Went outside & did the badminton court. Went & talked to Mrs Miles & then came home for tea. After tea got dressed & went to the flicks & saw "The Bridge of San Luis Rey". Very good. Came back home got dressed & went to the dance at the Mess. Had quite a good time. Peter [Emerson] danced with me once.'

(For her birthday, Margaret had bought a dress length for the derzi to make up, and a pair of slippers. She was already well developed, and Kitty Dudman had earlier provided her with a basic pattern to make a brassiere, from one she took to pieces. There were no such things available as disposable sanitary towels. The girls used rags that were washed and rewashed.)

On Sunday 9th February, she wrote: 'Got up early & went to church. Came back & had breakfast. After breakfast, Pat & I went to the range. Peter Emerson was there. Had a very nice morning & fired my first gun. Dudmans brought us home & stayed till lunch. After lunch got ready & went out on a picnic to Ram Bagh. The Dudmans came with us & we spent a very pleasant afternoon. Sat in the River Jumna and came home soaking wet but nevertheless had a very good time.'

Often at the weekends in winter, the men went off in the truck for shikaring (hunting), looking to shoot a buck or a duck. Occasionally wives and children went too; Barbara remembered being taken along. Bearers and cook usually accompanied the men, as it was their job to clean and lay out the birds, though they retained the entrails for themselves. Kitty Dudman revealed later that the servants would put the entrails into a curry to eat with friends, 'usually a feast'.

Another favourite pastime for the older girls was to go to the popular picture house, near the Sadr Bazar. Films were shipped over from England and provided a weekly and sometimes twice weekly focus. The girls would go with Jack and Norman, or with their mother. Sometimes, after a daytime get-together, Clare would go to the pictures with a friend such as Pat Rowlands, Harry's wife. This friend of hers lived out at Agra fort, and the two women made reciprocal visits: Clare also visited her in hospital during the days following the birth of her baby boy on 21st February.

Throughout March, Margaret continued to be assiduous in her diary keeping, even when the subject matter was mundane. On Sunday 2nd March she wrote: 'Got up fairly early. Went to church. Came back had breakfast and then watered the garden. Did this till lunchtime. Had lunch then lay down on the bed. The truck came and we went (Pat & I with Mary) to some unknown place. Had quite a pleasant afternoon. Came back and walked to the hospital with Mummy to see Mrs Rowlands. Came home and went to the show at the Mess. Had a fair time.'

A few days later, she wrote: 'Got up early went to school. Had a music lesson. Came home & played the piano. After that walked with Mum & Mary to the pig farm. Came home and practised on the typewriter. Jack and Norman came after dinner. Jack was drunk.' (It is worth observing that this was not the only occasion when he was the worse for drink.)

At the end of that month, on Saturday 29th March, she recorded: 'Did not get up early. Had breakfast then got dressed. Made cakes all morning then played the piano. Mummy went to see Mrs R. with Mrs M. As it was Jack's birthday Pat & I went in the afternoon & bought him something. Came home & got to bed. Read all afternoon. Got up in time for tea with J. & N. Went to the pictures & saw "Dragonwyck". Came home had dinner then went for a walk with Norman. It was a lovely night'.

March heralded the beginning of the Indian summer and, by the end of the month, it was so hot that Margaret recorded in her diary how she 'helped to take the beds outside and put up the mosquito poles'. Clare remembered later that during those months Barbara had been 'very ill'. Even when April arrived, she was still unwell and battling with the after-effects of the whooping cough. Its characteristic paroxysms of coughing caused her to vomit, and small holes were dug in the garden to get rid of the stuff as fast and as hygienically as possible. Barbara had lost weight and was by now, her mother remembered, a 'skinny young thing'. The doctor advised Clare to take Barbara to the hills to give her a change of air. From a geographical point of view, Naini Tal or Mussoorie were the most obvious possibilities. She and Hector were giving the matter serious thought when they received the news that Hector was to be posted to Madras in South India.

After the Easter holiday weekend, half-day school started on Tuesday 8th April. It was at about this time that the interminable heat of the summer months set in across the Ganges plain, sapping all energy so that, in the afternoons after lunch, the general habit for everyone, including Clare, was to 'go to bed' in order to rest or to read or sleep, often until teatime. Although tennis at the mess was to some extent still a feature in Margaret's life, vigorous games had by now mostly given way to regular swimming and refreshment at Laurie's Hotel.

Hector, though, continued to work on through the summer. That same afternoon on which school started again, news came that a fire had started at the ordnance sub-depot at the fort, and this meant all the ordnance men were put on duty to firefight throughout the night. The next morning, Hector and young Jack came home for breakfast, and that evening they went back on duty for about four hours. Clare took Pat and Margaret to see Mrs Rowlands, who was still coping with a young baby, and to have tea and dinner with that family.

They saw the remains of the fire: by then it had been damped down, but it was still smouldering badly due to the composition of the stores that had been set alight. According to Pat, there was no ammunition stored there.

The next day, 10th April, brought more change. The school bus did not come, and for the following weeks it became more and more unreliable. It seemed the service was being affected by the increasing political unrest. Meanwhile, the ordnance officers had not yet been able to extinguish completely the fire at the fort. On 14th April, Pat Rowlands came and spent the day at the Perks house, and when she and Clare went off to the pictures together, Pat and Margaret – as she recorded in her diary – had 'a lovely time' looking after the new baby boy together. On 20th April, a Sunday, they went swimming and while they were there, the fire alarm went again. It was another fire, this time at the central ordnance depot, and the news left many people wondering whether this could be arson. After all, in just a few weeks, this had been the second fire to break out in Agra army storage facilities. Everyone was aware that feelings were running high and that the situation was potentially volatile.

Other feelings, too, were starting to smoulder. Jack Stacey asked Pat to marry him. He had asked Hector's permission and on 22nd April, they became engaged. Perhaps he was spurred into action by the fact that the family was leaving the next day. In her diary, Margaret recorded that it was time to start packing and soon the family was on its way again – this time to the south of India.

TWENTY-SIX

BREAKING NEW GROUND

Leaving Agra for the second time was harder than it had been to leave the first. The cook was in tears, and he asked Clare: 'What is going to happen to us when you are all gone?' She gave him and the bearer a small sum of money. That was on Wednesday 23rd April 1947, when the Perks family said goodbye to everyone at their quarters and piled into the truck with bedding rolls and luggage. Jack and Norman came with them.

En route, they made a short stop at the Dudman bungalow near the Sadr Bazar. After saying goodbye to the Dudmans, the family continued to the cantonment station, making sure they arrived in plenty of time to catch the train. The goings on at this Indian railway station would have been all too familiar to the children. By now they were seasoned travellers and used to taking journeys over great distances, which might last for two or three days.

Typically, at whatever time it was, whether night or day, people were scattered about the station complex, among them whole families. Some were squatting, but many were fast asleep amid piles of luggage and bedding, quite content to wait for many hours – even days – before 'train time'. By day the whole place felt dead, more often than not, except perhaps for monkeys or the odd dog wandering around looking for food, while beggars curled up in the shade. In the evening, however, it was a different story, for this was when the stations, part of the great social fabric of the land, came to life.

The layout of the railways of Agra was quite complicated, with the Great Indian Peninsular Railway (GIPR), Bombay, Baroda & Central India Railway (BB & CIR) and East Indian Railway (EIR) lines all coming into the city. Whenever a train drew in, there was a crescendo of noise and the movement of hundreds of passengers along the platform, among them people of all different ages, castes and creeds. Many carried large items of luggage or bedding on their backs or heads. There too, jostling for custom in the chaos, were the char-wallahs and pani-wallahs (selling tea and water respectively) and others selling sweetmeats, chapattis and monkey nuts. These station vendors vied with each other for custom, and each had his own identifying call.

The army took responsibility for conveying families from their quarters to the station, and once there, railway coolies (porters) in red shirts were on hand, fighting between themselves for business, to carry the huge loads of luggage. But it was down to Hector to ensure the family was kept safe on their journey, and to see that the heavy luggage was safely secured with locks, and booked to proceed by the same route as the family. Clare often said how good it was to travel with him, 'a proper family man' and 'so strong with the baggage'. Her mother, Mary Perren, had also noticed this.

Most journeys on sleeper trains began at night when travel was cooler. Clare, for her part, remembered that nearly all their journeys in India were by sleeper. As usual, a self-contained compartment had been booked for them, and it was fitted with a throw-over catch that barred entry from the outside. It was also possible to latch the glass windows. (These had Venetian blinds for daytime shade and privacy at night.) Each compartment had its own external door, entered via the platform, and was fitted with its own sink, lavatory and sleeping accommodation. There were four couches, two up and two down, and each was long and generous enough to sleep two small people in a top-to-tail position. By day, the two upper couches were strapped to the wall while those below provided the seating.

The family was about to embark upon another lengthy train journey of nearly 1,200 miles, but while it was almost impossible to keep out the all-pervading dust, the sleeper trains were typically quieter than others due to the absence of corridors, which meant no disturbances from passers-by. In addition, the broad-gauge of the rolling stock provided a more comfortable ride.

Having arrived early, the family had some time to settle into the compartment before their excitement rose again as the train prepared to pull out. Then, before the last doors slammed shut and the whistle blew, Pat and Margaret said their goodbyes to Jack and Norman. Margaret wrote in her diary: 'Kissed both of them goodbye. Felt very miserable. Norman gave me book & a photo.' Pat would have felt no less miserable and possibly more so. As the wheels and pistons of the great steam engine gathered pace away from Agra and the United Provinces, Pat felt as though she was leaving behind a memorable period of her life, including 'all the boys we had known at the dances'.

The family headed south that night on a direct train service between Delhi and Madras that passed through Dholpur, Gwalior and Datia to Jhansi Junction Station, the centre of that Great Indian Peninsular Railway system, some 133 miles from Agra. On Thursday 24th April, the following day, Margaret recorded the boredom of the journey after the initial excitement: 'Travelling all the time. Felt very miserable. Read most of the day & drank cups of tea. Started writing a letter to Norman.' It was hot, too – blisteringly hot, with no form of air conditioning. The train continued southwards through central India and the Tropic of Cancer (the latitude passing across the northern fringes of Calcutta) to Bhopal. From there it headed for Itarsi Junction Station, arriving about a day into the journey, and from Itarsi onwards through Nagpur, the capital of the Central Provinces.

Arriving at a station was quite an event. The chances were that the whole place would be swarming with people, and anyone who wanted to change trains at a station would be forced, at night, to pick their way over the mass of sleeping bodies littering every platform. Hector and Clare had one very effective tactic to deter others from thinking of trying to come aboard into their compartment, even if they could find a way in. They got all of their children to put their heads out of the window so that everyone could see it was already well occupied. By now, the children also knew the importance of keeping all small articles in their carriage out of the reach of thieves when the windows were open on account of the heat. However, opportunist kite-hawks could pose a threat when the children leaned out of the window while eating their sandwiches.

Wherever a train stopped, beggars (many children among them) would plague the passengers, extending their outstretched hands and beseeching most plaintively until the very last moment before the train gathered speed and pulled out of reach. When the train was stationary, there were cries from the hawkers of 'garrum char' (hot tea) as well as 'Hindu char' and 'Muslim char' (like the water carriers calling 'pani', they sold to Hindus and Muslims separately).

From their compartment window, the children could observe vendors and recognise their familiar calls of 'pahn, biri'. Biri were cigarettes and pahn was the leaf of the Piper betel plant. The seller would spread a little pasty dressing of shell-lime, perhaps some spices, and finally an areca nut onto a fresh leaf before wrapping it for the customer. This product satisfied a common and ancient habit of Indians, mostly men, to chew it as a digestive. The chewing led to red-stained lips and teeth, and the associated spitting left messy deposits on most surfaces in public places. It also eventually caused tooth decay.

Clare's rule for her family was never to buy anything edible at Indian railway stations. This was a sensible precaution against the risk of upset stomachs or something worse, such as typhoid or dysentery. It did mean, though, that she had to be thoroughly prepared beforehand, packing enough bread, hard-boiled eggs, fruit and other supplies to last seven people on a long journey.

From Nagpur, it is uncertain which, of two possible routes, they then took to get to Bezwada junction, to connect with the Madras and South Mahratta main track at a point just 200 miles short of the journey's end. When the family arrived at what was one of the largest railway stations in India – Central Station, Madras – they were tired and listless, but with some residual enthusiasm about the new chapter of life awaiting them.

The family arrived on the evening of Friday 25th April 1947, two days after setting out from Agra. Madras was India's fourth largest city, located on the east coast of India and nearly 1,200 miles south of their last home. They were staying in a hotel in the city over the weekend, and on that day, Margaret recorded: 'Travelling most of the day. Could not get any tea. Finished my book. Arrived in Madras at half past seven. Went to Mackeys Gardens.' (She was referring to the Mackay's Garden – a hotel named after a former mayor of Madras.) She continued: 'Pat & I were given a lovely room. Went & had dinner. Came back to the room & finished my letter to Norman.'

The next day, she wrote: 'The bearer brought the tea at half past seven. Got up & had a bath. Got dressed then went to Mummy's room. Went & had breakfast then waited about for the Colonel. He did not turn up but the lady Supt. came & asked if we would like to go out in the afternoon to the sea.' It seems as though on that first day in Madras, Pat and Margaret discovered that although they had left behind their boyfriends, there would be opportunities to meet friends – including boys – here. Her entry concludes: 'After lunch went out & had a lovely time. Met a new boy called Dennis Reid. Very Nice. Had tea out there. Came home had a bath had dinner then went to a dance.'

The following day, a Sunday, was very similar. 'Did not go to Church,' wrote Margaret. 'Had tea at half seven. Had a bath then went for breakfast. After that at 10 went again to the sea for the whole day. Had a lovely time. Came home had a bath had dinner then went to bed.' Two baths in the day may have reflected the heat in Madras, and perhaps its dustiness, or the need to relax after a tiring day.

The start of a new week heralded more changes. Again the girls got up early and had tea at 7am. When all the family had taken their baths, Clare went to see their new quarters at Avadi, some 17 miles west of Madras, and the two older girls were left in charge of Barbara and Mary. 'Looked after the babies all morning,' wrote Margaret. 'Mummy came home & told us about it. Had lunch then packed up & got into the truck to take us to Avadi. Arrived there and Mum and Dad went on to the house or bashas while we went to Mrs Phipps house. Had tea there and she told us all about Avadi. Came home & felt very miserable, as there was nothing in the house. Went to bed early.' Margaret was not the only one in the family who felt 'very miserable'. All of them felt as though they had come to the back of beyond. Here there were no fine old buildings to capture the imagination, and no bustling commerce; not even a tonga.

The most intriguing thing about Avadi, the Perks children found, was that it had been an Italian POW camp during the Second World War, for the thousands captured by the Allies in Africa. Not wishing to take them to Britain which itself was undergoing austerity and rationing, the Allies shipped out many of them to India to be kept there for the duration of the fighting. Officially, it was 206 Base, Ordnance Depot, Avadi on the site of No4 Reserve Base, which was one of the three large bases constructed during the war after the formation of SEAC (South East Asia Command) in 1943. It had held stores for war including mechanical transport spares for the entire force of 20 divisions based in India. A large and mostly open-storage vehicle depot was also established here which, early in 1946, had been chosen to hold War Office stores of mechanical transport and technical stores.

Now Avadi had become a military establishment with living quarters, and some facilities such as a canteen and post office. It came under the command of senior officers of the military headquarters based on the sea front at Fort St George in Madras, the earliest important settlement of the original East India Company in the most southerly state of India. From 26th April onwards, Hector was to be the major in charge of the entire administrative function of the station, a job that involved supervising staff pay, recruitment, welfare, feeding, clothing, security and discipline.

This appointment no doubt reflected the experience he had acquired at Agra and other stations at which he had performed these duties from time to time in his career. With renewed vigour, he began duties that would have been familiar to him, trying to disregard the general feeling among regular officers of the Indian Army that they were not required any more and that, in due course, the officers of the Indian National Army would be replacing them. However, he evidently formed the opinion at this juncture that this would, and in any case should, be his last posting.

There were other considerations on his mind at such a time of uncertainty and change; primarily to do with the future of each of his children, all of them at such varying stages in their lives. It became increasingly obvious to Hector and Clare that Avadi was no place to further the education of their three youngest children, since the nearest school was in Madras, too far away. Furthermore, life in India presented poor career prospects for Pat and Margaret.

In that first week, there was a lot to adjust to. Instead of a bungalow, the family had been allotted one of the basha huts, which, from Peter's recollections, had been the billets for the officers of the Italian POW camp. These dwellings, wired for electricity but otherwise relatively crude, were laid out in generously-spaced rows and constructed of brick for roughly a third of the wall height, the remainder being made of matting. The huts had corrugated roofs that leaked badly, as the family was soon to discover. On Tuesday Margaret wrote: 'Got up early & had tea made by ourselves as we had no servant. Had a make-do breakfast. Had no rations or anything but the QM (quartermaster) came so we got a few things. We were all very miserable.'

Just a week after the move, on 1st May, Pat and Margaret were excited to receive a visit from their soldier boyfriends. Given the girls' new situation, the visit may have made them even more homesick for Agra, but in the event – as they were later to discover – it was to be the last time that Pat saw her fiancé Jack Stacey. The visit, which included an excursion into Madras, comprised the last few days of a beautiful friendship.

The time was approaching for Jack and Norman to leave the country. Pat did not keep a diary, so it is not known whether she or her fiancé had discussed or given any thought, prior to this visit, to the way that recent events – brought about by peacetime and by the growing pressures for the independence of India

– would affect their relationship. However, a more decisive factor intervened to determine that Pat would not see Jack again: he wrote and told her that he was ending their brief engagement. It seems he had been influenced by his mother, who felt he was not old enough (at twenty-one) to get married. Jack's mother also wrote directly to Hector, stating exactly this view.

It is not easy to relate how upset Pat may have been at this revelation, at the time. She and Jack had been close friends for two years or more. However, later in her life, reflecting on events, Pat said the broken engagement did not upset her beyond the point of hurting her pride, and recalled that she felt that until meeting Jack, her life had been somewhat sheltered and narrow – he was the one who introduced her to a wider world. It had been a case, she said, of 'being in love with love', but it was still a loss.

The younger children were somewhat oblivious to the events going on in their older sisters' lives; they were busy exploring their new environment. Like Agra, Avadi had its own varieties of pests and other wildlife, notably marsupial bandicoots. These rat-like creatures with short tails were thought to be of the 'lesser' type found all over India, although some here in the south were larger. At night they scampered noisily along the exposed wooden rafters above where the family was sleeping, and during the day they proved a real pest to local farmers, though they were harmless enough generally.

There were other visitors, too, including chameleons – or 'bloodsuckers', as the children called them, because of the way they changed colour about the neck when they were excited, from a dirty yellow or grey to a dark red. These large lizards were harmless, too, liking to bask in the heat of the sun until they were sniped at by a potshot from Peter's catapult. By contrast, the snakes were extremely poisonous, such as the fairly small but very alive specimen at which Clare found little Mary poking one day, outside, with a stick. Fortunately, she found her daughter before anything could happen.

The situation with servants was far from satisfactory. In May, Clare managed to engage a cook who was erratic and unreliable, 'a lot more off than on, before he disappeared altogether'. Fortunately, she had brought the three-burner stove with her from Agra. Here in Avadi, the hut came equipped with an oil-burning range that had a propensity to flare up close to the matting wall behind, to the extent that it nearly set fire to the hut (which itself was something of a tinderbox).

The only provisions available came from the canteen. Many were tinned, including milk and butter that was, according to Clare, 'ghastly' and 'like cart grease'. Hector arranged to have these provisions sent over daily for the first week, after which Pat, Margaret and Peter were allowed to go to the canteen, unaccompanied, to pick them up. As in Agra, there were limited supplies of water, available only for the first few hours of the day. This meant the family followed a similar regime, with the new mehtar (sweeper) filling the dual-purpose galvanised bathtub in the mornings and putting aside water to rinse out the commode in the day.

However, having a bath in Avadi did provide a new source of distraction and delight: small green frogs, which would jump up around the edge of the bath, just inches away from the children as they sat soaking themselves. Barbara and Mary, who were small enough to share the tub together, loved to sit still and to watch them. At the same time, they held their breath and hoped these little creatures would not dare to hop in.

In other places where the family had lived, there was a system for hiring extra furniture – a blessed optional extra for a mother and father with a family of seven. Here in Avadi, there was no such thing. There were sufficient beds, and the other basics that existed would just have to do. One extra item had, however, become by now a necessary piece of furniture in the Perks household. Having been procured by Hector, miraculously, it caused some excitement when it arrived on 10ᵗʰ May: a baby grand piano, no less. In fact, one leg was missing, a situation hastily remedied when it was propped up with books. This was the piano at which Margaret and Pat attempted to teach their mother and Barbara to play, although the progress they made was limited. Even so, the lessons did arouse in Barbara the desire, even an ardour, to learn to play by ear.

Things started to get better when it emerged that there was weekend tripping here, too, organised by Colonel Stevenson, a large, friendly and florid-faced man who, with his jeep, flying-officer moustache, and fancy for the ladies, was something of a character. For the Perks family, it was a new and thrilling experience to go to the seaside most Saturdays, usually after lunch (as opposed to Sunday outings in Agra), and they travelled in a similar fashion by army truck, along with a number of newfound friends and neighbours. These included Captain and Mrs Hadden, and Major and Mrs Phipps who were childless, but had a dog. The favourite spot was Diggers Dive, on a stretch of beach south of Madras, deserted except for local fishermen.

Known as the Coromandel Coast, this eastern stretch of India bordered the huge plateau called the Deccan, a fertile green flatland flanked by hills and peaks. Some outer aspects of the port of Madras were faintly visible to the north, but Diggers Dive itself was, by now, quite well established as a resort for army officer beachgoers. It seems that this was where the family had gone for that first weekend in Madras, with transport arranged especially for them by the colonel, from the hotel in which they spent their first two nights. Ocean-loving members of the army élite had constructed a wooden platform of generous proportions on the beach, supporting a little enclosure with a low roof. This was the only structure in sight, and conceivably it may actually have belonged to the hotel in Madras.

Clare remembered that bearers – again, possibly from the hotel – catered to patrons at small tables set out in the shade of the building. It seemed this place was for officers with or without wives and children, and it served teas, 'proper' meals including curry and rice (which must have been cooked at source and somehow kept hot), and 'lovely' salads. The view from this open and airy gallery was magnificent. Sitting with your tea at this spot on the flat eastern coastland composed mostly of dune and lagoon, you could survey a vast expanse of the Bay of Bengal. However, the sands were often too hot to be stepped on in bare feet and the seas were rough – the very best most children could expect was to be able to frolic and play in the shallows and the pools left by the outgoing waves.

Along that surf-beaten coast, swimmers were warned about various hazards, although this did not deter some, like Peter, from going in deeper. Notices clearly stated: 'Beware of Sharks and Undertow'. However, there was no such caution about drifting jellyfish, as one of the ladies of the group found out rather painfully while wading through the water. So rough were the seas, in fact, that until the beginning of the 20th century when breakwaters were built, ships at Madras and elsewhere along this coast anchored a mile or so offshore and were loaded and unloaded rather dangerously by surf-boats.

In the 1940s, local shark fishermen pushed and paddled their boats, often with some difficulty, out over the huge breakers; later the waves would bring them back into shore with their catch at points where their huts were dotted in small communities behind the beach. Mostly they caught the hammer-headed variety. Sometimes they attracted the interest of the beachgoers who waited eagerly to see what kind of fish they had landed; not surprisingly, the fishermen were usually very happy to sell directly to any of the bystanders, and on 28th June Hector himself bought a shark which Peter was keen to gut. The big challenge, with no ice in Avadi, was to keep it fresh for as long as possible.

Having unloaded their catch, the fishermen would beach their banana-shaped boats, which comprised several logs lashed together and equipped with outriggers. The children, especially Peter, liked to watch as the men then dismantled the boats in order to dry out the wood, and prevent it becoming waterlogged.

As the tide receded along the beach, it left pools here and there in which the children, treading delicately, would hunt for tropical shellfish and wonderful sea life, which they subjected to close examination. The heat soon caused the water to evaporate, however, leaving a pungent, heavy smell of salt and decay. Crabs scuttled over the sands, much as the children did to avoid its surface heat, but if approached, they would burrow fast and deep into the sand. For the children, of course, this was all the more reason to ferret after them.

By now Barbara was seven years old and, typically for a little girl, her time on the beach was enhanced by the excitement of searching for shells that the surging sea had cast up and left along its reach. While there were many beautiful shapes and colours, the real challenge was to find one of the more exotic shells that had been pitched out of deeper waters. One of Hector's officer friends saw Barbara's keen interest and made her a splendid gift: a large, heavy, pearl-coloured shank shell to add to her collection. It was shaped like a spindle, and was apparently of a type considered to be sacred and used in Hindu worship. When the shell's original occupant decayed, there was an unpleasant odour for some time, but Barbara held on to it, knowing that later and throughout her life, it would conjure in her mind pictures of that earthly paradise. Just how this kind man came by his unusual find is not known, but he was careful not to cause sibling rivalry, giving Barbara's younger sister Mary a nautilus shell at the same time.

A spectacle that was to make a lasting impression on Barbara occurred on one of the family's early visits to the beach. As the army truck neared the shore, passing through the staggered growth of coconut and banana palms, the beach party observed the body of an Indian man hanging by the neck from a horizontal branch of a different type of tree. He was evidently dead and they could hardly believe their eyes. Perhaps to lighten the moment, one of the officers remarked: 'He's just on an endurance test!' Just as mysteriously, when the party returned by the same tree later, the body had gone. Nevertheless, the homeward journey was traditionally the time for a hearty singsong to round off the day and to see everyone through the following week, and – despite the drama – this one proved to be no exception.

According to a timeworn adage, Madras is reputed to have three different types of weather: hot, hotter and hottest. In fact, the family found it no hotter that summer than the climate in any of the Indian cities where they had lived before. The city was, however, on the eastern coastal plain and on the leeward side of the Western Ghats. In June and July, the rains would bring little more than a few inches to this rain-shadow area where the Perks family now lived. However, although the cloudiness of the southwest monsoon air stream produced a decrease in temperature, the humidity of the air of those months made them very trying and uncomfortable.

The days were long and it wasn't surprising that Clare soon began embarking on impromptu visits to her new friends, as well as welcoming them into her own home. All of these social times provided good opportunities for the women to air their anxieties and doubts about the future, to listen to news or advice, and to reveal their plans. According to Margaret's diary, Clare also got involved in voluntary work at the cantonment and took strolls to the officers' shop. Sometimes, like her children, she simply walked 'up and down' for exercise, just as people had done at the officers' quarters in Agra.

On Sundays, there was church, which at first proved difficult to find. The chapel, a fair distance on foot or in an army truck each Sunday, was actually a school room, and while the mass was in Latin, there were readings from the Epistles and Gospels in English. This was largely due to the efforts of Christian missionaries who were the first to provide western education in India, especially after1815, when the ban against private enterprise in education was removed. With this new freedom, they were able to continue in earnest the work which, in small ways, they had already begun. Furthermore, after 1833, when the India Act abolished a licence held by the East India Company and all British subjects were given the right to enter India, missionaries were free to come and go without restriction. The British government then decided that, while they would maintain strict neutrality in religous matters, they would join together with the missionaries to provide education throughout India along western lines and in English. (It had evidence that Indians no longer wanted to be educated in Indian lore.) Now, in this state of Madras, far more people than in any other, could read and write English. Most of the local people were Tamils, a people with darker skin than in northern India and with a different language. Most, too, were Hindus, but there was a Christian presence. Tradition has it that Thomas the Apostle was martyred in 78AD at Mylapore, a suburb of Madras now known as St Thomé.

Though linked with the city of Madras, Avadi was quite separate. This meant there was a buffer against urban political turbulence, but it also meant the family was isolated – an ongoing reality for all of them. The main concern for Hector and Clare was that there was no school close enough for the children to attend, so that for the time they lived there, they could not go. Peter, Pat and Margaret had bicycles, acquired by Hector. These they used aimlessly and, in part, as exercise around the cantonment. They could go for a swim in the water tank built into the ground some distance away, though it wasn't too far and even the little ones could walk there. The tank, which was essentially there in case of fire, provided an easier-to-reach alternative to the sea. Filled with water to a depth of about 4ft, it was entered down a fixed iron ladder.

The 'babies' could join in the fun with their older siblings on the strict condition that they do exactly as they were told. On one occasion, however, Mary flouted her older sister Pat's instruction to 'sit still at the edge' while she herself had a quiet swim. Instead she slipped down into the water, and for a while it seemed that this incident would jeopardise future outings for both Mary and Barbara. There was another alternative, though: a swimming pool being built by the army at the cantonment, to be completed by the middle of May that year. Alas, it had a disappointingly short life, for not long after the grand opening, the pool developed a severe crack, and in the end parts of it finally caved in.

Clare saw the outcome of this 'proper amateurishly built' pool as 'a disaster'. In the interminable heat, the loss of the condemned pool – not just to one disappointed family but to the whole station community after weeks of excitement watching it being built – led Clare to appraise the merits of using instead a 'pukka' pool. This one was 'a rather posh affair', she thought, and lay further out at a remote spot. On the odd occasions when the family went, during the week, they had to travel by truck, but by this time Clare herself was determined to join in.

By now she was nearly forty, but she had made an effort and bought herself a new green swimming costume. She felt sure that this was the start of a new and pleasurable pastime, only to find – upon immersing herself up to her waist – that the water left her feeling very disorientated visually. Perhaps this was why she had steered clear of water previously. In any case, she reflected later that she had never been able to overcome this reaction, beyond a light paddle in the shallows of the River Jumna or by the sea, and this one dip was to mark her boldest attempt at swimming.

The fact was, however, that the children were not receiving schooling or work experience. On 27th May 1947, Margaret wrote in her diary: 'We are going home', meaning that they would go back to Britain post-independence. However, Auchinleck had instructed Hector and all his British fellow officers of the Indian Army that, despite the fact that leaving was inevitable, it would be their 'bounden duty' before they left to do all they could 'to ensure the continued well-being and efficiency' of the men and the army they had loved so well and for so long. He said that they were to pass on their knowledge and experience, 'unselfishly and willingly', to those who would replace them at higher commands and appointments. All this meant, for Hector, that he might have to stay on. If this was to happen – and it looked increasingly likely – they would have to consider the possibility that Clare might need to go to England with the children ahead of him. It was a prospect she little relished.

In preparation for their departure, Pat began receiving lessons in Pitman's shorthand and in typing, from a clerk who worked at Hector's office and occupied a neighbouring basha hut. He was one of the Indian civilians in the army branch of the civil service, a service much reduced in numbers since recruitment ceased in 1939 when war was declared. In general, the loyalty of these Indian civilians had become rather strained, if not divided, in the task of trying to administer a regime it would soon be their function to supersede.

It was somewhat ironic that by July, the family was starting to feel more at home here in Avadi, despite the matters they were forced to consider. 'Most evenings', according to Clare, they would gather and sit out at the tiny officers' mess. On 11ᵗʰ July, the focus was the celebration of Mary's fifth birthday. At one stage, the guest of honour was found to have disappeared, causing some anxiety, but little Mary was soon discovered sitting in a deserted dining room in the 'Colonel's chair' at the head of the laid table, enjoying the novelty of having the bearers hovering around and making a fuss of her. Finding the attention pleasurable and wishing for more of it, she went around telling everybody she saw that it was her fifth birthday. Evidently she beguiled her listeners, for in the days that followed, she received a number of fine gifts from officers and their wives. Colonel Stevenson himself sent a quality set of china crockery with a nursery design.

For one so young as Mary, there was nothing in the world to worry about. To her, everything in the garden was rosy.

TWENTY-SEVEN

WHAT PRICE INDEPENDENCE?

Outside the safe limits of the officers' mess, there was growing unrest and uncertainty in the rest of India. Occasionally, during the sleepy days of summer, Clare would take her family on a shopping excursion from Avadi station into the city, and it was then that the children – already feeling unsettled after leaving their beloved home in Agra – became more aware of what was going on in the outside world.

The nature of a journey by 'day' train was not altogether familiar. It was not very pleasant, either: as some of the very few if not only British people on board, they were lumped shoulder to shoulder with Indians and jammed into the carriage, watching as more and more people got on – or, during the short last hop into the centre, hung precariously to the outside of the train. As if the heat and dust weren't enough to contend with, some Indians took it upon themselves to sneer at Clare and her family, an attitude that demonstrated the general vulnerability of British people within the larger towns and cities (though it was still worse in the north than the south). Clare didn't go into Madras very often, however, and usually left her younger children behind.

It was a critical time in India, and the unrest was becoming widespread. There is evidence of this in a letter Mary Perren wrote to her 'affectionate niece' Annie Cecilia Heckels (Nancy) in Newcastle, who was in fact the granddaughter of one of her sisters and thus a great niece. This letter, dated 6th May 1947, refers to the severe English winter just past and its effects, and continues:

What a dreadful time you poor dear folks have been having in the old country. We read about it in the papers & also heard it on the Radio. It made me shiver to think of that cold, & we have been sweltering in a humid temperature of 108° (43°C) & over... It is distressing to think of the shortage of foodstuffs caused by the abnormal winter & all the damage, which will be felt for a few years to come...

...We are still having lots of trouble in India & especially in Calcutta, every day there are cases of stabbings. Poor Hester went to Market with a friend one day & saw a poor fellow who had been stabbed to death. She came home quite unnerved. We are under Curfew & it is such a nuisance.

Clare & her family have been transferred to Madras. I don't know when they will be going to England. They are finding it difficult to get a place to go to but they have to go as Clare's husband finishes his time in the Army soon.

In her letter, Mary mentioned her own unease, and the fact that Bill (or Billy, as she called him) had been transferred from Bombay to Bangalore – less than 200 miles from Madras – where all ranks of the 2nd Battalion were undergoing intensive training 'for duties in aid of the civil power'. In view of the increasing tension throughout India, the authorities wanted to make sure there were sufficient fighting forces capable of maintaining law and order. She wrote:

I expect he will go to England with his Regt. when the Army leaves India. I don't know what we poor folk will do as my Son-in-law Frank does not want to give up his good job here, in which case we shall be left to the not tender mercies of the Indians & poor Hester is very frightened with so much strife and hooliganism.

This 'strife' included the activities of lawless mobs, groups of people that took the call for political freedom as a licence to murder, burn and loot. Nevertheless, the process of independence for India was by now well underway. The deadlock that had stumped Wavell was broken by the British Labour government in February 1947, when it promised to hand over power in India 'by a date not later than June 1948'. It also undertook to arrange this transfer of responsibility to whichever authorities were ready to receive it, and sent out Louis Mountbatten, a cousin of King George VI, to succeed Wavell as Viceroy of India and oversee the changes.

Mountbatten was to be the last in a long line of British rulers going back to Robert Clive and Warren Hastings, the first governors of Bengal; and viceroy, of course, was the highest position an Englishman in India could hold, bearing an equivalent status to that of a monarch. Less than a year after leaving the east, having served as the head of SEAC (South East Asia Command), Mountbatten arrived in Delhi on 24th March 1947 to be sworn in amid the vice-regal pomp that had been passed down and established over the last century. However, he was now invested with new powers that allowed him to be wholly independent of the India Office in London, part of the British government.

There was a sense of urgency as he began his task. It was an awesome one: to guide the destiny of a fifth of humanity, some 400 million people speaking 23 languages and 200 dialects in more than 500 semi-independent princely states under the direct rule of the British. The people were diverse, firstly in caste (about 3,000 castes existed for occupational, territorial, tribal, racial or religious reasons) and in religion (there were 250 million Hindu people, 90 million Muslims and six million Sikhs living in India at that time). In addition, there were Buddhists, Christians and members of sects who had been united up until now only by the British Raj and a shared wish for freedom.

The desire of many people was to preserve a united India. However, when Mountbatten arrived in March, he found the situation was more serious than anyone had previously realised. Should things flare up, the lives of British subjects would be at risk – and as it was, most of these subjects already felt that the country was on the verge of a civil war, with good reason. That same month, more than 200 people were killed during incidents in Lahore, Multan and Rowalpindi, as well as Amritsar (notorious for being the scene of a massacre in 1919). A further 1,000 were wounded by the time the army restored order in all these places, which led Mountbatten to advise the British government to transfer full power as soon as possible.

Within two weeks of his arrival, the date of this transfer was brought forward to 31st December 1947. However, things were still not moving fast enough. By May 1947, after numerous meetings with leaders of both sides (including

Jinnah, Gandhi, Nehru and another very important figure in the Congress Party, Sardar Patel), Mountbatten feared the danger of political collapse was real and pressing. Conflict over two key provinces – Bengal and the Punjab, always the centres of trouble – seemed impossible to resolve.

Despite efforts to the contrary, the British government concluded that India would have to be divided. More than any other man, it was the Muslim leader Muhammad Ali Jinnah who made this move inevitable by demanding a new 'Pakistan' for the minority of Muslims who would otherwise, he said, be swamped by the Hindu majority in India.

Millions living in the middle of the subcontinent were Hindu, but the Muslim minority was concentrated in two widely separated areas. This would lead to the creation of a divided Pakistan, West and East. (The word Pakistan means 'land of the pure', and is composed of letters taken from the names of regions including Punjab, Afghania, Kashmir, Iran, Sindh, Tukharistan, Afghanistan and Baluchistan. In 1971, following a civil war, East Pakistan – also known as East Bengal – became Bangladesh.)

The next step was for Mountbatten to submit a Plan of Partition for the agreement of the Indian leaders, and on 4th June he gave a large press conference in Delhi to make its details and implications clear. For the first time, he also referred to the fact that the day of independence was to be brought forward from December to 15th August 1947. This would give him just nine weeks in which to divide the subcontinent and all governmental assets, including the army and the civil service, and to arrange for a smooth transfer of power.

At the end of June, Bengal and the Punjab voted for the partition of their own states, which meant that West Punjab and East Bengal would secede from India. Then Sind voted to join Pakistan, and Sylhet, part of Assam, voted to join (now-Pakistani) East Bengal. The new state of Pakistan, which was in essence two states separated by some 1,100 miles of Indian territory, was to be created at the same time as India gained independence from Britain. However, Kashmir and the North-West Frontier Province had not yet decided which way they would go.

The situation was not at all clear-cut. As Philip Warner remarked in his book *Auchinleck: The Lonely Soldier*,

There were many Hindus in what would become Pakistan, and many Muslims in India. People who had lived and worked amicably together for generations were now becoming conscious of their differences, and of new grievances. Certain areas would have to be divided; thousands, if not millions, of people would have to move.[99]

Things were further complicated by the fact that India was a patchwork of many different powers. There were princes with varying degrees of authority, as well as maharajahs, rajahs and nawabs, khans and lesser rulers. More than 500 dominions existed: some covered huge areas while others were no bigger than large estates of land, and contingents from all these dominions had served beside the British and Indian armies in both world wars. Now they would, in theory, be independent of Britain but they were urged to accede to one or the other of the new dominions, since Britain would be renouncing all her treaty rights with them.

There were other unhappy tasks to perform. It was the responsibility of Claude Auchinleck, the commander-in-chief, to preside over the dismantling of the Indian Army, an all-British officered body of soldiers - both Indians and Gurkhas - whose members came from families that had sent generation after generation of sons to join this force, more for the prestige of belonging to the profession than for the money. As Charles Chenevix Trench pointed out in his book *The Indian Army and the King's Enemies 1900-1947*, Hindus, Sikhs and Muslims served side by side 'in the closest and most trusting comradeship'.[100]

This was the army that at the start of the 20th century, according to Chenevix Trench, had 'united into a single force for the first time since the British had arrived in the sub-continent'.[101] Remarkably, the Indian Army had been the largest volunteer army in history, apparently without a single conscript. It was an army frequently at war on the North-West Frontier and played a large part in protecting and promoting 'British and Indian interests in a dozen countries east of Suez'.[102] Without its existence and abilities, the Japanese could have overrun India, and would probably then have linked up with German forces in Iran. It is possible that, without its actions, the world would have come under the domination of the 'axis' alliance of Germany, Italy and Japan. This was the army to which Auchinleck, Hector and many others had devoted their lives.

However, in 1947 there was little opportunity for nostalgia. As early as 12th June, the authorities had halted the demobilisation of British troops. Auchinleck was convinced that, for the division of the Indian Armed Forces to succeed, it would be necessary to retain British officers and enlist their 'willing cooperation'. They would be asked to remain in their positions of command and on the staff during the period of reconstitution. Auchinleck hoped that a requisite number would wish to stay on, temporarily, from 15th August: he was opposed to any idea of compelling them to do so.

Hector was among those who decided to stay. Bill, on the other hand, would with many other British troops start moving out of India on 15th August, although with the limitations of shipping, withdrawal would be phased over a period of six months. Auchinleck stipulated that after this date, British troops could be employed to protect British lives and property, but they must not participate in settling communal disturbances unless British lives were in danger. Additionally, Mountbatten urged indigenous governors not to ask for the support of British troops, as this would interfere with the reconstitution of the Indian Armed Forces.

Events in India and Britain had taken on a momentum of their own and on 18th July, the Independence Bill that had been pushed through Parliament became law. Among other things, it abolished the post of Commander-in-Chief, India. Less than a month later, at midnight on 14th August 1947, India gained its independence and Pakistan became a separate (and divided) country. Most of the princely states acceded to this new India, except for Hyderabad and Kashmir. (At first, the Nizam of Hyderabad refused to join either India or Pakistan even though the majority of the state's population was Hindu, but eventually the Indian Army occupied this state, and it became part of India. With India holding the east and south and Pakistan the north and west, Kashmir, which was a predominantly Muslim state with a Hindu maharajah, remains to this day the subject of bitter dispute between the two nations.)

It was the end of nearly 200 years of British rule in India. By coincidence, Independence Day on 15th August was also the wedding anniversary of Hector and Clare Perks. They had been married for 19 years.

Under that charged Indian sky, the day itself brought momentary and much-needed relief. There was an air of excitement and anticipation, and in Avadi Pat and Margaret joined their parents for an Independence Day celebration organised for the military and civil personnel of the control office section of the ordnance depot. Lunch was a 'first-class' curry served by Indian soldiers from large pots (dechsies) to everyone who was sitting outside the building at long trestle tables. Each person was given a small silk replica of the official national flag of the new India, which showed three horizontal stripes in saffron, white and green with the Ashoka Chakra emblem in the centre – the Buddhist Wheel of Life and Cosmic Order. (Ashoka the Great was the ruler of the Maurya Empire in the 3rd Century BC, between 273BC and 232BC.) The flag purportedly bore no religious symbolism.

Captain and Mrs Hadden accompanied Clare and Hector on an excursion into Madras, where citizens had taken to the streets to welcome independence. There was great revelling among the Indians, although some were not as pleased as others. In particular, 'working class Indians' (those employed by the British) and Anglo-Indians (recognised as being 'of mixed descent' and according to Clare, who felt sorry for them, a people who 'didn't belong in one place any more than they did another') faced something of a dilemma. However, most were delighted.

Amid the general air of celebration in Madras, each of the two men decided to buy a watch for his wife to mark such an historic time. Taking things one step further, both Clare and Mrs Hadden decided it would be nice to choose identical gold-plated models. Each watch cost one hundred rupees (£8) and Clare's was to last her for 37 years, providing a poignant reminder of that day. She also remembered her children, buying gifts that included 'the sweetest pair of red aeroplane hair-clips' for her second-to-youngest daughter, Barbara.

Millions celebrated in India that day, but there was a special focus on New Delhi. The building of this capital city had been completed 16 years earlier at a cost of £15m, and it was designed to accommodate the seat of government as well as some 70,000 inhabitants. It was a 'ready-made capital' and on 15th August – an auspicious day according to astrologers – amid scenes of great joy, the formal handover to India's new leaders took place. Jawaharlal Nehru, head of the incoming provisional government, became the first Indian prime minister. Mountbatten, who from this day forward was no longer the viceroy, took office as the first governor general of the independent India, a non-executive role. Meanwhile Jinnah, a happy man, was installed as the governor general of the new independent Muslim dominion of Pakistan. Mahatma Gandhi, clearly a very unhappy man, 'wept in Calcutta over the violence, the division of India, and the loss of human compassion'.[103]

Even before the cheers of that day had died away, the realities were beginning to set in. Vast hordes of refugees were on the move. Because partition had come simultaneously, independence was not simple – it would be a bloody, hate-filled and chaotic business, leading those who had previously been part of a composite culture, tolerant of religious differences, to slaughter each other by the thousands. Two boundary commissions had drawn up the new frontiers and inevitably, despite their best efforts, control of some areas was bitterly disputed, just as the commissions had predicted. Over the next few months of crisis there was to be constant rioting between Hindus and Muslims.

Muslims were stranded in India and Hindus, likewise, in Pakistan. In the months that followed, order more or less ceased to exist across the north of India. In September 1947, there were serious riots in Delhi and 500,000 homeless people advanced on the capital, having nowhere else to go. This created a difficult task for the fledgling government: how to house, feed and clothe people on the brink of disaster, and prevent the spread of cholera and other diseases. They set up large camps on the outskirts of the city, but conditions there were fairly horrific for some time.

Partition had removed two great pieces of India's territory. Almost a quarter of the country was torn away to form West and East Pakistan, areas separated from each other by a vast tract of land. The Punjab in the northwest and Bengal in the east had been split into two parts. In the eastern provinces of Bengal and Assam, the new boundaries were accepted with less trouble, although the exclusion of Calcutta from East Pakistan made it a flashpoint, which led to an inevitable loss of trade.

Gandhi stayed in Calcutta (now the capital of West Bengal only) to ensure that there was no repetition of the horrors of 'Direct Action Day' the year before, when many thousands of people in the city had been killed and wounded in riots between communities of Hindus and Muslims. To their credit, men in the Indian Army remained firm and disciplined, though they did not always know what was happening in their own villages. Occasionally, though, news came through about the now-divided Punjab (the province which was home to most Indian soldiers), where communities were fighting each other with considerable ferocity, leading to some horrific massacres.

In the Punjab, the boundary line cut through the traditional homeland of the Sikhs. These people tended to be closer in outlook to the Hindus than to the Muslims, whom they generally disliked, but the boundary line left many Muslims among the Sikhs on the Indian side of the border, and the Sikhs started to drive them out. On the Pakistani side of the boundary, the Sikhs began to slaughter the Muslims who in turn retaliated, wherever they were in the majority, by killing Hindus. These were the Punjab Massacres of August and September 1947, in which some 500,000 people died.

Meanwhile, some 4.5 million Hindus and Sikhs fled from Pakistan to India, while six million Muslims went the other way from India to Pakistan. This mass movement of the population only added to the problems with which the newly established governments were grappling. In addition, British troops could no longer be used for peacekeeping. However, there were some transitional measures.

Auchinleck, who had recently been promoted to the position of field marshal, was made the temporary supreme commander, taking central administrative control of the new armies of India and Pakistan, although this was only until they could be sorted out into two distinct forces and the two governments were in a position to administer them properly. On partition, most British officers were automatically transferred into the British Army, but a significant proportion had applied and been accepted to remain with Indian forces during the entire period of transition. Hector had elected to stay and, like all such volunteers, he came under Auchinleck's command.

Hector was one of about 2,800 officers, out of a rough total of 8,000 officers from various echelons, who volunteered to stay in India in an advisory capacity to ease the handover of power. (These troops were not involved in any way in matters of policy and direction.) Hector was accepted for service from 15th August until 31st December 1947, a date on which he would be permitted to volunteer for further service. However, it was made clear to all officers that despite their seniority and experience, they would no longer take precedence over Indian officers. One of the first tasks for the ordnance directorate of the new Indian Army was to move Indian officers into various senior appointments to fill the gaps created by the departure of British officers. After so many years in which Indians were subordinate, this must have been quite an adjustment for Hector and his colleagues to make. Still, he hoped his extended service would clock up two years of 'rank element' instead of one and so enhance his service pension.

Clare, worrying about the unstable conditions and her children's lack of education, decided she must bring her family 'home to England'. She had briefly lived in England during two quite separated leave years, staying in Plymouth near to Gus and Emily, but she knew that life there permanently would be nothing like living in her native India. However, her home country was metamorphosing into something quite different than previously, and the evidence appeared to indicate that, after these recent changes, it could never be the same again. Her mother Mary Perren, sister Hester and brother-in-law Frank had decided to stay indefinitely in India, and for their sake she hoped and prayed that the country would one day right itself.

During this period of handover, many other families were heading in the same direction. In Avadi, there was a grand farewell for Colonel Stevenson who was replaced by a smart, Westernised Indian. While the Perks were still at the base, the new colonel's wife gave birth to a baby and to ensure a regular fresh supply of milk, her husband invested in a cow. As it produced more than the little family required, Clare was among those who benefited from the surplus, and fortunately the small amounts she was given had little chance to turn rancid in the heat.

Equally, the jasmine and the sharp-smelling marigolds, as described in Kipling's novel *Kim* ('stronger even than the reek of the dust'[104]) did not wither away in the hot weather. Marigolds were held in high esteem all over India, being used in religious ceremonies and at celebrations, including that held for Colonel Stevenson's farewell staff photograph. Together with the colonel and the 139 Indians pictured, Hector posed with a garland of tightly-strung marigold blossoms around his neck. As long as she lived, said Clare, she would never forget the heavy scents of marigold, jasmine, gardenia and verbena, as well as the beautiful roses and other intensely fragrant flowers which had grown in some of the gardens she had known since her childhood days in Simla almost 40 years before. It was this memory of the senses, as much as anything else, that spoke to her so evocatively of India, her home country, the land of her birth.

TWENTY-EIGHT

PACKING FOR ENGLAND

As the sun went down on the Raj, the summer conditions gradually gave way to the great reversal of wind. The southwest summer monsoon penetrated progressively less into the heart of India, and the southeast winds of the Bengal Sea branch of the summer monsoon no longer reached the Ganges Basin: instead, they curved back out and down to the eastern side of the great Deccan plateau, bringing considerable rainfall to southeastern parts of the peninsula and Ceylon; diminishing rapidly inland. The bulk of the rain in Madras comes during this period of the retreating monsoon, from mid-September to December. However, as things turned out, the Perks family would never experience the entire season in this part of the subcontinent.

The prospect of leaving prompted mixed feelings – deep sadness, relief, excitement, and anxiety, but for the Perks children this combination was leavened by the surprise arrival of their grandmother, Mary Perren. She had come to say her farewells in the belief that she might never see this side of her family again.

Young Barbara volunteered to give up her bed for the seventy-two-year-old, and slept instead on a mattress that occupied the space under the bed. Surprisingly, although they were outside, protected only by the roof of the trellis-screened veranda, and seemingly more vulnerable to the ingress of the heavy downpours, these two beds provided somewhat more of a refuge than those inside. When it rained, as it often did now, those who slept under the main part of the tin roof would often be awakened by a racket, and then by the necessity of moving their beds to a drier position, where the large drops would not drench the bedding.

Since Barbara had given up her bed and consequently slept closer to her grandmother, it seemed right that she should have the privilege and the pleasure of taking her a cup of Horlicks in bed each morning although, being seven years old, she may have not been trusted to heat the drink herself. The children delighted in showing their grandmother Diggers' Dive one warm day in September, an event preserved in a snapshot which was clearly taken at a time of the day when it was tolerable enough in the heat to sit out in the open. The picture shows the whole family, including Hector, sitting on beach chairs at the edge of the shark-infested waters.

With her familiar deftness, Mary set to helping her daughter's family pack for the journey to England. Their luggage included items such as heavy coats for Barbara and Mary, which Clare had commissioned from a derzi (tailor) in Avadi, foreseeing a cold winter ahead; and trousers for Pat and Margaret, the first they had ever worn, which were fashioned out of some sage-green woollen blankets. Out came the family's old tin trunks, and leather and canvas cases, containers that by now were as well travelled as the family, having been hauled by steam across the huge expanse of India several times, and frequently manhandled onto and off trucks and trains by soldiers and by coolies.

Careful thought was given to what was packed where; whether this garment or that was right for the luggage to be marked Cabin, or whether it should go in the case marked WOV (Wanted On Voyage). Anything NWOV (Not Wanted On Voyage) was consigned to the ship's hold, but even these possessions had to be packed with care in wooden crates. They included quality Indian bed linen and towels, Clare's precious Singer sewing machine, a tiffin carrier, a brass tray, a brass gong and lots of brass ornaments and silver-plated tableware, much of which had been given to Clare and Hector on their wedding. There were other artefacts and useful items too, many of which later became treasured objects reminding the family of their beloved India.

It had only been six months since the family had moved from Agra, and since they had trimmed down their possessions for that long journey, there was not too much to dispose of now. In any case, as Peter once remarked of his parents: 'They had never had too much stuff'. It was Peter, now a teenager, who took on the painstaking job, while the family was still in Avadi, of stencilling in white paint on every crate, case and trunk the address in England to which the family was bound: Major H R Perks, 21 Durnford Street, Stonehouse, Plymouth, Devon. This was the home of Uncle Gus and Auntie Em.

At about this time, two crates turned up which held Hector's once-precious radio equipment. This was his pre-war pastime, and the contents included his transmitter and aerial, both of which had been impounded for the duration of the war. By now, though, he had lost interest in being a radio ham and so, apart from putting aside some useful instruments and bits and pieces which he wanted to keep, he disposed of it.

He had other things to think about, matters that were more pressing. While Mary Perren was staying, he was called away for several weeks to attend a court martial, possibly held at the army headquarters in New Delhi. All around, the country remained in a thoroughly disturbed state and by now, as a British officer, he would have lost status in the eyes of many of Indians. In this climate of madness, it seemed that respect had largely disappeared. Even in his uniform, Hector was forced to carry a gun at his side at all times to protect himself from troublemakers. On trains, particularly in the far north of the country, it was rumoured that Indians and refugees were being attacked with impunity by armed gangs. When Hector returned home and removed his revolver, he reminded the children of the strict instruction he had given on previous occasions, when he returned from operations, on the Burma fronts for example, that they were not to go near it.

It was not the best of times, but the days passed quickly and after a week or more, the time came on 6th October 1947 for Mary to go back to Calcutta. The distance from Madras to Calcutta was an astonishing 1,039 miles and the journey an incredible 39 hrs. It seemed cruel that in her seventies she should have to endure that tedious and wearying ride home, knowing it was likely she would never see her dear family again. Hector was still away and would be absent for several weeks, which meant he was unable to join his family in seeing Mary off at Madras station that day.

In such an uncertain climate, both mother and daughter were worried about each other and, given the upheaval going on all over the country, travelling felt more risky than usual. For Clare, who had so many other things on her mind, this was a difficult parting, though she had the comfort of knowing that her mother would be cared for very well by Hester and Frank. Mary, who had seen her own mother-in-law leave India for New Zealand with her husband William's sister Fanny, must have felt as though history was repeating itself – except that this time it was she who was staying, and the younger generation who were leaving India behind. She had already lost one son to death, and another – temporarily – to the horrors of the Thai camps, although he too would soon be leaving India. During her stay, she sensed Clare's anxiety and her concerns about how she could supervise her five children without Hector there to keep them safe, and would have done what she could to alleviate it.

Now, at Madras railway station, Mary told Clare not to worry but to put her trust in God. She vowed, as always, to pray for them all. She boarded her carriage and as she leaned down to hold the hands of her grandchildren through the open window, she must have felt bewildered by the change going on around her, and powerless to control it. Eventually the train departed, leaving the family bereft and with heavy hearts, mother and daughter believing they might never see each other again. Despite the distances in India, they were a close family, and for some time to come each of them would feel this void deeply, believing they had parted forever.

Mary's journey was not without excitement, both before and after the station of Waltair, where the Madras and South Mahratta Railway's northeast section joined the Bengal-Nagpur Railway bound for Howrah station in Calcutta. Fortunately, it had been arranged for Mary to be accompanied on this long journey by a certain 'Mr Mac', who had been paid to look after her.

On 9th October, the day after she arrived back in Calcutta, Mary was anxious to put pen to paper in order to let her younger daughter know of her arrival. 'Just a line to let you know I arrived safe & sound yesterday afternoon 3 hours late,' she wrote. 'Frank was at the Stn to meet me with the Car. It was a very tiring journey but fairly comfortable. We had two Indians in the compartment going to Pakistan, they were not bad, only for a short run we were crowded, four more Indians got in. One train crasher got in at one Stn on the off side without a ticket but Mr Mac handed him over at Waltair.'

The trip was otherwise uneventful and Mary did not worry unduly. She was, after all, a veteran of Indian travel. 'Our train was held up at Karagpur for one hour owing to the brakes having failed,' she wrote. 'Anyway we got here safely which is the main thing. Mr Mac was very good and looked after my comfort.'

The next part of her letter expressed, perhaps more fully than usual, her feelings about their parting.

> Now Darling I am very anxious to hear from you as to whether you got home alright. I miss you all very much & feel this parting more than I can say. My Heart feels very sad at times, it is just one of the trials we have to face. I shall often look back on the very happy & peaceful time I spent with you all, my darling, & thank one & all so much for making me happy & comfortable & for all the arrangement for my safe return to Cal.

Though she was unable to say goodbye to her son-in-law at the station, she wrote: 'I am very grateful to dear Hector. I wonder if you have heard from him & if he is returning to you soon.' On her return, she had also found a letter from her son Bill, who was still in Bangalore, and she wrote to Clare that he would soon be sailing for England (ahead of Clare and the children) on 7th October 1947, with his unit. Mary added:

> You may also have heard that he received all the birthday letters that you & the children sent. It will take me some days to settle down to the old life here. It is very hot & sticky, much worse than Madras & Avadi. Off came my vest on arrival. Hester & Frank sent their very fond love to one & all & Hester thanks you very, very much for all you have sent & says you must please let her know how much to send you for them. Only one of the dogs made a very big fuss of me on my arrival & that was Victor. The others were matter of fact. I will not stop to write more this time, my Darling, as I must post this letter now by Gulah. All my fondest love & heaps of kisses to each of you dear ones. My darling my heart & prayers are always with you, darling. Fond love & kisses from your ever fond loving mother. P.S. Tell Barbara I missed her this morning with the Horlicks. I hope Mary is good. Peter must be happy with his swimming now. Fondest love & kisses & God Bless you all, Mother.

Back in Avadi, there was no farewell party for the Perks family, and no garlands. Everyone was leaving – everyone who was British, that is – and Indian officers were taking up their posts. None were more directly affected by the break-up of the Raj than those serving in the Indian Army and the Indian Civil Service, as Charles Allen has noted.[105] The political failures that caused such abrupt division and turmoil within Indian society had also led to disappointment and bitter resentment among British officers. They felt that everything they had worked for and served over so many years was being condemned. Before independence, the army had been united under regimental colours and a single flag, regardless of caste, colour or creed. Now, that 200-year history had disappeared with the stroke of a pen.[106]

For Hector and other British officers, there was no future in joining up to serve with either of the two new armies. Others faced an even more difficult dilemma. Many in the Anglo-Indian population felt that they had to decide, once and for all, whether they were Indian, Pakistani or British; they felt pressured to nail their colours to the mast. However, some sections of the British community were likely to remain in India for the long term, including businessmen, planters and missionaries whose wish it was to continue their prime role in providing education along Western lines and a health service of sorts, as well as to spread the Christian gospel.

As October drew on, and farewells were said, if not celebrated, the Perks family prepared to leave. Like other officers who had volunteered for duty until the necessary replacements and handovers had taken place, Hector was staying on, but in the meantime he planned to travel with Clare and the children by train to Deolali. They would remain there in transit until they received orders to sail, though it seemed at this stage that Hector would not be travelling with them to England. It was an unnerving prospect, and one that Clare hardly dared to think about. No doubt Hector too was far from sanguine about the prospect of his wife and children embarking on an inter-continental voyage to establish a new home without him. Despite the fact that, to a great degree, they would be overseen by the army authorities on the voyage and supported by his brother and family upon arrival in Plymouth, it was difficult to see them off on their own, since he had shepherded them on all earlier journeys both within and beyond Indian shores. He must have felt torn between taking moves to ensure the safety of his family and provide for their welfare on the voyage, and the need to secure their future by remaining in India, for the time being, to maximise his pension.

Most army officers and officials were tired after working in extreme, stressful conditions for the past eight years. Hector was no exception. Few had been able to take home leave, and many were keen to get some rest and to see their homeland and families again. Even so, there was much regret in the going, especially for those with ancestral roots in the land. Clare and Hector were among those who had buried the bones of loved ones (some small and tender) in Indian graveyards, and it was hard to leave these behind. The children sensed that great changes were afoot – that in the coming weeks, they would have to adapt to new circumstances and rebuild their lives in a colder and perhaps harsher climate. While they had all envisaged leaving India one day, the sudden end of the Raj came, inevitably, as a shock.

Hector was engaged in 'extended service' to split the old Indian Army: its officers, equipment, depots and everything else. Nevertheless, despite busy times at work, he accompanied his family and all the luggage on that last long haul, a mere 840 miles over two days. Upon leaving Madras at the end of October, the family once more embarked by train, traversing the extensive Indian railway system that had been laid out by British engineers initially as a way of uniting India. Having been overworked and run down during the recent war, however, the system was now under huge strain from the process of partition. Special refugee trains transported millions of people who were quite literally fleeing for their lives (the worst area for conflict being the Punjab) but at that time all journeys were dangerous, with frequent line-side ambushes. Facing an additional voyage across the sea, without her husband, Clare was very apprehensive. No wonder Hector felt he had to accompany them as far as he possibly could.

From Madras they headed northeast over that great southern peninsula of India, the Deccan, on the main line to Bombay. Along the way they passed the junction stations of Arkonam, Reginunta and Guntakal, and here the bustle and bedlam contrasted greatly to the open country in between. Looking out of the carriage window, seven-year-old Barbara was struck by the stillness and quietness broken only by the powerful rhythmic pulses of the giant steam-driven train. For mile upon mile she gazed out, soothed by the never-ending line of telegraph poles, noticing how the telegraph line rose and sank from pole to pole.

After Raichur, the train crossed the Krishna river over a grand bridge nearly a mile long. From there it went on to Wadi, which marked a near-halfway point of the journey. The Nizam's state railway ran east some 115 miles from Wadi to the city of Hyderabad, and on to Secunderabad, another six miles. This of course had been, for more than four years, the stamping ground of one dashing young trooper in the 4th/7th Dragoon Guards: Hector Perks. It was the first place he had lived in India, at the start of his career. Could he ever have imagined, in those long-ago days, that he would carve out for himself such a happy and settled life in India? He had become an accomplished soldier, a trusted servant of the Indian Army Ordnance Corps, and above all, a family man.

Travelling from Wadi up to Sholapur, the great steam locomotive pressed on past Poona, a place which roused in Margaret and Peter special feelings of elation, for this was where they had been born, respectively, 15 and 13 years before. Soon after, the Deccan plateau gave way to a dramatic descent over the Bhor Ghat. This was 15 miles long, with precipitous hillsides of sheer rock, as well as great ravines and waterfalls, and led down to Kalyan junction at the foot of the great Western Ghats. These, of course, were the giant hills rising three, four and five thousand feet, that were annually fed by the air stream of the Arabian Sea branch of the southwest monsoon. After another 34 miles, they arrived at the end of the line in Bombay.

However, this was not their destination – not yet, at least. The next train, Calcutta-bound, would take them almost back on themselves up the Thal Ghat, the second of these two spectacular and heavily engineered mainline mountain passes, and beyond. Some 80 miles on was Deolali, the place they were to stay for now, a hill-resort patronised by the Parsi population. Parsis were and are adherents of Zoroastrianism, and descendents of those Zoroastrians who fled to India from Muslim persecution in Persia during the 7th and 8th centuries AD; they were popular with many others who lived in Bombay.

Deolali itself had a large barracks and was the first staging post in the transit of servicemen and families who awaited embarkation. (Previously it had been a halting- place, during both world wars, for troops arriving from or returning to Europe.) On arrival, Clare was relieved to find that food and meals were provided in the large communal canteen and dining hall. However, when the time came for Hector to leave to return to his duties in south India, having settled her in with the children, she could not help weeping. This was a parting unlike any other before, and coming on top of the recent separation from her mother Mary, it must have been very hard. She wondered how she would manage all that was ahead of her without him.

With its cooling mountain breezes, however, Deolali was a pleasant enough place to pass a few last weeks in India. Pat managed to continue her shorthand studies with the help of a Burmese couple also waiting to depart, and the picture houses played films intended to enable those stationed there to feel closer to 'home'. On 20th November 1947, people gathered round the wireless sets to hear the live broadcast of the wedding of Princess Elizabeth, heir to the throne, to Philip Mountbatten (the Duke of Edinburgh and also the nephew of the last viceroy of India). Not long after, the picture houses played the film of the actual event, which uplifted people's spirits amid all the grave and dismal political reporting. Nevertheless, despite the common-spirited approach to life, the place had its limitations and it was hard for anyone to forget for long that this was only a temporary camp, with everyone waiting to leave. The main focus was the large outdoor notice board, to which was pinned lists showing who was next in line to move to the port of embarkation.

On a wider scale, hostility was growing in government circles (both in India and Pakistan) to the continuing presence of Claude Auchinleck as supreme commander. He was higher in rank than the commander-in-chief of the new dominions; furthermore, many Indians considered him biased towards the Pakistanis. Under pressure from India's new political leaders to close the supreme headquarters at the earliest possible date, Mountbatten wrote to Auchinleck advising him to propose this, and then resign.

Auchinleck had drafted a long report for the British government, dated 28th September, which suggested withdrawing British officers from Indian units. Feelings were running so high between India and Pakistan, he indicated, that British officers remaining in these units were likely to have no choice but become involved in a war. The report he wrote clearly demonstrates how rapidly changes had already taken place:

> Those officers are now asking to be released from their contracts under the three months' notice clause in ever increasing numbers. One of the chief reasons for this is because they hold that they volunteered to help in Reconstruction and not to help the new Governments keep law and order in their own territories. The conditions of massacre and bestiality of the worst kind, in which many of these British officers have been working continuously for many weeks, have sickened them. They have lost faith in their cloth and in their men, of whom they were so proud a short two months back.

Some officers, attempting to prevent massacres, had already been killed, and on 1st October 1947 Auchinleck wrote 'General Routine Orders' which, among other things, laid out plans for the disengagement of remaining British officers. He gave all of the volunteers three months' notice, allowing them to be released from duty by the first day of the new year. He had already brought forward the closure of his headquarters to 31st December, as advised by Mountbatten, but decided on 21st October that even this was too late. On 30th November the headquarters were replaced by Command for British Forces, India and Pakistan, a temporary organisation that would look after and be responsible for all British officers as well as other ranks and their families. This organisation itself, however, would close on 31st December 1947.

These changes were important for Hector. On 13th October he received instructions in a GHQ Signal that all volunteers (other than those who had been accepted for service with the dominion governments after 31st December on different terms) were to be despatched immediately or sent to either Deolali or Mauripur to await embarkation.

Hector may have felt some relief that he would, after all, be escorting his family on their voyage to England, but he also regretted the need to wind up so hastily a military career in which he had taken considerable and justified pride. Aside from the loss of opportunity to enhance his pension, the circumstances of his enforced retirement felt inauspicious, given the sense of duty and satisfaction which he and his fellow soldiers had accumulated during their times of peace and war on the subcontinent, and considering his lengthy commitment to his adopted country. A career that began with seven years in a British cavalry regiment and continued with 21 years of service in India, together with advancement in his ordnance specialism, was not something he could so lightly set aside, whatever the political imperative.

News travelled fast: in a letter from Calcutta dated 5th December – a date by which supreme headquarters had closed for good and Auchinleck had left India – Mary Perren wrote to her daughter, and expressed the hope that her husband would soon join her, though she already knew Hector was coming.

> My own darling Girlie, My fond love & ever so many thanks for your dear welcome letter received a few days ago. I was so glad to know that you are all well. I hope Hector has arrived in Deolali safe and well. I am so very glad to know that he is to be with you all. I hope you received the parcel and registered letter from Hester. Auntie Lizzie has also sent a parcel to you on Monday or Tuesday. She was here with May & Mrs Johnstone on Wednesday evening, & she and May sent their love very fond love to you all. Auntie is not keeping too well and has a cold... I am so glad that Pat is able to keep up her shorthand studies, it will help her a lot. I should be glad to hear that Peter was doing some study, he will have a long way to make up & will find it very hard when he returns to school...

Her letter betrays some anxiety about the situation, and also about the changes and upheavals with which she herself was coping. Frank's brother Cyril had apparently resigned and hoped to leave India in March, while his niece Beryl and her husband were also planning to go.

> Beryl & Aubrey have not yet arrived from Ranchi. They all seem to be clearing out of this country. I wonder how many will come back sadder & wiser... Give my love to Emmie & her family. I am so glad you are going to be near her on your arrival, she does really seem to be a real good sort, as you say.

Mary added:

I have not heard from Bill again since he joined up after his leave. I am expecting a letter daily. He was very sorry that he did not take a sports jacket home with him to go with his grey flannels. He says he can't get one in England as they give no coupons to the Army. I don't suppose it would be possible to get one there for him before you leave... Hester & Frank send their very fond love to each one. I wonder if I shall be able to send you any more letters before you leave & if you will receive this. Give my fond love to Hector & tell him I wrote to him in Avadi but I am afraid he left before it arrived... If I cannot write to you again in Deolali, my darling, you will find an air letter awaiting your arrival in England & you will all be in my daily prayers & thoughts always... Give my fond love to each of the dear children with lots of kisses, they must be having a good time there. No more this time darling with all my fondest love & heaps of kisses from your ever loving Mother.

Leaving his unit on 27th November, Hector arrived to join his family in Deolali and was met with a surge of warmth, affection and relief; they would now travel to England together. In all, Clare and the children spent six weeks in Deolali, 2,000ft above sea level, and Hector was there just for the last two.

At last their names came up on the list. They all travelled back by the same rail-route, westwards this time, taking the awesome and thrilling track down the sharp Thal Ghat incline. According to Pat, this journey included many uncomfortable jerky stops and starts because the driver of the train – sensitive to the dangers of the gradient – was taking care to apply the brakes at every opportunity. (It was just the opposite of going up, when high tractive power was needed to pull the heavy trains up the slopes.) The weather was hot, adding to the discomfort of the children, but soon they were on the coast at their next temporary camp.

This was Colaba, on the southern strip of Bombay, a peninsula that was originally one of a group of 12 islands separated from the mainland and from one another. The family thus completed all their years of railway travel in India with an arrival at the city's GIPR terminus, one of the grandest of Indian stations opened on the day of Queen Victoria's Golden Jubilee in 1887. With a central dome, stained glass and solid-cut stonework, the station – as Barbara remembered it later – seemed more like a cathedral.

Clare's brother Bill had left India in early October, on the SS Asturias. By now, thousands of other people were desperate to depart from these shores for 'the homeland'. Hector remembered later how the commandant at Colaba camp 'was being pestered by many anxious to get home'. With the transport arranged centrally by the remainder of the British operation in India, all anyone could do was to sit and wait. For the children, though, it was a time of some excitement, and a new place to explore. As in Deolali, meals were served at a large canteen, but Pat, Margaret and Peter, enjoying the fresh air of the coast, also took the younger girls out for walks along the land that skirted this narrow-necked promontory. As they and their sisters looked out across the vast Arabian Sea, they were already dreaming of their new life to come.

To the very last, they sang songs as they walked, songs that were certain to raise their spirits. (These usually remained high, in any case.) Some of the songs came from the years in Shillong and Agra, while others were learned more recently. When later in life she brought to mind the time of their departure, Barbara would always remember *Five Minutes More* (1946), *Mairzy Doats* (1943), *Swinging on a Star* (1944), *Darling Je Vous Aime Beaucoup* (1935), *K-K-K-Katy* (1918) and *I'll be Seeing You* – a song revived in 1944 just as *J'attendrai* was in 1945, and *Yours* in 1941.

By now Christmas was just days away. So much else had been going on that there had been scarcely any mention of presents, but Hector and Clare had not forgotten the importance of the occasion and they made it a priority one day to venture into the busy streets of Bombay to search – very successfully – for delights. The day they went into the city as a family was to be their last shopping trip in India. After a week at Colaba, it was time to go home – to England.

TWENTY-NINE

FAREWELL GREAT JEWEL

S o it was that on the evening of Sunday 21st December 1947, the Perks family prepared to leave India. It was nearing 7pm and as dusk closed in all around on that great subcontinent, hundreds of passengers lined the deck rails to watch and wait for the moment when their ship, the ocean liner SS Ormonde, left shore.

While the passengers on board were almost exclusively army officers and their families, among them were 373 Polish displaced persons from camps in India. It seems they were part of the 5,000-strong Polish community in India whom Claude Auchinleck, the former commander-in-chief, had wanted to remove from the country – an intention he had stated back in June 1947. These people had been evacuated to India from Britain during the war, under the authority of the British government, following an influx in 1939 when Germany invaded and occupied the western two-thirds of Poland while the Soviet Union occupied the remainder.

More than 160,000 Polish men had fought alongside the British forces in Europe during the war, and during that time they and their families became aware of the atrocities visited upon their compatriots during the Nazi occupation. In the post-war settlement, the prospects for their homeland looked no less bleak when a puppet, communist government was installed in Poland by the Soviet Union. Unsurprisingly then, many refugees, including 40,000 wives and dependent relatives, pressed to be allowed to remain in Britain or at least to be helped to settle in other Commonwealth countries. It was apparent from the SS Ormonde's passenger list that most if not all of the Poles on board were wives and dependents. According to this list, they intended England as their 'permanent residence' and gave their address as the Polish Resettlement Corps in London.

As for the ship itself, the SS Ormonde had undergone one of the longest and most varied careers of any of those on the Orient Line (of the 57 ships on this line, the first was built in 1871 and the last in 1953). The SS Ormonde had only just returned to India that year from government service: from the start of the war, she had been running continuously as a troopship or assault ship to all parts of the world, and before that had been plying the route back and forth to Australia (normally via the Cape), doing a total of 75 round voyages on the 'Australian run' as a vessel for the British government's emigration scheme to Australia. She took part in the evacuations from Norway and France and, in November 1942, was present at the North African landings, then Sicily and Italy. She came through all this unscathed and later carried troops mostly to India and the Far East.

The SS Ormonde was designed as a troopship, and was built by John Brown & Co on Clydebank between the years 1914 and 1917, being completed in June 1918. With the peace, she was refitted as a passenger vessel for immigrant traffic. In total, she had seven holds and five passenger decks and made her maiden voyage to Australia in November 1919. She was undoubtedly the finest ship on the run and recognised as the ultimate in Australian mail liners.

As far as Clare was concerned – bearing in mind her memories of the troopships of earlier passages to England – this was 'a first class ship'. Neither she nor anyone else on board had any idea that in 1952, just four years later, this beautiful and well-known vessel would be taken to the ship-breaker's yard at Dalmuir in Scotland and broken up to be sold in parts.

For the Perks children, leaving on board the SS Ormonde was a grand way to depart. Slowly, to the sound of singing, the ship drew away from the dock as the clock struck the hour. The singers were Polish, and the song on their lips was a haunting Polish rendition of 'Now is the Hour', a Maori farewell song. It was a poignant moment, especially for Clare, who realised even then that she would probably never return to India – and might never see her mother or sister again. Such emotions, heightened perhaps by the apt lyrics of that song, must have tempered any excitement that the family in general may have felt about their adventure. For certain members of the family, there may have also been a degree of resentment and a sense of powerlessness and loss. However, there was also relief that the last stage of the journey was finally underway.

Bombay was the city at which Clare's grandparents John and Susannah Perren had arrived seventy-four years earlier, in 1874, on their big adventure. To them, the sights and sounds of Bombay must have been awe-inspiring and exciting as the ship approached the quay: the noise, the bustle, the vivid colours and bright light. Above all, there was the heat. Now, all these years later, Clare was returning to the land her grandparents had come from, a land which her father William – John and Susannah's first-born son – had yearned with all his heart, unsuccessfully, to reach before he died. With Clare's return, a great enterprise embracing four generations, had come full circle.

As darkness fell, the ship cruised south out of the shelter of Bombay's vast and beautiful land-bound harbour. Covering the fine expanse of water of this great inlet, which in places was nine miles wide, the SS Ormonde glided past the shadowy images of the crowded buildings of the harbour's inland shore to the west, and on towards Colaba Point. At the southernmost tip of this point lay the old European Cemetery, the final resting place of many who had not been as fortunate as John and Susannah, those who had been struck down by cholera, plague or malaria 'as soon as they entered the harbour'.[107]

Colaba Point was the entrance into the open sea. Leaning over the rails of the deck like everyone else, the children took this last opportunity to wave goodbye to the land they knew so well. For Barbara, it would be a chance to breathe a different kind of air: Clare remembered later that 'everyone' (those who had shared her worry over Barbara's slow recuperation, evident from her persistent leanness and want of 'building up') thought the sea voyage would do her good.

The journey was to take more than two weeks, and the seven family members were sharing space again, this time in a six-berth cabin. The cabin was a retreat from the rest of the world, where the affairs of family life could be maintained, while the public parts of the ship became a pleasure ground. All passengers were listed as travelling Tourist Class and there was no requirement for saluting, although one of the most important duties, for everyone, was to learn the lifeboat drill.

There was one thing Clare hated about travelling by sea. Once again she was seasick as the ship rolled and pitched, for it was said that while the SS Ormonde was an excellent sea boat and easy in the seaway, she could be 'rather tender' under certain conditions. In fact, Clare was so badly afflicted at times that either Pat or Margaret had to take over care of their younger sisters, although little Mary had bouts of seasickness too. Even Peter nearly succumbed, having eaten a dish of tripe for breakfast on a particularly rough morning: only a hasty flight up the stairway onto the airier deck – which was sluiced daily – alleviated his symptoms. Tripe and seasickness aside, Clare remembered one of the family's favourites on board the ship was bread and butter, more delicious and fresh than any they had eaten before.

Generally there was not much organised amusement, though various forms of physical recreation were on offer, such as exercises and daily walks round the deck to keep fit. Within the shelter of the glass deck screens, there were other more sedentary pursuits, including card playing in the lounge areas. There was also a barbershop and the chance to browse in a shop selling sundries, souvenirs and chocolate. One day Barbara struck lucky when a man whom Hector knew bought her a whole bar of chocolate. This man was one of the 271 army personnel on board ship and, like Hector and the others, he went about garbed in his uniform. It wasn't until later that these men would have to go to London to be kitted out in 'civvies' – a 'demob' suit, trilby hat, etc. In any case, troops always wore uniform on troopships that were going out from or returning to Britain; it was in India, after all, that khaki dress first enjoyed general use. Initially, tropical uniform was worn on deck and a pair of shorts was worn below deck, but later in the voyage these were exchanged for home-service serge dress issue (battle dress).

Another officer, popular on board, was 'the gallant' Archie John of the Black Watch who had lost his left hand as a result of wounds sustained on the Burma front. He was the only son of Field Marshal Wavell, and was possibly by this stage a major himself; so Peter thought, at least. Archie was a kind man, later agreeing to Peter's request that he get his famous father's autograph on a copy of the very last dinner menu of the voyage, which had already been signed by a number of other selected fellow passengers.

By now the ship had made her run across the Arabian Sea and the family had seen flying fish and porpoises along the way. The ship's arrival at Aden on the 25th

December 1947 meant that the longest leg of the voyage was now behind her and Christmas had arrived. In all of the ship's to-ing and fro-ing throughout the year, this was the voyage on which the ship's company truly rose to the occasion and the passengers, isolated from the rest of the world (for on this journey, no one was allowed to go ashore at any time), were all too ready to join in.

While Father Christmas did not actually appear in person, Barbara and Mary were still of an age to be convinced by the idea that it was this venerable man who had left them each a life-sized baby doll. In fact, these dolls had been earmarked for the two little sisters since that last day of shopping in Bombay, and they were real enough to become the almost constant centre of attention, especially when dressed in the beautiful outfits Clare painstakingly knitted. Pat and Margaret both received a Parker pen, each one engraved with her name, while Peter was given a 'Frog' aeroplane powered by elastic bands. The children had not bought gifts for their parents, though Pat later remembered that they would have made things, as usual, to give Hector and Clare. It was a day of celebration, spent surrounded by comfort and lovely furnishings (Orient liners were said to set the highest standards), and it provided the family with a hearty interlude in what otherwise might have seemed a longer and perhaps less pleasurable time on board.

They departed from Aden on Boxing Day and covered the length of water that runs up to the Red Sea, arriving in Suez on the 29th December. From there, many passengers lined the decks to watch their ship's slow passage up the canal to Port Said. To all those homeward-bound from British India, this was the place where the East ended and it was here, in keeping with tradition, that tropical wear was put away for the last time and exchanged for the cold and wet weather wear brought up from one of the holds of the ship. Pat and Margaret were keen to don their new warm sage-green trousers, but the novelty soon wore off because these trousers had to be worn a lot and were quickly found by both sisters to be rather shapeless.

It was also at Port Said, before the ship moved on the following day, that some Egyptians, known as 'gully-gully' men, came on board while the ship was anchored offshore. With their patter they drew quite a crowd, and their slick conjuring of noisy yellow baby chicks (and eggs) from here and there among the audience held Barbara spellbound. She and Mary were focusing on every move of this astonishing act when suddenly one of the men plucked out an egg from inside her cardigan!

That same day, there was chance to do a little shopping from one of the small

Egyptian 'bum boats' that drew alongside the SS Ormonde. 'Very cheap, very cheap' was the claim, and if one intended to buy, it was possible to bargain for the goods, some of them crafted from leather. When a bargain was struck, the item was placed in a basket attached to a rope that the vendor had first thrown up the side of the ship, establishing a pulley system, although the money for the item had to be sent down in the basket first.

Bit by bit, the family was adjusting to the idea of a new life in England. When the sea was quiet, everyone could relax and spend 'nice times' chatting; and these would, of course, be among the last opportunities for the Perks children to mingle with other children leaving British India, as well as for Clare and Hector to talk with familiar army people before confronting the responsibilities and the rigours that lay ahead. The new year of 1948 was welcomed in with much frivolity, especially by those eligible to attend one of the 'lovely' moonlight dances of the voyage – a highlight for Pat and Margaret.

After passing through the Straits of Gibraltar into the Atlantic, the ship proceeded north to where the seas got rough again in the Bay of Biscay. A combination of westerly winds, heavy waves and tidal currents working together made this part of the voyage so stormy that only the hardiest of those on board escaped bouts of seasickness. Everyone was glad to leave the bay behind and to reach the relative calm of the English Channel.

At last, on 8th January 1948, the SS Ormonde approached the shores of England before edging cautiously up the River Thames, and as the early morning light grew stronger, the children began to see that this was nothing like the country they had left behind.

It was a cold, bleak and drizzly day.

THIRTY

ADJUSTMENT

One of the first things Peter noticed on arriving alongside Tilbury Landing Stage was that the coolies here (or rather, the dockers) were white. Eventually, after some hours of waiting around, Hector, Clare and the children took their leave of the SS Ormonde down the gangway to a crowded dockside. For Barbara and Mary, it was the first time they had set foot on English soil. In the busy customs shed, when the officer saw the size of the family and the amount of luggage, he marked all items with an 'x' and told them to pass straight through.

Later in life, Barbara came across an old Orient Line Special Train luggage label and began to wonder how her family had got from Tilbury to Plymouth. She contacted John Slater, editorial consultant of *The Railway Magazine*, who has an extensive knowledge of train history from the 1940s. 'I doubt you would have got a through train from Tilbury Docks to Plymouth,' he told her. 'Trains from Tilbury in the late 1940s all went to Fenchurch Street, from where you would have had to take the Underground or a taxi to Paddington or Waterloo for another train to Plymouth. The Orient Line may well have arranged to convey your specially-labelled luggage between Fenchurch Street and Paddington or Waterloo.' A few days later, however, he came back to her with revised information. Before the war at least, he said, 'Orient Line boat expresses from Tilbury to London travelled via Barking and South Tottenham to St Pancras. From there you would have taken a taxi or the Underground to Waterloo or Paddington.'[108]

Plymouth was the place that Hector and Clare had decided the family should settle into their 'very different life'. It was somewhere they already knew well, and it was also the home of Hector's brother Gus and his wife Emily, a couple acknowledged by all as 'the salt of the earth'. Since Hector had been released from active military duty following disembarkation, and would hereafter be either on leave or receiving his pension, he had no need to be in London or anywhere else.

For the night journey down to Devon, the family managed to secure an entire carriage compartment, which necessitated some of them sleeping on the floor between the seats, and eventually they arrived in Plymouth at about 6am the next morning. Hector's brother was expecting them but the family's arrival on the doorstep at such an unseemly hour must have caused a stir. Nevertheless, exhibiting a generosity of the kind they had shown ten and 20 years before (when there were fewer members of the family), Gus and Em flung the door open wide and welcomed them in. (This was despite the fact that their own children, Joan, Stanley and Betty, were now grown-up and were also living there.) Em cooked a hearty English fried breakfast for everyone. Then, stout-heartedly, she and Gus took the entire family and its possessions into the basement rooms of their four-storey, terraced house until Hector and Clare could find a place of their own. Pat and Margaret slept upstairs in the attic room.

In preparation for the arrival of her brother-in-law's family, Em had already consulted a town councillor some months before, and this person was influential in obtaining somewhere for the family to live – a house to be built in the suburbs, which the family would rent. Em also helped Clare to obtain ration books with the pages of coupons the family would need to buy food. Not only was the country grieving for 400,000 people killed during the war, but it was also gravely impoverished, having lost a quarter of its national wealth, and was undergoing a period of economic and financial stringency. This meant rationing of certain articles, imposed during the war, remained in place in the immediate post-war period. Such articles included sugar, butter, meat, bacon, ham, eggs and even clothes.

Plymouth had suffered severe war damage, which was evident in several districts not least Stonehouse, close to the naval dockyard, where Gus and Em lived. The immediate surroundings were, therefore, dismal and discouraging. For Pat, especially, these first few months living at Stonehouse and walking around the sea front (near Devil's Point) made a sorry impression. For the rest of her life, she never forgot how dispiriting it was, for body and soul, to be in England after leaving her shining India. Nearby Devonport had lost nearly all of its main entertainment houses, including Clare's favourite The Hippodrome, and in Stonehouse itself thousands of buildings had been demolished or were in need of repair.

When Gus took the children up onto Plymouth Hoe for the first time, Barbara, too, was struck by how sombre and colourless was the landscape compared to the refulgence of India. The weather was grey and it was plain to see how the German bombing raids had flattened and burned the city.

For its size, Plymouth had been subject to a degree of devastation hardly exceeded by that in any other provincial British community. Even Promenade Pier, a seafront landmark that had been enjoyed for many years by summer visitors, was now no more than a twisted mess of metal, later dismantled. Other Blitz victims included churches, schools, theatres, cinemas, shops and pubs. Stanley's school – the boys' grammar on the Hoe – had been completely destroyed and the Notre Dame Convent School in Wyndham Square that Joan attended as a day pupil had been damaged. As a consequence of this, Notre Dame was evacuated to a large house at Teignmouth until after the war and this meant both Joan and Betty had to board. They were billeted out with different families and both found this difficult.

The scars of Plymouth were recent and obvious: more than 1,100 civilians here had died as a result of bombing, and many others were seriously injured or still struggling to accept the implications of loss. On top of this, a great number of servicemen and women had lost their lives. However, by 1947 there were some encouraging signs of recovery. That year, despite Britain's economic problems, authorities in Plymouth unveiled an elaborate and innovative programme to rebuild streets, shops and houses from the rubble and ashes of this wasteland.

The beginning of their new life in post-war Britain presented challenges to all the family and decisions had to be made that would impact on their futures. The disrupted schooling of the youngest three children – Peter, Barbara and Mary –

the limited resources at Hector and Clare's disposal, both potential and actual, it was difficult for them to reconcile their aspirations for themselves and their children with reality, not least when it came to housing and education. There was much to catch up on, and perhaps it was this perceived lack of knowledge that led Hector and Clare to decide that it was wiser to spend money on their children's education than to invest in buying a house of their own. A Catholic education was an imperative, but much of what was available came at a cost. Having decided to defer buying a house, they instead took advantage – with Em's assistance – of the chance to rent a new three-bedroom house on one of the post-war reconstruction estates on the northeast outskirts of Plymouth.

With the first term of 1948 already underway, Peter launched straight into the third form at St Boniface's College at Beacon Park and took to it enthusiastically with both academic and sporting success. It soon became apparent that Peter was enjoying school for the first time in his life. Meanwhile, Barbara and Mary went to St Boniface Primary School, the school their elder sisters had attended ten years before when the family lived in Plymouth for a year. Later they were to complete their studies at Notre Dame High School.

For the older girls, the transition was different and in some ways less easy. Grounded in the British education system while living in India, they now applied themselves to the task of securing an occupation. Margaret, like Pat, had the same job of launching herself into the big wide world. Pat joined the staff of Spooners, a department store, and Margaret became a nursery nurse.

Hector, too, had to adjust. The day after he disembarked from the SS Ormonde, he was released from active military duty, which meant he needed to make a trip to London to collect his 'civvies'. Following this initial release came 56 days of 'release' leave, then 100 days of 'overseas' leave. His leave expired on 13th June and, having served for 28 years, he was formally discharged from the services. He had started as a trooper; and went on to win the War Medal; the Burma Star or Campaign Medal 1939-45; the India Service Medal 1939-45; and the medal for Long Service and Good Conduct.

However, leaving the service also brought a big disappointment. Hector had pinned his hopes on receiving an annual army pension of £316, but instead he only received £304. He had been a major for two years, but the government of India claimed there was a shortfall of four days in his service at this level, and refused to pay the full amount, though he went on contesting this figure until January 1950. In fact, the documents show that although Hector was a captain in the army, he was only ever an acting or temporary major. Having been given 'acting major', he must have felt it would only be a matter of time before the rank became substantive, but the political situation changed and India became independent and he never got it.

Nevertheless, a letter he received from the Commonwealth Relations Office in Whitehall on 21st January 1948, soon after his return, referred to his release from military duty and conveyed the gratitude of His Majesty's Government for the 'valuable services' he had rendered his country at a time of 'grave national emergency'. It added: 'At the end of the emergency a notification will appear in the London Gazette (Supplement) granting you the honorary rank of major. Meanwhile, you have permission to use that rank with effect from the date of your release.'[109]

Hector may have been right to feel angry and wronged by the British government, who refused to pay him the annual rate of pension he felt he was due morally, if not by the letter. However, a far greater injustice was done to the 2.5 million Indian soldiers who fought on the side of the British during the Second World War, in the (British) Indian Army. The British government appeared to forget their deeds and bravery – the fact that they had volunteered to fight for the British Empire remained a sensitive issue long after India became independent – and they were sidelined, and received no pension.

In contrast, the veterans of the anti-British Indian National Army were celebrated as the heroes of independence. The last British soldiers left Indian soil on 13th February 1948, but they were hardly able to prevent the carnage, which by now was happening all around them. A million people were murdered in a hideous war between factions. Feelings on both sides of the borders of India and Pakistan ran high over the division of the assets inherited from the British, and there were bitter squabbles over disputed areas such as Kashmir.

Meanwhile, the diminutive Gandhi was tireless in his efforts to end Hindu-Muslim violence, and in January he threatened to fast to death to induce the government of India to deal fairly with Pakistan and reduce violence between communities. Achieving these aims, he ended his hunger strike on 18th January but was assassinated twelve days later in New Delhi (his killer was an extremist Hindu who hated Gandhi's attitude towards the Untouchables). He did not long survive to enjoy the independence to which he had contributed so much. His friend Jawaharlal Nehru (known as Pandit or Pundit, Hindi for 'teacher') told the Indian people in a broadcast: 'The light has gone out of our lives and there is darkness everywhere.'

Yet good was to result from the death of this man whom millions of Hindus regarded as a saint. Gandhi was a man whom many Europeans also came to value as truly great. In the hearts of the horrified people, high and low, his murder provoked shame and a sense of revulsion against the extremists. This was seen in the great demonstrations of feeling at his funeral, incredible even by Indian standards, when his cremated ashes were cast into the River Jumna. Hindu and Muslim people, however embittered, now sought a new tolerance towards each other, and put aside their hatred towards the British. At least for the time being, each of the two dominions – India and Pakistan – would remain within the Commonwealth of Nations.

In Plymouth, change was afoot. As early as 1943, a 'Plan' had been drawn up to address the serious housing problems emerging in the city as a result of the destructive effects of the Blitz and the inadequacies of pre-war dwelling stock; its basic proposal was to reduce, to a large extent, the density of the older inner-city areas. This included the removal of most houses in Stonehouse, south of Union Street, and the 'pruning' of other dwellings on the northern side. Among other things it meant the clearing of Chapel Street and parts of Emma Place, both familiar to Hector and Clare from their past stays in the city. Although much of Union Street survived, it was no longer the centre of entertainment it had once been – although it remained popular with servicemen and others. Eventually the seedy nature of activities that took place there led the street into decline, and many considered it a 'no go' area, especially at night.

For the authorities in Plymouth, the next stage was to decentralise the population by moving people into new housing estates that were being built on the city's perimeter. The idea was to build some 20,000 new homes over ten years, redistributing 60,000 people, and for these new estates to become suburban extensions to the city's northern edge in the form of a series of self-contained satellites separated by green belts. This would ensure that each community had its own defined geographical space and its own village green and range of facilities such as shops, a school and a church at the centre, which in turn would promote community life and prevent the new estates becoming 'dormitories'.

Hector and Clare were among those to benefit from the building of the new estates: the so-called 'neighbourhood units'. Their unit, begun in December 1945, was the first to turn theory into practice and by the spring of 1948 – just a couple of months after the family arrived in England – it comprised a series of brand new houses. The children were so excited about their new home that even before their parents were given the keys, the whole family went to peep in through the ground floor windows. On 9th April, they were all ready to move.

Their house, designated 183 Pike Road, was built on the hilly Efford Estate and was the end house in a block of four two-storey dwellings, situated three miles or so northeast of the city centre. Previously, Pike Road had been open fields, which were home to an American military camp during the war years.

Although Hector and Clare were indebted to Gus and Em for putting them up, each family was relieved to have its own space once more. As others moved into their new houses all around, the family was constantly meeting new neighbours, and Barbara and Mary had a ready supply of playmates and friends. A large green space opposite the house provided a safe area to play and to learn new games. (In addition, the house was just a few minutes' walk away from one of the more established residential areas on the outskirts, home to a boy named Michael – a boy Barbara would later marry. As they were growing up, they probably crossed each other's paths countless times.)

Despite the children's excitement, these first few months in particular were a testing time for Hector and for Clare. However, Hector was successful in securing a position in 'civvy street' with the Plymouth City Architect's Department, where he worked until his retirement at the age of sixty-five.

Clare, though, living in a wholly new country, found it harder to make the adjustment. Having been accustomed throughout her life to a domestic arrangement supported by a variety of servants, she now had to fit into the economic and social culture of provincial Britain and learn how to perform all of these domestic duties herself. She needed to get to grips with cooking, cleaning and shopping, a series of repetitive tasks that seemed endless. (She was also persevering in her task of restoring Barbara to her proper weight by feeding her rich English dairy milk and homemade clotted cream.) Nevertheless, she succeeded in her endeavours to adjust to this unfamiliar, less sheltered civilian life, and this was vividly demonstrated in the ensuing years with the development of a very happy, love-filled home and a healthy, united and successful family.

In those first few months, though, she must to some extent have missed the social life she had enjoyed in India. There was no officer's mess just across the road, and there were no army wives nearby with whom to share experiences. However, two ex-Indian Army ordnance families had also come to live in Plymouth: the Suttons from Quetta days and the Daws from Summer Hill, Simla. As it happened, Lieutenant Colonel Daw and Hector both took up their new appointments in the city architect's office on the very same day in September 1948.

While Hector and Clare met with Mr and Mrs Daw only infrequently, there was nearly always a Christmas get-together at one home or the other and at the Christmas office social the Perks had allies in the Daws with whom to share new experiences and reminisce over old times. The Suttons, on the other hand, settled close by, and this meant more frequent visits between the families. For a time, the eldest son Ronald was courting Pat and the youngest, John, found he had something in common with Barbara when he visited Pike Road. Both children had been used to having a piano in the house and shared an ambition to be able to play by ear. On these visits, the two young people played together and alone, displaying their increasing abilities.

There were other reunions. For the first time in many years, Hector met up with both of his brothers when his younger sibling Ralph travelled down from Birmingham with his wife Gladys and sons. A photograph of the three brothers, taken at the time, portrays Hector still in the uniform that he kept for many years. Gladys told Barbara much later that Ralph was immensely proud of his brother Hector's achievements as a cavalryman and soldier out in India. Both Clare and Stanley (Gus's son and Ralph's nephew) later recalled Ralph as being a very funny man, sometimes putting on a posh accent for comic effect. In appearance and manner, he reminded them of the American stand-up comedian George Burns.

Even better, from the children's point of view, were the frequent visits from their beloved Uncle Bill. Having remained a bachelor, he came to stay with them whenever he was on leave and never arrived empty-handed, for his small case always contained various chocolate bars and thoughtful gifts. Like Hector and Clare, he had come back to England following independence in India, and at first he was part of the new 1st Battalion of the Royal Leicestershire Regiment. This was reformed on 6th June 1948 from the amalgamated 1st and 2nd battalions and based at Glen Parva Barracks in South Wigston near Leicester, but when in May 1949 it was uprooted once more and sent to Hong Kong, Bill – not wishing or able to go back to the Far East – transferred to the 1st Battalion Royal Warwickshire Regiment.

It was a sad parting, for 'Jock' had to say goodbye to the band and all his old pals, as well as to sever the connection with his regiment. He had been with the Leicesters for 20 years and in this time he had gained the Indian General Service Medal 1936 and Clasp; the NW Frontier Medal 1937-39; the 1939-45 Star, Pacific Star and the War Medal 1939-45; and, like Hector, the Long Service & Good Conduct Medal with Gratuity. In order to continue as a bandsman, he joined the Warwickshires at Budbrooke Barracks in Warwick, and from

21st January 1951 until 14th April 1953 saw service as part of a contingent of occupying British troops in Austria. However, on 24th March 1954 he decided it was time to leave the service, and relinquished the rank of bandsman (clarinet-player). Subsequently he retired from the army on 28th September, that same year. He was forty-one years old.

By then, Bill's new battalion had already departed for the Middle East a month before, and at the home depot the band was waiting to hear a 'hard and fast' date to join them. Meanwhile, its spokesman found time to write in the November Regimental Journal, *The Antelope*, a short dedication to Bill and Corporal Thomas, another 'stalwart' who had recently left the service. This spokesman, employing the pseudonym 'Harmony', wrote: 'Perren enlisted as a Boy in the Royal Leicestershire Regiment in 1929 and during the war was taken prisoner by the Japanese. He joined the Band in 1949 when his own Band went out to the Far East, the reason that he came to us was that he was medically unfit for Far East service owing to jungle ulcers, a souvenir from his POW days.' He added: 'Both were very good Bandsmen as well as good sportsmen and will certainly be missed. So we say cheerio Tomo and Jock and the very best of luck to you in your civilian ventures...'

In a final assessment, his commanding officer stated that Bill was a private of 'exemplary' military conduct and character and testified he was 'a thoroughly loyal and hard working man who has rendered extremely good service while a member of the Band of the Royal Warwickshire Regiment. He is smart, alert and intelligent and he can be relied upon to do a job on his own without supervision. His example to younger soldiers has been exemplary and I recommend him to his future employer as an exceptionally trustworthy and reliable man.' Always humble, Bill had declined promotion in the army.

Initially, having left the army and until he found lodgings, he lived for a short while with his sister Clare's family, crammed into Peter's small box room. He was to spend nearly all of the remaining 30 years of his life living in lodgings, and although he usually spent his leisure hours in the family home, he would walk or take a bus to his lodgings for the night. Later he would live with his widowed sister Hester. He kept his nickname, Jock, but for the rest of his working life he held a modest occupation, that of a factory cleaner, with duties that included sweeping the floors and lighting the factory boilers at the start of every day, a job for which he had to be up at the crack of dawn.

Such commonplace jobs were often the lot of long serving and severely tested soldiers. Bill, being a mostly self-effacing man, may not have seen it in this light, but it hardly seems appropriate for men who had made such sacrifices for their country to have ended their working lives in this kind of ignominy. He had shown outstanding courage under fire in Malaya as a first-aider and stretcher-bearer, and like thousands of other prisoners of war under the Japanese he had endured and survived ordeals and agonies which, by his own declaration, had 'knocked the stuffing' out of him. Perhaps this was why he now chose an undemanding occupation, and while he rarely if ever spoke of his terrifying and arduous experiences, his warmth, generosity, modesty and gentleness won him affection, admiration and love from all with whom he came into contact.

In 1955, the Perks family were astonished and overjoyed to learn that Hester, Frank and the now-elderly Mary Perren were coming to settle in England. Hester and Mary had been enduring some of the most trying times of all the years they had lived in India and Mary, especially, kept in touch with Clare by letter. For some time, her letters had expressed dissatisfaction with the state of affairs in India: she was unhappy with the changed political climate and the fact that life had become very difficult for many people, not least for Anglo-Indians such as Frank.

More than this, it was clear that she was no longer thriving and was feeling the effects of her advancing years. She was enduring Calcutta's seasonally intense heat and humidity less successfully and found it exhausting. The 'awful climate', she said, had contributed to her difficulties in recovering from influenza and bronchitis, and she expressed a yearning for some of England's cool air. It was clear that age was starting to limit her, especially as she revealed that she did not get out much any more.

In the end, the three of them had decided to make 'a clean break of it' and set sail for England from Calcutta on 1st September 1955, travelling on a cargo ship with many stops along the way. Their arrival at Tilbury, in a land new to Hester and Frank, must have felt uncertain and unfamiliar. For Mary, though, it was a return to her home country after 52 years away, 'to lay' her 'weary old bones'. Frank and Hester, whose marriage had suffered in recent years owing to his occasional straying, went to live in London where Frank secured a job as a technical writer with Foster Wheeler.

After so many years with Hester and Frank, Mary now went to live with the Perks family in Plymouth. Clare welcomed her dear mother into her home, and the elderly Mary spent the rest of her days with almost daily visits from her own son Bill. From time to time, Frank and Hester visited them all and even they eventually retired to Plymouth in the 1970s. By then, however, Mary had passed away. She died in 1967 at the grand old age of ninety-two.

It was a glad end to the story, for in those last years the reunited Perren family members (Mary, Clare, Bill and Hester) continuously rejoiced in their unexpected but close proximity. Sometimes they were saddened to remember William, whose end had been so very tragic, and to think of young Jackie, their brother lost to typhoid at the age of fourteen. However, mother, son and daughters were sustained by a deep love of God and of each other and by shared memories of a solid, happy upbringing in Simla. It had been the most famous of British Raj hill stations in the Punjab, the land of the five rivers, which Kipling described as 'fairer than all'. It was, he said, fairer even than the fair and most beautiful land of Hind.[110]

Of course, the remaining members of the Perren family also shared a strong sense of loss of their Indian life, along with Clare's own family, but this was relieved by the long and happy hours they stole together to reminisce and retell the great fund of tales from their India days. Hector could be persuaded easily to re-enact some of his colourful experiences, capturing the attention of family, visitors and – after his retirement – the friends he had made at his local pub, to whom he was affectionately known as 'the Major'.

It was Margaret who made perhaps the easiest transition to life in England and elsewhere, for within four years she had met and married a Canadian naval officer who had been seconded to a naval college in the city. She soon left with him for Canada, to set up home there and raise a family of four. Her husband had a further period of service in England but, after their departure for the second time, she kept well in touch with home.

Peter, meanwhile, completed his schooling and went on to gain a degree in engineering. He embarked on a long and mostly satisfying career with Rolls Royce, married a Welsh girl, and with her raised three children. He was a keen sailor and eventually retired to the banks of the River Tamar with his boat and his wife!

Frank died in 1975, having reached the age of seventy-five, but Hester lived on for another 11 years, passing away in 1986 at the age of eighty-one. By then Clare's children had already lost their beloved Uncle Bill, who had died in 1983 at the relatively young age of sixty-nine.

Barbara decided to embark upon a career in nursing. Later her younger sister Mary followed her into the profession, but before this Pat – Barbara's eldest sister – realised that she, too could make a go of nursing. She abandoned her job at the department store and, as she was already old enough to start her nurse's

Bill, 5 months after his release from captivity during WW2. Calcutta, January 1946.

Bill's reunion with his sister Clare and her family in Agra in May 1946.

Some of the many dead of the Calcutta massacres. August 1946

Peter and Bruce Blair at the Taj lit by moonlight.

The Perks family at the officers' mess in Agra on
Christmas Day 1946.

An occasion for Hector to be garlanded
with marigolds at the farewell of
Colonel Stevenson. Avadi, 1947.

Bill with his two youngest nieces Barbara and Mary at their new house in
Plymouth. The girls are pictured with the Christmas presents they received
on the SS Ormonde while in transit. A first summer in England for the three
exiles from India. September 1948.

Hester and Frank at home in Calcutta.
November 1950.

Mary Perren on her 81st birthday, a few months
after her return to England after 51 years in India.
Pictured with her grand daughter Pat at the family
home in Plymouth in 1956.

training, went ahead with it two years before Barbara was even eligible. Perhaps surprisingly, she was the only one of the three women to keep it up until her retirement.

Despite this, it could be said that Pat had the most difficult transition of all. She left India at a time in her life when many girls of nineteen have in some way dreamed of, if not actually mapped out, their futures – and she left behind a love affair that had come to an abrupt end. She never married and lived in the family home for the rest of her life, becoming a nursing sister in a Plymouth hospital where she specialised, for many years, in the care of premature babies. Sadly she died in 2004, aged seventy-five.

Barbara married a customs and excise officer, Michael – who had grown up so near to her own home in Plymouth – and travelled with him around the country while raising a family of three children. Eventually she and her husband retired to Bath, where Barbara became a keen family historian. Her younger sibling Mary married a naval man, like Margaret had done, but Mary's husband was British and her life followed the pattern of moving around from place to place that was usually associated with that profession. She had her own family and lives in Northamptonshire.

Clare, though she made a full life for herself in England, found that it could never transcend her affection for traditional India, with all its sights, sounds and smells, together with its timeless mystery and beauty. For her, as for so many others, it had been the brightest jewel in the crown of the British Empire. Even so, she made her home at 183 Pike Road, and became the heart of that house for the last 40 years of her life.

Steadfast, gentle, eager to listen and with an understanding mind, she was slow to prescribe but always quick to praise and encourage. Throughout those years, she and Hector gave incalculable amounts of love and comforting, tactile endearments to their children. Devoted to each other, Hector and Clare enjoyed a long retirement in their house (which they eventually bought) until Hector passed away in 1984. Clare survived him by ten years and missed him dreadfully: when they were both gone, their children felt bereft. Even so, the house they left seemed suffused with the special qualities of their lives, and with the memories of all those who had lived there or passed through.

Many years later Barbara, a lucky India-born child of the Raj, would sit contemplatively at home and put on her reading glasses to look into the treasured photograph albums again, and to think of those cherished loved ones. She would take comfort in all she had discovered about her family, and in those descriptions or pictures that had been preserved in print where her own memories had faded. Having settled not far from Corsham, Wiltshire, herself, she undertook to find the resting place of her forefathers, and, after a great amount of research, visited the small decaying graveyard of the old Independent Church in Corsham, a church sadly now deconsecrated.

One of the stones stood out among the others, bearing the following epitaph:

In memory of Ann, wife of William Perren, died December 17th 1884 aged 84 years
Also William Perren, died February 23rd 1886 aged 84 years
Also Ann Garner Perren, died October 23rd 1884 aged 41 years
Also John Perren, died November 11th 1885 in the East Indies, aged 40 years.

Here was where it had all started, the family of John Perren – William's father and Clare's grandfather – whose members had all died within scarcely more than a year of each other.

Feeling very moved, Barbara found it hard to contain her emotion upon seeing this stone, and its commemoration of the adventurer John Perren. He had set out for India with his new bride in 1874 and died just 11 years later, and clearly his loss had been felt, for his untimely death had been cut here in stone above the grave holding the bones of his mother and, eventually, his father.

More than a century later, as she stood there at the graveside, she realised how poignant it was to be visiting this place, to have returned to the same soil. A great-great-granddaughter had come home.

ACKNOWLEDGEMENTS

In writing this book, I have drawn upon a number of sources that have been especially useful.

Among those that have shaped my thinking are *Beneath the House Flag of the P&O* by Peter Padfield, *Queen Charlotte's – The Story of a Hospital* by Professor Sir John Dewhurst, *The Indian Army* by T A Heathcote, *Plain Tales from the Raj* by Charles Allen, *A History of the Army Ordnance Corps* by Brigadier B Rao, *The War in the Far East* by Basil Collier, *Death Railway* by Clifford Kinvig, *The Royal Leicestershire Regiment* by WE Underhill, *Auchinleck: The Lonely Soldier* by Philip Warner, and *The Indian Army and the King's Enemies 1900-1947* by Charles Chevenix Trench. © 1988 Charles Chevenix Trench and reprinted by kind permission of Thames and Hudson Ltd, London.

I am also grateful to Pat Barr and Ray Desmond, the authors of *Simla: A Hill Station in British India* and to Vipin Pubby, the author of *Shimla Then & Now*, for their fascinating insights into life in that fashionable settlement perched in the foothills of the Himalayas. Perhaps the most famous of all the British Raj hill stations, it also happened to be the birthplace of some of those among three generations of my family.

I am indebted to all these and the other authors to whose work I have given bibliographical reference. Their meticulous research has influenced my account. If there are any errors and misinterpretations they are probably mine and are likely to have arisen because of the many years of research and revision I have devoted to my story.

I am especially grateful to my editor Rachel Jones for her professional guidance and I value her kindness and understanding of my personal thoughts and approach to the work. It has been a joy to work with her. I also thank Douglas Hill, a regimental historian who had, at his fingertips, all the answers to my questions about the dragoon guards who went to India early in the 1920s. My most heartfelt thanks go to those who, like him, took time to speak to me about their experiences in and recollections of India.

I especially acknowledge my late, dear mother Clare who gave unstintingly of her time during our countless conversations over many years. I extend similar sentiments to my late, dear father Hector, and my sisters Pat, Margaret, Mary and brother Peter.

Although I have made great efforts to acquire permission to reproduce any protected material, the tracking down of some references has presented insurmountable problems with regard to time and distance. If I have overlooked any duty as a consequence, I would be more than happy to rectify this in future editions on receipt of an email (barbaradinner@live.co.uk).

BIBLIOGRAPHY

Abram, D et al, eds (1997). India, The Rough Guide. London: Rough Guides.

Adams, Geoffrey Pharaoh (1973). No Time for Geishas. London: Leo Cooper.

Allen, Charles (1979). Raj: A Scrapbook of British India. London: Penguin.

Allen, Charles (1975). Plain Tales from the Raj. London: Deutsch/BBC.

Bamfield, Veronica (1974). On the Strength: The Story of the British Army Wife. London: Charles Knight & Company.

Barr, Pat & Desmond, Ray (1978). Simla: A Hill Station in British India. London: The Scolar Press.

Barr, Pat (1989). The Dust in the Balance: British Women in India 1905-1945. London: Hamish Hamilton.

Bernardi, Debra et al, eds (1984). Fodor's Travel Guides: India, Nepal and Sri Lanka. London: Hodder and Stoughton.

Bhandari, R R (1983). Kalka-Simla and Kangra Valley Railways. New Delhi: Northern Railway.

Buck, Edward J (1904). Simla Past and Present. Calcutta: Thacker, Spink.

Calvert, Mike. (1973). Slim. London: Pan Books.

Collier, Basil (1969). The War in the Far East 1941-1945. London: William Heinemann.

Connell, John (1969). Wavell: Supreme Commander. London: Collins.

Dewhurst, Professor Sir John (1989). Queen Charlotte's: The Story of a Hospital. London: RCOG.

Donnison, Jean (1988). Midwives and Medical Men: A History of the Struggle for the Control of Childbirth. London: Historical Publications.

Francis, Charles Edward (1848). Sketches of Native Life in India with Views of Rajpootana, Shimlah etc. London: Publisher unknown.

Heathcote, T A (1974). The Indian Army. London: David & Charles.

Howarth, David and Howarth, Stephen (1986). The Story of P&O. London: Weidenfeld and Nicolson.

Karney, Robyn, ed (1995). Chronicle of the Cinema. London: Dorling Kindersley.

Kinvig, Clifford (1973). Death Railway. London: Pan Books.

Kipling, Rudyard (1989). Kim. London: Penguin.

McIntosh, E, ed (fourth edition). The Concise Oxford Dictionary. Oxford: Clarendon Press.

Murray, John (1929). A Handbook for Travellers in India, Burma and Ceylon. Calcutta: Thacker, Spink & Co.

Nicholson, Louise (1998). Delhi, Agra and Jaipur. Hong Kong: Odyssey.

Padfield, Peter (1981). Beneath the House Flag of the P&O. London: Hutchinson.

Parkinson, David (1995). History of Film. London: Thames & Hudson.

Pubby, Vipin (1996). Shimla Then & Now. New Delhi: Indus Publishing Company.

Rao, Brigadier B (1987). A History of the Army Ordnance Corps. Delhi: AH Wheeler & Co.

Robertson, Patrick (1980). Guinness Book of Film. Middlesex: Guinness Superlatives.

Singer, André (1984). Lords of the Khyber. London: Faber.

Trench, Charles Chenevix (1988). The Indian Army and the King's Enemies. London: Thames and Hudson.

Underhill, WE, ed (1957). The Royal Leicestershire Regiment (book written entirely by officers of The Royal Leicestershire Regiment)

Walker, Alexander (1978). The Shattered Silents. London: Elm Tree/Hamish Hamilton.

Warner, Philip (1981). Auchinleck: The Lonely Soldier. London: Buchan & Enright.

Whatmore, Rev L E (1973). Recusancy in Kent: Studies and Documents. Publisher unknown.

Yule, Henry and Burnell, A C (1985). Hobson – Jobson. London: Routledge & Kegan Paul.

ARTICLES AND JOURNALS

4th Royal Irish Dragoon Guards Regimental Magazine, June 1922: 5

4/7th Dragoon Guards Regimental Magazine, June 1925, Vol 1 No 1

Quarterly Magazines of the Leicestershire Regiment, *The Green Tiger*, February 1939, Vol 18 No 1: 11-16, May 1939, Vol 18 No 2: 48-52

Dunn, Cyril. 'The Lingering Twilight of the British Raj' (Australian Magazine, 1967): 28-37

Madras Independence Day Newspaper Supplement, *The Mail*, August 1947: xvii

NOTES

1   Charles Allen, *Raj: A Scrapbook of British India* (London: Penguin Books, 1979), p14.

2   Peter Padfield, *Beneath the House Flag of the P&O* (London: Hutchinson, 1981), p24.

3   *Ibid*, p41.

4   Pat Barr & Ray Desmond, *Simla: A Hill Station in British India* (London: The Scolar Press, 1978), p7.

5   *Ibid*, p8.

6   *Ibid*, p7.

7   *Ibid*, p18.

8   *Ibid*, p26.

9   *Ibid*, p26.

10 Rudyard Kipling, *Kim* (London: Penguin, 1989), p193.

11 Barr & Desmond, *Simla*, p26.

12 Cyril Dunn, 'The Lingering Twilight of the British Raj' (Australian Magazine, 1967), p28.

13 Barr & Desmond, *Simla*, p39.

14 Barr & Desmond, *Simla*, p27.

15 Vipin Pubby, *Shimla Then & Now* (New Delhi: Indus Publishing Company, 1996), p67.

16 Barr & Desmond, *Simla*, p72.

17 T A Heathcote, *The Indian Army* (London: David & Charles, 1974), p24.

18 Revd L E Whatmore, 'Our Oldest Missions' (The Southwark Record, October 1952): Vol xxv1 No 302, p208.

19 Revd L E Whatmore, *Recusancy in Kent: Studies and Documents* (Publisher unknown, *1973*), p31.

20 Prof Sir John Dewhurst, *Queen Charlotte's: Story of a Hospital* (London: RCOG, 1989), p6.

21   Jean Donnison, *Midwives and Medical Men* (London: Historical Publications Ltd, 1988), p38.

22   Dewhurst, *Queen Charlotte*, p42.

23   *Ibid.*

24   *Ibid.*

25   *Ibid*, p69.

26   *Ibid.*

27   *Ibid*, p72.

28   Dunn, 'Lingering Twilight', p37.

29   Barr & Desmond, *Simla*, p41.

30   Vipin Pubby (1996). Shimla Then & Now. New Delhi: Indus Publishing Company, p66.

31   Heathcote, *Indian Army*, p21.

32   *Ibid*, p22.

33   John Murray, A *Handbook For Travellers in India, Burma and Ceylon* (Calcutta: Thacker, Spink & Co, 1968), p261.

34   Barr & Desmond, *Simla*, p39.

35   Rudyard Kipling, *Kim* (London: Penguin, 1989), p196.

36   *Ibid.*

37   Official Programme of the Royal Review at Delhi on 14th Dec 1911.

38   Barr & Desmond, Simla, p24.

39   *Ibid.*

40   Andrew Wilson. Barr & Desmond, *Simla*, p24.

41   R R Bhandari, *Kalka-Simla and Kangra Valley Railways* (New Delhi: Northern Railway, 1983), p11.

42   *Ibid.*

43   Edward J Buck, *Simla Past and Present* (Calcutta: Thacker, Spink, 1904), p41.

43a   Barr & Desmond, *Simla*, p32.

44   Heathcote, *Indian Army*, p22.

45   William John Perren's service book.

46   Charles Edward Francis, *Sketches of Native Life in India with Views of Rajpootana, Shimlah etc.* (London, 1848). Publisher and page number unknown.

47   Barr & Desmond, *Simla*, p91.

48   E McIntosh, *The Concise Oxford Dictionary* (Oxford: Clarendon Press, 1951), p211.

49   Vipin Pubby, *Shimla Then & Now* (New Delhi: Indus Publishing Company 1996), p84.

50   *Ibid*, p91.

51   *Ibid*, p92.

52   *Ibid*, p72.

53   *Ibid*.

54   *Ibid*, p68.

55   *Ibid*, p68.

56   Kipling, *Kim*, p194.

57   D Abram et al, *India, The Rough Guide* (London: Rough Guides, 1997), p437.

58   Kipling, *Kim*, p194.

59   Barr & Desmond, *Simla*, p26.

60   *Ibid*.

61   4th Royal Irish Dragoon Guards Regimental Record (June 1922), p5.

62   Douglas Hill. Regimental Historian. The Royal Dragoon Guards.

63   4/7th Dragoon Guards Regimental Magazine (June 1925), Vol 1, No 1.

64   John Murray, *A Handbook For Travellers in India, Burma and Ceylon* (Calcutta: Thacker, Spink & Co, 1929), pxlvi.

65   Alexander Walker, *The Shattered Silents* (London: Elm Tree /Hamish Hamilton 1978), p4.

66   *Ibid*, p27.

67   *Ibid*, p10.

68   Robyn Karney ed, *Chronicle of the Cinema* (London: Dorling Kindersley, 1995), p211.

69   Walker, *Shattered Silents*, p202.

70   *Ibid*, p202.

71   Patrick Robertson, *Guinness Book of Film* (Middlesex: Guinness Superlatives, 1980), p179.

72   David Parkinson, *History of Film* (London: Thames & Hudson, 1995), p86.

73   Allen, *Raj*, p21.

74   *Ibid*.

75   Debra Bernardi et al, *Fodor's Travel Guides: India, Nepal and Sri Lanka* (London: Hodder and Stoughton), p528.

76   Murray, *Handbook for Travellers* (1929), p496.

77   *Ibid*.

78   Bernardi, *Fodor's*, p529.

79   Charles Chenevix Trench, *The Indian Army and the King's Enemies 1900 – 1947* (London: Thames & Hudson, 1988), pp136-137.

80   Basil Collier. *The War in the Far East* (London: William Heinemann Ltd, 1969), p49.

81   André Singer, *Lords of the Khyber* (London; Faber, 1984), p173.

82   Chenevix Trench, *The Indian Army*, p209.

83   Heathcote, *Indian Army*, p58.

84   *The Observer* newspaper, 24th January 1988, p45.

85   Clifford Kinvig, *Death Railway* (London: Pan Books, 1973), p39.

86   *Ibid*, p42.

87   Geoffrey Pharaoh Adams, *No Time for Geishas* (London: Leo Cooper, 1973),   p58.

88   John Connell, *Wavell: Supreme Commander* (London: Collins, 1969), p243.

89   Chenevix Trench, *The Indian Army*, pp261-262.

90   Book written entirely by officers of '*The Royal Leicestershire Regiment*', p126, and entitled as such and Edited by W. E. Underhill, 1957. No apparent copyright.

91   *Ibid.*

92   Murray, *Handbook for Travellers* (1929), p278.

93   *Ibid*, p270.

94   Kipling, *Kim*, p105.

95   Michael Calvert, *Slim* (London: Pan Books, 1973), p131.

96   Underhill, *Royal Leicestershire Regiment'*, p239.

97   Henry Yule and AC Burnell, *Hobson – Jobson* (London: Routledge & Kegan Paul, 1985), p427.

98   Underhill, Royal Leicestershire Regiment, p243.

99   Philip Warner, *Auchinleck: The Lonely Soldier*, (London: Buchan & Enright, 1981), p206.

100 Chenevix Trench, *The Indian Army*, inside flap of front cover.

101 *Ibid.*

102 *Ibid.*

103 Louise Nicholson, *Delhi, Agra and Jaipur* (Hong Kong: Odyssey, 1998), p18.

104 Kipling, *Kim*, p110.

105 Charles Allen, *Plain Tales from the Raj* (London: Deutsch/BBC, 1975), pp252-258.

106 *Ibid*, p252.

107 Bernardi, *Fodor's*, pp305-308.

108 Taken from letters from John Slater written July 2003.

109 Document from Commonwealth Relations Office, Whitehall, dated 21 January 1948.

110 Kipling, *Kim*, p194.

Lightning Source UK Ltd.
Milton Keynes UK
UKHW011526150921
390625UK00001B/316